Uninvited Neighbors

Race and Culture in the American West
Quintard Taylor, Series Editor

Uninvited Neighbors

*African Americans in Silicon Valley
1769–1990*

Herbert G. Ruffin II

University of Oklahoma Press : Norman

This book is published with the generous support of
Edith Kinney Gaylord.

Library of Congress Cataloging-in-Publication Data

Ruffin, Herbert G., 1969–
Uninvited neighbors : African Americans in Silicon Valley, 1769–1990 / Herbert G. Ruffin II.
    pages cm. — (Race and culture in the American West)
Includes bibliographical references and index.
ISBN 978-0-8061-4436-8 (cloth)
ISBN 978-0-8061-5417-6 (paper)
1. African Americans—California—Santa Clara Valley (Santa Clara County)—History. 2. African Americans—California—Santa Clara Valley (Santa Clara County)—Social conditions. 3. African Americans—California—Santa Clara Valley (Santa Clara County)—Politics and government. 4. Santa Clara Valley (Santa Clara County, Calif.)—History. 5. Santa Clara Valley (Santa Clara County, Calif.)—Race relations—History. I. Title.
F868.S25R84 2014
305.896'073079473—dc23
2013039142

Uninvited Neighbors: African Americans in Silicon Valley, 1769–1990 is Volume 7 in the Race and Culture in the American West series.

The paper in this book meets the guidelines for permanence and durability of the Committee on Production Guidelines for Book Longevity of the Council on Library Resources, Inc. ∞

Copyright © 2014 by the University of Oklahoma Press, Norman, Publishing Division of the University. Paperback published 2014.
Manufactured in the U.S.A.

All rights reserved. No part of this publication may be reproduced, stored in a retrieval system, or transmitted, in any form or by any means, electronic, mechanical, photocopying, recording, or otherwise—except as permitted under Section 107 or 108 of the United States Copyright Act—without the prior written permission of the University of Oklahoma Press. To request permission to reproduce selections from this book, write to Permissions, University of Oklahoma Press, 2800 Venture Drive, Norman OK 73069, or email rights.oupress@ou.edu.

Contents

List of Illustrations   vii
List of Tables   ix
Acknowledgments   xi

Introduction   1

PART I. African Americans in a Frontier Valley, 1769–1941

1. Origins of Santa Clara Valley's Black Community, 1769–1900   15
2. African Americans in the Valley of Heart's Delight, 1900–1941   48

PART II. African Americans and the Suburban Dream, 1941–1990

3. World War II and Postwar Santa Clara County, 1941–1953   73
4. Urban Sustainability and Race in Santa Clara County, 1945–1968   92
5. Sunnyhills: Race and Working-Class Politics in Santa Clara Valley, 1945–1968   122
6. The Santa Clara County Civil Rights Movement, 1949–1966   138
7. The Revolt of the Black Athlete and Its Accomplishments, 1956–1987   163
8. The Third Great Migration: Black Suburbanization in Silicon Valley, 1968–1990   201

Notes   229
Bibliography   299
Index   329

Illustrations

Figures

Black Student Union members at Stanford University	2
Garden City Women's Club, ca. 1985	9
James Williams, 1905	30
Reverend Peter Williams Cassey	36
St. Philip's Academy and Institute	38
Advertisement for Jacob Overton's catering business	46
Orchard scene, ca. 1920	50
Anna Stokes McColl, ca. 1905	68
Anderson family, ca. 1919	79
Inez Jackson	87
Mary Anne Smith	99
Joseph Eichler	104
Benjamin Franklin Gross	128
Local 560 purchasing the original "Sunnyhills"	133
Dr. James Blackwell, leading a freedom march through downtown San Jose, 1963	152
A child peering from behind an American flag at a rally at St. James Park	153
The Good Brothers, ca. 1960	166
Civil rights rally, San Jose State College, 1964	174
Speed City, San Jose, March 1968	177
Dr. Harry Edwards and President Robert Clark at September Hearings	187
The Olympic Project for Human Rights, 1968	191
John Carlos and Tommie Smith, 2003	192
Dr. Charles Murray	195
Charles Alexander and Dr. Harry Edwards, ca. 2008	198
Milpitas High School principal Charles Gary with student	208
San Jose NAACP Youth Group at 1992 Freedom Train	227

Maps

Santa Clara Valley and surrounding communities	xvi
Black communities in New Spain	16
Northside San Jose, 1860–1970	51
African Americans in West County Palo Alto, 1910–ca. 1970	60
Redlining in Santa Clara County, ca. 1937–1950s	76
Black communities in Northern California by 1990	225

Tables

1. Black People in the Santa Clara Valley, 1777 — 17
2. Castas: Racial Classification System in Colonial New Spain — 19
3. African American Population in California, by County, 1850 — 28
4. Population in the Santa Clara Valley, by Race and Ethnicity, 1860–1900 — 42
5. Populations of Color in Santa Clara County, 1900–1940 — 53
6. Populations of Color in California, 1940–1950 — 74
7. Black Population in Santa Clara County, 1940–1980 — 95
8. African Americans in Santa Clara County, by City, 1970–2010 — 203
9. Median Owner-Occupied Home Prices, by County, 1980–1990 — 216

Acknowledgments

Unwelcome Neighbors is a result of eighteen years of researching and reflecting on African American history and scholarship in the American West, U.S. urban studies, and Africana studies. My attraction to the topic emerged from informal conversations with the late Charles J. Murray, my mentor at San Jose City College, in 1995, before I transferred to the University of California at Santa Cruz. What sparked my initial interest was an odd story about the first blacks whose presence was publicly recognized in the Santa Clara Valley: several hundred members of the United Auto Workers from Richmond, California, who retained their jobs after Ford Motor Company moved the plant to the San Jose region during its early phase of suburbanization in the 1950s. Without going any further with this history, which is examined in chapter 5, I want to thank several people and institutions for providing me invaluable assistance on this project.

During the course of writing this book I have incurred many debts. Intellectually I owe a great debt to Sidney Lemelle at Pomona College and David Yoo at Claremont McKenna College (now at UCLA), and to Hal Barron at Harvey Mudd College. I especially thank Sid and David for critically and editorially shepherding the book when it was a dissertation and encouraging me to think about the big picture for publication. I also owe a huge debt to people who gave me an academic direction. These include Charles J. Murray, Albert E. Dippipo, Reginald Lockett, and Anne Heffley, San Jose City College; David Anthony and Edmund "Terry" Burke, University of California at Santa Cruz; Janet Brodie, David Hinds, and Dean McHenry, Claremont Graduate University; Jose Calderon, Pitzer College; Rita Roberts, Scripps College; and Miguel Tinker-Salas, Victor Silverman, and Phyllis Jackson, Pomona College.

Others who played a critical role in my intellectual growth include African Americans in the West historians, trailblazers, and mentors

Quintard Taylor at the University of Washington, Albert Broussard at Texas A&M University, Ronald Coleman at the University of Utah, Lawrence de Graaf at California State University at Fullerton, and Matthew Whitaker at Arizona State University. Just as important, Taylor embraced the book before it was a doctoral thesis, which gave this project a clear path and had an immeasurable effect on how I wrote my dissertation. Other scholars whose influence played a crucial role in inspiring and shaping this book include (in alphabetical order): Abdul Alkalimat, Michael Duchemin, John Hope Franklin, David Hamilton Golland, Gerald Horne, Hasan Kwame Jeffries, T. Hasan Johnson, Robin D. G. Kelly, Patricia Nelson Limmerick, Daniel Lind, Dwayne Mack, Manning Marable, Delores Nason McBroome, Bobby McDonald, Kevin Mulroy, Becky M. Nicolaides, Chris Niedt, Colleen O'Neill, Robert Self, Amilcar Shabazz, Michael "Cowboy Mike" Searles, Urla Taylor, Joe William Trotter, Andrew Weise, Cornel West, Richard White, and Rhonda Williams. I thank the people who allowed me to interview them for this book, including Charles Alexander, Gloria Anderson, Kenneth Blackwell, Albert Camarillo, Clayborne Carson, Gordon Chang, Harry Edwards, Sofia Fojas, Helen Gaffin, Charles Gary, Cazetta Gray, Ben Gross, Urla Hill, Cass Jackson, Barbara Kinchen, Jean Libby, Ralph Libby, Ken Lowe, Steve Milner, Ray Norton, Sr., Allisa Owens, Patricia Perkins, Clifford Price, Monica Ramos, William Ribbs, Sr., Ellen Rollins, Herb Ruffin I, Talya Ruffin, Steve Staiger, Orvella Stubbs, Ocie Tinsley, Mattie Briggs Tinsley. At the Smithsonian Institution these people include Diana Baird-N'Diaye, John W. Franklin, Mary Monseur, and Carla Borden at the Center for Folklife and Cultural Heritage; and Niani Kilkenny, Kimberly Kelly, Alonzo Smith, Spencer Crew, and Lonnie Bunch at the National Museum of American History.

 I would also like to thank Patricia Perkins at Evergreen Valley College in San Jose for her overall assistance, especially with the oral interviews. As a member of three of the oldest black families who still live in San Jose (the Andersons, Dollarhydes, and Ellingtons), she interviewed some of the region's oldest African Americans for the project, and she and her family were interviewed on several occasions. Invaluable in this endeavor have been oral interviews with people such as former Milpitas mayor Ben Gross and black athlete revolt co-organizer Dr. Harry Edwards; and interviews and vignettes taken from the Garden City Women Club's *History of Black Americans in the Santa Clara Valley* (1978). Moreover, I would like to thank people and institutions that contributed images for this project, such as Charles Alexander and History San Jose. Without your stories and images, this project would be a dry demographic assessment augmented by secondary sources.

At the University of Oklahoma Press, I am particularly grateful for Jay Dew and Steven Baker's editorial guidance and support, which was crucial at every stage of this project. Thanks are also due to Steven Danver at the *Journal of the West* and Ingrid Banks at the U.C.–Santa Barbara Center for Black Studies Research for allowing me to adapt for this book my articles "Sunnyhills, Race, and Working Class Politics in Postwar Silicon Valley," and "San Jose and the Great Black Migration, 1941–1968." In addition, I am appreciative of Genevieve Beenen, who edited the early drafts of this book; and for Norma McLemore, who edited the book's final draft.

I am also grateful to the many librarians and historical society archivists who have been gracious with their time and have provided materials for this project. They include librarians Ruth Schooley, Kimberly Franklin, Adam Rosenkranz, and Mary Martin at the Honnold-Mudd Library at the Claremont Colleges and its interlibrary loan staff and special collections staff. I would also like to thank the staff of the Bird Library and Martin Luther King Library at Syracuse University; the African American Museum and Library at Oakland; Bancroft Library at the University of California, Berkeley; California History Center at De Anza College, Cupertino; the California Room and Sourisseau Academy for State and Local History at San Jose's Dr. Martin Luther King, Jr., Library; California State Library at Sacramento; Claremont School of Theology Library; research librarian Jim Reed at History San Jose; Inez C. Jackson Historical Library at the African American Community Service Agency, San Jose; Michigan State University Libraries; Milpitas Public Library; Moorland-Spingarn Research Center at Howard University, Washington, D.C.; Mountain View Historical Society; National Archives at College Park, Maryland, at San Bruno,

California, and at Washington, D.C.; Oakland Museum of California; Oakland Public Library; Palo Alto Historical Association; San Diego State University Library; San Francisco African American Historical and Cultural Society; research librarian Danielle Moon and staff of San Jose State University Special Collections at San Jose's Dr. Martin Luther King, Jr., Library; Santa Clara City Library; Santa Clara County Archives and County Clerk Office; Santa Clara County Historical and Genealogical Society; Stanford University Archives; Sunnyhills United Methodist Church in Milpitas; Sunnyvale Library; University Archives, Santa Clara University Library; Reverend Jerry Drino and staff at Trinity Episcopal Church; and Walter P. Reuther Library at Wayne State University, Detroit.

As a first-generation scholar, I have found other kinds of help to be essential for this book. I would like to thank San Jose City College President Del Anderson; Linda Tursi, Cheryl Perazzo, and the Karl S. Pister Leadership Opportunity Award Program at University of California at Santa Cruz; Pamela Hudson and Catherine Harris at the Office of Fellowships and Grants, Smithsonian Institution; Claremont McKenna College History Department; former Claremont McKenna College Dean of Faculty William Ascher; Ronald Teeples, American Jazz Institute, Claremont McKenna College; and Claremont Graduate University Dissertation Fellowship Committee.

Moreover, Syracuse University's support has allowed me to research, teach, participate in conferences, and go to South Africa as a historian delegate. I would like to thank Syracuse University's Department of African American Studies, the College of Arts and Sciences, the Office of Chancellor Nancy Cantor, the Department of History, and the Africa Initiative. Finally, I would like to thank university cartographer Joseph W. Stoll for editing the maps used in this book.

Family and friends have sustained me emotionally through this project to its completion. They include my parents, Sadie and Herb Ruffin; my wife, Tanya; and my siblings, Talya and Michael, and their families. I thank all for their patience and support but especially Tanya, who has had to directly endure my many moments of deep immersion in research. I extend a heartfelt thank-you to friends T. Hasan Johnson, Daniel Lind, and (in alphabetical order) Jenny Bahn and family,

Ariana Brooks, Daniel Cady, Dawn Dennis, Wendell Eckford, Kimberly Ellis, Mike Elliot and our colleagues at the University of the West Indies at Cave Hill, Barbados, Amy Essington, Salim Faraji, Kimberly Coleman Foote, Elmo Frazier and family, Jerry Gonzalez, Naomi Hall, Urla Hill, Marsha Horsley, Robert Jefferson, Robert Johnson, Bomani Jones, the Keels family, Willow Lung-Amam, Dwayne Mack, Sandra Mayo, Casey Nichols, Bernadette Pruitt, Jamal Ratchford, Rochelle and Darrell Sivad, Tharon Smith, Kimberley Stanley, Krista Thompson, Dwight Watson, and Natale Zappia. I would also like to thank Kelly King, Peter Harris, the Interdisciplinary Department of Black Studies at the Claremont Colleges, Gerry Murray, Michelle Murray, Alissa Owens, T. J. Owens, Hughes Suffren, and Tamara Woolfolk.

This book is dedicated to the thousands of black westerners and suburbanites like the Ruffin family whose lives still await introduction as historical subjects.

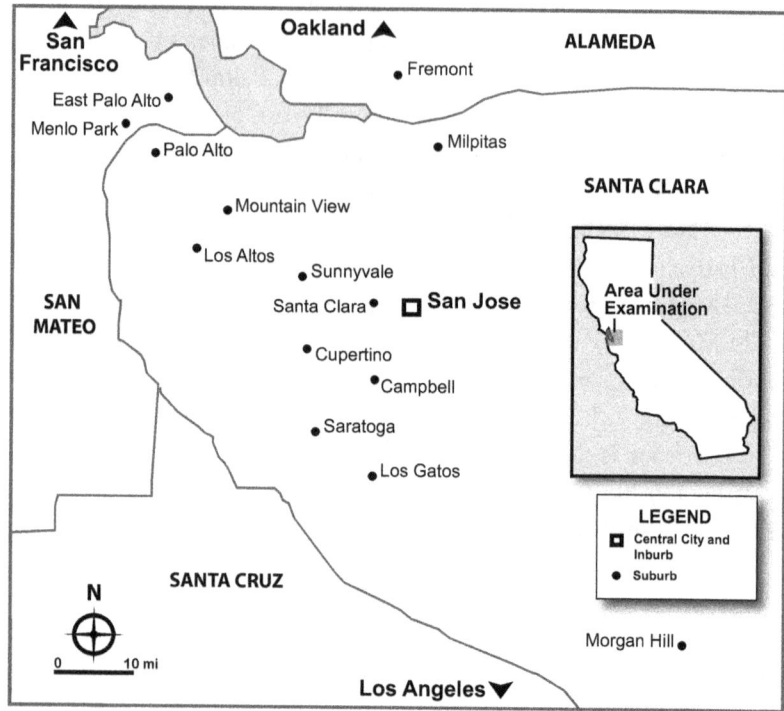

Santa Clara Valley and surrounding communities. Copyright © 2014 by the University of Oklahoma Press.

Introduction

ON APRIL 8, 1968, FOUR DAYS after Dr. Martin Luther King, Jr., was assassinated, Stanford University canceled its classes and held a campuswide discussion on racism at Memorial Auditorium.[1] As university provost Richard Lyman began to speak about increasing black enrollment, African American students—mostly members of the campus's Black Student Union—took over the microphone. The union's president, Keni Washington, said to the surprised audience of faculty, staff, and students: "Put your money and your action where your mouth is." He then handed the microphone to Black Student Union representative Frank Satterwhite, who read a list of ten demands that needed to be met immediately. The speaker assured the crowd, "We're not going to hurt anybody—but we are going to have our say. . . . We're tired of listening." The demands included "increasing Stanford's minority enrollment, recruiting heavily from surrounding communities like East Palo Alto and East Menlo Park . . . hir[ing] more minority professors, offer[ing] more grants and introduc[ing] a curriculum relevant to minority groups." Other complaints ranged from a lack of black administrators to general frustration with campus culture and with residential discrimination that prohibited blacks from having access to housing in the Santa Clara Valley.[2] When the black students were finished, they received a standing ovation.

The school's response to the demonstrators' demands was immediate and surprisingly favorable—this was the first time Provost Lyman was not tough on protesters and took positive steps to meet activists' goals.[3] In a 2002 interview, Lyman acknowledged Stanford's errors: "The University thought it was doing more than we really were. . . . Progress was trickling and people had lost patience."[4] Soon after, the incidence of black student protest at Stanford declined. By then, however, the students had won African studies and black studies programs and enough resources to temporarily sustain several other

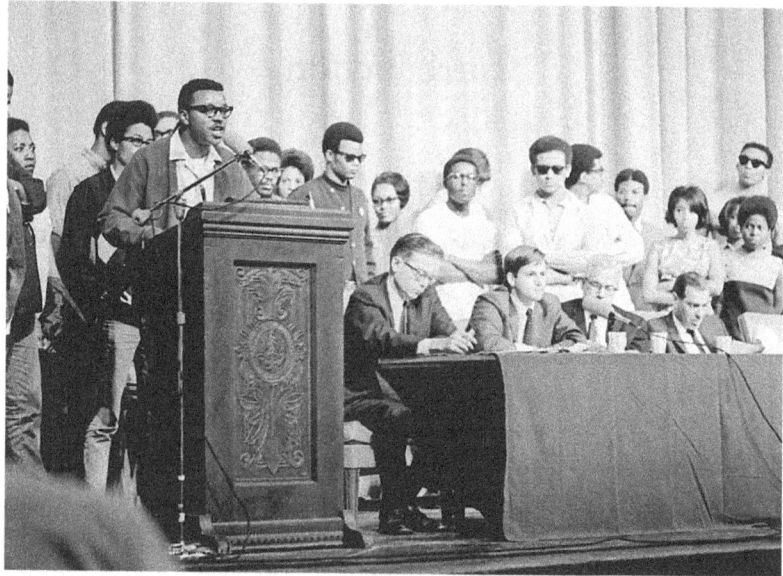

Black Student Union members at Stanford University take over the stage at a memorial for Dr. Martin Luther King, Jr., 1968. Courtesy Stanford News Service Library.

black student groups created from 1968 to 1970, such as a committee on black performing arts, Ujamaa House, Kuumba Dance Ensemble, and a gospel choir.[5]

Stanford's example is representative of the overall African American experience within the Santa Clara Valley. Blacks' perceptions and concerns have largely been ignored—or, better yet, placed in interstitial space where matters of race have for the most part been handled without headlines or historic record.[6] This pattern can be traced back to the 1890s, when most forms of racial discrimination were legally abolished in California's constitution and racism toward African Americans was thought to have been ended by legal reform. Unlike the well-defined social order of black subservience to whites in the South, race relations in the West were always in flux and conflicted by the region's insincere embrace of racial tolerance and social equality. From 1890 to 1990, discrimination in the South Bay was administered by custom, complacency, and indifference. Before 1960, for example, Stanford

University had only two black students enrolled. By 1966, it had thirty-five. By the next year, the combination of the civil rights movement, urban uprisings, and the Black Power movement had pressured Stanford's administration into enrolling sixty-five black freshmen for the 1967–1968 school year. However, Stanford had no institutional black presence associated with the university until the 1969–1970 academic year, when it hired black sociologist St. Clair Drake to chair its black studies program and began gradually increasing its minority enrollment (which included Mexican American students).[7]

Throughout this work I explore how blacks in the Santa Clara Valley faced the predicaments of having an obscure presence by engaging in political expression and community formation. By focusing on these actions, my research provides a promising model for exploring small black communities as well as de facto racial discrimination—customary and institutional racial discrimination that existed in practice and structure rather than by legal prescription. Chronologically, this history ranges from California's Spanish era of the 1770s to the emergence of the World Wide Web in 1991. My interest in studying black urban and surburban formation along the lines of community formation and political expression within late-blooming Santa Clara County derives from a desire to understand the dynamics that allowed African Americans to migrate and live in a place that became a high-tech suburban metropolis in the post–World War II era.

THIS IS THE FIRST ACADEMIC STUDY undertaken on the movement of blacks into the Santa Clara Valley. Thus this project necessarily presents the African American experience in a new way, with a focus on how a minute population forged communities and overcame socioeconomic restrictions as the area suburbanized and industrialized. It explores Santa Clara Valley blacks' quests for the postwar American dream, which most have defined as the freedom to live the way that they anticipated living, and how that pursuit produced mixed results because of social isolation and de facto racial discrimination in housing, employment, education, and law enforcement. This book addresses the scattering of the black community during the South Bay's late but rapid urban growth after 1950, which led to the creation of several distinct black communities rooted in Northside San Jose, East San Jose, downtown Palo Alto, Barron Park (Palo Alto), East Palo Alto (on the outskirts of the county), and, after 1955, Sunnyhills (Milpitas). Implicit in this discussion is a challenge to a popular notion among suburban scholars that most suburbanites started feeling socially isolated after 1980 and that Santa Clara County blacks reflected that trend. Instead, that trend dates back to 1950, when the South Bay began to suburbanize and blacks began living in white neighborhoods uninvited and struggling to build a strong sense of identity through cultural community—a pattern that arguably occurred in other late-blooming areas such as Anaheim, California; Arlington, Texas; Las Vegas; Phoenix; and San Diego.[8] Finally, *Uninvited Neighbors* is a study of how blacks survived and formed their own political traditions in a peculiar region conflicted by its embrace of racial tolerance and social equality.

Methodologically this study intersects two distinct bodies of literature pertinent to the contemporary American experience. The first is the large body of work examining the twentieth-century city and urban fringe from within the disciplines of history, sociology, cultural anthropology, and urban planning. The second is the literature on black migration and community formation in twentieth-century urban America, especially the work of Joe William Trotter, Albert Broussard, Lawrence De Graaf, and Quintard Taylor.[9] Trotter's work has helped me to ground my research in traditional urban studies. As a postwar study of black history, my work goes beyond the telling of a modern African American history derived from southern and inner-city experiences and focusing on such topics as Jim Crow (de jure) racial discrimination, the southern civil rights movement, and ghettoization. Similarly, Broussard's landmark study of San Francisco blacks has informed my work. In many ways my study extends Broussard's notions into the South Bay, which was dominated by agricultural pursuits prior to its hasty transformation into a suburban high-tech region after the mid-1950s. In addition, the works of Lawrence de Graaf on African American suburbanization in postwar California has provided my work with a strong model for researching the subject that has its roots in my brief but significant study of the subject under De Graaf's supervision.[10] Finally, Quintard Taylor's examinations of the urban black West offer one the most complete resources for how to conceptualize the history through the frameworks of community formation and "African American West logic." For instance, my work examines South Bay blacks' political expression and community life through essential black institutions like churches, social clubs, and economic organizations as the focal point of the community.[11] This is an emphasis sorely lacking in many urban and suburban histories that define the black community by denial, exclusion, and juxtaposition to explain the creation of whiteness in post–World War II suburbia. Moreover, African American West logic is central to my theoretical framework because it conceptualizes the U.S. West as a *place* in which race, social history, and urbanization are essential explanatory tools, as opposed to a *process* that celebrates European American conquest and westward migration from the East. Within places such as San Jose, U.S. West history since 1986 has increasingly seen people of color and women as agents in their own development and survival; slavery and Jim Crow did not predominate in most regions, and the West has always been multiracial. Combined, these social and historical differences have created a different racial atmosphere for African Americans.

The recording of African Americans as subjects in Bay Area scholarship covering 1941 to the present was nonexistent until three decades ago. A more general shift from objectifying blacks began with the emergence of sociological and autobiographical accounts written by and about blacks during World War II. After the 1965 rebellion in the black section of Los Angeles known as Watts, several popular causes—the push for equal educational opportunities, the Black Panther Party for Self Defense, and the black studies movement—led to a crucial shift in urban studies from merely objectifying inner-city residents to recording their agency.[12] In Bay Area historiography, these trends were different from national developments in urban scholarship prior to the mid-1980s, which overexamined the black urban experience between 1890 and 1930 and often failed, as Quintard Taylor noted, "to ask significant questions concerning the [contemporary] African American urban experience."[13] By the late 1970s, scholars were covering a wider range of black California experiences.

The traditional interpretation of the black West traces its roots to Fredrick Jackson Turner's work. In Turner's writings on the American frontier, which has had tremendous influence on historians of the U.S. West, he never acknowledged African Americans, and thus their history was not adequately documented. Postwar scholars writing in the Turner tradition, such as Walter Prescott Webb, contended that the presence of blacks in the American West as a frontier was not recorded because they were insignificant and passive before World War II.[14] No one challenged this traditional interpretation of the post-1941 African American experience in the Bay Area until 1984.[15]

That was the year Albert Broussard's essay "The Politics of Despair: Black San Franciscans and the Political Process, 1920–1940" was published, an event that, within black Bay Area historiography, marked a major academic shift from demographics toward examining the lived experiences of African Americans in twentieth-century urban history.[16] This article is important because it went beyond detailing African American migration into the 1940s Bay Area, examining black political leadership and community formation a generation prior to the Second World War. Its basic argument is that African Americans in the Bay Area had an active political tradition prior to the 1940s and that this tradition became the foundation for the local black activism that flourished from 1942 to 1970.[17] Since publication of Broussard's seminal essay, contemporary literature on Bay Area blacks has become increasingly rich and complex, focusing on topics including African American migration, art, black self-determination, education, fair housing, industrial and capital relocation to suburbs, labor union racism, prisons, and white and middle-class flight.[18]

In black Bay Area literature, the main victims of labor union racism, deindustrialization, white flight, and urban redevelopment were young, educated African American families migrating into the Bay Area who were fully capable of working skilled jobs. During the Second World War, they worked in the shipyards and were upwardly mobile; a broad-based black middle class seemed to be emerging. Consequently, when the postwar years brought them mass unemployment, unfulfilling employment, and continuing residential segregation, those conditions created an impoverished, frustrated, and disaffected population in culturally concentrated urban areas such as the Fillmore District in San Francisco, West Oakland, and North Richmond. This telling of the American West challenged traditional scholarship, which interpreted blacks as passive victims, the U.S. West as untamed frontier, and its urban centers as belonging to "the North," as though the West was locked in the U.S. North-South paradigm.[19] In this new millennium the historiography of the U.S. West needs a fresh discussion addressing its urban experience, one that can speak to blacks living in suburban sites such as Santa Clara Valley, who are popularly viewed as living the American dream despite their lived reality of being persistently confronted with institutional racism, stereotyping, and social isolation.

In California, San Francisco–Oakland and San Jose have two of the seven largest suburbs in the state.[20] This physical area symbolizes the middle-class pursuit of the American dream, which includes homeownership, disposable income, and occupational status. According to historian Lawrence de Graaf, "Between 1950 and 1970, 83 percent of the nation's population growth occurred in suburbs, and by 1990, for the first time in history more than half of all Americans living in urbanized areas resided in suburbs."[21] During the first wave of suburban growth from 1945 to 1970, most blacks were excluded and relegated to overcrowded, rapidly deteriorating central cities.

In regard to the Santa Clara Valley, the history of business and technology in the making of Silicon Valley and the high-tech global economy predominates historical research on the region. As a result, the history of the people and community has largely been ignored. Instead, the intense focus on business and technology that began in the 1950s with city boosters, businessmen, electronic engineers, and local media intent on creating an importance for their cities and themselves has since the mid-1980s expanded into the domain of scholars. Since 2000, people have been included in scholarly works only in regard to Silicon Valley, or the post–1971 period, by authors who have written about environmental injustice and the absence of labor rights in the high-tech industry. Notable examples in this much-needed and emerging field are David N. Pellow and Lisa Sun-Hee Park's *The Silicon Valley of Dreams* (2002), Ted Smith's collection *Challenging the Chip* (2006), and Elizabeth Grossman's *High Tech Trash* (2006). However, in its focus on Silicon Valley and the development of the high-tech industry rather than on the Santa Clara Valley, the social history of the region prior to 1971 continues to go unrecorded, with the exception of a few texts such as Stephen Pitti's *The Devil in Silicon Valley* (2003) and Glenda Matthews's *Silicon Valley, Women, and the California Dream* (2003). As a result, the formation of Silicon Valley has become synonymous with Santa Clara County in the minds of most nonresidents.[22] By examining the critically important history ranging from the initial formation of the South Bay black community in the 1860s to the Third Great Migration of the 1970s and 1980s, this book attempts to salvage some of what has gone unrecorded and was thereby rendered insignificant in the histories of the Santa Clara Valley, California, the U.S. West, and African America.

The only comprehensive history examining Santa Clara County blacks was the Garden City Women's Club's *History of Black Americans in the Santa Clara Valley* (1978),[23] which documents the African American families who lived predominantly in San Jose from 1850 to 1970. It was published during a period when local media outlets such as the *San Jose Mercury News* were taking a renewed interest in San Jose's African American heritage, after a ten-year hiatus following the black athlete revolt of the late 1960s. Similar to Delilah Beasley's *The Negro Trail Blazers of California* (1919), *History of Black Americans in the Santa Clara Valley* attempts to center African Americans in local memory through oral history, public history, and chronology. According to the *History of Black Americans in the Santa Clara Valley*, the Santa Clara Valley has a smaller and more scattered African American population in the Bay Area than do San Francisco and Oakland. Many of the valley's pre-1940 migrants came from historically southern states (especially Missouri, Kentucky, Georgia, Arkansas, and Virginia) and moved into downtown San Jose's Northside area in East Santa Clara County, or East County.[24]

In the 1940s and 1950s most blacks came from the Southwest. After the 1960s, opportunities for people of color increased in the West generally, and the black population of the Santa Clara Valley

Garden City Women's Club, ca. 1985, several years after the publication of the *History of Black Americans in the Santa Clara Valley*. Charles Alexander Collection.

exploded from 730 people in 1940 to 56,211 people in 1990, attracting African Americans from all parts of the United States.[25]

For this work, East County designates the more diverse, urban, and inner suburban half of the Santa Clara Valley, located east of the Guadalupe River, and all county flatland areas north of Capital Expressway. West County designates the white, affluent suburban areas located on the Peninsula, the outskirts of San Jose, and in inburbs (or suburbs within the central city) such as South and West San Jose. Before the 1950s, around half of the county's African Americans were clustered in the Northside, while West County's African Americans lived around Palo Alto's University South area (east of Stanford) prior to Stanford's expansion in the 1940s.

During the postwar period, older Santa Clara Valley blacks' sense of belonging was increasingly challenged by newer black southwestern migrants in search of decent housing, skilled employment compatible with their educational training, and social justice. These were blacks who initially came to California to work in the defense industry in San Francisco and East Bay and migrated to South Bay after being laid off, which typically occurred after the Second World War ended and white veterans returned to their homes. Racial tensions arose, and there was also a tension within the African American community because established residents felt it a burden to acculturate newcomers to local norms. Many established black residents, including San Jose resident Mattie Berry, resented the more racially hostile social climate and put the blame on these newer black migrants, whom they called "suitcase Negroes."[26] The newer black migrants had a larger and younger population that was not content with racial injustice and menial jobs.[27]

Significant black intraregional migration from inner city to suburb began with African American Ford autoworkers in the mid-1950s. From then through the 1960s, the Milpitas subdivision called Sunnyhills became home to senior UAW members, white and black, who had moved from Richmond, California, as Ford Motor Company phased out the plant there and replaced with it with one in Milpitas. But Sunnyhills didn't exist when the process began, and housing initially threatened to become a major obstacle. In Richmond, they had lived close to the plant. But closed housing ordinances in the proximity of the Santa Clara Valley made local housing difficult for the black workers, and a daily commute from their homes in Alameda and Contra Costa Counties (aka the East Bay) was not feasible. Many eligible African American workers fell victim to regional apartheid and remained working at the Richmond plant until it closed in the mid-1950s. The lives of those who didn't—the blacks who ended up with housing in the proximity of the South Bay and retained their jobs—are an interesting study that forces the observer to re-explore traditional notions of class and find a more fluid conception of the term. Their conception of class represented an alternative notion grounded in racial differences but mollified by union solidarity, homeownership, and middle-class consumption in suburbia. To Sunnyhills' residents, they were all engaged in the same employment, alongside similar people, as had been the case in Richmond during the 1940s; however, their standard of living had vastly improved, and they had become homeowners with greater disposable income. Ultimately, these were people in transition to becoming middle class. Their political-economic experiences and community formation made Milpitas vastly different from the more typical all-white middle-class suburbs of the time.

UNINVITED NEIGHBORS IS DIVIDED INTO two parts. In Part 1, "African Americans in a Frontier Valley, 1769–1941," this book addresses the background of the Santa Clara Valley and its Spanish-speaking African population, slavery, and the forging of an African American community in the late nineteenth and early twentieth centuries. The first chapter of Part 1 outlines the Santa Clara Valley during the Spanish and Mexican periods, slavery and freedom in gold rush San Jose, and black community building in the Santa Clara Valley from 1860 to 1900. Chapter 2 examines South Bay blacks from 1900 to 1941 in terms of their neighborhood development and growth. What I find is that, contrary to what most twentieth-century scholarship on blacks in urban America concludes, the existence of black community was not a reaction to such outside forces as residential segregation, economic discrimination, and political impotence but rather was something that began with the people themselves and was consciously chosen.

Part 2, "African Americans and the Suburban Dream, 1941–1990," examines blacks' pursuit of the American dream in Silicon Valley through migration and resettlement, housing, labor relations, black politics, and, after 1970, the quest for freedom while continually being challenged by social isolation and de facto segregation in a post-suburban Santa Clara County that transformed into Silicon Valley. Chapter 3 critically discusses the dramatic transformation of the Santa Clara Valley and examines how blacks were affected by its hasty shift from a rural region dominated by agricultural pursuits to a suburbanized area whose economy was taken over by the electronics industry and the military-industrial complex. Chapter 4 is crucial to understanding this history because it addresses residential apartheid and the struggles to eradicate this exclusionary custom and law on local, state, and federal levels. Chapter 5 looks at labor, civil rights, and race relations in the South Bay after Ford Motor Company relocated its local plant to Milpitas. Moreover, this chapter explains how Santa Clara County evolved into a region bifurcated by white- and blue-collar suburbs and how this split informed racial divisions and community growth throughout the valley. The forming of various African American communities and political traditions are further discussed in chapters 6 and 7 through the lenses of a fragmented civil rights movement within the South Bay and the "revolt of the black athlete," which sparked a domestic and international movement that transformed campuses and urban areas and opened positions in coaching and the front office for people of color. *Uninvited Neighbors* then ends with a concluding chapter on African Americans' attempts to live the American dream while being confronted with social isolation and customary racism during the Third Great Migration era.

It is my hope that *Uninvited Neighbors* will significantly contribute to the black urban and suburban historiographies and will firmly place the African American experience in the history of the American West rather than denying blacks their place in that history, as has been all too common.

Part One
African Americans in a Frontier Valley, 1769–1941

Chapter One
Origins of Santa Clara Valley's Black Community, 1769–1900

AFRICAN AMERICANS WERE intricately interwoven into the fabric of nineteenth-century Santa Clara Valley as settlers, institution builders, and freedom rights activists, yet their story is not commonly known and is rarely told.[1] Their saga began with ethnic Africans accompanying the first Spanish expedition along coastal Alta California in 1769. In that year, Gaspar de Portola explored the San Francisco Bay Area for the Spanish, followed by several other expeditions led by explorers and priests such as Pedro Fages, Juan Crespi, and Juan Bautista de Anza, whose initial aim was to locate the port of Monterey and secure it for Spain.[2] This quest ultimately included finding an overland route running from San Francisco to Mexico, and developing inland missions and pueblos to serve the coastal presidios and missions of San Francisco, Monterey, and San Diego. From fall 1769 to 1776, mulatto soldiers and other racially intermingled peoples with some African ancestry joined the Spanish expeditions into the Santa Clara Valley.[3] Ultimately these excursions led to the Spanish settling in the region.

The first Spanish settlement in the South Bay was Mission Santa Clara de Asis (Mission Santa Clara), established on January 12, 1777. This was one year after the Spanish founded a mission and presidio at San Francisco. Mission Santa Clara officially existed as a Christian agricultural commune serving the immediate population of Native American, Spanish, African, and Asian peoples. But the mission became a platform used by the Spanish to take everything away from the sole group that preceded them, the Ohlone Native Americans, including their religions, their livestock, the land they had been living on, and ultimately their lives. This mistreatment, which continued with American settlers, didn't let up until the Ohlone had virtually disappeared from the region by 1870.[4]

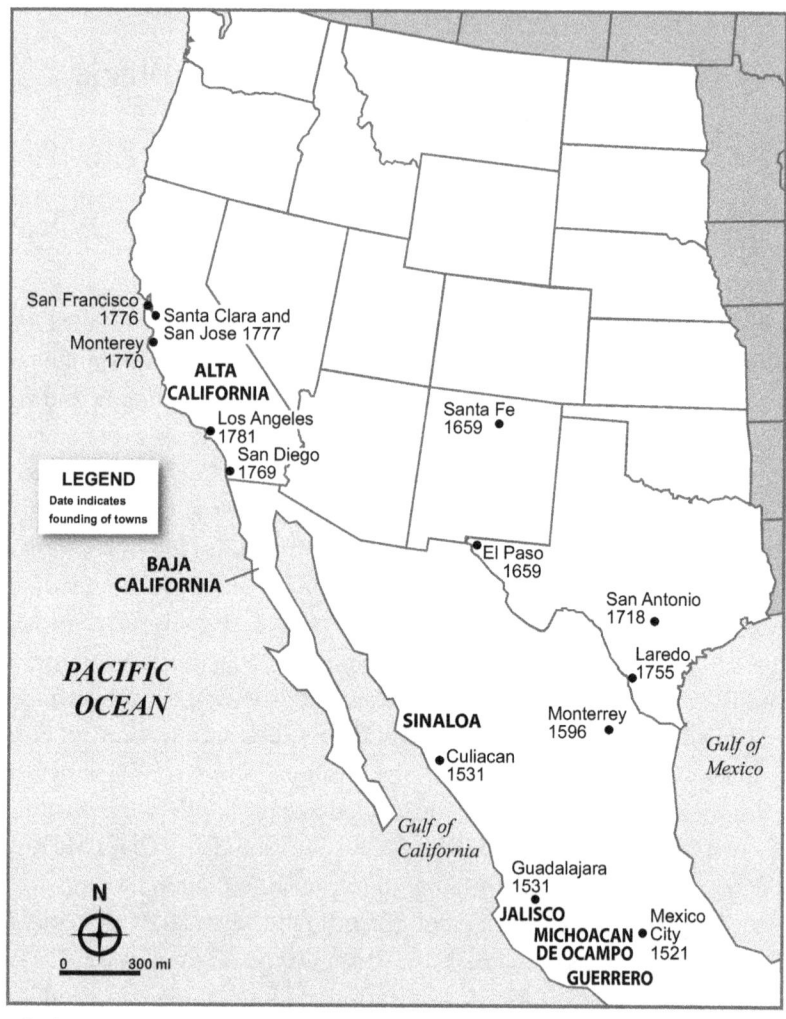

Black communities in New Spain. Copyright © 2014 by the University of Oklahoma Press.

TABLE 1 Black People in the Santa Clara Valley, 1777

	Age
Amesquita, Manuel (Mulatto, widower)	21
Joaquin Gabriel (Amesquita's son)	1
Basques, Tiburcio Joseph (Mulatto)	25
(Maria Bojorques, Mestiza) (Basques' wife)	19
Ygnacia, Maria (Basques' daughter)	1
Romero, Joseph (Mulatto)	35
Maria Petra Azebes, Mulatta (Romero's wife)	17
Tapia, Philipe	42
(Juana Cardenas, Mestiza) (Tapia's wife)	30
Maria Rosa (Tapia's daughter)	16
Joseph Bartolome (Tapia's son)	12
Juan Joseph (Tapia's son)	11
Juan Cristobal (Tapia's son)	10
Maria Manuela (Tapia's daughter)	9
Joseph Franco (Tapia's son)	8
Maria Ygnasia (Tapia's daughter)	7
Joseph Bito (Tapia's son)	3

SOURCES: Oscar Osburn Winther, "The Story of San Jose, 1777–1869, California's First Pueblo, Part I," *California History Magazine* 14 (1935): 3; Edith Smith, *Some Early African American Settlers in the Santa Clara Valley* (San Jose: Sourisseau Academy, 1994), 2; Tiburcio Joseph Basques, "Chapel Dedication Communication Sent by Mission of Santa Clara to Mission of Purisima Concepcion: February 8, 1812," in "Translations of Spanish/Mexican Archives: Pueblo of San Jose, 1792–1859" (California Room, Dr. Martin Luther King, Jr., Library, San Jose), 339–340.

NOTE: The first persons of African descent recorded in the Santa Clara Valley's list of first settlers (1777) were mulatto and mulatta *pobladores* (citizens) and their children.

Later in 1777, Lieutenant Don Jose Joaquin Moraga established El Pueblo de San Jose de Guadalupe (or San Jose), Alta California's first civil settlement.[5] During the Spanish era, San Jose was an agricultural settlement, or pueblo, in which its settlers produced food for soldiers in the Presidio of San Francisco and for bureaucrats in Spanish California's capital at Monterey.[6] San Jose was founded on the eastern bank of the Guadalupe River adjacent to Mission Santa Clara, which was founded on the western bank of the river.[7]

Persons of African descent were crucial to San Jose's founding and development. Of the sixty-eight original settlers, fifteen were people of African ancestry; in other words, 22 percent of the founding population was categorized as having African lineage.[8] Of the original fifteen families, four were headed by men of African descent, which amounted to 27 percent of the founding population. Within New Spain's porous racial classification system called the *sistema de castas* (system of castes), most of these persons of African lineage were identified as mulatto or racially intermingled Hispanicized citizens of predominantly African heritage. According to historian R. Douglas Cope, "the *sistema de castas* was a hierarchical ordering of racial groups according to their proportion of Spanish blood."[9] In this system, notable categories with significant meaning were Spaniard, *castizo, morisco, mestizo,* mulatto, Indian, and Negro (or African).

In the sistema de castas's most extreme application, there were more than forty classifications, with Spaniard the most desirable and Negro the least preferred.[10] San Jose's settlers of African descent were categorized between Spaniard and Negro. Socially they were marginalized in Mexican affairs and were constantly victimized by institutional discrimination. Afro-Mexicans came to San Jose from Mexican states on the Pacific Coast, including Sinaloa, Jalisco, Michoacán de Ocampo, and Guerrero. The initial recruits for frontier settlements such as San Jose were light-complexioned Spanish colonists, but many of them declined to participate because of "low pay, poor uniforms, antiquated weapons, insufficient housing, extended absences from families, and the overall unattractiveness of the Spanish military" and settlement.[11] This placed great burdens on racially marginalized colonists such as mestizos and mulattos to serve in colonial Spain's front

TABLE 2   Castas: The Racial Classification System in Colonial New Spain

Male	Female	Offspring
Spaniard	Indian	Mestizo
Spaniard	Negro	Mulatto
Spaniard	Mestiza	Castizo
Spaniard	Mulatta	Morisco
Morisco	Espanola	Chino
Chino	Indian	Salto atras
Salto atras	Mulatta	Lobo
Lobo	China	Gibaro
Gibaro	Mulatta	Alborazado
Alborazado	Negro	Cambujo
Cambujo	Indian	Zambaigo
Zambaigo	Loba	Calpamulatto

SOURCE: Leslie B. Rout, Jr., *The African Experience in Spanish America* (Cambridge: Cambridge University Press, 1976), 130.

lines, fighting wars and battles for settlements they probably did not adequately understand.

In the Santa Clara Valley during the Spanish era, few "Spaniards" were of pure European lineage.[12] As a result, intermarriage with Native American women was encouraged by Spanish officials, especially given the dearth of Spanish-speaking women to help populate the newly conquered region.[13] The task of populating the region fell on a wide array of racially intermingled Hispanicized people with backgrounds of Native American, European, African, and Asian descent.[14] According to historian Jack Forbes: "This frontier population also became 'whiter' as Indians and mulattoes declared themselves mestizos, and mestizos described themselves as espanoles. . . . Whitening occurred throughout Spain's empire, for a person's social status or *calidad* was never fixed solely by race, but rather defined by occupation and wealth as well as parentage and skin color."[15]

Consequently the goal for most people in New Spain was to become espanol for sociopolitical purposes. Race, color, and physical features in this society mattered then as they do today. For non-espanoles, California was not a racial paradise. Spanish colonies like San Jose offered limited socioeconomic mobility to men of African descent; for example, few Afro-Mexicans rose above a *cabo* (corporal) in the Spanish army; higher ranks were primarily reserved for *criollos* and mestizos.[16] Nonetheless, the sistema de castas allowed persons of African descent to socioeconomically elevate themselves more frequently in Spanish California than in the United States at the end of the eighteenth century. In one example, mulatto Pedro Huizar was able to become a don (Spanish nobleman) at Pueblo San Jose and thus change his status to espanol. Huizar was born and raised at Aguascalientes, Mexico, and he there acquired many skills in the arts and building trades. Around 1778, Huizar journeyed north. First he went to San Antonio and then to San Jose, where he worked as a sculptor, mission carpenter, and surveyor. Along the way, his race changed. Quintard Taylor notes that from San Antonio to San Jose, even though Huizar was initially "listed as a mulatto in the 1779 census, by 1793 he had become an *espanol*"—a switch that became more common after 1800 as racial lines became so blurred that they became useless to Spanish census takers and other Iberian officials.[17]

The racial classification system was not the only Spanish institution endangered by 1800. Spanish America under Charles IV (1788–1808) was becoming a place of political and economic instability because of socioeconomic unrest in the colonies and European activities abroad, such as Spain's internal economic depression, which eroded its ability to administer its colonies. This instability sparked the Mexican War for Independence (1810–1821).[18] In this period, Spanish Santa Clara Valley was a stagnant society of citizens remote from the war. On the eve of Mexican independence in 1821, San Jose had a small *castas* population of approximately 240 persons and a larger indigenous population, whereas Mission Santa Clara had a Spanish population of two (both Franciscan fathers) and a native population under mission instruction of almost fourteen hundred.[19] Outside of a few calls to arms for San Jose's militia, the wars waged within the valley were for social reforms, such as San Jose's attempts to maintain law and order by prohibiting the sale of alcohol to Native Americans and its own inhabitants.[20] Within this environment most castas of African descent, such as Tiburcio Basques, continued ignoring their African heritage and placed heavy emphasis upon the "perfect blend" of their Spanish and indigenous lineages until the sistema de castas collapsed under Mexican rule in 1829.[21]

The fall of the racial caste system was one of Afro-Mexican president Vicente Guerrero's reforms, and it prohibited "the use of race in any government document or in church records of baptism, marriage, and death."[22] In doing this, his administration transformed the racial caste system into a social system celebrating racial pluralism under the rubric of Mexican nationalism, and it restructured the country's social hierarchal order to privilege *ladino* (Spanish-speaking) civilization against non-*ladino* (indigenous) civilization. Africans within this scheme became Mexicans with *moreno* (brown) complexions, with no public mention of their African roots.[23] After 1829, the process of integration through intermarriage, de-Africanization, and Mexican citizenship hastened for most persons with African ancestry. In California, the collapse of the sistema de castas transformed castas into *Californios*.

ONE OF THE MOST NOTED Californios in the Santa Clara Valley was Antonio Maria Pico, who came from a family of African ancestry. Pico lived in San Jose from 1833 to 1869. Like most Californios, he came from a family that denied its African lineage, which in Pico's case traced back to the late 1700s to the offspring of his mestizo grandfather, Felipe Santiago de la Cruz Pico, and mulatta grandmother, María Jacinta de la Bastida.[24] Well connected, Pico came to San Jose as a soldier of Mexican descent and quickly became a leader in Bay Area affairs as lieutenant of San Jose's National Guard in the late 1830s and as owner of the 35,546-acre Rancho Pescadero (which means "fishing place"), a Mexican land grant in San Joaquin County and Alameda County. During the Mexican-American War (1846–1848) Pico served Mexico's Upper California Territory as an *alcalde* (judge) in San Jose and as colonel in the Mexican army. After California statehood (1850), he was a delegate to the first California Constitutional Congress, a prefect, a member of Santa Clara County's General Assembly, and the 1860 Republican candidate for presidential elector for the California Republican State Convention.[25]

Pico represents one of three different types of persons of African descent emerging within Mexican California: the Californio elite, whose power and privilege was rooted in family networks and the land grants that formed the nucleus of their ranching empires in the 1830s and 1840s. More common was the experience of Californios like the Romeros, who lived modest lives and had a lineage tracing back to two Pueblo San Jose founders, the mulattos Joseph and Maria Petra Azebes Romero.[26] The third type of people of African descent found on the South Bay's Mexican frontier consisted of self-identified blacks who had fled their owners and tested Mexico's commitment to emancipation.

In 1829, the same year in which the Spanish caste system collapsed, Mexico legally abolished slavery and granted Hispanicized persons of African and Native American descent civil rights. This legislation struck fear in U.S. slaveholders during the antebellum period. Within Mexico's anomalous state of legal antislavery and inconsistent enforcement, a few enslaved Africans from the United States were able to achieve freedom in the Santa Clara Valley. In Mexican San Jose, two examples were William Warren and John Caldwell.[27] According to historian Rudolph M. Lapp, Warren was probably a runaway seaman who came to California in 1828. For two decades, Warren appears to have lived as a freedman in northern California, making it possible for him to participate on his own behalf in the 1848 gold rush at Coloma—the gold discovery that triggered the famous California gold rush in 1849. After leaving the diggings, he moved to San Jose, where he lived out his life known to locals as "Uncle Billy."[28]

Meanwhile Caldwell, a cook on the frigate *California*, deserted ship at Monterey in 1832. The ship's captain demanded that authorities seize Caldwell, but to no avail because slavery had been abolished there by then. Caldwell ultimately made it to San Jose, arriving at the farm of someone who was possibly a former acquaintance, John Burton, who later was suspected of hiding Caldwell from slave catchers for an indefinite period.[29] In 1847 Burton, as a San Jose judge, heard a landmark case of an enslaved woman named Mary—who "may have been the first black woman from the States to come to California," according to Lapp.[30] Mary had accompanied her owner from Missouri to San Jose in 1846. Upon arrival she sued for her freedom in Burton's court and won without contest because her owner surrendered his property rights.

The California in which Mary was emancipated was on the verge of dramatic change. In 1846, the United States provoked Mexico into war, seeking to obtain California and western territories by military conquest. California fell immediately under U.S. military supervision until February 2, 1848. This was the date that Mexico officially ceded the area comprising what is now the Southwest United States, following the coerced signing of the Treaty of Guadalupe Hidalgo. Mexico was immediately reduced by about half as the United States took over lands that, in addition to California, are now Arizona, Nevada, New Mexico, and Utah and make up parts of Colorado, Kansas, and Oklahoma.[31] Rural regions within California, such as the Santa Clara Valley, were relatively unaffected by the war until the 1848 gold rush, when economic incentive became intricately linked to political changes.

During the early phases of the gold rush (1848–ca. 1854) the Santa Clara Valley did not attract most of the migrants contemplating quick riches through placer mining. Towns such as San Jose, Santa Clara, Milpitas, Mountain View, and Sunnyvale functioned as trade centers, agriculture centers, and rest areas between San Jose and the Sacramento Valley, San Francisco, and East Bay. San Jose's population became white and hypermasculine almost overnight as its population doubled, increasing from four thousand people in 1850 to eight thousand in 1852.[32] This population was a result of gold rush sprawl—or miners looking to settle as farmers—and San Jose's position as the state of California's first capital (1849–1851), which attracted people with political and entrepreneurial ambitions.

In addition, this period ushered in the first significant thrust toward urban development within the valley since the Spanish era. Inspired by potential commerce, population growth, and political acumen, San Jose was the South Bay's "beacon city," leading the way in urban growth, institution building, and the use of new technologies such as the telegraph, gas lamps, and, after 1880, an electric light tower that attracted a delegation from Paris prior to the construction of the Eiffel Tower in 1889.[33] Despite such advances, Santa Clara County did not register in the popular black consciousness until the 1860s, when Reverend Peter Williams Cassey opened St. Phillip's Mission School, a black secondary school, and a separate group founded the First African Methodist Episcopal Zion church.[34]

In fact, the California gold rush did not have special appeal for African Americans until California became a free state in 1850, representing socioeconomic freedom for free blacks and emancipation for those enslaved. Unfortunately for most African Americans, the gold rush was the catalyst for revolutionary change in nineteenth-century California when "the world rushed in" and, with it, chattel slavery and legal oppression imported from the East.[35] In this period of extreme greed, hardship, and despair for the people involved, California was significantly altered demographically, politically, economically, and socioculturally. It reinforced Anglo-American values and norms, even though they were never absolute. The state's large multicultural population and U.S. law intermingling with Mexican law became barriers to total Anglo domination throughout the state. Closely following such changes were drastic alterations in popular perceptions, attitudes, and beliefs. White supremacy emerged on the Californian frontier in the second half of the nineteenth century. For recent Anglo migrants such as Governor Peter H. Burnett, a San Jose resident, California was not about idealistic virtue. It was a place to create a white civilization on the Pacific coast, one superior to white communities in the East, which carried the stain of racial intermixture connected to slavery in the South and racial segregation in the North, and the hierarchal ordering of native-born white Americans, European immigrants, Native Americans, and African Americans. According to Governor Burnett in his first annual message to the California Legislature in 1851:

> Although it is assumed in the Declaration of Independence, as a self-evident truth, that all men are born free and equal, it is equally true that there must be *acquired* as well as *natural* abilities to fit men for self-government. Without considering whether there be any reason for the opinion entertained by many learned persons, that the colored races by nature are inferior to the white, and without attaching any importance to such opinions, still it may be safely assumed, that no race of men, under the precise circumstances of this class, in our State, could ever hope to advance a single step in knowledge or virtue. Placed by our institutions and our usages (stronger than law) in a degraded and subordinate political and social position, which reminds them at every step of their inferiority, and of the utter hopelessness of all attempts to improve their condition as a class, they are left *without motive* to waste their labor for that improvement, which, when attained, *brings them no reward*.[36]

Such California nativists as Burnett were strongly influenced by their mining experiences, slave-owning practices, and cultural prejudices, all of which led to contempt, hostility, and indifference toward black people, an attitude historian Eugene Berwanger framed within the U.S. West context as "Negrophobia" or "we don't want them here."[37] White supremacists believed that people of color were inferior Others who were unfit for self-government. And since they were not recognized by white society as free labor, they deserved no respect as first-class citizens living in a democratic, capitalistic, and Christian society. Thus for California nativists, individuals fitting within the black–indigenous people paradigm had to be either excluded from the state or demographically contained within white society and thus relegated to inferior status by law, custom, and enslavement.

During the California gold rush, blacks were confronted by a massive body of racially discriminatory laws aimed at reducing the African American population to total exclusion. As political agents similar to other people of color such as the Chinese and Native Americans, African Americans were banned from suffrage, citizenship, testimony against whites in court, jury service, intermarriage with whites, fair education, public accommodations, and homesteading.[38] Essentially California was a peculiar paradise from 1850 to 1893, representing to African Americans the potential to achieve the American dream of freedom and equality, yet restricting such mobility to European Americans. This compromised freedom traces back to September 9, 1850, when California entered the Union as a free state as part of the Compromise of 1850. To achieve this status without first becoming a territory, California lawmakers passed a weak antislavery constitution and a de facto (customary) anti-immigration bill, which left "the status of slaves who arrived before and after admission undefined, and no provision was made stating how long blacks could be held in slavery" until the enactment of the California's Fugitive Slave Law in 1852–1855 and 1858.[39] This law haunted free blacks, because the burden of proving one's freedom rested on the person accused of being a runaway slave, who was required to present manumission papers to legal authorities.[40]

California's Fugitive Slave Law worked hand-in-hand with the California Testimony Ban, in which African Americans, Native Americans, and Chinese could not testify against a white person.[41] For example, in 1850, a street fight in San Jose occurred between an apparent fugitive slave and a man claiming to be his master. The black man had the white man on the ground until a third party came to the aid of the white man, violently beating the black man with a club "so mercilessly that the gathered crowd cried, 'Shame!'"[42] The incident was broken up by the town marshal, who took the white man and black man before the judge. "To the dismay of San Jose citizens, a great many of whom were . . . of African ancestry, the *alcalde* ruled in favor of the white man, telling lawyers from both parties that the black man was a slave and that the white man was the rightful owner."[43] One spectator, however, reminded authorities that California was a free state and asked to purchase the slave outright and be allowed to leave the state with him, which the authorities agreed to.

Under most circumstances slavery spread easily across what would become the continental United States, but it was halted from becoming a dominant institution in part by political decisions such as the Missouri Compromise and antislavery constitutions in states like California. Slavery was not restricted because of improper climate, soil, arid land, or "natural limits" in the American North and West, as most scholars and public intellectuals had thought in previous years.[44] Slavery in California easily adapted to ranching, mining, and urban life, and antislavery legislation was lightly enforced. By 1852, about three hundred slaves worked in the goldfields, and an undetermined but sizable number were house servants in California cities.[45]

For San Jose resident Mattie Reed Lewis, slavery was a customary part of California life during the Mexican-American War. Her father owned several slaves who were brought into San Jose from Illinois in 1847. He later purchased several others in San Jose to work as domestic servants and to be hired out for extra income, a common practice in the South Bay.[46] Ms. Lewis first recognized just how extensive slavery was when her family visited Sacramento in 1847 and she saw several Malayans and Kanakas Native Americans serving men of European descent. What Ms. Lewis discovered on this trip was that even prior to total American domination and the influx of enslaved blacks from the East, men with lighter complexions, such as Captain John Sutter, commonly enslaved Native Americans, including the Kanakas and Ohlones of the Sacramento and Santa Clara Valleys. In the late 1840s, the practice of enslaving Asian Indians and Hawaiian natives as servants emerged for a short period in California until they were replaced by African Americans in the 1850s.

In antebellum Santa Clara Valley, a combination of enslaved African Americans and free blacks coexisted (1848–1865). According to South Bay historian Harriet Arnold, "some of the early settlers that came to San Jose were slaves who traveled with white settlers to the West, while others were free men and women."[47] In most instances, black Santa Clara Valley residents initially came to California to work the diggings for their owners. After slavery was abolished when

TABLE 3   African American Population in California, by County, 1850

	Free Total Population	Free Black People[1]	Free Black Males	Black Females	Slaves
California	92,597	962	872	90	NA
Los Angeles	3,530	12	5	7	NA
Sacramento	9,087	212	195	17	NA
San Diego	798	8	6	2	NA
San Francisco	NA	NA	NA	NA	NA
Santa Clara[2]	NA	NA	NA	NA	NA

SOURCE: *Historical Census Browser: County-Level Results for 1850–1960* (Charlottesville: University of Virginia Library, Geospatial and Statistical Data Center, 2005).
[1]The 1850 Census referred to "Free Black" as "Total Free Colored" population, males and females.
[2]The Santa Clara County portion of the federal census was lost.

California entered the Union in 1850, its practice continued in places like San Jose, which was a criminal society with an understaffed police force of questionable legal status until the mid-1850s. In the early 1850s, slave owners, taking advantage of the fact that San Jose police did not enforce California's antislavery law, concealed their slaves in the city for domestic work or hired them out for manual labor.[48] For many Santa Clara Valley slaveholders, slavery was an institution of both convenience and socioeconomic power. Common was the example of the Bascom family, who came to San Jose from Kentucky in December 1849. Upon Dr. Louis H. Bascom's arrival, he paid $800 for a black cook. In spite of California's antislavery law, the cook remained with the family for four years because in San Jose the ordinance was not enforced until the mid-1850s.[49] According to San Jose resident Mattie Reed Lewis, once California became a state, blacks were the preferred domestic servants. As for the Chinese, Lewis said that when her father "brought [the] family to San Jose, Chinamen were never seen in the house. People feared them."[50]

SANTA CLARA VALLEY BLACKS IN THE second half of the nineteenth century confronted political and legal restrictions through community building and political activism. For South Bay blacks, San Jose was the community where most former enslaved African Americans settled. During the gold rush era, this type of migration into Santa Clara County usually took place after African Americans worked in the Sacramento Valley as miners or as domestic servants.[51] James Williams—said to be the first African American in the South Bay— came to California enslaved in May 1851, working for his manumission at the diggings at Negro Hills, a small mining enclave for blacks at Sacramento. After being swindled out of $600 in wages for six months' labor in the mines and being manumitted, he moved and settled at Murphy Ranch (Milpitas) around 1852, where he found employment. Williams later started his own whitewashing business and operated freight teams between Hollister and San Francisco. A newpaper story from 1979 said of Williams, "Though considered well off by others in the black community, he died penniless."[52]

In a few reported instances, black abolitionists such as the Reverend Peter Williams Cassey and Harriet Davis purchased slaves in the early 1860s and immediately manumitted them in San Jose. Once free from slavery, many African Americans chose to live in San Jose because racial laws and the courts there were more flexible and perhaps more sympathetic to their plight than in larger cities such as San Francisco and Sacramento. Blacks came voluntarily and involuntarily to San Jose from all over the United States, with a huge proportion of the total coming from Missouri in the early 1850s, enslaved and serving their masters as farmhands and servants.[53] Of the forty-nine non-Spanish-speaking African Americans recorded as living in the South Bay around 1852, only one was indigenous to California.[54] In earning their living, Santa Clara Valley free blacks integrated into a diverse range of economic institutions related to their previous occupations in

James Williams, 1905. Courtesy History San Jose.

the North and South, as "farmers, laborers, gardeners, porters, waiters, barbers and cooks."[55] Several African Americans from northern states also appear to have created niches for themselves as bricklayers, restaurant owners, and merchants.[56] However, the serious drawback to blacks living within the valley was the fact that most economic pursuits were dominated by agriculture, an industry that formerly enslaved blacks associated with the antebellum South. Moreover, the South Bay was relatively isolated, its pace was slow, and its urban infrastructure was rudimentary in comparison to that of San Francisco, the preeminent urban center in the American West during the second half of the nineteenth century.

Central to African American community development in nineteenth-century California were the family, social justice politics, risk taking, and community activism, all centered on consciousness raising, self-determination, and survival. Within the sphere of black politics, community development began with cultivating a black consciousness. This was achieved by establishing African American institutions and honing skills that blacks had acquired in slavery and later as free women and men. As an economically marginalized people, gold rush–era blacks had to be alert for jobs and constantly hustle to earn a living. Sociopolitically, black Californians responded to racial degradation by developing separate communities geared toward promoting their humanity to themselves and within white society. Black Californians like Mary Ellen Pleasants and the Reverend Cassey often pooled their resources to cope with the weakness of blacks' economic foundation, which was marginal to the state's urban and mining economies and offered them little hope of amassing wealth from landownership—African Americans were excluded from California's homestead law until 1863, when they could contest white claims in court following the repeal of the anti–black testimony law.[57] Nonetheless, African American institution building flourished during the gold rush era beginning with the family, church, schools, barbershops, newspapers, and state political conventions. By the late 1850s, San Jose's black community was one of more than thirty in California that were intricately interwoven within a sociopolitical network led by black San Franciscans. Through racial unity, black uplift, and black pride, these communities influenced state and federal legislation in a manner disproportionate to their minute populations.

In black California, the foundation of institution building was the black church. Blacks established the African Methodist Episcopal (AME) Zion and Bethel churches and the Baptist church, with AME churches being the most dominant institution in terms of proliferation and political activism. The first black churches founded in California were the San Francisco and Sacramento AME churches in 1852. Later, AME churches were established in smaller rural towns with sizable African American populations, such as Stockton, Marysville, and San Jose. In San Jose in 1864, nine determined men who believed that blacks needed their own space for worship founded the First AME Zion Church on land donated by wealthy landowner and cofounder John Madden. The other founders, all northerners imbued with black uplift ideology and social justice politics, were John Williams, a former valet to Union General Ulysses S. Grant; William Smith and James Lodge, the church's first deacons and trustees; and Henry Venable, William H. Davis, George Caples, Howard Franklin, and Reverend William H. Mitchell. Prior to First AME Zion, blacks had to attend white churches, which some felt were indifferent to their needs, or go to San Francisco. During the gold rush era the only other Santa Clara Valley black institution to rival and collaborate with First AME Zion was Reverend Cassey's Christ Episcopal Church and St. Phillip's School.[58]

In nineteenth-century California, black Southern Baptist churches were established at a much slower pace. In the Santa Clara Valley, black Baptists did not have a church until 1893, when Antioch Baptist Church was formed.[59] They had to worship at Baptist churches either in San Francisco or Oakland, traveling by horse and buggy, or at First Baptist Church in San Jose, a predominantly white Baptist church where they were barred from leadership roles.[60]

The black church kept African Americans in California spiritually and materially grounded. Its existence was their collective response to being second-class members in white churches, in seeking property ownership, and in having limited civil rights, employment, and educational opportunities. More important, the black church fostered black unity, self-help, race pride, and leadership development as well as community action, moral reform, independent worship, and education. The black church was also the hub of a complex underground network that coordinated political strategies, "sending petitions to the state legislature . . . [and] letters of protest to news journals enlisting the aid of sympathetic whites" while transmitting local and statewide events to captivated African American audiences in code through ministers and barbers.[61] Ultimately, black churches were "communities within communities" directly rooted either in slave religion and independent black Baptist churches of the South or AME proliferation in the North.

IT IS NOT INSIGNIFICANT that the establishment of the black church and of a unified black community in South Bay occurred during the Civil War. For many black Californians, the war represented the hope of a new beginning on American soil. And with that hope came a call for civic responsibility and dignity. Peter Bell, editor of African American newspaper *Pacific Appeal*, wrote in 1864: "A new era has dawned, and it is with yourselves to decide as to whether you or your children shall be made capable of assuming the responsible positions which already are available to you. The federal government and the good and intelligent among the American people are endeavoring to help you."[62]

Essential to black Californians' premature optimism was the repeal, on March 21, 1863, of the state's testimony ban.[63] A key figure in opposition to the ban was San Jose abolitionist, politician, and *San Jose Mercury News* publisher James Jerome ("J. J.") Owen. On March 4, in a riveting speech to the California Assembly, Owen argued that "all men born beneath the protecting egis of the American flag, who can speak [English] . . . irrespective of color, condition or caste, [are] entitled to equal political privileges," and that such protection

> can only be guaranteed by admitting [people of color] testimony in our courts of justice. . . . That republican governments are made for white men only is a paradox too inconsistent to require serious reflection. We, as a people, will yet be made to recognize this truth: that the strength

and durability of republican governments depends solely on the universal intelligence and equal liberties of the people. I comprehend the gulf that a century of fraud and injustice has opened up between the races on this continent; and I comprehend also the slow process by which men unlearn error. The time has arrived for us to take the first step in the direction of justice. Let us not hesitate.[64]

This speech received unanimous support from the state's African American communities and was printed in the black newspaper *Pacific Appeal*. Owen, reared in upstate New York amid Radical Republican politics, had long supported abolitionism and racial equality before the law, and his outspokenness set the tone for black optimism to be a matter of fact in San Jose during the years he lived there, from 1861 to 1884.[65]

The repeal of the testimony ban allowed African Americans to sue and contest white claims in California courts over issues such as slavery, exclusion from streetcars, segregation in public education, and suffrage. The combination of these efforts ushered in a new phase of politics centered on black freedom rights activism and the creation of stronger communities. Moreover, black Californians, especially those living in San Francisco, stopped talking about leaving to escape fugitive slave law, and they became interested in new settlements. They discovered black communities in California and developed stronger ties to such communities, sometimes by resettlement but often by extending their institutions. Because of this refocus, San Jose became a major player in community building and African American politics in the second half of the nineteenth century through the efforts of such leaders as Richard Shorter, the Reverend T. M. D. Ward, William A. Smith, Cassey, Sarah Massey Overton, and Jacob Overton.

The seeds of black San Jose's influence on black California politics were sowed in 1857 by the Convention of Colored Citizens of the State of California (CCC; 1855–ca. 1865). The CCC was the first successfully organized abolitionist and civil rights group in the U.S. West. In 1857, Richard Shorter represented Santa Clara County as an officer on the convention's State Executive Committee. In this early phase, the convention connected with satellite black communities like San Jose through officers like Shorter. After 1860 the CCC created a network that included CCC officers, black institutions, and subscription agents who also worked as stringers for black newspapers *Mirror of the Times* and *Pacific Appeal*, such as William A. Smith and the Reverends Ward and Cassey.[66]

THE REVEREND PETER WILLIAMS CASSEY was a founding father of black San Jose. Born on October 13, 1831, and raised in Philadelphia by a prominent African American activist family, Cassey at an early age became deeply committed to black uplift, equal citizenship, and the eradication of social injustice. During the California gold rush, he evolved from barber to abolitionist, minister, educator, institution builder, and freedom rights activist.[67] In essence, he was one of the few "race men" in nineteenth century California to have made a living pursuing institutional activities geared toward black uplift.[68] Cassey's grandfather, the Reverend Peter H. Williams, was a fair-skinned man who chose not to pass for white and benefit from white privilege. Instead he fought racial injustice from the trenches as the founder of St. Phillips Episcopal Church in New York and as a leading philanthropist from the late 1700s to 1824.[69] Cassey's father, Joseph R. Cassey, was a student activist in the Free African School movement in New York City. The school was the training ground for leading black abolitionists and freedom rights leaders including Alexander Crummell, Henry Highland Garnet, and Philip A. Bell.[70] In addition, Cassey's grandfather and father were renowned businessmen, abolitionists, and anti-colonialists staunchly opposed to the white supremacist group known as the American Colonization Society. Cassey's grandfather and father also supported the independent AME church movement, black education, black voluntary migration, black suffrage, manumission societies, and black newspapers such as *Freedom's Journal*.[71]

When Cassey initially migrated to California in 1853 as a twenty-two-year-old barber, he hoped to capitalize on rumors of easy riches. In San Francisco, Cassey formed a partnership with Charles H. Mecier that led to their establishing a barbershop in the basement of

Reverend Peter Williams Cassey. Courtesy Trinity Episcopal Church.

the Union Hotel on Merchant Street.[72] According to a 1996 newspaper story, the two men "became part of a network [of politically active African Americans] that passed along reports, in code, on legislation being considered in Sacramento that might be detrimental to blacks. This underground network also collected and distributed information on acts of cruelty and discrimination."[73] More important, Cassey was closely connected with the CCC's Executive Committee. That group later provided him with crucial organization and administrative assistance and donated money to Cassey's St. Phillip's Mission School for African American children at San Jose during a period of nonwhite exclusion from California's public schools.

St. Phillip's Mission School was the first black institution in Santa Clara County. Cassey opened it after his ordination in December 1861 in downtown San Jose. He had left San Francisco and moved to San Jose a year earlier in response to the pleas of African American families in the area to open a secondary school for their children.[74] At the time only a few secondary schools had been established in California, and white children were the only ones allowed to legally attend in most school districts until 1874.[75] As early as 1854, the CCC formed "colored schools" in Sacramento and San Francisco primarily in reaction to African American tax dollars being used to finance white-only public schools. These schools sought to instill racial uplift, promote academic excellence, matriculate public funds for black education, and pressure local school boards to integrate public schools while "pointing to New England, where such schools were operating successfully."[76] In the late 1850s, this black school movement extended into Oakland and Stockton, and it had come to San Jose by the early 1860s.[77]

St. Phillip's presence gave most black Santa Clara Valley residents hope and a sense of belonging in black California affairs. The school was closely aligned with Trinity Episcopal Church, a white church in San Jose founded in 1860.[78] Financially and institutionally, St. Phillip's initial opening was supported by Cassey, Trinity Episcopal Church, the CCC, and a white music teacher by the name of Mr. Higgins. Higgins taught at the predominantly white local public school and taught music to black students as an unpaid volunteer; he organized

The two-story building on the outskirts of San Jose (in the center of this sketch) was where the Casseys rented the Bascom Home for the St. Philip's Academy and Institute. Information courtesy Reverend Jerry Drino. Courtesy Trinity Episcopal Church.

fundraising recitals at Town Hall for St. Phillip's.[79] The school was housed in several different locations during its ten-year existence, with the Cassey home on Fourth Street, between Reed and William Streets, being the space most commonly cited by scholars.[80] St. Phillip's was sometimes referred to as the Phoenixonia Institute (after December 22, 1863) or St. Phillip's Mission at Phoenixonian Hall. The *San Jose Mercury News* instructed its readers to call it "the School for Colored Children."[81]

The Phoenixonia Institute functioned as a secondary school, boarding school, and library.[82] The boys and girls attending St. Phillip's came from the greater San Jose area, other parts of California, and as far away as Portland, Oregon, and Panama.[83] The school's operational expenses were paid primarily by fees for board and tuition. These ranged from $12 to $20 per person for four weeks, or from $100 to $160 per term in 1866 and 1867.[84] Expenses were supplemented by the CCC, private donations, the Rev. Cassey, and common city school funds from 1866 to 1871. From December 1861 to 1871 more than two hundred students attended school at St. Phillip's.[85] Within this period, from twenty-eight to thirty-five children were enrolled at St. Phillip's at any given time.[86]

Critical to St. Phillip's success was its superb education. Teachers trained young people to read and write English and learn music. Lessons were taught Monday through Friday and sometimes on Saturday.[87] According to local historian Deborah LeFalle, on Sunday the space occupied for secular education was transformed into a Sunday school that Cassey called St. Phillip's Mission. On the same day, Phoenixonian Hall became the Santa Clara Valley's third African American institution, called Christ Episcopal Church; the only other place of worship in the region prior to the establishment of Antioch Baptist Church in 1893 was First AME Zion Church.[88] More important, St. Phillip's was the training ground for future black leaders in the South Bay, including early-twentieth-century African American women activists Sarah Massey Overton and Julia A. Shorey, a founder of Antioch Baptist Church.

The Phoenixonia Institute regularly brought national attention to blacks in the Santa Clara Valley. It recruited students through its fabulous reputation, black networks, and African American newspapers. As a lead organizer for the 1863 Annual Convention of Colored Citizens of the State of California in San Jose, Cassey made education and suffrage critical topics for convention delegates, and his priorities were echoed at other colored conventions throughout the United States. Convention delegates saw learning and literacy as highly valued in the African American community. And yet African Americans were being taxed to support public schools that excluded them.[89] For many black leaders, integrated education was paramount to the eradication of race prejudice in the state.[90] Convention delegates considered the Phoenixonia Institute to be a valuable institution that went beyond educating African American youth excluded from Santa Clara Valley public schools: it was, in the 1860s, the pulse of the black South Bay. Through a unanimous motion the convention passed a resolution "to tax each black person in the state one dollar to support the school."[91]

In hindsight, the resolution was apparently a success, given that St. Phillip's taught African American children until 1874.

However, St. Phillips confronted tremendous barriers daily that challenged its existence. The school was constantly endangered by shortages of money, limited time for development, and California legislation. The year 1866 was transitional for both Cassey and his school. Cassey broke racial barriers on September 13, 1866, by becoming the first person to be ordained as a deacon of San Jose's predominantly white Trinity Episcopal Church and hence the first black person in California to become a deacon at any predominantly white church. Conducting the ceremony was Bishop William Ingraham Kip, the first Episcopal bishop of California and a strong supporter of Cassey's.

The year 1866 was also transitional for Phoenixonia Institute because California passed legislation that year that recognized that a child of African, Asian, or indigenous descent had the right to a public education.[92] For the first time, provisions were made for a separate system that permitted people of color to attend their own publicly supported schools. California also stipulated that in districts in which school trustees did not vote to establish a separate "colored school," black children could not attain a basic education unless they attended a private institution such as the Phoenixonia Institute. The San Jose Board of Education responded by becoming one of the first school districts in California to open a state-supported colored school. They did so through an agreement with Cassey. He would become principal of the state-supported public school, San Jose School for Coloreds, in return for common school funds from the state to financially support St. Phillip's until there was no need for private colored schools in San Jose.[93] This arrangement ended in 1874 when the San Jose Board of Education voted to stop appropriating state funds to St. Phillip's and open a public colored school controlled by the city.[94] Thus for Cassey, what appeared to be an unequal partnership with the San Jose Board of Education, in which St. Phillip's enrollments steadily declined because African American children were being steered to the public "separate school," actually formed the core of a complex CCC strategy aimed at equal education in California. In the following year (1867), the CCC responded to Cassey's success by holding the conference in

San Jose and passing resolutions that made the fight for equal education a top priority.[95]

In the 1870s Cassey's focus became divided between San Jose and San Francisco. According to the Reverend Jerry Drino of Trinity Church, Cassey, acting at the request of Bishop Kip, in 1870 founded a small Episcopalian mission known as Christ Mission Church for Colored People in San Francisco.[96] In the following year, he fully relocated his parish membership to San Francisco, while his wife ran St. Phillips and remained a San Jose resident until her death on September 3, 1875. In 1881, Cassey left California to become the rector at St. Cyprian's Church in New Bern, North Carolina. However, before leaving California, he helped to establish another legacy in the South Bay, through black California's suffrage movement.

THE MOVEMENT TO OBTAIN THE BLACK vote in California began during the Civil War. On March 13, 1863, a group of San Jose African Americans sent a suffrage petition signed by seventy-five people to the California governor and to President Lincoln. They received no reply.[97] Petitioning for the vote became a central issue for the CCC in 1863 and 1865. After the Civil War, the suffrage movement became a national movement among both African Americans and white women. In 1865, the CCC's petitioning encouraged California Senator John E. Benton to propose an amendment to the state constitution to give blacks the right to vote, but the proposal failed in the state's Judiciary Committee, which was controlled by white supremacists in the Democratic Party.[98] This failure was actually a political success for black Californians, whose appeals for suffrage nationally exposed California as a state hostile to Reconstruction's post–Civil War goals of economic and racial justice. Federally, the black suffrage movement was strengthened by the passage of the Thirteenth (1865), Fourteenth (1868), and Fifteenth (1870) Amendments to the U.S. Constitution, which, respectively, abolished slavery, established national citizenship, and gave black men the right to vote.[99]

In the Santa Clara Valley, caterer and community leader Jacob Overton responded to the passage of the Fifteenth Amendment by

TABLE 4   Population in the Santa Clara Valley, by Race and Ethnicity, 1860–1900

	1860	1870	1880	1890	1900
Black	87[1]	173	161	989	251
Total population	7,309	26,246	35,039	48,005	60,216
White	NA	24,536	32,110	NA	NA
Native American	NA	12	73	19	NA
Chinese	NA	1,525	2,695	2,723	NA
Japanese	NA	NA	NA	27	NA

SOURCE: *Historical Census Browser: County-Level Results for 1850–1960* (Charlottesville: University of Virginia Library, Geospatial and Statistical Data Center, 2005).
[1] Only blacks who were free were counted in the 1860 census.

immediately organizing prospective black male voters. Of the ninety-four potential African American male voters in the valley, sixty-five attended the first meeting in a courtroom lent to them by a judge.[100]

What the group decided was that they would vote as a unit and try to get some political patronage in return for their electoral support. The initial implementation of the black male vote was challenged by San Jose's city clerk's office. On April 1, 1870, Cassey and an unnamed friend were turned away from the clerk's office when they attempted to register. The deputy clerk "claimed he had no authority to register them."[101] This decision was reinforced by County Clerk John Littlefield, who rebuffed their appeal "but agreed to take the matter under advisement."[102] Unsure, Littlefield telegraphed U.S. Secretary of State Hamilton Fish about the status of the Fifteenth Amendment and for possible instructions.[103] In reply, Fish placed the responsibility of registering African American voters on the office of the county clerk. The next day, blacks registered. The deputy clerk invited the first African American man walking by the county clerk's office to register. The man, Peter Wagner, was a forty-six-year-old Kentucky native and former slave who registered as a Democrat. Soon after Wagner registered, twenty other African American men registered, most as Republicans.[104] White San Jose mostly responded favorably to the black vote and to federal law superseding state law.[105] In the Santa Clara Valley, the *San Jose Mercury News* reporting perhaps prevented a white backlash by noting that the black vote was nonthreatening because of the smallness of South Bay's African American population.

The African American vote in Santa Clara County was largely symbolic. On the surface, it appeared to signal the dawn of a new day for racial equality and social justice for California. In reality, the black vote of the postbellum period (1865–1900) did not result in political patronage and had little influence on California public policy. The state did not have an African American representative until 1918, when Frederick M. Roberts of Los Angeles was elected to the California Assembly. In the Santa Clara Valley, the first black nominated to public office was Ben Gross, who in 1961 was elected as Milpitas city councilman. Still, suffrage was a crucial step in the black quest for first-class citizenship and social justice in the United States.

On April 7, 1870, African Americans rejoiced in their men's being able to vote by holding religious services at San Jose's AME Zion Church. This was followed by a San Jose ratification celebration at the Pleasure Garden. At the garden they heard J. J. Owen and Judge Robert F. Peckham speak.[106] The night ended with a grand ball at Phoenixonian Hall that was attended by both blacks and whites.[107] Despite the South Bay's optimistic mood on race relations, many racist comments were made during the ratification celebration and after the event in newspaper editorials in communities surrounding San Jose, reminding black and white liberals that the color line in the Bay Area was firmly in place. In one instance, a white Democrat allegedly approached an African American man either during the Pleasure Garden event or at the polls and said, "Now that you have got the ballot, I suppose next you will be wanting to marry our daughters." "No," the black man answered, "and we don't want you to marry ours."[108] This was followed by editorials denouncing the grand ball in newspapers in Nevada City, Sacramento, San Francisco, and Sonoma as a miscegenation ball. A *Mercury News* editorial in support of the ratification ball said, "There were carriage loads of as beautiful, intelligent, and well-dressed women and children as we ever saw in any 'white' procession."[109] Offended, Nevada newspaper editor A. M. Morse published the statement with this response: "This self-stultifying statement of the San Jose man shows to what degrading depths of falsehood and blindness a man may be brought to by Radicalism. This poor *Mercury* editor asserts that he never saw any white woman who was more 'beautiful and intelligent,' than the negresses in the procession of which he speaks."[110]

In Santa Clara County, any attempt to generate a white backlash fell on deaf ears as fifty black men voted in San Jose without challenge. Most white Democrats in the valley protested being on equal terms with African Americans at the ballot box by refusing to vote.[111] However, in most California counties white Democrats did vote, and they did so as a conservative bloc that was united in opposition to the black suffrage movement and Chinese immigration.[112] More significant, "San Jose's municipal election marked the Fifteenth Amendment's first test in California" and possibly one of the first places in the United States.[113] According to historian Steven Millner, "The openness of the community brought San Jose notice throughout the country."[114] Word of the African American vote and Santa Clara Valley living conditions ("some of the best housing in the country," according to Millner) were disseminated by train through black porters, letters, churches, and the black press. However, this did not create a mass migration of African Americans to Santa Clara County for four reasons. First, local white Democrats counteracted the black and Republican vote by increasing its voter pool with European immigrant males through the use of nativist rhetoric.[115] Second, from 1848 to 1900, economic opportunities for South Bay blacks were limited to domestic work, manual labor, and a small pool of skilled professionals and entrepreneurs. Third, the Reconstruction era (1863–1877) brought hope to blacks living east of the Mississippi River and halted their outmigration to Canada, Mexico, and the U.S. West from the North and South; this is in contrast to the prior era (1850–1863), when African Americans were trying to escape chattel slavery in the South, or to avoid accusations of being fugitive slaves, or to acquire easy riches during the numerous gold and silver rushes throughout the West. Fourth, blacks tended to migrate to cities with major railroad connections and waterfront employment opportunities, like Oakland.[116] When African Americans did migrate to rural areas, they did so seeking to establish their own base of land and communal power in black towns like Nicodemus, Kansas; Boley, Oklahoma; and Allensworth, California. This is not to say that Santa Clara Valley blacks lacked their own base of power.

The political culture that began with the CCC during the gold rush continued in the South Bay up to the turn of the twentieth century. From 1870 to 1900, a new generation of African Americans emerged in downtown San Jose, replacing the gold rush generation who were either passing away, retiring, or moving on to new challenges elsewhere. Among this new generation were people like Jacob and Sarah Massey Overton.

JACOB, A FORMER SLAVE FROM Kentucky and high-profile caterer, served the South Bay as a subscription agent and stringer for the *Pacific Appeal*, a voting rights activist, lodge leader in the Colored Odd Fellows and Masons, and local Afro American League president in the 1890s; it was under Jacob's leadership that the league fought for women suffrage.[117] In the 1880s, Jacob's wife, Sarah, a former St. Philip's student, became a leading activist in the fair public education movement while also working as a caterer and raising two children.[118] This battle for fair public education was partially won following the *Wysinger v. Crookshank* decision by the California Supreme Court in 1890, which allowed African American and Native American youths to desegregate public schools. The verdict, however, also upheld the "separate but equal" doctrine, reserving for the California legislature the right to reimpose de jure (legal) segregation in public education whenever it wished.[119] In the following decade, Sarah extended the CCC tradition to the women's rights struggle, starting with her cofounding of the San Jose's Garden City Women's Club in 1906 and lobbying for the formation of interracial women's club coalitions to support women's suffrage. Sarah was also in the forefront of registering male voters to support women suffrage on the state level through the Political Equality Club of San Jose. This hard work in intersecting the black and women

Advertisement for Jacob Overton's catering business. From *Hidden Heritages: Six African American Families; San Jose, 1860–1920* exhibit at San Jose City Hall, 2009–2010. Photographer Herbert G. Ruffin II. Courtesy Sourisseau Academy, San Jose State University.

struggles catapulted her to vice president of San Jose's interracial Suffrage Amendment League and, later, president of the all-black Victoria Earle Matthews (Mothers) Club, which aided young black women and girls who had been sexually abused or who were threatened with sexual abuse. In the story of black freedom politics, the Overtons were two of many South Bay blacks who continued the CCC tradition of making California live up to their expectations of legal and social justice. In the 1890s, California was a peculiar state that led the nation in anti-immigration legislation but also in racial desegregation. In 1893, the state barred segregation in public accommodations.[120] Some of the African American pioneers who worked with the Casseys and Overtons in agitating for legal equality were related to the Breckenridges, Browns, Casseys, Coopers, Floyds, Maddens, Maddoxes, Overtons, Speights, Turners, Vennerables, and Whitings. According to the manuscript census, almost all of the adults in this group came from northern or southern states east of the Mississippi River, whereas most of their children were born in California. Most of these blacks also made their living working as laborers, domestic servants, bootblacks, and barbers; a few were farmers and farm laborers working in isolation from other blacks in Gilroy, Los Gatos, Milpitas, San Jose, and Santa Clara. Most African Americans lived around today's San Jose State University and in a community called the Northside. By the turn of the twentieth century, most blacks had been steered into clustered communities in and around the Northside.[121] At the time, the neighborhood was a small, vibrant working-class community centered on Tenth and Washington Streets and situated north of Santa Clara Street. During the age of Jim Crow, the Northside became the place where African Americans forged the core of San Jose's black community and politically mobilized toward breaking the county's color line.[122]

The next chapter will examine the development and growth of San Jose's Northside from 1900 to 1941 and of black communities outside of San Jose, such as Old Palo Alto, whose AME Zion church was ground zero for a small yet significant and forgotten black community that lived and owned property near Stanford University in West Santa Clara County.

Chapter Two
African Americans in the Valley of Heart's Delight, 1900–1941

BLACK WESTERNERS IN THE EARLY twentieth century have been overlooked in the American West by western regional historians and historians of African America because of their relatively small population. California in this period continued to be a land of compromised freedom predicated on racial segregation and white privilege, which contradicted its popular image of racial tolerance and multicultural inclusion. The traditional interpretation of blacks living in American West communities like San Jose before the 1940s has contended that African American westerners were insignificant, passive, and involuntarily "excluded from many spheres of the region's activities."[1] This argument has led Richard Dalfiume, Gerald Nash, and many other scholars to overestimate the effect that World War II and the postwar era had on African American communities in larger metropolitan areas in the West.[2] Excluded from this interpretation are smaller urban spaces such as San Jose, Santa Clara, and Palo Alto in the Santa Clara Valley, which in the first half of the twentieth century were transformed from agricultural communities with a modernizing central business district in downtown San Jose into a suburban metropolis after World War II. In 1900 the South Bay African American population was little more than a fourth what it had been ten years before. Though hampered by outmigration, the black community continued to focus on the formation of black institutions and political organizations. This chapter examines African American life and the development of black institutions in the South Bay from 1900 to 1941. In this period, black institutions and political organizations were crucial to African Americans in the Santa Clara Valley in transcending racial barriers and demographic stagnation and in creating a sense of belonging in a place where economic empowerment was elusive.

From 1880 to the mid-1950s the Santa Clara Valley was predominantly a large farming community that fed the nearby metropolitan areas and industrial centers of San Francisco and Oakland. At the turn of the twentieth century, boosters aptly termed the region the "Valley of Heart's Delight," a direct reference to the South Bay's warm weather, placid valleys, fruit trees, and residents, who were supposedly always flourishing with youth and vigor.[3] The South Bay's agricultural industry developed simultaneously with the railroad industry and new techniques in food preservation, including refrigerated railcars and dried fruit packing in the 1870s and canning in the 1890s. A viticulture industry also developed during the same period. Before the 1940s, the South Bay's urban development and heavy industrial growth beyond San Jose's central business district ranged from gradual to very slow.

Employment and housing within the South Bay's agricultural industry were segregated along strict lines of race, ethnicity, and nationality. European immigrants, especially the Portuguese, replaced Chinese laborers after the 1880s. These immigrants moved up the local social and economic ladders by becoming U.S. citizens, farmers on choice fertile soil, and "Caucasians" in a pseudo-scientific racial hierarchy that privileged whites over people of color—all within one generation.[4] In terms of skill, first-generation Japanese immigrants (the *Issei*) could have rivaled Portuguese immigrants as farmers; however, the California Alien Land Law of 1913 and federal naturalization laws of 1790, 1922, and 1924 prevented an economic and social rivalry from occurring—underscoring the continuation of white supremacy.[5] As for persons of Mexican ancestry, most were restricted to working-class urbanizing communities like East San Jose and areas dominated by large food producers including Libby, McNeil & Libby at Sunnyvale. Neighborhoods within East San Jose include Alum Rock, East Foothills, Evergreen, King and Story, Little Portugal, and Meadowfair. Mexican Americans commonly worked on farms as day laborers and at canneries between 1914 and the early 1930s.[6] Most African Americans participated on the periphery of the local agricultural industry, working in the downtowns of San Jose and Palo Alto as domestics, entrepreneurs, laborers, service workers, and skilled tradesmen.[7] The few who participated in the agricultural industry mostly worked

Orchard scene, ca. 1920. Courtesy History San Jose.

as farmers and day laborers on the outskirts of downtown San Jose in the townships of Alviso, Burnett, Gilroy, and Milpitas. Otherwise, most South Bay blacks lived in the downtown San Jose community called the Northside.[8] This semiurban community centered on Tenth and Julian Streets. The Northside was one of several communities in the South Bay that symbolized progress and vertical social mobility for Santa Clara Valley blacks prior to the suburbanization of the region in the 1950s because it was absent a ghetto, and many African American homeowners could compensate their economic marginalization in the local economy by building their own homes and community institutions.

San Jose in the early twentieth century was an agricultural metropolis with walking city and streetcar suburb components within its central business district. Known for its farms and orchards in the areas beyond the downtown, San Jose was called the "Garden City." San Jose grew rapidly in the early twentieth century because of its relative monopoly in providing services and goods to an isolated South Bay

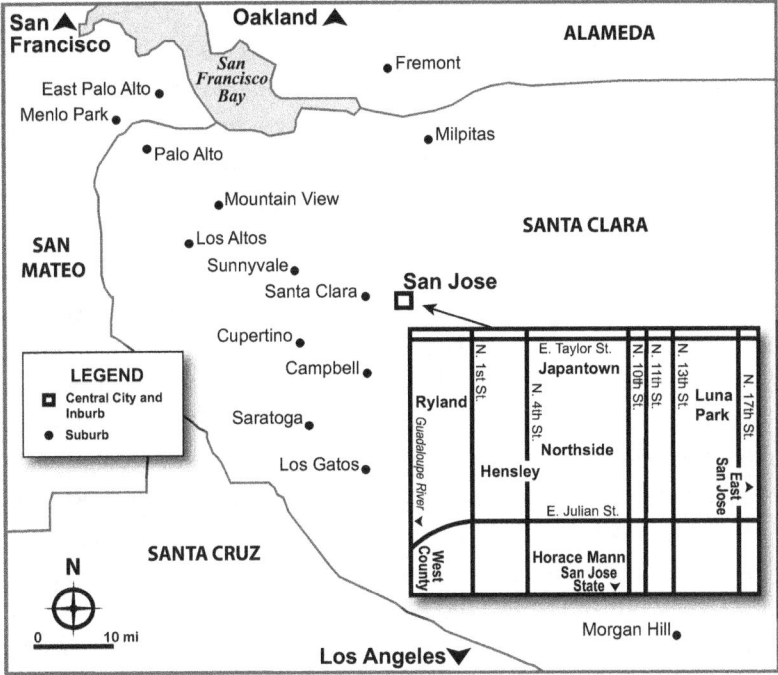

Northside San Jose, 1860–1970. Copyright © 2014 by the University of Oklahoma Press.

region. Crucial to San Jose's rise in local preeminence was its infrastructure and management: downtown was accessible from most parts of the valley by electric streetcars; and it was the first South Bay city to provide electric street lights, hire a city manager, and implement city planning, all of which occurred from the turn of the century to the 1910s. According to the *Los Angeles Times*, San Jose at the turn of the twentieth century attempted to mirror Los Angeles' phenomenal growth as a former pueblo turned enterprising city.[9] This movement peaked around 1912 and ended during the Great Depression, when San Jose's hopes to construct a deepwater seaport and major railroad terminus at Alviso were dashed by two realities. First, small farmers were resistant because development of nearby open space and higher residential densities would diminish their economic independence and quality of life. Second, San Jose could not annex Alviso, the most natural harbor on the bay in the Santa Clara Valley; only much later, in 1968, would a vote for annexation succeed. These failures stunted San Jose's urban growth and chased away potential investors, leaving the city unable to develop a major transport system that would have allowed it to store and ship surplus goods throughout the South Bay.

One can only imagine what course the Santa Clara Valley's history might have taken if the deepwater seaport and major railroad terminus had become realities. But without them, people in the South Bay remained predominantly committed to rural-agricultural pursuits, a commitment that stunted black population growth up to the 1960s. In 1890, Santa Clara County had the third-largest African American population among counties in California, with 989 persons.[10] This was a significant jump from the 161 blacks who resided in the valley just a decade before. However, by 1900, the county's black population was reduced to 251 people, primarily because African Americans coming of age found better residential and work opportunities in the rapidly urbanizing and industrializing Alameda and Los Angeles Counties. Four decades later, in 1940, the Santa Clara County black population had risen to 730 people.[11]

Prior to World War II the pattern of gradual demographic growth of persons of African descent in California was not uncommon. With the exception of Los Angeles and lesser-known enclaves scattered throughout California, most communities became almost exclusively white. Blacks were discouraged from coming to the Bay Area primarily by distance, paternalism, de facto segregation, socioeconomic glass ceilings, and the entrenchment of exclusively white trade unions in urban industries: the West was not beyond the racial frontier prevalent in the East.[12] Perhaps the most important factor influencing African Americans prior to 1942 was distance from the eastern United States, with the West Coast being seen by blacks as "the end of the line" within a series of migrations.[13] These migrations started with circular movement from the rural to urban South, then became an increasingly linear exodus to larger metropolitan areas in the North like Chicago. If the northern cities didn't meet blacks' socioeconomic needs, this migration was followed by a more permanent resettlement pattern to the urban West.

TABLE 5 Populations of Color in Santa Clara County, 1900–1940

	1900	1910	1920	1930	1940
Black	251	262	335	536	730
Other people of color	NA	3,428	3,428	9,394	5,298
Total	60,216	83,539	100,676	145,118	174,949

SOURCE: *Historical Census Browser: County-Level Results for 1850–1960* (Charlottesville: University of Virginia Library, Geospatial and Statistical Data Center, 2005).

Black Bay Area residents in this period were always on the periphery of the region's economy, with the greatest potential for economic freedom occurring in Oakland, which was urbanizing and industrializing. Socially, most Bay Area migrants of European descent did not leave their Eurocentric beliefs and Jim Crow traditions at the California border. From 1896 to 1968, legal racial segregation was a national phenomenon interwoven throughout California with preexisting discriminatory practices (i.e., de facto racial discrimination and the exclusion of nonnaturalized citizens). However, in pre-1942 California, this racialized behavior primarily targeted the Chinese, Japanese, Filipinos, and persons of Mexican descent. From 1900 to 1940, there is very little documentation that mentions what relations were like between different ethnic groups in the Santa Clara Valley. The evidence that does exist suggests that although blacks lived near other people of color, language barriers and cultural differences limited interracial interaction. As a result, most South Bay blacks were racially tolerated and lived relatively isolated lives. They defined themselves "around themes of collective destiny, flight from bondage, and liberation," or biblical Exodus in which the Santa Clara Valley represented a promised land.[14]

IN SAN JOSE, SOME OF THE black families that migrated to the city during the early twentieth century were the Berrys, Bosts, Boyers,

Isums, Ellingtons, Jordans, Masts, McCalls, McColls, Mosses, Ratliffs, Ribbses, and Turners.[15] Most of these migrants came from families in which it was common to have more than six siblings—some of whom settled into the South Bay because it resembled their communities of origin, which were mainly in the South. One such settler was Henry William Ribbs, who saw the Santa Clara Valley as a fresh beginning in which Jim Crow conditions could be challenged with minimal fear of white violence. Ribbs arrived in San Jose in 1920 after receiving a death threat in Shreveport, Louisiana, from two white men. Ribbs, who was twenty-one at the time, had been minding his own business hauling bales of cotton for a local farmer when one of the white men interrupted him with the opening line, "hey, nigga, nigga, nigga" and orders that Ribbs "fetch someone to [his] telephone." Ribbs responded by telling the white man to "go to hell" and demanding that he be called by his name. The white man proceeded to threaten Ribbs with a pistol and again called him "nigga." The other white man responded to the exchange by saying, "Nigga, I give you five days to get out of this county."[16] Tired of southern racism, Ribbs left Louisiana hastily and went to California with few resources, hoping to cultivate a new beginning in a place where he would be treated like a man. The event haunted Ribbs, who tried his best to stand like a man and not be expected to endure racial insults made all the more unendurable because they came from racist thugs.[17]

Initially Ribbs intended to travel to Hawaii, but he reconsidered after a black porter on the Southern Pacific informed him that San Jose was "the finest town" in the American West. If San Jose was not to his liking, the porter then suggested, he should try out San Francisco or Oakland before sailing off to Hawaii. After spending several days in San Jose, Ribbs examined his options in San Francisco and Oakland. Both had pros and cons. But Ribbs favored Oakland because it had a black presence, and San Francisco did not.[18] Disoriented, Ribbs ultimately settled on San Jose. The city was slower paced than Oakland and was less sprawling, with a gentle, countrylike social atmosphere—an assessment that his brother Clyde and sister-in-law Ola apparently made a year before Henry's arrival. As a farmer raised in a family with ten siblings, Ribbs also found the Santa Clara Valley to be the closest Bay Area region resembling home. More important, Ribbs immediately found a support network in Antioch Baptist Church. He also quickly found employment as a rancher and plumbing apprentice under Thomas Moss in exchange for a minimal wage and room and board. For Ribbs, "San Jose was alright."[19]

FOR MOST SOUTH BAY BLACKS, earning a living wage was a constant challenge. At the turn of the twentieth century most African Americans earned a living in a range of jobs similar to what their predecessors had been restricted to in the nineteenth century, such as "farmers, laborers, gardeners, porters, waiters, barbers and cooks."[20] A small percentage of blacks worked as professionals and served the African American community, which formed the foundation of a black middle class. Such was the case with doctors Milton Combs and D. W. Boyer, photographer Charles Overton (son of Jacob and Sarah), notary public Benjamin Gray, and clergymen at San Jose's Antioch Baptist Church and Palo Alto's AME Zion Church.[21] In the 1920s and 1930s most black Santa Clara Valley residents found work opportunities in San Jose's expanding central business district. According to longtime resident Mattie Berry, the St. James Hotel on St. James Street regularly hired black men, including Sam Quinn, her former husband, as waiters in its restaurants and black women as domestics. Berry had the distinction of being one the few African Americans to work at the prestigious Hale Brothers Department Store.[22]

Prior to the 1970s, South Bay industrial unions customarily locked African Americans into low-skilled employment through membership exclusion. Prior to the 1940s, these unions were in the ironworks industry, construction industry, and minimally in the food production industry, which briefly emerged as a force in the mid-1930s and is where most blacks eligible for unionization would have worked.[23] From 1900 to 1930 there were little more than a dozen black men working as skilled tradesmen in the valley. In San Jose they were Steve Alexander (plasterer), Jacob A. Ferguson (cement construction contractor), Baby Hall (carpenter), James Harton (cement mixer), James Howard (blacksmith), Richard Izor (bricklayer, plasterer, concrete construction owner), Andrew Mast (teamster), D. Sandy (painter), Willie Thompson (cement construction), and Joseph Vashon (machinist); and in Palo Alto, John Brown (carpenter), Eugene Edwards (mortar mixer), and John Pickett (painter). Most of these men were middle-aged and from the South, with the exceptions of Brown (from British Canada), Sandy (from Haiti), and Thompson (from Jamaica). The majority of them were similar to black professionals in that they were homeowners and thus found ways to break the local residential color line and lived in neighborhoods southeast of San Jose State (by Kelly Park) and San Jose's East Side.[24]

Most African Americans who came to the South Bay had some trade skills. Typically these skills extended beyond janitorial and domestic service. In addition, a handful of blacks acquired a trade through education and job apprenticeships. Until the 1970s, however, white businesses in the South Bay had an unwritten code that excluded African Americans from certain types of employment. San Jose Northside resident Rosalind Taylor found this out the hard way as a recent graduate of Superior Business School poised to work in mainstream San Jose during the Depression in an entry-level position. Responding to a newspaper advertisement, Taylor applied for a stenotypist position, a job she was qualified for, at Food Machinery. While attempting to turn in an application at the company's central office, three whites ignored her until she interrupted with the comment: "I think it's a job I am interested in doing."[25] After getting their attention she left her information, but was never contacted.

Within the South Bay only a small percentage of African Americans were entrepreneurs or skilled professionals. Mattie Berry was an exception. She ran the only concession stand owned by a black person in the St. James Hotel Lobby, selling newspapers, cards, and stamps. Clyde Ribbs, Henry Ribbs's brother, was the only African American to own and operate an express company—the Jones Transfer Company. Clyde is interesting because he represents the process that many black men underwent in becoming entrepreneurs. After migrating to San Jose in 1919, Clyde for several years worked the typical bottom-rung jobs designated for black men: janitor, night watchman, chauffeur, and shoe shiner. He worked at white establishments such as the Elks Club, the bus depot, and Hour Shoe Hospital. Clyde's business opportunity came after his close friend Spencer Jones, founder of the Jones Transfer Company, passed away. Jones's daughter, Mildred Jones Baker, sold the company, one of San Jose's oldest black-owned businesses, to Clyde for an undisclosed amount. Essentially Clyde bought a truck and a stand and then made an agreement with the drugstore at Morehead and Fleming asking that his calls for orders be processed at its location. Not to be outdone, Henry Ribbs became the second African American plumbing and heating contractor in Santa Clara County when he received his plumbing license in 1927. Henry's secret to socioeconomic success was in believing he could do anything he wanted and in seizing opportunities when they passed before him. After apprenticing under Thomas Moss from 1921 to 1927 for a dollar a day plus room and board, Henry went solo to become a plumbing and heating contractor. Throughout Ribbs's career one episode of institutional discrimination stood out. While working out of his Alum Rock shop in an exclusively white San Jose community on the Westside, Henry was harassed by a city inspector who would not pass his job because Ribbs used taps from an Alabama company rather than the more expensive taps loosely required from a local foundry. After Ribbs stood up to the San Jose inspector, the inspector said, "Ain't no nigga goin' to talk to me like that," and a minor scuffle ensued at a job site. The altercation was eventually broken up by San Jose's city manager, Clarence Goodwin, who tried to calm both men down in his office. Uncommon in an era of very hostile race relations nationwide, Henry was able to get the city manager to stop the plumbing inspector from harassing him after threatening "to kill the son-of-a-bitch" if he were to cross him again. When reminded of the consequences of murder, Henry replied, "I don't give a damn where I go, go to hell! I'm already in hell!"[26]

Part of the hell Ribbs was referring to was the housing discrimination that urban blacks were subjected to in the form of restrictive covenants. Prior to *Shelley v. Kraemer* (1948) most African Americans, with the exception of servants, found themselves confined to living in communities like the Northside because of restrictive covenants, real estate practices, and homeowners refusing to sell property to minorities out of fear of miscegenation, declining property values, and crime.[27] In spite of a local myth denying that restrictive covenants existed in San Jose, deeds within the Santa Clara County archives show that these covenants were common throughout the county in the early twentieth century. The most common racially restrictive deed stated, "No person of any race or nationality other than of the Caucasian race shall be allowed to own, lease or occupy any of said real property or any part thereof, except servants who may be permitted to live upon the premises occupied by the owner or tenants thereof."[28] As a result, most blacks lived in Northside homes that they either rented as tenants or built from the ground up.[29]

According to elders like Mattie Berry, the Northside prior to the 1950s was a racially mixed neighborhood of "Italians, Chinese, some Negroes and Mexicans—and *we had no racial problems.*"[30] Longtime resident Helen Gaffin agreed that there was little friction among the races, but the neighborhood as she described it was one in which racial groups kept to themselves and broke color lines only as students attending integrated public schools, customers in local stores, and for specialized services such as dressmaking.[31] Within the South Bay there was an unspoken agreement between black and white communities that stipulated that the southern and western parts of the valley, centered on downtown San Jose, were off-limits to African Americans. This included communities west of the Guadalupe River (i.e., West San Jose and Santa Clara), and neighborhoods within San Jose's Southside and below. Boundaries marking the Southside, within the white-controlled central business district, included south of Santa Clara Street, Naglee Park, and the campus community (San Jose Normal School/San Jose State College). According to Joyce Ellington, the Southside was "considered the fancy side of town. Lots of doctors settled there, and they didn't want houses sold to blacks." One of the few exceptions of an African American family living in the Southside was done through stealth. Joyce Ellington spoke of an unknown black man (probably photographer Charles Overton) who had a white man buy a home on South First Street for him.[32]

Beyond San Jose's Northside, African Americans were building communities throughout the western and eastern half of the Santa

Clara Valley, in areas that urbanized after the 1910s, such as Alum Rock (San Jose), Lakewood (Santa Clara), Mountain View Park, and downtown Palo Alto.[33] Among these communities, downtown Palo Alto was the most notable in the early twentieth century. In Palo Alto, a black community developed around University South, Crescent Park, and Old Palo Alto, which neighbored one another east of Stanford University and, together, formed the core of the African American community in West Santa Clara County (or West County).[34] According to Octavia Jones, whose family moved to Palo Alto in 1927, "Black families were clustered primarily on Fife, a two-block street between Boyce and Lincoln Avenues; on Ramona Street; and in the former town of Mayfield, now part of south Palo Alto."[35] African American pioneers who settled in Palo Alto included the Basses, Bromleys, Brookins, Browns, Edwardses, Flowers, Francises, Hallidays, Harrises, Hellens, Hinsons, Fosters, Greens, Joneses, Kingsburys, McCaws, Mouldens, Natises, Neelys, Nichols, Stokes, Wades, and Williamses.[36]

Most black residents of Palo Alto, like those of San Jose, came from the South. However, San Jose offered blacks greater opportunities to be homeowners and entrepreneurs. In 1930, 63 percent of San Jose blacks were homeowners, 30 percent were renters, and only 7 percent were live-in servants; whereas 27 percent of Palo Alto blacks were homeowners, 46 percent were renters, and 27 percent were live-in servants. In other South Bay communities with an African American presence (such as Burnett, Campbell, Gilroy, Los Altos Hills, Mountain View, Santa Clara, and Saratoga), only 10 percent of blacks were homeowners, 30 percent were renters, and 60 percent were live-in servants.[37] The handful of black people residing in these much smaller communities usually worked as servants or as farm laborers. In contrast, most of the black workforce in San Jose and Palo Alto worked as cooks, domestics, and porters, with Palo Alto having far more African Americans working in the service industry for private families, restaurants, and Stanford University fraternities and sororities. San Jose had far more black entrepreneurs in the service industry, and several of the skilled tradesmen in the city owned their own companies; Jacob Ferguson's construction company was one of the largest employers of South Bay blacks from 1930 to the 1960s.[38] To rectify

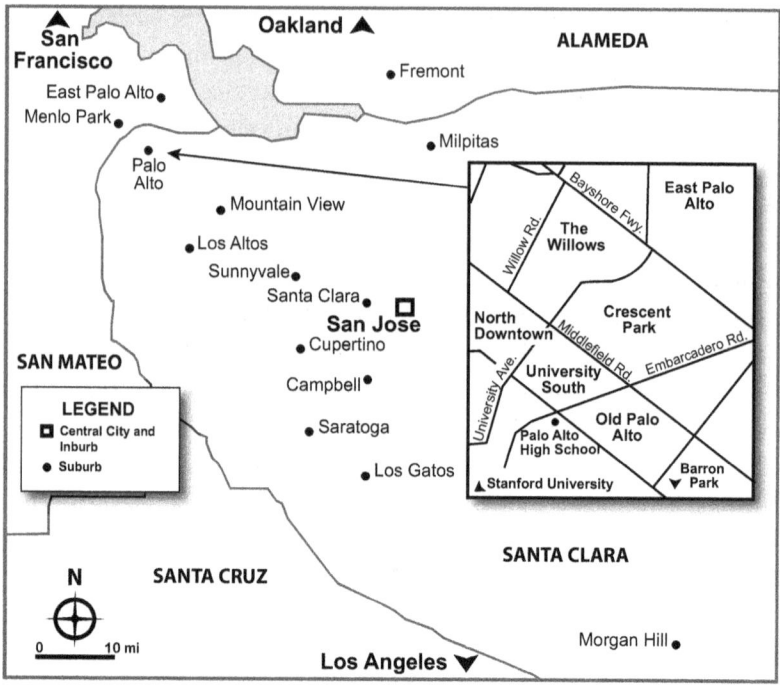

African Americans in West County Palo Alto, 1910–ca. 1970. Copyright © 2014 by the University of Oklahoma Press.

their feelings of disempowerment in restricted homeownership and in employment, black residents of Palo Alto focused on family and community as sources of self-esteem and social standing. They made sure that their children received a quality education within the integrated Palo Alto School District. Such was the case with Frank ("Mac") and Pearl Moulden, whose son William graduated from Palo Alto High School in 1934.[39] To keep the Palo Alto public schools in check, concerned parents like Pearl Moulden used the Community Activities Committee of the Excelsior Club (which she cofounded) to promote first-class education for West County African American youth. The other way that West County blacks were able to empower themselves was through the Palo Alto African Methodist Episcopal Zion Church (aka University AME Zion Church).

The AME Zion Church was the first black church in Palo Alto. During the early twentieth century it was the only black church between San Mateo and San Jose. In West County it served as the religious, social, and cultural center for black communities in Palo Alto, Los Altos Hills, Mountain View, and neighboring San Mateo County.[40] In 1918, AME Zion became the central institution for West County's small but growing African American community. In this year its congregation was organized by the Reverend J. W. Byers, Jennie Moore Bass, Melvina McCaw, Maude Natis, and Isaac MacDuffey Hinson, and it met in Fraternal Hall on High Street and University Avenue. In 1925, following a successful fundraising drive, the church moved to 819 Ramona Street.[41] In the 1920s and 30s, the church played a crucial role in promoting dialogues among African Americans, European Americans, Chinese Americans, and Japanese Americans as racial progressives supported the church financially and morally. These supporters included the Palo Alto Ministerial Association, Japanese American Methodists, the Chinese American community, Stanford University professors, the American Legion, the Shriners, the Kiwanis Club, the Rotary Club, the *Palo Alto Times*, and the local business and financial community. Their support relieved many working-poor blacks from having to fully shoulder the burden of financing the church, which was crucial because most of these African Americans made just enough money to support their families. Ultimately, the coalition played a huge role in the African American community, and the church paid off its mortgage on July 8, 1939.[42]

AFRICAN AMERICANS LIVING IN Santa Clara Valley from 1900 to 1940 survived discrimination and other hardships by remaining united and adapting to their circumstances.[43] They sustained themselves by believing that the Santa Clara Valley was a relatively racially tolerant region and by participating in African American institutions like the Antioch Baptist Church and University AME Zion Church.[44] They knew the limits circumscribing their lives, and they focused on their freedoms. This attitude was expressed well by Joyce Ellington: "When we were kids, we knew there were places where we were not going to be accepted and so we just didn't go there. . . . They had teen dances at O'Brien's Confectionery [in downtown San Jose] that we knew we couldn't go to so we never tried."[45]

South Bay blacks' accommodation to de facto segregation led whites to perceive the black community as complicit in their subtle form of racism. But although the Santa Clara Valley black community was small, its members confronted racism whenever it became obvious. Several African Americans there also vehemently tried not to be categorized as a racial minority to escape the discrimination that blacks often faced in urban America—residential apartheid, poverty, educational discrimination, and exclusion from public accommodations. Mattie Berry once stated that she "never encountered much prejudice here, because [I] wouldn't stand for it. . . . I am a human being. They try to put us in a minority. I am a majority—I am Mattie Berry. . . . I don't understand why we accept that anyway."[46] For local African Americans like Berry, racial discrimination was a matter resolved on an individual basis, such as the one instance when a white man called Berry a "nigger," and she retorted by spitting in the man's face, a response that went unchallenged. But although blatant insults sometimes met with pointed resistance, institutional discrimination was often understated by blacks in the valley.

During the Great Depression, accommodating the local color line became difficult to maintain in Santa Clara Valley. Local black attitudes shifted during this period to a more radical posture that resorted to collective action and collective violence, often in league with whites and people of other ethnicities. The Depression brought unprecedented economic hardship and social strain, and in its worst years, 1931 and 1932, most local governments had no welfare programs and instead promoted voluntarism and personal responsibility, reasoning that poverty existed because of moral laxity and that relief would undermine citizens' free and independent character.[47] As a result, when the Depression hit the eastern and southern parts of the county, citizens of every stripe felt abandoned by local government officials, and many took the law into their hands. St. James Park, in downtown San

Jose and adjacent to the county's old courthouse, became the center for civil liberty demonstrations, labor rights protests, protests on behalf of homeless Bay Area residents and community sharing, and vigilantism.[48] The duress brought on by the Great Depression broke down racial, economic, and religious class divisions as tents lined the valley and masses of homeless people wandered the region.[49] They had come from other parts of the Bay Area and, after 1937, from the drought-devastated Dust Bowl. Early in the Depression, South Bay blacks participated in the area's relief efforts by providing food and possibly shelter at the Antioch Baptist Church.[50] That was before 1933, the year a lynching destroyed Santa Clara County's reputation for tolerance and support for civil liberties.[51]

PRIOR TO 1933, SAN JOSE WAS known as the fruit-growing and -processing capital of the world.[52] To African Americans, the region had been known for its fluid and flexible race relations ever since black men first received the ballot in 1870. But in 1933, after several years of farmworkers' agitation for the restoration of 1920s wages and better work conditions, strikes broke out among fieldworkers and cannery workers under such labor organizations as the Cannery and Agricultural Workers Industrial Union.[53] A few blacks participated in the labor activism, which included Italians, Mexicans, Filipinos, and Puerto Ricans. To combat this progressive coalition, large agribusinesses and state and local law officials encouraged antiunion and anti–civil liberties vigilantism among Bay Area citizens under the guise of deterring the spread of communism and disorder.

This explosive struggle between progressive and reactionary forces came to a head on November 9, 1933, when John Holmes and Thomas Thurmond kidnapped twenty-two-year-old Brooke Hart for a ransom of $40,000.[54] All of the men involved were white. Holmes and Thurmond were the black sheep of relatively well-off families. Hart's family was wealthy; his parents owned a popular department store in San Jose. Brooke Hart had worked at the store since he was little, learning the business from the ground up; he was well liked, and the store had many customers in San Jose. When a radio station reported, two weeks after Brooke's disappearance, that his remains had washed ashore and were discovered by two duck hunters, tempers in the South Bay approached a boiling point, and a sizable reward was offered for the kidnappers' capture and transport to San Jose. Boiling turned to mayhem after Santa Clara County Sheriff Emig transported the kidnappers from a San Francisco jail to his county jail—immediately across the street from St. James Park and its revolutionary ferment— to be tried for conspiracy to extort.[55] The crowd didn't want to wait for a trial, and radio stations and public readings of newspaper articles and editorials were feeding the crowd's fury. Emig, sensing the danger, frantically phoned Governor James Rolph to request that he call in the National Guard, but he was rebuffed, with Rolph saying he would pardon anyone involved in the lynching of Holmes and Thurmond. On November 26 a radio station advertised that the lynching of Holmes and Thurmond would occur at 11 p.m. The crowd attracted by this advertisement, estimated at ten thousand people, consisted mostly of white men, but it drew some women and children and many high school and college students. By 8 p.m. a mob had converged at the jail, and they rammed the door with materials from a nearby construction site. They broke out Holmes and Thurmond—badly injuring the sheriff, his deputy, and his jailer in the process—and lynched them in the park.[56]

An estimated one hundred people participated directly in the lynching as African Americans like Mattie Berry looked on in horror from their windows, listening to the carnival-like atmosphere reminiscent of the lynchings of blacks in the South. "We didn't live far from there," Berry said, "and neighbors came home saying they had cut up part of the [lynching] tree to take some of the famous tree."[57] Another woman wrote in her diary, "One thinks that a revolution might come about . . . there was something in the air."[58] What was in the air was in fact a white conservative backlash that by 1936 had severely weakened local unions and civil liberties groups through the systematic purging of progressive activists and intellectuals who were labeled as communists and San Francisco Great Strike radicals.[59]

To many South Bay blacks segregated by custom in every facet of their lives, the reactionary politics sweeping through the South Bay was considered to be "white folks' business." The mob violence of the Holmes and Thurmond lynching had a deeper effect on them, however, because for the first time a critical mass of white residents outside the South, right in their own county, showed what they were capable of doing in desperate times. In addition, the lynching was a humbling moment for some African Americans. Mattie Berry was raised in the Santa Clara Valley and professed to a strong sense of individualism and ideological belief in the American creed that "All men are created equal." However, for recent black migrants to the Santa Clara Valley like Henry Ribbs, who had lived the harsher realities of Jim Crow segregation, the lynching confirmed their belief that whites were not to be trusted and that local African Americans had to be more cautious in the South Bay to prevent racial hatred. Ultimately, in the latter half of the 1930s, South Bay blacks became more deeply involved in trying to figure out the state of the black nation and where it was headed in their clustered communities and institutions.

Santa Clara Valley blacks in the early twentieth century had put their faith in ensuring a quality education for their children in integrated public schools and in participation in black churches and social clubs. Institution building was important to them. It seemed a way to make some security for themselves even in uncertain times and an expression of black aspirations that were surely above reproach. Their institutions ensured that most African Americans in the area knew one another, which united them in community and created a sense of solidarity. In the 1920s, black consciousness, which engendered racial uplift and racial pride through black culture, was augmented in Northside San Jose by an African American history class taught at Grant School by Minnie Darling. Adults and children attended. It was basically a training course for leaders, and out of that course of study came future local activists such as Lucille Lawson and Bertha Stafford Ellington.

Black consciousness and community growth were also nurtured within Santa Clara County black churches. Antioch Baptist Church, founded in August 1893, was the first black Baptist church established in the South Bay. At the turn of the twentieth century, Antioch easily eclipsed the San Jose AME churches as the leading black institution in the Santa Clara Valley. Antioch was founded by seven people at the Henry Hawkins home: Deacon Henry Hawkins; Treasurer W. M. Mast; M. E. Hawkins, Ellen Davis, L. Walker, Ellen Hawkins, and E. Pinkson. Their purpose was to organize a Missionary Baptist Church with a consistent presence in the South Bay. Originally pastored by the Reverend C. C. Laws, Antioch held its services in the Northside area called the "Tar Flats," which was around Tenth and Julian Streets. It was given its name because of "ill-smelling tar weed that grew rampant in the area." From 1893 to 1908, church services alternated between the Hawkins home and the Colored Odd Fellows Hall. In 1908 Antioch outgrew this arrangement and constructed a church building that would become the center of the neighborhood, a community presence at which various other African American organizations and political movements would get their start, such as the Garden City Women's Club and the Order of the Eastern Star.[60]

African American women were crucial to Antioch Baptist Church's daily operations and to broadening its public arm. Their participation within the church went hand in hand with their participation in the black women's club movement.[61] In the early twentieth century, three black women's clubs predominated in San Jose: the Garden City Women's Club, the Victoria Earle Matthews Club, and the Mothers' Club. Of these, the Garden City club was the oldest and most influential. The South Bay black women's club movement came out of the 1895 Conference of Colored Women led by Josephine St. Pierre Ruffin, president of the Women's Era Club of Boston.[62] The 1895 conference was an African American middle-class movement that exuded a respectability that in many ways mirrored that of their white counterparts.[63] After the conference, delegates such as Detroit's Elizabeth P. Boyer went back to their communities with renewed vigor in their struggles against lynching, segregation, and gender discrimination. They also intensified their activism for daily community uplift and outdoor relief, providing clothes and food for the poor, building homes for the elderly and orphans, and raising money for local causes.

The black women's club movement came to California at the inauguration of the California State Association of Colored Women's Clubs at Oakland on August 6, 1906. Its motto, adopted by black women clubs throughout the state, was "Deeds, Not Words." Listening intently at the meeting was Elizabeth Boyer, who in 1898 migrated to San Jose from Detroit with her husband, Dr. D. W. Boyer. Encouraged by what she heard, Boyer, then in her early forties, cofounded the Garden City Women's Club. The club was born in the immediate aftermath of the San Francisco 1906 earthquake and fire, which devastated the entire Bay Area. In the South Bay, the most damaged areas were the Northside, Agnews Insane Asylum, Palo Alto, and parts of downtown San Jose.[64] While the cities were in chaos, the Garden City Women's Club provided safe spaces for African American women to meet. Initially twelve to thirty-five members over the age of eighteen met on Sunday mornings at Antioch Baptist Church. The club's agenda eventually grew to include literary activities and sociopolitical activism for black liberation, women's suffrage, temperance, and (during World War I) the Red Cross. The club was one of only a handful of South Bay institutions that provided a public platform for black freedom fighters to speak; Marcus Garvey of the Universal Negro Improvement Association spoke under the club's auspices in 1922.[65]

In the same period, the only male institutions to nurture black consciousness and community growth was R. C. Marshall Lodge #15, established by Theodore Moss in 1917, and the Civic E. Social Club founded by Henry Ribbs and Walter Thompson in the early 1920s. Little is known of the R. C. Marshall Lodge because its members were sworn to secrecy in the Prince Hall Grand Lodge tradition. All that is known is that they combined civic duty, black male fraternity, and membership in an African American church.[66] Similarly, very little is known about the Civic E. Social Club beyond the fact that it was a black middle-class men's social group whose members were full-time skilled and semi-skilled workers and entrepreneurs from San Jose, Palo Alto, and Mountain View whose wives were engaged in similar activities.

The only African American institution outside of the church that was not gender specific was the Order of Eastern Star, No. 30,

Portrait of Anna Stokes McColl, ca. 1905. McColl was a founding member of the Garden City Women's Club and San Jose Chapter of the National Association for the Advancement of Colored People. Courtesy History San Jose.

founded by Theodore Moss in June 1924. Prior to 1942, the Eastern Star functioned as a mutual aid and benevolence society that engaged in small-scale civic activism in conjunction with other black institutions. One such occasion occurred in 1939 when Henry Ribbs's son "Bunny" (William T. Ribbs) and a Japanese youth were restricted from swimming at a public pool during a class picnic at Alum Rock Park out of fear that they would contaminate the water. The two children were the only people of color at the picnic. This infuriated Henry Ribbs, who, like many African Americans in the South Bay, had overlapping memberships with institutions such as the Eastern Star and Antioch Baptist Church to which they turned when confronted with social injustice. Ribbs contacted Antioch's minister, the Reverend William Allen Magette, who got in touch with City Manager Goodwin, who in turn contacted the mayor. The situation was immediately corrected. Similar reports of successful small-scale activism as well as Moss's connections with black institutions throughout California attracted new members to the Eastern Star (estimated in the hundreds) in the South Bay, some from as far away as San Francisco and Chico.[67]

IN 1932, SANTA CLARA VALLEY BLACKS waged their largest political mobilization up to that time by becoming independent voters swinging their support to the New Deal Democrats of Franklin D. Roosevelt. Within African America this political realignment was revolutionary as "black voters were responding to years of neglect from the 'party of Lincoln' and more directly, to the strain of the Great Depression and lure of New Deal economic benefits."[68] Santa Clara County blacks were especially neglected because they made up less than 1 percent of the county's population.[69] Fully aware of the imbalance of political power, black voters knew they could demand nothing that most mainstream officials would respect and respond to except on a small-scale basis like the swimming pool incident. The voting patterns of South Bay blacks were in line with most Santa Clara County voters—they posed no threat to the established order. But Santa Clara Valley blacks' political realignment was in tow with similar political shifts that made it clear that African Americans were conducting serious dialogues among themselves about U.S. politics in relation to their lives. This included talks of political alignment with the Communist and Socialist Parties through the Eastern Star and the Brotherhood of Sleeping Car Porters in the East Bay.

African Americans' radical shift in voting paralleled political developments affecting California and Santa Clara County as a whole.[70] In 1930, 78 percent of registered voters in the South Bay were

Republicans, with strongholds in the western and southern parts of Santa Clara County—Willow Glenn, Gardiner, Hester Hanchett, and College Park—or the whitest and most affluent sections of the valley. When in 1932 the county voted for Franklin D. Roosevelt, it was the first time a Democratic presidential nominee had carried the county in the twentieth century.[71] In 1936, registered Democrats were in a slight majority in the county. By 1940 that had become a sizable majority (around 60 percent), which reverted back to the Republicans after Roosevelt's death in 1945. South Bay residents backed Roosevelt because the economy had collapsed under his predecessor, Herbert Hoover (a Palo Alto resident). And they, like most of the country, were captivated by Roosevelt's economic programs and his promise to help the "forgotten man" in his New Deal.[72]

What Santa Clara Valley blacks discovered was that New Deal Democrats were as indifferent to them as the Republicans had been. Although the New Deal was disappointing to them, one positive element they took away from politically realigning with New Deal Democrats was growing optimism that a new political order would help dismantle the entrenched discrimination that had confronted their community since the 1890s. The early twentieth century was a period when most South Bay blacks settled into the region. Their recollections of the black gold rush generation were either faint or nonexistent, since most people of that era no longer lived in the Santa Clara Valley. As a result, the political renaissance that many South Bay blacks would embark on in the 1940s was an expedition into the unknown.

Part Two
African Americans and the Suburban Dream, 1941–1990

Chapter Three
World War II and Postwar Santa Clara County, 1941–1953

WORLD WAR II WAS A WATERSHED for African Americans throughout the nation and particularly for those in the West.[1] In the Bay Area, most blacks bypassed the South Bay's orchards for the North Bay's and the East Bay's urban appeal, shipyard opportunities, and unprecedented access to government-subsidized housing. During this period the black population in the West grew by 33 percent in the 1940s, as 443,000 African Americans migrated to the West Coast to work in war production industries.[2] California gained 338,000 of this population, which amounted to a 272 percent increase over the previous decade.[3] In the South Bay, the black population grew from 730 persons in 1940 to 1,718 by 1950. Much of this population migrated into the area as young families from San Francisco and the East Bay—after being released from war production employment—in search of a new beginning and jobs that paid a living wage.[4]

Although black population growth in the South Bay was minute in comparison to that of San Francisco, Oakland, and Richmond during this period, the 1940s and 1950s saw the beginning of a numerical resurgence for African Americans in Santa Clara County. Its black population had not been so high since the Spanish era, when blacks accounted for more than 20 percent of San Jose's population; in 1890 African Americans numbered 989, the third-largest black population in California behind San Francisco and Los Angeles. This population resurgence did not begin until after World War II when companies in San Francisco and the East Bay laid off people of color and white women in massive numbers. As a result, an intraregional migration of black people to the Santa Clara Valley more than doubled their numbers in every decade from 1940 to 1980. This increase acted as a catalyst for political change.

TABLE 6 Populations of Color in California, 1940–1950

	1940			1950		
	Black	Total	Other People of Color	Black	Total	Other People of Color
California	124,306	6,907,387	186,318	462,172	10,586,223	208,878
Alameda	12,335	513,011	10,531	69,442	740,315	16,042
Los Angeles	75,209	2,785,643	50,392	217,881	4,151,687	55,862
Orange Co.	287	130,760	2,151	889	216,224	1,698
Sacramento	2,156	170,333	11,384	7,499	277,140	10,742
San Diego	4,444	289,348	5,276	17,030	556,808	6,811
San Francisco	4,846	634,536	26,989	43,502	775,357	37,967
Santa Clara Co.	730	174,949	5,298	1,718	290,547	8,400

SOURCES: U.S. Bureau of the Census, *1950 Census of Population: Volume 11, Characteristics of the Population, Part 5, California* (Washington, D.C.: U.S. Government Printing Office, 1952), 5–21; *Historical Census Browser: County-Level Results for 1850–1960* (Charlottesville: University of Virginia Library, Geospatial and Statistical Data Center, 2005).

This chapter examines community building in Santa Clara County in the context of the Second Great Migration (1941–1970) in the 1940s. It argues that Santa Clara County black community development can be best understood as a process of its residents "working together to survive and thrive" amid institutional and customary racial discriminatory barriers in housing and employment. This form of development reflects a national trend during the postwar period, but black community formation in Santa Clara County was unique in several ways. First, African American migration into the South Bay occurred after World War II as part of an intraregional migration from industrial city to semirural city, in which the rural parts of the Santa Clara Valley became suburbs by 1970. Second, the largest waves of black migrants came to the South Bay for family, familiarity, and social justice. Third, South Bay blacks were attempting to cultivate African American community in a social geography in which persons of Mexican and Asian descent have always been the larger populations of color, and this led to a pattern of race relations in Greater San Jose different from that in the urban North and Jim Crow South.[5]

PRIOR TO THE 1940s, MOST African American communities did not constitute population majorities anywhere in the West. Instead they were clustered in what often became racially segregated and isolated areas in the postwar era. The exception to this claim was Los Angeles, which already showed signs of becoming racially segregated and isolated in the 1930s.[6] Like other clustered communities, black Santa Clara Valley was a close-knit community formed from necessity to resist their total exclusion from the region and to combat de facto racial discrimination: actions that directly contradict the common claim by traditional western scholars including Walter Prescott Webb that black westerners were passive actors in their own community development.[7] From the late 1870s to the 1950s, about 40 percent of South Bay blacks lived in single-family homes in the Northside. Before 1937, residency was limited by restrictive covenants and unspoken agreements that made the southern and western parts of the valley off-limits to African American residency.[8] After 1937, San Jose "redlined" persons of color and the working poor to encourage homeownership on open land that became suburbs in the 1950s.[9]

Redlining was the practice of systematically denying home loans to people in residential areas considered to be high economic risks because they were people of color, working-poor people, and were living on property that had mixed land uses (i.e., housing near businesses). Central to this suburban policy bias was the Federal Housing Authority (FHA) mortgage program.[10] The FHA's participation in the postwar housing market profoundly restructured race relations in a damaging manner by restricting people of color to central cities and allowing whites-only access into newly developed suburbs. In 1934, the FHA was created to stimulate employment (especially in

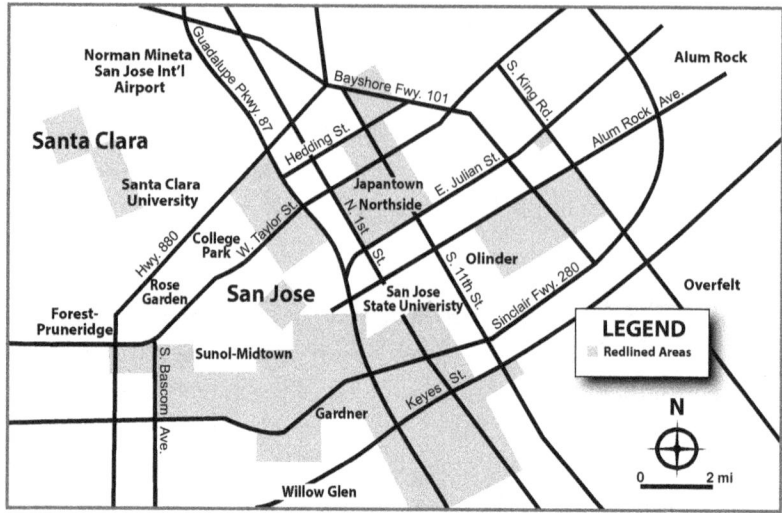

Redlining in Santa Clara County, ca. 1937–1950s. Copyright © 2014 by the University of Oklahoma Press.

construction), inspire homeownership, improve housing standards and living conditions, and stabilize the mortgage market by reviving the housing industry and relying on private enterprise rather than direct government spending to achieve that objective.[11] In practice the agency insured long-term loans for owners made by banks for home buying and housing construction.[12] During the postwar era, redlining replaced restrictive covenants to become the largest discriminating factor in the housing industry through the FHA's openly screening out mortgage loan applicants and subsidizing whiteness.[13] Much of the FHA's discriminatory behavior was adopted from savings and loans, the construction industry, and the Home Owners' Loan Corporation of the 1920s and 1930s. What the federal government sequentially did was nationalize preexisting residential discriminatory practices such as the color-coded valuation of property used by the Home Owners' Loan Corporation, in which the best property value was coded green, red was the worst, blue was the second best, and yellow was just above red.[14] How this translates for Santa Clara County was that African Americans were redlined in the Northside and in East San

Jose, Mexican Americans were redlined in East San Jose, and Japanese Americans were restricted to downtown North San Jose until internment in 1942.[15]

What partially bound South Bay blacks of the pre- and post-1940s is that all African American migrants were confronted with de facto racial discrimination in housing, employment, education, and police misconduct. While this was not the better-understood de jure racial discrimination, it was an oppression of a long-lasting sort that was institutional and still is a major constraint leading people of color to feel they have not fully achieved first-class citizenship. Crucial factors in making African American pioneers feel like second-class citizens were their being restricted to particular communities and working in positions well below their education and skills. According to Maurice Hardeman, the first African American municipal court judge in Santa Clara County, and the Reverend C. W. Washington of Antioch Baptist Church, blacks during the Second Great Migration generally did not work in department stores, major grocery stores, banks, hospitals, municipal government, or in the telephone and gas companies.[16] They were employed as manual laborers, domestics, or service workers, or they created alternative paths that fostered economic self-sufficiency as small-business owners.

Similar to blacks nationwide, South Bay African Americans overcame residential and economic racial discrimination by "working together to survive and thrive." For Kenneth Blackwell, a San Jose native, that was an expression rooted in black southern traditions of self-sufficiency and community solidarity—one he learned from his father, Deelvin Blackwell—which formed the theoretical framework for black San Jose self-reliance after the 1940s during a period of overt racial restrictions.[17] Prior to the 1940s, South Bay blacks were racially tolerated because the smallness of their population made minimal demands on white people and on Santa Clara County's system of governance. After the 1940s, this treatment noticeably changed with the unprecedented growth of the African American community and rapid urbanization. Many of the African Americans who lived in and around San Jose migrated from Oklahoma to be among family members who had been migrating into the region since the late 1920s and after the war to resettle in a reputedly racially tolerant region that reminded them of home.[18] Within the scope of pre-1940 black San Jose, the black Oklahoman contingent did not stand out because they were part of a larger movement of African Americans who came from towns and farms throughout the South and Southwest in the 1910s and '20s. They began to stand out in the 1940s, when the South Bay black population doubled from 730 people to 1,718, and by 1960 had grown to 4,187.[19] This meant that during the 1940s many African Americans who came into the South Bay knew immediately where they could live, work, and go to school because they were already part of a community network. For long-settled African American migrant Helen Gaffin, this migration felt as if "Oklahoma took California without firing a shot" because many of its migrants grew up together in central and eastern Oklahoma, had similar experiences of racism and poverty, and were determined not to let San Jose become like Oklahoma in regard to its legal and customary discrimination.[20]

Black Oklahomans like the Andersons, Dollarhydes, and Blackwells came to dominate black migration to San Jose by networking and informally marketing the valley's economic opportunities, social environment, and mild weather to kinfolk still suffering the aftereffects of the Dust Bowl and Great Depression. According to Earlsboro, Oklahoma, native Orvella Stubbs of the Dollarhyde family, the Great Depression was more devastating to her family than the Dust Bowl had been. The Dollarhydes' Oklahoma roots began in the 1890s with Tom Dollarhyde, a former slave, escaping plantation life in Arkansas and resettling in Earlsboro, Oklahoma. Of his twelve children, eight settled in San Jose in the 1930s and '40s. In the 1890s, Oklahoma was Indian Territory, and the African Americans who migrated there were fed up with sharecropping and black codes in the South, and they looked to Oklahoma as a promised land where they could farm free of white intrusion.[21] Dollarhyde purchased six hundred acres in Earlsboro. By the Great Depression, this land had passed down to Orvella Stubbs's father. The Dollarhyde farm saved the family from starving because they grew their own food and were not dependent on wages to pay bills. Essentially, the Oklahoma Dollarhydes followed a pattern set by Lenora Sypert-Anderson and Edna and Gertrude Dollarhyde

The Anderson family, ca. 1919. First row *(left to right)*: John Anderson, William Anderson (child), Hattie Anderson-Lee, Jo Anderson, Bill Anderson. Second row *(left to right)*: Ethel Anderson, Nittie Anderson-Logan. Top row *(left to right)*: Lenora Sypert-Anderson, Elroy Anderson, "Big John" Anderson, Sally Michaels Anderson, Forest Anderson, Willie "Mack" Anderson, Carl Anderson. Courtesy Patricia Perkins.

during the Great Depression and Dust Bowl in the late 1920s and early '30s—people who brought their families to the South Bay and conveyed the region's prospects through letters, telephone conversations, and interactions at family reunions in Oklahoma.[22]

According to Patricia Perkins, who is an Anderson, the Anderson movement to San Jose began with Lenora Sypert in the late 1920s. Lenora was an Anderson through marriage to Pat's grandfather, John, son of Forest Anderson, the black millionaire who, according to *Ebony* magazine in 1949, was one of the ten richest African Americans in the United States.[23] He made most of his money from farming, real estate, banking, and ownership of two oil wells from which he sold crude oil to petroleum companies. After John's death, Lenora married Ernest Sam Cross, who worked for the railroad, and they and their youngest son, Felton (nicknamed "Man"), and his sister Gladys (nicknamed "Babe"), all came to San Jose.[24] In 1942, Lenora's other two children moved to San Jose. They were followed by Lenora's brother, Frank, his family, and Grace Echols and her family. All the Andersons and Dollarhydes migrated to San Jose prior to the war's end in 1945. According to Vern Wilson, who was a descendant of the Dollarhydes, when many of these black Oklahomans came to the Northside, there were very few homes available for them to purchase. Most immediately resolved this problem by purchasing single-family homes in adjacent Japantown, which were vacated during Japanese American internment (1942–1945)— which according to historian Quintard Taylor was a phenomenon that occurred in almost every city on the West Coast.[25]

DURING THE WAR YEARS, at least fifteen San Jose blacks were hired at the Kaiser Shipyards at Richmond, fifty-three miles away, and made the daily three-hour round trip. When Great Migration histories examine African American shipyard workers, they primarily focus on workers living in communities close to shipyard factories like North Richmond and West Oakland.[26] In none of the black urban histories have scholars addressed African American shipyard workers coming from relatively distant suburban metropolises like San Jose.

Some of the South Bay blacks who worked at the Kaiser Shipyards went by first names. They included Helen, Gertrude, Buster, Dale, and Ms. Matilda. Helen was a welder working swing shift on Liberty Ships. Her time was consumed by working, commuting, and sleeping. The daily trip to Kaiser Shipyard #2 was made often in two or three Buicks and Fords. Sometimes Clarence "Buster" Johnson, a cousin, drove them in the bus he had brought from Shawnee, Oklahoma. With the long commute, they did not have time for union activities. They paid their union dues for access to the shop floor, worked, and went home and slept. According to Helen, none of her cohorts was aware of labor discrimination by blacks being restricted from the full benefits of union membership in auxiliary units.[27] They were also unaware of the

California Supreme Court decision *James v. Marinship* (1944), which dismantled the racist auxiliary structure that forced blacks to pay full union dues and join racially segregated unions to work on shop floors without the ability to vote on union activities and stop union officials from laying black workers off by simply abolishing the auxiliary union. That the shipyards hired African Americans for well-paid employment was a pleasant surprise for many of the black Oklahomans who came to California to reunite with family. They were also handsomely compensated with gas stamps for their long commute up Oakland Road. This was almost two decades before the 880 Freeway was completed (in 1958), which shortened the round trip by an hour.[28] The commute was one that many South Bay residents made to the shipyards, as there were only two ways to get back and forth from the Santa Clara Valley to Richmond. Helen and her family never moved to Richmond, though, because they considered San Jose to be home.[29]

Most Santa Clara Valley blacks like the Andersons never seriously considered working in South Bay factories producing for the war effort because most were not given access to the shop floors of existing plants, even though, according to Gretchen Lemke Santangelo, "between 1941 and 1945 the federal government invested over $70 billion in California aircraft, shipbuilding, food processing, clothing manufacturing, and other war-related industries."[30] In the South Bay those industries included food processing, ironworks (engine building for Liberty ships), and aerospace. African Americans had employment opportunities in food processing, token access into Food Machinery Company and the Hendy Iron Works as janitors, and very minimal, if any, undocumented access into aerospace at Moffett Field and Lockheed Aircraft. The exception to this rule was that a few blacks, among them Bill Moody and Lucille Bunch, were hired by Food Machinery Company as welders, after passing a very hard welding test. According to Helen, Moody and Bunch were exceptionally good and part of an elite group of welders who were much better than most welders building Liberty and Victory Ships at the shipyards.[31]

Employment opportunities were quite different for African Americans in the North and East Bay areas, where shipbuilding employment predominated. Four major shipbuilders were located in the region: Bethlehem-Alameda (Oakland), Kaiser Company (Richmond), Marinship (Sausalito), and Moore Drydock (Oakland). Arguably, the most inclusive of these employers was Kaiser Shipyards, which had four shipyards.[32] The unprecedented demand for a diverse labor force to fill vacant positions in wartime defense contracts included other people of color and women of all colors. A major barrier blocking access of African Americans and other people of color to industries with war contracts were white trade unions like the International Brotherhood of Boilermakers of the exclusionist American Federation of Labor. In the Bay Area, the boilermakers union dominated the shop floor through an unprecedented closed-shop agreement with shipbuilders that gave them jurisdiction over 65 percent of the dockworkers on the West Coast except for Seattle–Tacoma—other ports include Portland, San Francisco–East Bay, and Los Angeles–Long Beach. Within this arrangement, African Americans, for most of the war effort, were restricted to auxiliary unions designed to have them pay full union dues to work on the shop floor in temporary low- to semi-skilled jobs with only moderate pay and without full union benefits and protections.[33] Racial discrimination at companies with defense contracts was somewhat tempered by federal oversight agencies created by Executive Order 8802 legislation (est. June 25, 1941), such as the War Manpower Commission, which recruited and placed workers; and 8802's investigative body, the Fair Employment Practices Committee (FEPC), which reminded employers that they risked losing their lucrative contracts if they discriminated.[34] This legislation in turn politicized black dock and factory workers who used the FEPC to investigate discrimination in the defense industry and to build cases, such as *James v. Marinship* (1944), solid enough to carry over to state and federal courts.[35]

Contrary to the traditional Great Migration narrative, in South Bay manufacturing industries, the FEPC, and the trade unions failed to function as galvanizing forces for blacks. Black San Jose residents Julia and Daisy Dollarhyde, for example, attempted to make industrial labor more central to the black community. They appealed in writing to President Franklin D. Roosevelt through the FEPC, suggesting that African Americans could help the war effort if they were given secure industrial work of the sort that people of European descent already enjoyed.[36] In the food-production industry, the FEPC had a minimal presence because during the war African Americans were hired mostly to fill labor shortages in stereotypical "person of color" employment (as fieldworkers, cannery workers, and dry packers), day-labor jobs for which Mexicans were preferred during peacetime.[37] Also, union representation in the food-production industry was not an issue after the fall of San Jose's United Cannery, Agricultural, Packing-house, and Allied Workers of America because agricultural workers were minimally organized.[38] The FEPC had no jurisdiction over the workforce in the Armed Forces so, unless African American civilians worked at Moffett Field during the war, the FEPC had no reason to be involved there. At Lockheed Aircraft, a handful of janitorial positions became available to blacks, perhaps because of pressure from the FEPC. As for blacks working on Lockheed's shop floor as skilled laborers, the aircraft producer had an abundance of labor that it favored. These preferred laborers consisted of white Bay Area residents and white Dust Bowlers; the latter were mostly farmers and farm laborers originally from Oklahoma who migrated to Central California before resettling in Greater San Jose in the late 1930s.

At Hendy Iron Works a great opportunity to democratize an inclusive South Bay industrial workforce beyond food processing was lost. Hendy and food producer Libby, McNeil & Libby held economic hegemony in Sunnyvale until Westinghouse took over Hendy in 1947. Hendy's presence in Sunnyvale dated back to 1906, when it moved from San Francisco after the earthquake and fire. This fledgling ironworks business was saved from bankruptcy by World War I, which also assured its solvency during the intervening period of peace and then enabled it to become one of the main employers in the valley during World War II. As a defense contractor, Hendy manufactured ship engines and iron and steel armaments for the Navy.[39] There is no mention in records that African Americans were employed at Hendy during WWI; however, someone who worked at Hendy during WWII later remarked that it was not uncommon to see white working-class men and business professionals working side by side with white women and blacks.[40] Only a few African Americans and women worked on

Hendy's assembly lines. Most were relegated to labor assignments based on racial prejudice and stereotypes, such as cleaning engines and performing janitorial duties.[41]

To escape the indignities of working in spaces like Hendy, many South Bay blacks survived and thrived as common laborers working for relatives and extended kin in small black companies founded during the immediate postwar era. Some of these businesses include Jacob Ferguson's cement and construction business; Emmitt Dollarhyde's steam-cleaning business, called Dollarhyde House; and Mr. Graham's Shell gas station (est. 1951). According to Kenneth Blackwell, prior to the 1960s "any black person could find a job if they were willing to work."[42] In 1946, Blackwell's father, Deelvin (aka Mr. D), founded the janitorial service Blackwell and Sons, which is still running strong. Of the businesses mentioned, the largest employers were Ferguson's cement and construction business and Blackwell and Sons. According to Kenneth Blackwell, Patricia Perkins, and her mother, Gloria Anderson, everyone who needed a job worked for Mr. D.[43]

Prior to the founding of Blackwell and Sons, only a handful of African Americans worked as janitors in Santa Clara County. Deelvin Blackwell had lived in several places in Oklahoma—Brooksville, Shawnee, Earlsboro, and Boley—before traveling to the West Coast to resettle. Similar to many men who made this trek, Deelvin worked his way to California, temporarily resettling in Arizona before migrating to San Jose for economic opportunities. Once he was rooted, his family drove twenty hours nonstop to San Jose. The path they took was Route 66 and the former route of U.S. 40 (1925–1964), which was common for most Oklahomans. In San Jose, Deelvin first worked in agriculture but then found his niche as a janitor under a white man by the name of Johnson. Deelvin did his job so well that Johnson let him work unsupervised and increased his responsibility. The places where Johnson had contracts recognized Deelvin's work and encouraged him to start his own janitorial service.

Other notable African American businesses in the Northside and East San Jose in this early period include Henry Ribbs's plumbing company; Thomas Moss's plumbing company; beauty shops operating out of private homes; Fisher's barbecue restaurant and several other restaurants; Walter's shoe shine service; and juke joints such as Cherry Inn and Hollywood Inn. At the Hollywood Inn, owned by Helen Gaffin's mother, a diverse cross-section of people listened to live music played by Duke Ellington and other notables, and they danced, drank, and partied into the wee hours of the morning. These businesses fostered a sense of black community, independence, and pride, and the money they pumped into the economy made homeownership possible; most African American migrants of the 1940s and '50s invested in property throughout the Northside and in parts of Alum Rock in East San Jose. Pat Perkins described this world of working together the best, when, she said, everyone knew everyone else and "supported one another until somebody did them wrong."[44]

IN THE IMMEDIATE POSTWAR PERIOD African Americans in the Santa Clara Valley worked together to make significant inroads into becoming first-class citizens. In employment, this began with new African American migrants who outnumbered their established neighbors. They were also more unapologetically southern, younger, relatively more educated, and were not content with racial injustice and menial jobs.[45] During World War II, most of these blacks migrated to California for shipyard employment, and they lived in central cities. After the war, they were the first factory employees to be laid off, along with white women. Most of these African Americans remained in the cities of their former shipyard factory employers. Others migrated within the region from cities like Oakland to cities and towns such as San Jose and Palo Alto, which represented their most favorable path toward achieving socioeconomic justice. Many established black residents, including early San Jose resident Mattie Berry, voiced their resentment toward this new group and the South Bay's abrupt shift toward a more racially hostile social climate by blaming it on this new wave of African American migrants, whom they called "suitcase Negroes."[46]

Among these newcomers, the first African Americans to politically agitate for equal opportunities were people such as Inez Jackson. Jackson was born and raised in Terrell, Texas. In 1944, she came to California to reunite her family with her husband, Leon, who worked at the Oakland shipyards.[47] In 1945 the Jacksons moved to the South Bay. Inez Jackson, an experienced schoolteacher with a credential from Langston University in Oklahoma, wanted to live in California during the war years because she had heard that discrimination did not exist there and that she could teach in an integrated setting. She was disheartened when she found that California in many ways was no better than Oklahoma, where she and Leon's family were terrorized by white supremacists during a race riot in the mid-1930s.[48] She was told by San Jose's school board that "black teachers were not hired," and she was instead offered a job scrubbing floors.[49] Insulted, she never pursued teaching again. In San Jose, she picked prunes and worked in canneries for several years before she was hired as a clerk for the U.S. Postal Service in 1949. This sour experience in the job market prompted Jackson to critique postwar South Bay in a manner that would be echoed by other politically conscious African American migrants when she said, "People had always talked about segregation in the South but this was worse."[50]

For Jackson, what was worse about the racism that she and her family experienced in the Santa Clara Valley was its subtlety, which often left doubt in the minds of black people because of its arbitrary nature. Jim Crow segregation was much more straightforward. What Jackson and other South Bay blacks encountered was de facto racial discrimination, which was far more difficult to detect because it occurs institutionally and in the customs of people who *may* or *may not* intend to be racially offensive, people who are accustomed to being culturally privileged as white people. To make the region live up to their expectations and fight for the hope of acquiring the American dream, southern black migrants like Jackson worked with settled African Americans in established institutions within black enclaves such as San Jose's Northside and downtown Palo Alto: the Garden City Women's Club, Antioch Baptist Church, Prayer Garden Church of God (San Jose), the Afro-American Center (San Jose), and Palo Alto AME Zion Church. New African American migrants were also the driving force behind the founding of the Santa Clara County chapter of the National Association for the Advancement of Colored People (NAACP).

Inez Jackson, ca. 1987. Charles Alexander Collection

The Santa Clara County NAACP was founded on February 8, 1942, at Anna B. McCall's home by 103 paying members.[51] Its first president was Antioch minister J. W. Byers. The county NAACP was made up of working-class people and a few professionals. It included maids, domestics, butlers, a few teachers and clergymen, an expressman, chauffeur, machinist, printer, carpenter, and lawyer. Most members were domestics and manual laborers. There was no gender or class discrimination except perhaps in leadership during the 1940s. Representative of this group was Emmitt Dollarhyde, who migrated to the South Bay from Earlsboro, Oklahoma, before the war, during the Dust Bowl, in either 1933 or in 1940.[52] Emmitt came to the South

Bay in search of farm work. According to Helen Gaffin and Orvella Stubbs, both of whom were Dollarhydes, Emmitt was a calm and forthright person who differed from his brothers, who were said to be hell-raisers.[53] Immediately upon coming to the valley, Emmitt created his own vertical mobility in the workforce from picking prunes to becoming an entrepreneur owning Dollarhyde House.[54] In Emmitt's spare time he was a political activist who was nominated as Reverend Byers's successor as Santa Clara County NAACP president.

In Dollarhyde's first year of leadership, he and Antioch's minister, C. W. Washington, negotiated with San Jose mayor Clark L. Bradley to establish Negro History Week, which has occurred in the first week of February since its beginning in 1947.[55] In this same year the Santa Clara County NAACP also created an interracial forum to discuss and improve race relations in the South Bay. This increase in community activism correlated with the rise in local NAACP membership, in which most of its members were from the Northside and downtown Palo Alto.[56] Perhaps for that reason, the branch went into 1951 overconfident and ended the year in a tailspin. On November 29, 1951, it was accused of overstepping its political boundaries for its attempts to sue the all-white Elks Club and ban all Elks-sponsored minstrel shows at the San Jose Civic Auditorium.[57] The crux of the issue was that whiteness and race-based citizenship directly connected to minstrelsy had existed in the South Bay from 1880 to 1965, and no one had ever protested its existence prior to the Santa Clara County NAACP protest.[58] According to historian Stephen Pitti:

> While apparent for a time in the late nineteenth century, anti-Italian and anti-Portuguese nativism did not dominate political concerns for long in Santa Clara County, and the widespread acceptance of European immigrants and their U.S.-born children as "white Americans" emerged hand in hand with more salient hostilities towards those considered to be nonwhite. Along with other images of black primitivism, minstrel shows shaped a sense of whiteness among local European immigrants and their children by the 1920s.[59]

The Santa Clara County NAACP in this instance wanted minstrel shows banned because, it said, they contributed to the forging of a local white supremacist identity by characterizing African Americans as people unfit for first-class citizenship because they were "lazy, ignorant, unfaithful to marriage vows, afraid of ghosts, given to unintelligible jabbering, given to razor wielding and chicken stealing, and endowed with other negative traits."[60] Defendants of the Elks included Mayor Clark Bradley, City Manager Anthony P. Hamann, Auditorium Manager Jay McCabe, and all the members of the city council. Some of them, including Mayor Bradley, went on record as being "friends of the Negro" when it came to resolving insignificant social issues. However, the NAACP's attack on an institution so deeply ingrained as minstrelsy turned "friendship" and supposed white tolerance of the local black population into white backlash. Dollarhyde immediately lost most of his customers and was forced to temporarily close Dollarhyde House.[61]

In 1952, several months after the minstrelsy protest, the Santa Clara County NAACP split into San Jose and Palo Alto–Stanford branches over political tactics. Immediately afterward, membership in both branches declined. The San Jose branch had started with 108 members. Its president was former Santa Clara County NAACP president Emmitt Dollarhyde (1952–1955). In 1953, he briefly stepped down during a period in which the San Jose branch membership declined to fewer than fifty people—the minimal number for maintaining an NAACP branch. Dorothea Leath took his place. Similar to blacks in Palo Alto, many San Jose African Americans lost interest in the local NAACP until 1960 because there was too much focus on membership drives, and most members were not prepared to consistently commit to large tasks such as fighting for fair employment and fair housing. Nonetheless, the NAACP's importance to the South Bay in the 1940s and 1950s stemmed from the fact that it replaced the mutual aid society the Order of Eastern Star. The Eastern Star was helpful in the 1920s and 1930s because it engaged in political activism and linked small black populations such as the Northside San Jose to other African American places throughout California. With that said, the NAACP was a new political entity within the valley representing national concerns for black freedom, similar in some ways to the Colored Convention Movement of the 1850s and 1860s.

IT COULD BE ARGUED THAT, for African Americans in suburbanizing Santa Clara Valley, no issue was more critical than understanding the nature of the community they were becoming. What they knew was that "suitcase Negroes" were in the valley to stay. They also knew that Santa Clara County's color line was hardening and that real estate agents and property owners were openly excluding blacks during the area's golden era (1945–1970), in which a new American way of life was being constructed, called suburbia. Yet the one peculiar saving grace for most blacks in the South Bay was that the region was ambivalent in its commitment to racial justice, and its customary segregation was always in flux. Though this indecisive posture empowered the white majority because customs of whiteness usually trumped racial justice, it also empowered racial liberals who were willing to take the myth of racial tolerance and racist customs to task through public demonstration and negotiation. This was a strategy that nineteenth-century abolitionists and civil rights activists had used to fight slavery and legal racial discrimination in California. This tactic was rediscovered during the 1940s as the black population radically increased and refused to go back to the Jim Crow South physically or conceptually. This combination forged a new chapter in Bay Area politics.

African American urban scholars would also add that the rise of the urban black working class in manufacturing industries with federal government contracts was an important factor to the modern African American political resurgence. However, in the Santa Clara Valley, blacks were marginal to the industrialization process of the 1940s.[62] Their political activism was instead fueled by the quest for social and political freedom—a quest that became the most feasible political tactic for many African Americans, who had lost their base of political empowerment through unionization and industrial work after World War II. Going into the 1950s, in the South Bay, the black community remained publicly active until its momentum was derailed by policy makers and internal divisions that weakened political organizations like the Santa Clara County NAACP. This temporarily set back a burgeoning black freedom movement and subdued the African American community presence in most parts of Santa Clara County until civil rights activism reemerged in the valley during the 1960s. The next chapter will explore the postwar urban development of the Santa Clara Valley and the struggle to either eradicate housing discrimination or codify it into local and state law.

Chapter Four
Urban Sustainability and Race in Santa Clara County, 1945–1968

> *Certainly, as we talk seriously of going to the moon, we ought to be ready to straighten out our living conditions here first.*
> California assemblyman William Byron Rumford

IN THE POST–WORLD WAR II ERA, perhaps the most urgent civil rights issues confronting African Americans in most urban communities outside the South were residential segregation and the struggle for affordable quality housing.[1] In the Santa Clara Valley this struggle was critical, because communities shut people of color out of their housing markets primarily because of race prejudice and not to prevent a decline in property values. To understand this fact is paramount, because the fight against residential segregation in the postwar years played a huge role in blacks' gaining access to housing in suburban areas such as the South Bay after 1968.

From 1945 to 1968, residential segregation was fought nationwide by loosely connected state and local fair housing movements. In Santa Clara County, the fair housing movement began in 1949 with the San Jose Council for Civic Unity. Three years later San Jose's newly formed NAACP forged alliances with the Brotherhood of Sleeping Car Porters, the Council of Churches, the Catholic Interracial Council, and the Quakers (American Friends Service Committee) in order to counter residential discrimination.[2] In the following year San Jose NAACP president Dorothy Leath wrote a letter to the San Francisco chapter expressing how problematic closed housing was in the South Bay. "Housing is most definitely at its worst as far as segregation and discrimination are concerned," she said. Although open housing might lead to a decentralized African American community, with blacks dispersed and a sense of community diminished, "most [South Bay blacks] decided that the most important issue was for Black people to be able to make their own choices about where they wanted to live and not have others making that choice for them."[3] By 1959, the local fair housing effort made considerable headway as about two thousand San Jose homeowners signed an "open housing covenant," declaring: "I hereby bear witness that I am ready to welcome into my neighborhood residents of whatever race, creed or national origin."[4] In 1962 fair housing activists pressured San Jose into becoming the second city in Santa Clara County to try to resolve residential apartheid with a fair housing ordinance—the first city was nearby Milpitas, which had a fair housing ordinance built into its municipal codes before it incorporated in 1954.[5]

On the state level, passage of the California Fair Housing Act of 1963 (also called the Rumford Fair Housing Act) made California central to the success of the fair housing and civil rights movements. On February 16, 1964, at the Negro Consolidated Realty Board of Los Angeles installation banquet, Dr. Martin Luther King, Jr., acknowledged California's importance to the civil rights movement. At that time the movement was fighting the repeal of the Rumford Act through Proposition 14, which would outlaw fair housing in California. In King's address he said the repeal of the Rumford Act would be "one of most shameful developments in our nation's history." He also condemned people who said that "civil rights cannot be legislated, [while] asserting that segregation can be."[6] The fair housing movement peaked in 1968, when the federal government made Federal Housing Authority (FHA) insurance more accessible to black home buyers and passed the Fair Housing Act of 1968, or Title 8 of the Civil Rights Act of 1968.

RESIDENTIAL CONSTRUCTION IN postwar America was concentrated on the fringe of central cities called suburbia. It was triggered by the availability of inexpensive rural land, federal housing and highway policies that promoted suburban growth, the redlining of older neighborhoods, and the amenities offered in suburban housing.[7] According to the U.S. Census Bureau, nearly 33 million families—or 62 percent— owned their own homes in 1960, the highest level of homeownership since 1890. In the same period, two million African Americans—or 25 percent of all black families—owned their own homes.[8]

Despite the fact that there was a 5 percent homeownership increase for African Americans in the 1950s—the largest in their history—the huge disparity in homeownership and the quality of housing in black and white America widened. Most new homes were built in suburbia and were purchased by white Americans.[9] This unprecedented opportunity elevated many whites into the middle class and dynamically increased their net worth with little effort. The opposite held true for most people of color living in ghettoes and, after 1950, "ring suburbs" or minority middle-income neighborhoods on the fringes of the inner city, who either built their own homes or purchased existing homes in urbanizing communities within East San Jose.[10] Ultimately, people of color fell victim to the policies and customs created by the real estate and home buyer industries to support the popular belief that the more homogenous a community is, the better its chemistry will be.[11]

Residential and industrial development from 1945 to 1990 transformed Santa Clara County entirely as orchards were replaced by subdivisions, high-tech companies, strip malls, and industrial parks. This new economy made the South Bay into a self-sustaining region, one no longer reliant on larger nearby cities such as San Francisco and Oakland. In the valley, residential development was controlled for the purpose of preventing sprawl and creating better quality of life. But this was not true in many areas on the outskirts of downtown San Jose and some parts of Santa Clara, where a mixture of controlled and haphazard planning resulted in an urban growth rate that occasionally challenged that of metropolitan San Jose in the 1950s and 1960s.[12] Consequently, new housing, job growth, and a stable economy triggered an intraregional and global movement into the South Bay. From a homeowner's perspective, the valley prior to the 1970s was appealing because homes there were relatively large yet less expensive than older homes in more established metropolitan areas like San Francisco and Oakland.[13] Moreover, the housing costs-to-income ratio in most parts of the valley was moderate, though rising, up to the late 1960s. Until then, most homeowners did not have to spend the bulk

TABLE 7 Black Population in Santa Clara County, 1940–1980

	1940	1950	1960	1970	1980
Total black population	730	1,718	4,187	18,090	43,716
Total population	174,949	290,547	642,315	1,064,714	1,295,071

Total increase in black population, 1940–1980: 98%

Total population increase from, 1940–1980: 86%

SOURCES: U.S. Bureau of the Census, *1950 Census of Population: Volume 11, Characteristics of the Population, Part 5, California* (Washington, D.C.: U.S. Government Printing Office, 1952), 5–21; U.S. Bureau of the Census, *1970 Census of Housing: Volume 1, Housing Characteristics for States, Cities, and Counties; Part 6, California* (Washington, D.C.: U.S. Government Printing Office, 1972), 7–10, 14–15, 453; U.S. Bureau of the Census, *U.S. Census of Population and Housing: 1980 Census Tracts* (Washington, D.C.: U.S. Government Printing Office, 1983), 215; *Historical Census Browser: County-Level Results for 1850–1960* (Charlottesville: University of Virginia Library, Geospatial and Statistical Data Center, 2005).

of their wages on a mortgage; with the exception of West County, the South Bay was one of the more affordable places to live in the Bay Area. Almost all prospective buyers in the valley expected to purchase a newly built home, and the vast majority of housing constructed in this suburban boom consisted of single-family homes.

Few of these prospective buyers were black, however. For African Americans, the ambition to move to the South Bay and purchase housing during its boom was halted by various barriers: race prejudice, state and federal policies, affordability, and de facto segregation in the housing and employment markets.[14] This combination of obstacles amounted to the exclusion of black mobility in most Santa Clara County communities during this first period of substantial suburban growth. African Americans in this period ranged from 0.6 percent of the South Bay population to 1.7 percent; in 1950, 1,718 blacks lived in Santa Clara County, and by 1970 this number had risen to 18,090.[15] Most of them lived in Northside San Jose, East San Jose, downtown

Palo Alto, Barron Park (Palo Alto), East Palo Alto (on the outskirts of the county), and Sunnyhills (Milpitas).[16]

Prior to the 1970s, this "virtual restriction" imbued the few black suburbanites with pioneer status. Residential scholar W. Dennis Keating traces this movement back to the 1920s as modern suburbs began to emerge—inspired by middle-class Americans wanting to move from congested cities, the mass production of the automobile, major development of roads and freeways, domestic petroleum booms, white flight in response to the Great Black Migration (1915–ca. 1930s), and public policy pushing to urbanize the countryside.[17] After World War II, the federal government played a huge role in jump-starting a second wave of modern suburbanization through its single-family housing and mass transportation policies, which popularized the movement in the 1950s. The real estate and banking industries also steered Americans' attention toward the suburbs. Real estate brokers and bank lenders worked with the FHA and Veterans Administration (VA) to build large subdivisions of single-family homes on relatively inexpensive rural land. In turn, most buyers were able to purchase spacious new homes in a sellers' market subsidized by the federal government on thirty-year installment plans with 10 percent down.

Manufacturers, too, drew people to the suburbs. Ford and GM relocated from nearby central cities to underdeveloped and often unincorporated areas like Milpitas and Fremont, where land for building factories was cheap, and taxes and city amenities were more favorable. Basically, the postwar suburb offered better housing, better schools, better amenities, better municipal services, and better employment.[18] To white Americans, that is. Most blacks, regardless of economic class, were restricted to the central city, which had lost many of its industries and jobs and, because of white flight, many of its public services. For urban scholars W. Dennis Keating, Andrew Weise, Robert Self, and Thomas Sugrue, this second wave of suburbanization (1945–1970) marked an era in which single-family homeownership was seen as an indicator of white supremacy, and minority exclusion was at its peak in modern American history.

The few African Americans given the opportunity to live in the suburbs prior to the 1970s often were steered into transitional housing in older declining areas that extended the ghetto by artificially creating one. Scholars such as Lawrence de Graaf, Bruce D. Haynes, and Sheryll Cashin called these communities either "ring suburbs" or "suburban black belts" to describe the post-1950s phenomenon of older suburbs taking on characteristics of the twentieth-century inner city once blacks moved in and whites and industry moved out.[19] Ring suburbs have historically extended the black community as African Americans moved either into adjacent older suburbs (e.g., South-Central Los Angeles to Compton) or into relatively distant older suburbs from which they could provide surrounding white communities with inexpensive labor (e.g., East Palo Alto to the South Bay and West Bay Area).[20] For example, after 1950, unincorporated East Palo Alto became a black community, fostering the dreams of African Americans who sought full inclusion into suburbanizing Santa Clara and San Mateo Counties. But East Palo Alto became a ghetto overnight, falling victim to white flight, capital flight, unfair taxation, debased city services, and divestment in the housing market. Consequently, East Palo Alto's limited job opportunities forced most of its African American residents to work as manual laborers and domestics, even though many were military veterans, tradesmen, or college graduates.[21]

To combat the residential apartheid developing in the Santa Clara Valley in the 1950s and 1960s, blacks and their liberal white allies fought for open housing on a variety of fronts: as civil rights activists, real estate agents, home builders, concerned individuals, and fair housing advocates. Among the civil rights activists were Inez Jackson and her husband (see chapter 3), who migrated from the East Bay to the South Bay in 1945 in hopes of benefiting from its urban and industrial growth.[22] It was while they were living in San Jose that Inez discovered that the housing market in Santa Clara Valley was about as fair as its job market, which had countered her application for a teaching job in the school system with an offer of a janitorial job there. She and Leon settled on a white wooden house in the center of the Northside. However, they quickly discovered that residential mobility for blacks was restricted to living in the San Jose downtown area north of Julian from First to Twentieth Streets and parts of the Eastside.[23]

Inez found the de facto segregation of California to be no better than the legally enforced segregation she had lived under in Oklahoma; in some ways, in fact, it was more intolerable because it was covert. Instead of moving on, she decided to make the region live up to her expectations. Central to her beliefs was that African Americans should be free to live anywhere they chose to live within their financial means. In 1958 she and J. S. Williams, a white Realtor, encouraged fellow activist and close friend Mary Anne Smith to become the first black real estate agent in the Santa Clara Valley. Williams hired her for his own firm and then went on to recruit and hire a second black agent, Berthina Nelson.

From 1958 to 1970, Smith, Nelson, and Williams were in the vanguard of desegregating exclusively white neighborhoods throughout Santa Clara County.[24] Similar to most African Americans in the South Bay who came to the region during the Second Great Migration, Smith and her family were from the South. She was born Mary Anne Spencer in 1917 to farmers in Patrick County, Virginia. Segregation in her community was not by residence, but by education, employment, and public accommodations. Although most of the family's neighbors were white, Mary and the other black young people in her area were required to attend a separate school. In 1942, she moved to Baltimore to work as a clerk for the Social Security Administration,[25] then on to Washington, D.C., where she met a sailor named Thomas H. Smith. In 1944, shortly after marriage, the Smiths moved to San Francisco, where Thomas was stationed at Treasure Island. Mary found work at the West Coast Regional Social Security office. In 1947, the couple moved to San Jose. The decision to move to San Jose was Thomas's. He was impressed by the region's warm and gentle social environment, its country appeal, and racial tolerance. Mary, on the other hand, had several notable brushes with racism in the Santa Clara Valley soon after moving there. Her first significant encounter occurred as she and her husband were trying to purchase a home and found themselves steered to what they thought was a house on South Thirty-Fourth Street in East San Jose. According to Mary, the broker took the couple

Mary Anne Smith, ca. 1987. Charles Alexander Collection.

to an empty lot that needed loads of fill dirt before any construction could begin. The broker also showed the Smiths "one other [lot] on Race Street by the railroad tracks, and told us that's all he had for us." Initially Mary did not know what he meant: "I didn't recognize the discrimination. I didn't know you couldn't live anywhere you want." Then in her painful recollection she recalled figuring out "that's all he had for *me* . . ." This matter was resolved only after the broker went to the house next door to the empty lot and asked the homeowner, an immigrant from Portugal, "if she wouldn't mind if Negroes moved in next to her."[26]

Smith and Inez Jackson met in 1947. Jackson had never learned to drive, and Smith would pick her up and chauffeur her to meetings of the NAACP, League of Women Voters, and Garden City Women's Club.[27] Eventually Smith became interested in these organizations and became an activist herself. Jackson took Smith under her wing and helped her understand the discrimination that was happening around her, especially in the residential market.[28] During this period, Smith met Williams at local NAACP functions. Williams had been desegregating South Bay neighborhoods since the late 1940s, starting with assisting "formerly interned Japanese to find homes and rebuild their lives."[29] In the 1950s Williams, an NAACP member, took his efforts further by joining a collective struggle against white flight and "block busting," a scare tactic used by unscrupulous real estate agents to goad white homeowners into panic sales of their properties, which the agents would then sell to minorities at inflated prices. Williams saw that the only way to put an end to the industry's corrupt practices was to have black real estate agents positioned within it.[30] Smith was immediately receptive to his message. "I didn't want what happened to me to happen to anyone ever again," she said later.[31]

Driven by the passion to open the Santa Clara County housing market to all cultures, Smith strove to make the South Bay inclusive and to prevent any area of the valley from becoming a ghetto because of discriminatory real estate practices. Her method to accomplish this was to encourage prospective homebuyers of different cultural backgrounds to purchase homes throughout the South Bay to avoid concentrating groups such as African Americans into areas like San Jose's Northside, which is what had happened from 1878 to the 1960s.[32] From 1958 to 1964, Smith worked for several brokers before opening her own practice on East Santa Clara Street between Thirty-Third and Thirty-Fourth Streets. Smith was a successful realtor because she chose to ignore the unwritten rules about where people of color should live. In the process she created a niche for herself. And some notoriety as well. In the early 1960s, she ignored segregationist practices by showing a black client a home in the exclusively white Willow Glen area (West San Jose). The next day, she received a phone call from a white agent at a different brokerage who did not know Smith's racial makeup. The woman proceeded to inform her of the unwritten rules governing real estate sales in San Jose. According to Smith, "She told me in no uncertain terms that there were areas where black people were not welcome, and that Willow Glen was one of them."[33]

The unwritten rules in Santa Clara County realty dictated that agents could show African Americans homes in the Northside or Eastside, which was mostly Mexican American or Portuguese American, but they couldn't show the all-white enclaves in West San Jose such as Willow Glen and Rose Garden or the downtown area surrounding San Jose State College.[34] From 1958 to the 1970s, Smith broke all those rules. She sold homes to blacks, relocated Ford and Lockheed workers of color, and worked for "mixed couples, white couples, Mexican clients, all kinds of clients."[35] Her biggest obstacle was finding friendly banks to get her clients' home loans approved. The lenders most willing to cooperate with Smith were located in San Francisco such as American Savings, San Francisco Federal Savings, and Bay View Federal Savings. These lenders ironically sent Smith the listings of available homes in hopes of increasing their business by undermining the discriminatory practices of their competitors in San Jose.[36] Essentially, Smith's profits were on par with white real estate agents. Though she made less money on commissions, she made up the difference in volume by selling homes throughout the Santa Clara Valley.

THE TYPICAL RESTRICTIVE HOUSING scenario was for white real estate brokers to tell prospective black homeowners that the homes they coveted had been rented or sold. After receiving this information and purchasing elsewhere, many blacks told Smith that they would go by the so-called rented or sold homes months later only to find that a for-sale or vacancy sign was still up.[37]

One group Smith worked with to combat residential segregation was the San Jose Council for Civic Unity (CCU). The CCU was founded in 1949 in First Unitarian Church of San Jose by white freedom rights activists such as San Jose State English professor Florence Banks Bryant, real estate agent Alden Campen, Robert Doerr (who would later become the mayor of San Jose), Unitarian Church minister Nat Laureat, and San Jose State professor of sociology Claude Settles.[38] The CCU's main goals "were to locate housing for minority persons and to defend them against discriminatory practices."[39] Their political strategies for resolving racial discrimination in the South Bay were oriented toward informing segregationists that their tactics were illegal. Basically, the CCU in the 1950s and '60s was doing what Black Power activists suggested their white counterparts do in the mid-1960s: instead of organizing the African American community, organize your own. Under Florence Banks Bryant's leadership, the CCU found low-cost housing for African Americans, investigated housing advertisements specifically aimed at blacks that promoted segregation, and presented a united front in opposing unfair housing legislation in the 1960s. According to Bryant, the organization's methods leaned more toward moral persuasion than direct confrontation:

> When we found a real estate company that was really discriminating or there was threatened discrimination in a subdivision, we didn't go and attack that person directly and personally. . . . I remember one case where a subdivision was being started in the West Valley. Of course, West Valley has always been a little more resistant to minority people than the Eastside, and still is. There were some Negro people who wanted to buy in this subdivision. . . . The people who [had] already bought homes set up a meeting to see how they were going to keep these "undesirable people" out. We [the CCU] heard about this and set up a meeting of our own in the same area and invited everyone to come. We held that meeting; it was very successful, very mild, very friendly and low-key. As a matter of fact, when this subdivision opened there were no scare tactics used, as they had intended.[40]

In investigating housing for rent in newspaper advertisements, the CCU looked for such catchphrases as "Whites Only," "No Colored," and "Look! Colored!" If the advertisement was race neutral, a member of the organization would call the advertiser and ask if he or she rented to minorities.[41] The most common responses were either a straight "We don't rent to Negroes" or "Somebody has already spoken for the apartment." Bryant once followed one of the "Look! Colored!" ads to the location given and found that it was filthy. "It was impossible for anyone to live there," she said. "There was garbage all over floor, and cans, and broken doors." She called the real estate agent and scolded him. "How can anyone have the nerve to advertise a place like that and say specifically that it is for colored people?" she said. "What kind of people are you?" The real estate agent nervously responded, "Well, I haven't seen the place." Bryant closed the conversation with a strongly worded criticism, "That is not the way to advertise, even if you had seen it."[42]

The CCU had major influence with the South Bay's religious community. Several of its members served on the boards of the Council of Churches, Catholic Interracial Council, and the American Friends Service Committee. For the CCU, the challenge in dealing with local religious liberals was to get them to become more politically active.[43] In the 1950s, the CCU's affiliation with the local Quakers made them coalition partners in the development of one of the first integrated subdivisions in America, at Sunnyhills, Milpitas. In the next decade the CCU joined black activists throughout the valley on numerous freedom rights projects ranging from public demonstrations to institution building.[44]

Moreover, the CCU and Mary Anne Smith worked with Doris Jones, who operated a civil rights and fair housing switchboard in the West Bay Area. Jones, a white retired engineer, was the Palo Alto–Stanford NAACP's housing chairman and editor of the chapter's newsletter, the *Beanstalk* (aka "human beings talk").[45] In 1963, she headed a coalition project run by a joint housing committee made up of the Santa Clara County CORE and the South San Mateo County and Palo Alto NAACPs.[46] By 1960, one major problem for blacks and working-class people looking for a home in the San Francisco Peninsula was that the cost of housing already rivaled race as an inhibitor for most African Americans attempting to move into urbanizing towns such as the white and affluent Palo Alto and Menlo Park.[47] Nonetheless, the NAACP switchboard consisted of listings of homes and apartments available to African Americans within the peninsula. Jones organized investigations of suspected residential discrimination whereby blacks and whites would call the same homeowner separately to assess whether discrimination was at work. She also provided information on housing laws to African Americans who were turned down

Joseph Eichler. Courtesy Palo Alto Historical Association.

by apartment owners. However, Jones, like the CCU in San Jose, only confronted the landlord with the results of her investigation and never threatened legal action; that part was up to the African Americans who were discriminated against. Nevertheless, Jones did connect blacks with lawyers willing to do pro bono work on housing discrimination cases. She said she found that there was about a 50-50 chance that a homeowner in Palo Alto would sell to an African American. "But apartment houses [were] almost 100 percent closed to Negroes." Jones saw the driving force behind racial animosity in the Greater Palo Alto area as landlords and homebuilders.[48]

THE EXCEPTION TO JONES'S observation was Eichler Homes, who worked with fair housing activists in providing single-family housing for African Americans who could afford to live in expensive communities like Palo Alto.[49] Joseph Eichler, the company's founder and president, was a liberal Democrat who contributed money to California Governor Pat Brown, the ACLU, and John F. Kennedy's electoral campaign for president. In the 1950s and '60s, Eichler Homes emerged as one of the largest builders in the United States, known for its innovative architectural design and community planning.[50] The company operated mostly in the San Francisco Bay Area and in Greater Los Angeles, where the lush geographical environment and open landscapes proved perfect for Eichler's cosmopolitan and liberal vision. Eichler Homes was the first large tract builder among American builders that specialized in single-family homes to administer an open occupancy clause. When this policy was first implemented in 1954, Eichler Homes referred to it as "silent reality": the company never sought publicity for being an open housing builder and in fact mentioned the policy only when customers asked about it, but most Eichler homeowners and prospective buyers knew that Eichler Homes did not restrict people on the basis of race.[51]

Eichler's open housing policy began in 1950 with the selling of a home to an Asian American family in Palo Alto. Some white residents were upset, but Eichler Homes did not lose any sales. The real test for the company came in 1954, when more African Americans were moving into the proximity of Palo Alto and East Palo Alto and were seeking housing in line with their professional status and income. A West Indian woman married to an African American professor at Stanford purchased a home in an Eichler subdivision in Palo Alto.[52] The wife was persistent, asking Edward P. Eichler (Joseph's son), "Do you discriminate in the sale of your houses? Do you sell houses to minorities?" Nervous because he never had to field these questions before, Edward responded by asking "if she was a minority who wanted to buy a house, or was she asking for academic purposes?"[53] What made this subject difficult for both parties was that there was no official law addressing open housing until the state sanctioned the Hawkins and Unruh Acts in 1959 and the federally sanctioned Executive Order 11063 in 1962.[54] This situation became more complicated for the younger Eichler after the woman informed him that her family lived across the street from a small Eichler home up for sale (with two bedrooms) and wanted to purchase it because it was a better home. By every standard aside from race—income, education, profession—this couple was qualified in Edward's mind.[55] Unsure how to respond, Edward called his father, who replied, "Why are you bothering me about this? I haven't got time for these little problems." As a result, the couple was sold the home. There was one notable objection from a white couple who had put money down on the house next door and expected the black couple to leave—the wife was "very disturbed about living next door to Negroes."[56] According to Edward, her anxiety was driven not by fears of declining property values, but by race prejudice. Without hesitation, Joseph Eichler returned the down payment to the white couple and resold that house to a white man who was not worried about living next to blacks. As it turned out, the new buyer and the black professor knew each other quite well, although they did not know until after the sale that they had become neighbors.

Joseph Eichler's casual approach toward systematically opening his subdivisions to people of color through the principle of "silent reality" set the tone for Eichler Homes and its purchasers. Open occupancy was mostly a business decision that also reflected the values and persona of Joseph Eichler, who knew as a large builder that he could absorb the initial economic setbacks that might destroy most small builders. In doing so, he slightly altered the housing market in affluent California communities such as Greenmeadows Street (Palo Alto), Torrington Drive (Sunnyvale), Cupertino, and West San Jose, although this was not an attempt to resolve any social problems. Neither Joseph nor his son Edward (who became president in the early 1960s) could see the day when there would be a "big rush of [blacks] to the suburbs," something that occurred only after 1980.[57]

Joseph and Edward Eichler maintained the attitude that if a person wanted a home, so be it—the Eichlers were out to build a community on the properties they owned by selling to qualified buyers, not to consciously develop an integrated community such as the United Auto Workers–sponsored subdivision in Milpitas called Sunnyhills. The Eichlers insisted that closed housing began and ended with the state and federal governments changing their practices and taking the lead to clean up the mess that the governments had a huge role in creating dating back to the 1930s. Moreover, for Joseph Eichler the mess was not a result of challenging popular mores by integrating communities, but rather had been created by the real estate industry's sales to unqualified whites, a practice that often resulted in massive foreclosures during economic recessions and the devaluation of white communities. With this said, the Eichlers were very cautious about bunching too many African Americans into one tract, and instead persuaded prospective black buyers to scatter throughout the Eichler communities. Eichler Homes set a goal for its black occupancy rate in a single subdivision at 6 percent. They did this to prevent potential white hostility directed toward African Americans and Eichler Homes from local homeowners and to thwart real estate brokers looking to create a panic that would create white flight and a massive loss of revenue.[58] After "silent reality" was established, selling Eichler homes went relatively smoothly, and values on his integrated tracts went up, not down, by $10,000 from 1954 to 1962 and kept pace with the South Bay's growth in the 1960s.[59]

SOUTH BAY BLACKS' REACTION TO discriminatory housing frequently reflected generational differences. For older African American residents who moved to the South Bay from the U.S. South, the area's subtle segregation was usually accommodated because it appeared to be better than Jim Crow, and was fought along the lines suggested by Francis Tanner: "I got respect because I demanded it and deserved it." Tanner was the first black police officer in San Jose in 1951, and he fought racism as an exemplary citizen and an individual integrationist.[60] However, the region's de facto segregation did not go over well with younger blacks and African Americans raised in the South and Southwest in the 1960s. According to Inez Jackson, the social and political climate within the Santa Clara Valley on matters of race followed national trends and became increasingly tense during the 1960s.[61] Former San Jose NAACP president T. J. Owens stated that this new generation of African Americans, which he led, often contemplated confronting racism with black insurgency—echoing racial altercations in nearby San Francisco and Oakland. Every step of the way they were blocked by older freedom rights activists whom they respected, among them Jackson and Smith, who reminded them that "San Jose was not always [bad] like this."[62] They were also informed of viable options in combating San Jose's subtle discrimination by "working together to survive and thrive," filing civil rights lawsuits, and engaging in nonviolent direct action protest.

Others, including a local black resident named Ms. Bremond, wrote public forum editorials in the *San Jose Mercury News*. Bremond questioned the goodwill of white people on the subject of racial integration and racial equality. In an article titled "Assimilate with You?" she made bold to critique the white segregationists. "What will you have us assimilate from you? That which we know of you? That strongly believed freedom . . . your strong moral fiber?" Bremond proceeded to identify efforts intended to ensure white supremacy. She pilloried whites for injustices ranging from slavery to racial segregation, for ineffectual elite white liberalism, and for the weak position that political moderates took in regard to race, a position she identified with the suburbanization, ghettoization, and white conspicuous consumption that occurred in the postwar period. Bremond concluded with an incisive question for the white community: "Have you ever stopped to consider that our relationship with you has been severely limited; nearly to the point that assimilation is almost impossible? What do we see of you? You think you look like a prince to us, wrapped in virtue. I see you as condescending. . . . I see you as hypocrites."[63]

Bremond's anger and frustration reflected a general feeling coming over many black Californians in the early 1960s, who saw their dreams of first-class citizenship far from being realized during a very prosperous period in a supposedly racially tolerant state. When the letter was published in June 1963, racial tensions were high as San Jose policymakers were going through the process of passing a municipal fair housing ordinance, and the state was getting close to passing the California Fair Housing Act of 1963.

The roots of the California Fair Housing Act date to 1946, when black assemblyman Augustus F. (Gus) Hawkins hastily initiated the battle for the Fair Employment Practices Commission (FEPC), and the measure was decisively defeated 2-to-1.[64] According to labor and civil rights leader C. L. Dellums, conservative leaders helped defeat the initiative by saying it was linked to communism. This loss set the FEPC movement back more than ten years, as it was declared to be a reflection of the California majority's will.[65] California's hardening color line was directly countered in 1951 by the California Committee for Fair Employment Practices (CCFEP). The committee included representatives of the NAACP, the American Civil Liberties Union, the California Federation for Civic Unity, the Community Service Organization, the Congress of Industrial Organizations, the Japanese American Citizens League, the Jewish Labor Committee, Assemblyman William Byron Rumford (D–Berkeley and West Oakland), and Christian church groups.[66] In 1957 the FEPC movement extended itself into a movement for fair housing. At the helm of this movement were Assemblymen Hawkins, Rumford, and Jesse Unruh. Within the Senate the CCFEP was assisted by a new wave of young, idealistic Democrats, led by Governor Edmund G. "Pat" Brown (1958–66), who supported civil rights programs and were referred to as "the club."

In 1959, CCFEP and "the club" spearheaded the passage of a fair employment practices bill and two fair housing bills in the Hawkins Act and Unruh Act.[67] The Hawkins Act (AB 801) restricted discrimination in public-assisted housing by banning discrimination in government-aided transactions, such as apartment housing insured by FHA, VA, and CalVet federal loans. It also covered "tract housing with five or more units insured by government loans, urban renewal developments and multiple dwellings with veterans' tax exemptions."[68] The Hawkins bill's initial effect on the housing market was minimal. According to Marshall Kaplan, it covered only around 20 percent of the state's housing.[69] Whereas the Unruh Act, by amending Section 51 of California's Civil Rights Act, had the potential to have a more serious influence on the housing market, if it would be more specifically worded and actually enforced.[70] The Unruh Act might outlaw discrimination in all business transactions, including the renting, leasing, and selling of housing. Private housing was in theory covered by Unruh because real estate brokers were licensed through the state, thus making any illegal business transaction—including discrimination by race, color, or creed—punishable by California courts. Unruh's greatest impact on housing transactions occurred in public housing when it combined with the Hawkins Act, which had FEPC enforcement powers. However, Unruh was very broad in what it addressed as a business transaction; for example, the law does not specifically cover, but only implies, private housing. Consequently, real estate business transactions were left up to the California legal system to interpret and enforce on a case-by-case basis. This confusion undermined early fair housing law in California on the local and state levels because the court process was very slow and expensive, and the reward for the plaintiff was minimal (i.e., $250 to $2,500).

In the Santa Clara Valley the implementation of Hawkins and Unruh was difficult because many of the homes available were single-family homes that were increasingly purchased through private lenders. One rare instance of how justice was pursued invoking the Unruh Act in the Santa Clara County involves Moffett Field in 1960. The administrators of Moffett Field demanded that the San Jose Superior Court stop all sales of homes in the Sun Valley residential subdivision on McKee Road until their African American employee Herbert Mills was sold a single-family home. The home that Mills and his family tried to purchase was advertised for $14,320 to veterans and nonveterans for $99 down, including closing costs. When he tried to purchase the home from Assurance Realty Company, Assurance Finance Company and Assurance Investment Company refused to sell. Mills charged institutional racism based on an illegal business transaction. Attorneys asked for $30,000 for general and punitive damages "and an injunction to stop discrimination against them [Mills and his family] and a court order halting further sales of homes in the subdivision until the home they offer to buy is deeded to them under advertised conditions."[71]

In another rare reported incident, Clarence Hudson, a black electronics technician working in Palo Alto, and his wife, Diane, publicly pursued residential racial justice invoking Unruh in 1960.[72] Their suit, filed in San Jose Superior Court, claims that they were refused the sale of a house in the newly built ten-thousand-home Tropicana Village in East San Jose based on residential discrimination. The Hudsons had made offers on a house in July and October 1959 and again in January

1960 but were turned down each time. What was different about the January rejection was that Tropicana Village started selling completed homes and was advertising in the newspaper, which is how the Hudsons knew that homes within the new subdivision were available. The Hudsons asked the court to freeze the sale of all homes in Tropicana Village until they were sold the home of their choice. In addition they wanted to be sold a home on the same terms and conditions accorded to whites.

Beyond these two examples of residential discrimination, an African American filing for residential-economic redress in the South Bay was rare. Many African Americans in the 1960s had too insufficient a sense of California housing law and of the protective power of the government to pursue redress from residential discrimination, even as local fair housing advocates were gradually making headway with white homeowners. Still, by 1962, San Jose became the second and last city in Santa Clara County to seriously try to counteract its residential apartheid with a fair housing ordinance; the first was Milpitas during its incorporation in 1954.

Rumblings of a fair housing ordinance were heard from the San Jose Human Relations Commission in 1961. This six-hundred-member board was the official spokesperson for owners and operators of three thousand apartment houses in San Jose. The board publicly viewed fair housing legislation as an outlet to teach race tolerance to San Jose's white public and place the burden to end residential discrimination on their shoulders, rather than relying on laws or resolutions to achieve that effect.[73] Its goal was to enact a voluntary integration housing ordinance conducive to changing local custom through legislation and moral suasion with a minimal degree of enforcement, such as refusing to grant business licenses to apartment owners who reportedly discriminate.[74] These rumblings immediately sparked a white backlash. The most high profile group to attempt to stop any open housing law from being enacted was a loosely organized federation of contractors, real estate agents, and apartment house owners calling themselves the Citizens League for Individual Freedoms.[75]

This league forestalled the San Jose City Council's adoption of an open occupancy code until March 12, 1962, when the city council officially sought a ban on housing discrimination on the basis of race, religion, national origin, or ancestry. Even though City Attorney Ferdinand Palla framed the ordinance to keep it in line with the Hawkins and Unruh Acts, the San Jose law would have been more potent. It was more clearly stated than the fragmented fair housing laws coming out of California's state capitol in Sacramento. More important, San Jose's proposed fair housing law was drafted to have enforcement powers administered through its legal and law enforcement system.[76] The major problems confronting its passage were finding money to finance the program and the fact that California courts still had problems clarifying the boundaries of the Unruh Act.

Nevertheless, on May 23, 1962, a marathon public hearing on fair housing, administered by San Jose's Human Relations Commission, was held from 4 p.m. to midnight at San Jose City Hall. Within this hearing, racial tensions in San Jose were at their peak, not just between blacks and conservative whites, but also between African Americans and Mexican Americans. The majority of city council members were in favor of fair housing, with one dissenter. Among the spectators, the group most vehemently opposed was the Citizens League for Individual Freedoms. According to a representative of the group, William P. Nelson, "Equality between races and individuals can never be a proper subject for legislative action."[77] As a resolution he challenged the commission to set aside the ordinance and seek a solution to residential discrimination through education rather than legislation. Then Nelson and several other members of his group suggested that the proposed legislation be called "the forced housing ordinance." The friction between African Americans and Mexican Americans was not necessarily personal but rather a response by persons of Mexican descent to how fair housing legislation was being framed, which centered on the concerns of African Americans and only marginally considered the concerns of people of color who had a much larger population in California.[78]

Supporters of fair housing at the hearing came from all areas of the political spectrum. These supporters included the American Jewish Congress, Anti-Defamation League, Antioch Baptist Church, B'nai B'rith, Central Labor Council, CORE, Council of Churches, NAACP,

United Auto Workers, Valley Committee on Open Housing, Wilsonian Democratic Club, and the Women's International League for Peace and Freedom. Those testifying ranged from people who believed that everyone should have the freedom to choose where they live; to activists, such as CORE, who were skeptical of the goodwill of white homeowners and pushed for a legislative approach; to members of the politically moderate Wilsonian Democratic Club, who supported fair housing on the basis of fair competition in the housing market.[79]

Most supporters vehemently denied the myth that people of color drove down property values, and several supporters claimed that residential discrimination led to the formation of ghettoes. Blacks, in particular, dominated the discussion, and they insisted that residential discrimination was entrenched in San Jose, especially in the city's Westside. According to census tracts used as evidence during the hearing, West San Jose had no blacks at all, whereas most of the city's African Americans resided in the downtown and Eastside. After this presentation, the Reverend C. W. Washington of Antioch Baptist Church declared that residential discrimination "intimidates many people who would like to live in decent housing, and [it] creates slums and crime."[80] Despite the unprecedented energy put into attempting to resolve the matter, the ordinance was superseded by California's Fair Housing Act of 1963.

THE CALIFORNIA FAIR HOUSING ACT of 1963, better known as the Rumford Act, was introduced amid controversy in the Assembly on February 14, 1963, after a regular general session of the California legislature.[81] The Rumford Act was seen as an important extension of the modern civil rights movement coming to California because it held great potential for exposing de facto segregation in California to further civil rights measures. It was a space where everyone on the state's political spectrum from the Left to the Right took an affirmative stand, including people looking for a middle ground, which usually meant siding with conservative forces because, to truly support fair housing, these "middle grounders" would have to give up some of their property ownership privileges, something most were not ready to do.

Within the Assembly, most Democratic Party members supported a stronger fair housing bill than Hawkins and Unruh had provided in 1962. Further support for a stronger bill came from Governor Brown, who asked for a government study; the study results indicated widespread discrimination in the housing market throughout the state of California.[82] The study also suggested that if something were not done about high-density areas that concentrated blacks in a discriminatory manner, such as in East Palo Alto and Watts, something explosive would happen in the near future.

As a result, Rumford easily passed through the Assembly during the 1963 session. Getting the bill through the Senate was a different story, because most senators strongly opposed fair housing in the private market. During the session, single-family home ownership and most forms of private housing were negotiated out of the Rumford bill. Assembly Rules Committee Chair Luther Gibson also blocked the bill from coming to the floor. With two congressional days remaining, he very bluntly stated his convictions to a reporter, telling him that "if I had my way about it, there would be no fair housing bill. I am against it on the principle that property rights come before human rights."[83] Gibson's comments sparked a massive protest at the state's capital. This activism along with pressure from liberal Democrats pressured the Senate into bringing the bill to the floor for a vote. On June 21, 1963, with fifteen minutes remaining before recess, the Rumford Act became law.[84] After seventeen years of struggle, the Rumford Fair Housing Act became effective on September 20, 1963, giving California a fair housing law that clearly covered public and private housing with stronger enforcement tools.[85]

The Rumford Act specifically covered public assisted housing, urban renewal housing, and privately financed housing that exceeded four units. It also applied to real estate brokers—Rumford's strongest addition to California fair housing policy—and was enforceable by the FEPC, which had undefined administrative enforcement powers. Missing from this legislation was anti-discriminatory coverage of bank lenders, private single-family housing units, small apartment buildings, and private property owners renting and selling homes. Thus the Rumford Act was not revolutionary; it was only one step toward expanding fair housing legislation into private housing throughout California. According to lawyer John Denton, who prosecuted Proposition 14, "Almost all housing included in the Rumford Act was already covered by earlier California law or by President Kennedy's Executive Order on Equal Opportunity in Housing of November 1962."[86] Nonetheless, what Rumford did was clarify California's fair housing policy, which strengthened its use in state and federal courts.

For African Americans in communities like the South Bay, the Rumford Act's impact was not properly tested because conservative forces immediately countered its legitimacy politically, legally, and in public opinion. A clear fair housing ordinance threatened the old order in California's housing market, and its detractors easily created a climate in which it could be quickly overturned. Most voting-age white Californians hated the Rumford Act, saying it was an infringement on their individual rights as property owners and potential homeowners. The bill was estimated to ban housing discrimination in two-thirds of the state's housing, a significant increase from around 30 percent prior to its enactment.[87] The forty-two-thousand-member California Real Estate Association responded by demonizing Rumford and vowing to eradicate all forms of fair housing in California six months after the bill's enactment.[88] They did so with a tactic off-limits to Rumford supporters in the use of the initiative process, which directly addressed the attitudes and prejudices of most Californian voters.

The California Real Estate Association made its public declaration to battle fair housing on March 22, 1964, at its three-day quarterly directors' meeting at the Cabana hotel in Palo Alto. This was also the first public battleground over the infamous Proposition 14. Outside the hotel was an orderly two-day demonstration in a rainy downpour of seven hundred "coat and tie" marchers, 25 percent of whom were African Americans. These demonstrators were church leaders, "civic leaders, politicians, and housewives clutching toddlers."[89] The consensus among the marchers, Governor Brown, and Assemblyman Rumford was that the association's anti–fair housing initiative was going to set back every Californian—socially and morally—and inevitably exacerbate racial tensions. This included the surge of hate groups such as the White Citizens Council from Mississippi who arrived in California in 1964, the rush of extreme conservatism from groups like the John Birch Society whose ideology deeply penetrated the California GOP in the mid-1960s, and the course of violence toward black people and their property in central-city communities like Watts in 1965 and Hunters Point (San Francisco) in 1966.[90]

From the time the Rumford Act became law in 1963 to the enactment of the 1968 National Housing Act, supporters on both sides of the fair housing debate drew a line in the sand, allowing little middle ground for political compromise. Supporters of Proposition 14 in and around Santa Clara County were the Citizens League for Individual Freedoms, the Santa Clara County Board, San Mateo County Board, Santa Clara County Apartment Owners Association, the San Jose Real Estate Board, Los Gatos–Saratoga Real Estate Board of Realtors, the Sunnyvale Board of Realtors, Bible Presbyterian Church, California Young Republicans, United Republicans in California, and the California Republican Assembly.[91]

Supporters of the fair housing movement in the Greater Santa Clara County could be found in almost every city, with the greatest concentration of activists stationed in the more diverse northern and eastern parts of the valley and centered on downtown San Jose. Countywide groups included Santa Clara County CORE and Santa Clara County Catholics who went beyond the general split among California Catholics that had led most members to take no stand on the issue.[92] Regional supporters in West Santa Clara County included the Mid-Peninsula Citizens Against Proposition 14, an umbrella group that came together in November 1963. The group specialized in organizing a cross-section of youth and church groups around Palo Alto–Menlo Park, including Protestants, Catholics, Buddhists, and Jews, and in time it represented more than seventeen hundred persons and about one hundred organizations.[93]

On the outskirts of the northeast part of the county above Milpitas, the regional supporter was the Tri-City Citizens Against Proposition 14, comprising residents from Fremont, Newark, and Union City. In San Jose, fair housing supporters included the Antioch Baptist Church, Assemblyman Al Alquist (D–San Jose), CORE, Council for Civic Unity, Garden City Women Club, San Jose Human Relations

Commission, San Jose Women's International League for Peace and Freedom, the NAACP (which also was represented in South San Mateo County and Palo Alto), and, surprisingly, the San Jose Republican Assembly, who thought that the Rumford Act should have been corrected by the legislative process rather than by an all-or-nothing repeal.[94] Lawyer guilds in the valley opposing Proposition 14 on legal grounds included the Bar Associations in Santa Clara County, Palo Alto, San Jose, and Sunnyvale.[95] In Milpitas, fair housing was supported by the United Auto Workers and the Quakers, who collaborated on developing Sunnyhills, one of the first planned integrated subdivisions in America in 1955–1957. In the Sunnyvale-Cupertino area, supporters were Citizens Committee Against CREA, and the Sunnyvale-Cupertino branch of the American Association of University Women.[96]

The lone southwestern county representative opposing Proposition 14 was the County Democratic Council, a fair housing referral service to buyers, sellers, renters, and real estate agents working through the First Methodist Church of Los Gatos. Moreover, on the eve of the November election an editorial in the *San Jose Mercury News* opposed the California Real Estate Association initiative for legal and moral reasons, urging readers to "Vote No on Proposition 14."[97] Finally, the initiative was opposed by racial-ethnic groups including the Japanese American Committee, Mexican Americans Against Proposition 14, Council of Mexican American Affairs, League of United Latin American Citizens, and Mexican-American Lawyers Club.[98]

Holding the electorate's attention was the constant bombardment of pro–Proposition 14 advertisements attacking the Rumford Act with the intent to confuse and arouse racial fears and distrust among white homeowners and small real estate investors by using such references as "property rights," "forced housing," "Repeal Rumford," and "Restore Property Rights."[99] This tactic was countered by pro-Rumford advertisements and public discussions that characterized Proposition 14 as what Governor Brown often called "the initiative to promote bigotry."[100] However, it appears that most white Californians in 1964 cared less about being nationally labeled as racists and bigots than they did about their individual homeowner rights and personal privileges.

According to the final vote tally, Proposition 14 passed almost 2-to-1, by an official count of 4,526,460 to 2,395,747, with suburbanites voting almost 3-to-1 in support of the status quo.[101]

The overwhelming support for residential segregation and individual property rights surprised many Santa Clara Valley political analysts, who predicted that the vote would be a toss-up.[102] Within Santa Clara County, Proposition 14 was hotly contested, passing 162,029 to 143,689; however, the lion's share of votes that took Proposition 14 out of contention came from Southern California, which by 1964 was undoubtedly the hotbed for new forms of hardline conservatism emerging on the state and national political scenes.

After Proposition 14 was passed, it became Article I, Section 26, of the California Constitution, which forbade fair housing from being legislated and discussed. California in turn was penalized by the federal government, which immediately froze all assistance for urban renewal projects and charged the state higher interest rates on federal loans already outstanding for urban renewal projects.[103] Simultaneously, the racial climate throughout the nation was getting more violent with black people arriving at their own political crossroads in terms of either continuing with nonviolent civil disobedience tactics or strategically implementing grassroots insurgency. These latter political strategies ranged from organized separatism to waging an urban war on their oppressors' property, as in the Watts rebellion of 1965.[104]

In 1966, Proposition 14 was overturned by the California Supreme Court following the activist efforts of groups like Palo Alto's Midpeninsulans for Fair Housing and the trial of six civil cases involving blacks who were evicted or refused rentals because of their race.[105] The most notable of these cases was *Mulkey v. Reitman* (1966), which declared that Proposition 14 was unconstitutional because it violated the Equal Protection Clause of the Fourteenth Amendment to the U.S. Constitution.[106] In June 1967, the U.S. Supreme outlawed Proposition 14 for violating the Fourteenth Amendment and the Civil Right Act of 1866, which "prohibits all racial discrimination in the sale or rental of property."[107] Moreover, the Court said that Proposition 14 went well beyond the Rumford Act and was applied to public assisted housing and housing financed with federal funds, making its application a federal offense.[108] For conservative policymakers, whose momentum to remove Rumford stagnated after this decision, attacking fair housing legislation did not end until the Fair Housing Act of 1968 was enacted.[109] According to California historian Lawrence de Graaf the passage of this law made FHA insurance

> more accessible to African American home buyers and lower-income families, and Congress subsidized home purchases and renting by low- and moderate-income families under sections 235 and 236 programs of the 1968 Housing Act. The culminating measure was Title VIII of the 1968 Civil Rights Act, which prohibited most forms of discrimination based on race, color, religion, or national origin in the sale, rental, or financing of housing.[110]

There was an unprecedented migration of black professionals into the South Bay who, for the first time, were invited to work in Santa Clara County. But because of Proposition 14, as African Americans they remained uninvited neighbors in white suburbs. Moreover, most black professionals who became the South Bay's first beneficiaries of affirmative action (after 1965) were recruited into the region to work at high-tech firms like Lockheed and IBM.[111] Most of these professionals initially failed to find housing where white recruits lived, such as in Campbell, Santa Clara, Saratoga, Sunnyvale, and West San Jose.

Ocie Tinsley was one of these professionals. In 1966, Tinsley, a native of Kansas City, Missouri, was one of approximately fifty African American engineers recruited to work in the high-tech industry in California. Though he had received offers from companies in Florida, Arizona, and his native Missouri, he settled in Santa Clara Valley at Lockheed and worked in research and development because he was fascinated by the National Aeronautics and Space Administration (NASA) program, which was booming. At the time, Lockheed was building Polaris missiles for the U.S. Navy. Like many of this new generation of black migrants, Tinsley initially failed to understand the South Bay's color line, which was far subtler and arguably more complex than Jim Crow discrimination had been in Kansas City. When he first came to the Santa Clara Valley, he moved to Sunnyvale, like white recruits within his cohort. But Tinsley was the only African American recruit, and unlike his cohort, who immediately found single-family housing, he stayed in hotels for two months until he figured out where most African Americans in the area lived: in the Northside, East San Jose, North Milpitas, and unincorporated East Palo Alto (in nearby Alameda County). This early experience of social isolation and difficult adjustment almost compelled Tinsley to leave the Bay Area. His culture shock did not just rest with his being excluded from most of the South Bay's housing market because of law and custom; it also extended to the region's inherent multiracial environment of Mexican Americans and Asian Americans, who were not people that Tinsley normally hung out with.[112] These feelings of social isolation subsided only when Tinsley came into contact with the African American community and began understanding how he could make the South Bay live up to his expectations.[113]

IN THE SANTA CLARA VALLEY, de facto segregation intersected race and class in the post–World War II period. After the 1968 Housing Act was passed, the cost of buying or renting a home was becoming as much a factor as race for residential segregation in most South Bay communities.[114] The increased cost of living was directly linked to rapid urbanization, industrialization, and mass migration into the region. Census tract statistics and census block data suggest that racism was a crucial dynamic in the makeup of most Santa Clara County communities, especially in traditional white neighborhoods in the western and southern peninsula parts of the region such as Los Altos, Cupertino, and Los Gatos. Communities with a notable black presence were San Jose, Milpitas, and Mountain View. Despite strong racial and economic resistance to African American occupancy in the Santa Clara Valley, since 1940 its black population has at least doubled in every decade leading up to 1980, with their numbers quadrupling in the 1960s. In 1940, only 730 blacks lived in the valley, 0.4 percent of the county's total population. By 1990, their numbers had risen to 56,211, or 3.5 percent of the county's total population.[115]

African American movement into the South Bay accelerated after 1965 when newly built housing such as the San Juan Bautista Apartments gradually began renting to blacks, and urban tensions in Watts, San Francisco, and the East Bay (1966–1967) inspired an intrastate and intraregional black middle-class movement into Bay Area suburbs.[116] California's fair housing movement assisted this migration process by putting in place a symbolic frame of reference informing white liberals about its minute black population and their agency and needs. Moreover, the 1968 Housing Act sparked an unprecedented movement of African Americans into the valley, which culminated in a spike in their purchase of new homes in eastern and northern parts of the Santa Clara County in 1969–1970.[117]

Perhaps the most important effect that the California fair housing movement had within Santa Clara County was to gradually change white attitudes and beliefs about people of color, by amplifying what local civil rights activists had been saying since 1960—that Santa Clara County was not as racially tolerant as most white people proclaimed.[118] Case in point was the county's vote, albeit by a narrow margin, in support of Proposition 14, which set back a local civil rights movement that had been growing since 1960. Chapter 5 will explore the radical cultural changes that occurred in a small white rural town called Milpitas when Ford Motor Company moved a plant there in 1955. Central to Milpitas's cultural diversification was the presence of an integrated community called Sunnyhills. Within the boundaries of Santa Clara County, this cultural incorporation into a town that had formerly been exclusively white marked African Americans' initial pursuit of the suburban dream.

Chapter Five
Sunnyhills
Race and Working-Class Politics in Santa Clara Valley, 1945–1968

THE EFFORT BY THE United Auto Workers' (UAW) to maintain worker solidarity through the racial integration of its Milpitas assembly plant and the housing development known as Sunnyhills represents unusual chapters in the histories of African Americans, the U.S. West, and American labor. This happened in a region, the Santa Clara Valley, that has proved to be just as resistant to racial integration as pre-1970s San Leandro in the East Bay Area and Orange County in Southern California.[1] The central theme confronting most twentieth-century labor historians concerns the relative weakness of organized labor and its lack of political influence in the United States.[2] The weakness of labor has been the strength of capitalism, which has systematically fragmented the labor movement by creating mostly nonmanufacturing jobs, raising the standard of living, and encouraging an acceptance of individualism, middle-class values, and corporate power. White worker racism and privilege have most often excluded African Americans, Latin Americans, and Asian Americans from accessing union jobs, a tactic that consistently damaged working-class solidarity.[3]

Following the Second World War, the federal government's support shifted away from industrial trade unions and toward big businesses. This reversed the government's previous position, which encouraged and supported unions during the years 1933 to 1945.[4] In response to the economic devastation of the Great Depression, government looked favorably on unions during the late 1930s and regarded labor's right to organize as a way to get people back to work with fair wages. An unprecedented shift in federal legislation that ushered in the New Deal favored social welfare in addition to labor's right to organize.[5] This adjustment made the labor movement more appealing to a new generation of trade unionists that included European immigrants, African Americans, and Mexican Americans, who were grassroots based with radical leanings toward the inclusive elements of socialism, communism, civil rights activism, and industrial unionism. Their involvement in trade unions led to a wave of strikes in the 1930s on waterfronts, steel mills, and agribusiness farms. These strikes were often led by upstart unions such as the Congress of Industrial Unions (CIO). According to labor historians Kevin Boyle, Mike Davis, and Leon Fink, most postwar labor unions moved from the political Left to moderate Center. Special-interest groups uncommitted to racial equality while protecting the rising living standards of their members quickly became exclusively white—following the Taft-Hartley Act of 1947 and red-baiting purges that connected civil rights activism and its participants to communism.[6] From 1945 to 1968, the UAW in Northern California was one of the few unions to keep its black workforce at full strength and keep its promise of relocating them from central cities such as Richmond to postwar suburbs like Milpitas.

AFRICAN AMERICANS' FIRST FULL inclusion into industrial labor within Santa Clara County occurred from 1955 to 1957 when several hundred black UAW members working at the Ford Motor Company plant in Richmond moved with the company to Milpitas and established an open occupancy subdivision called Sunnyhills.[7] The development of this housing tract brought national attention to newly incorporated Milpitas and its black inhabitants. From 1955 to 1983, African American access and integration into the South Bay's automotive workforce had been minimal with whites being the preferential hires, and the top people of color hires being local Mexican Americans. However, this was not initially the case in Ford's first decade in Santa Clara County. Between 14 percent and 25 percent of Milpitas Ford's fourteen-hundred-person workforce were senior workers of African descent relocated from Richmond's declining Ford assembly center fifty-one miles north, near Berkeley.[8]

This unique history of racial and working-class liberalism in the Bay Area automotive industry traces back to 1946, the year Walter P.

Reuther became UAW president.[9] Prior to 1946, World War II temporarily made Richmond into a thriving boomtown; after the war, however, black Richmond was hit by deindustrialization, residential segregation, capital flight, and white flight. The few fortunate blacks able to find factory employment during shipyard downsizing in the immediate postwar period found work at Ford, which reconverted its lines from military to automotive production and had an open policy in hiring black labor after 1945.

Going into the 1950s, Ford leaders began planning for long-term capitalization on the postwar economic boom and the relatively inexpensive urbanization of dense rural land. Central to their vision of industrial growth were new assembly plants and equipment on large tracts on the outskirts of central cities nationwide. Twenty of these factories were part of a nationwide expansion program schedule to either open or relocate after 1955.[10] The first of these plants to open were in Milpitas; Louisville, Kentucky; and Mahwah, New Jersey. Milpitas was a strategic location on the West Coast for Ford to enhance its sales in western states and Alaska and Hawaii. As an unincorporated entity, Ford initially pushed for Milpitas to become an "industrial unit of government," like nearby Emeryville in the East Bay, where the land base would favor industry over residences, and taxes would be kept low through maintaining minimal services that would be predominantly used by industry.[11] Milpitas founders wanted balanced residential and industrial zoning, adequate services for its residents, and low taxes.

After negotiations, Ford publicly announced its plans to move to a $50 million state-of-the-art assembly plant in Milpitas.[12] Billed "The Miracle at Milpitas," the Ford assembly plant functioned from 1955 to 1983 with more than seven miles of production lines producing almost five million vehicles.[13] Its lines made Falcons, Fairlanes, Cougars, Pintos, Comets, Escorts, F-Series pickup trucks, Edsels, and Mustangs. In 1961, during the plant's peak production, it employed between thirty-five hundred and five thousand workers on two eight-hour shifts with a daily output of 700 passenger cars and 180 commercial vehicles.[14] Prior to the Santa Clara Valley being renamed "Silicon Valley" in the 1970s, Ford dominated Milpitas's economy and was a major catalyst for phenomenal urban and industrial growth within the proximity of the city and the California auto industry.[15]

Ford predominance had an unprecedented influence on Milpitas's social and residential patterns. Prior to Ford and incorporation, Milpitas was an exclusively white rural town and the butt of jokes throughout the Bay Area to the mid-1970s; it was the scenic area one drove through on the way to San Jose or Oakland. From a racial standpoint, this soon changed primarily through the efforts of the International UAW and an emerging group of people progressive on racial issues in UAW Local 560, as several hundred well-paid blacks were imported into the valley in the mid-1950s.[16]

THE SOUTH BAY OF THE 1950s had a rapidly growing African American population. In 1950, 1,718 blacks lived in Santa Clara County.[17] They were clustered around the downtown areas of San Jose, Palo Alto, and were beginning to expand into East San Jose and East Palo Alto by the time the Ford assembly plant in Milpitas opened in 1955.[18] Fifteen years later (1970) 18,090 blacks were settled in the valley.[19] Compared with postwar communities in San Francisco, Oakland, and Richmond, the African American presence in South Bay was minuscule and even today is still inconspicuous in most parts of the county. Segregation in the Santa Clara Valley was a regional phenomenon that transcended county borders and began on the Peninsula (West Santa Clara County) at the Palo Alto–East Palo Alto border, and along the Highway 680 and 17 East Bay corridors as far north as the San Leandro–Oakland border in Alameda County. Within the county, blacks were excluded from communities west of downtown San Jose (around Meridian Avenue) or West Santa Clara County, and south of downtown San Jose (around Tully Road), which comprised the southern half of the county.[20] Unlike the pre-1970 U.S. South, where segregation was legally prescribed, in the Santa Clara Valley de facto segregation was arranged by custom and by clustering particular racial and ethnic groups into specific communities. The 1950s and 1960s were a period when homes in the South Bay were abundant, big, and inexpensive.

Electronics industry jobs that required an educated workforce were plentiful, yet most blacks with college degrees who applied were turned away—until approximately fifty African American engineers became the South Bay's first beneficiaries of affirmative action in the late 1960s and were recruited into the region to work at such high-tech firms as Lockheed and IBM.[21] From an economic perspective, poverty trumped discriminatory policy in the South Bay and reinforced the economics of the local industries. For example, most of the manufacturing and canning factories were in low-income areas such as East San Jose, and the more lucrative high-tech production was in white, homogenous, high-income communities heading toward Palo Alto.[22] Servicing many of these affluent households as domestics, manual laborers, and service workers were recent black emigrants from San Francisco and Oakland, who moved to the nearby deteriorating community of East Palo Alto.[23]

The introduction of Ford Motor Company into the Santa Clara County political economy disrupted patterns of racial exclusion in the local economy and housing market. Fueled by black workers with seniority and the principle of solidarity in the workplace, Local 560 secured a guarantee from Ford that union members would retain their seniority rights in Milpitas as an incentive to move there.[24] Otherwise, most African American workers would fall victim to residential apartheid and be forced to commute fifty miles to work for jobs that their white co-workers commuted to in three miles. According to the *Milpitas Post* editors, "African American Ford workers ran into evasions and deed restrictions and some outright snubs as they sought to look over the housing opportunities."[25] To win Ford's bid, the town of Milpitas agreed to help develop Sunnyhills, one of the first planned racially integrated subdivisions in the United States.[26] Sunnyhills was a unique community that dispelled many popular beliefs about what constituted the postwar suburb: as a spatially pleasant homogenous white area with expanded economic opportunities that go beyond industrial and manual labor.[27] For example, the community was developed at a time when less than 1 percent of housing built between 1935 in 1952 was occupied by nonwhites, and the lion's share of this new housing was built in suburbia.[28] The community was also a suburb dominated by working-class families employed by Ford or what sociologist Bennett M. Berger called the "working-class suburb."[29] He described it as a space in which industrial laborers predominated. Living in such communities grounded the suburban proletariat consciousness in values more working class and collective than middle class and individualistic. According to Berger, the first workers to move to Milpitas were in the early transition of inculcating middle-class values and mores. They lived more comfortably than their Richmond counterparts and were able to become homeowners; however, their neighbors and coworkers were the same people who resided in their working-class communities such as the bayshore flatlands in the East Bay. It took about a generation for most relocated Ford workers to acculturate into suburbia.[30] Ultimately, "racial liberals" within Local 560 or, more accurately, people progressive on racial issues and the Sunnyhills community, forced Milpitas to make race relations and open housing central to the city's core development.

Already in the late 1940s, the UAW had, under the leadership of Reuther, taken a progressive stand on race. After Reuther's election, the Fair Practices and Anti-Discrimination Department was established at UAW International in Detroit. The national director of the office, African American William "Bill" Oliver, started the quest for affordable integrated housing close to the Milpitas plant. This was followed by Local 560 President Vincent McKenna persuading the UAW's Fair Practices Department to acquire the necessary autonomy to create policy and develop affordable housing specific to Local 560 needs.

To carry out this plan, McKenna appointed Benjamin Franklin ("Ben") Gross, an African American, to chair Local 560's special housing subcommittee and teamed him with International UAW representative Arnold Callan to design a strategy.[31] In his capacity as special housing subcommittee chair, Gross made the ultimate decision for Local 560 housing to be built in North Milpitas. The plan Gross, Callan, and Oliver designed called for the construction of a racially integrated cooperative housing development that was both affordable and free of "ghetto" conditions in North Milpitas, which was three miles from the new plant.[32] According to Gross, "It was my insistence that

Benjamin Franklin "Ben" Gross at UAW International Headquarters, Detroit, December 2008. Herbert G. Ruffin II Collection.

we did not want discrimination in housing for workers. We get the same wages. We worked on the lines together."[33]

After this plan was drawn up, Gross and McKenna, representing Local 560, brought the issue to Reuther's attention. He supported the project by issuing an "order banning union support for any segregated housing developments" and, in an unprecedented maneuver, appointing a black person—Ben Gross—to develop an integrated housing plan with Milpitas, a city that, up to Ford's moving there in 1955, had no acknowledged African American presence.[34]

In March 1954, the housing plan started with Santa Clara County businessmen, Milpitas politicians, the county's Council of Churches, and the UAW commissioning the American Friends Service Committee of the Quakers to put together a report for agencies and groups concerned about problems that may stem from integration and rapid industrialization.[35] Questions emerging from the report asked: How does Milpitas integrate the rapid influx of blacks guaranteed to arrive in the upcoming years and prevent racial problems? Was it possible to construct comfortable suburban multiple housing units (a rarity in this period) at a price affordable to factory workers? And how could Milpitas bring a practical intersection between race and affordable housing to blue-collar workers? Crucial to answering these questions was the knowledge that no hard color line in the Northeast South Bay was ever constructed, Milpitas was underdeveloped and eager to do business with Ford, and the UAW under Reuther positioned itself within the rubric of worker rights and racial equality. Consequently, there was a probability that the housing which the UAW sought could be built. However, the UAW-led coalition had a hard time finding a tract of land in the proximity of Milpitas, securing start-up financing and long-term funding for the project, and locating builders willing to construct integrated housing with a sound plan.

Early efforts to find a land tract in the proximity of Milpitas for the UAW-led coalition were frustrated by systematic obstruction from those opposed to the project. The first obstacle arose when Milpitas abruptly rezoned a proposed site from residential to industrial use.[36] At another site, an eight-thousand-square-foot building space was rezoned from residential use to commercial use only. On yet another site the builder ran out of options on where to build after encountering governmental and customary roadblocks.[37]

A partial breakthrough for the coalition occurred when a meat packer named Joseph Kaufman offered to sell fifty-five acres of Rancho Agua Caliente (now Warm Springs, Fremont) to the FHA regional office in San Francisco during the summer of 1954 when he heard of the UAW effort. Initially the plan was for Kaufman to be the developer and provide the start-up money for a housing development with black occupancy in 268 homes. This was more than a fourth of the units scheduled to be built and was considered to be a fair representation of Local 560's black population. Immediately, local finance companies that were supposed to provide long-term financing backed out when they heard of the open occupancy policy, or they wanted premium arrangements ranging from 4.5 to 9 percentage points.[38] This would have made the housing unaffordable to most union members. After several frustrating months that included many delays because of flooding and ad hoc building codes and ordinances established to stop the project, Kaufman couldn't financially maintain the property and sold Rancho Agua Caliente to UAW International outright.[39]

During the latter half of 1954, financing the housing development became a central issue confronting the UAW-led coalition. In January 1955, the American Friends Service Committee found financing from Quaker-owned Metropolitan Life Insurance Company to cover the start-up costs with the agreement that any housing constructed had to be interracial and that UAW's sponsorship had to be publicly mentioned.[40] On January 26, 1955, the loan was approved, and the integrated housing project went public. Simultaneously, "UAW Local 560 collaborated with Ford to use [Local 560's] pension fund" to become the development's contractor so that the work would be subcontracted to companies who would answer to the local, and to control the terms of the development's mortgage.[41] This occurred after Local 560's executive committee rejected a construction firm that would build the development only if it consisted of two tracts under union sponsorship: one all-white and the other integrated, with white workers given the option of living in either complex.[42]

In addition, following several frustrating months of Local 560 and Ford dealing with the FHA, a long-term mortgage was obtained from the Federal National Mortgage Association (Fannie Mae) through a rarely used special co-op ownership program administered by the FHA's Cooperative Development office.[43] While parts of the agreement had to be created, enough of it fell under Section 213 of the Federal Housing Act of 1950.[44] Under this law, "each section of housing was organized legally as a cooperative with somewhat more liberal financing terms than were available under Section 203, the program under which most of the FHA . . . [single-family] housing had been built."[45] For example, instead of a thirty-year mortgage with a 5 percent to 10 percent down payment, which was standard for single-family homes, under the co-op ownership program the mortgage would be for forty years with a down payment of 3 percent. This unique arrangement opened FHA-supported housing to blue-collar hourly wage workers unable to qualify for or afford single-family housing under Section 203. It also temporarily broke a pattern established by the federal government in which residential segregation was used to manipulate the housing market for the greatest financial returns and to further perpetuate social inequities, tracing back to the FHA mortgage program's creation in 1934. According to historian Robert Self, "In the 1950s, before changes in Federal housing policy and the civil rights act of 1968, desegregation threatened the financial foundation of home building, because FHA and VA programs had virtually eliminated lending for mixed-race developments. Further, the universally accepted rationalization for segregation—that mixed-race communities depressed property values—circulated within the industry as an unchallenged truism."[46]

Despite finding a sizable tract and advantageous financing, the UAW-led coalition needed to find either more acreage to build integrated and affordable housing or a way to place their workers in an adjacent housing tract also called "Sunnyhills." This was the original Sunnyhills built in 1954. It was separated from the Agua Caliente development by Dixon Landing Road. Sunnyhills was developed by the San Lorenzo Homes Company, a major East Bay real estate developer and architect of all-white neighborhoods throughout Alameda County that in the mid-1950s was attempting to bring its segregationist operations and vision into the South Bay. Ironically, the original Sunnyhills was meant to be built exclusively for white occupancy.

Sunnyhills was a fledgling enterprise for San Lorenzo Homes Company because it had a problem filling vacancies. In addition, housing construction throughout the Greater San Jose area was fiercely competitive, and builders had been overbuilding since the early 1950s.

When the UAW went public with its proposed housing development, it immediately represented further financial loss for Sunnyhills both because it increased competition and created the possibility that African American buyers nearby would drive down its property values and trigger white flight. According to Ben Gross, this never happened because anybody in the Bay Area could become a co-op member and purchase a brand-new three-bedroom home with as little as $179 down, with monthly payments as low as $79, whereas monthly house payments in the region usually ranged from $300 to $500 in the early 1960s.[47]

The San Lorenzo Homes Company, which was committed to maintaining residential segregation for fear of financial loss, tried to prevent the construction of the UAW housing development. By creating opposition to that development among local developers, the company made it nearly impossible to find builders willing to construct integrated housing with a sound plan. Even when builders were willing to develop the Agua Caliente property, municipal codes and ordinances became roadblocks that drove up the costs of building to local and state code. Agua Caliente was also denied building permits and access to existing infrastructure systems such as water and sewage, which were necessary for a community to function.[48]

The UAW led a coalition of racial liberals. They responded to the San Lorenzo Homes threat by having California investigate Milpitas for institutional discrimination. They also formed coalitions to strengthen their political base and filed lawsuits over the refusal to extend sewage lines. On the charge of institutional discrimination, California investigators could not determine whether Milpitas was guilty or innocent. Nonetheless, the city became more cooperative with the UAW after the investigation. As for coalition building, the media coverage during the sewerage controversy created enough public sympathy to generate support from organizations, individuals, and builders positioned to help the effort. Included in the coalition were the Quakers service committee, the San Jose Council for Civic Unity, and the San Jose Council of Churches; the liberal wing of the California Democratic Party, led by future governor Edmund G. "Pat" Brown, the League of Women Voters, and the American Association of University Women; and the AFL Building Trades Council and other unions nationwide.

Local 560 purchasing the original "Sunnyhills" (December 1955). Local 560 president Vincent McKenna signs contracts to buy eight and a half acres just north of Milpitas for a union hall, recreation area, swimming pool, and more. Also pictured: (*seated to the right of McKenna*) Attorney Sanford for the Sunnyhills interests; Secretary Treasurer Jack Amiot; UAW subregional director Arnold Callan; (*standing from left to right*) Committeeman Joe Alvarez; housing committee chairman Ben Gross; President Reuther's assistant from Detroit, Bill Oliver; and UAW attorney Irv Bloom. Courtesy Walter P. Reuther Archives, Wayne State University, Detroit, Michigan

This coalition accomplished two huge feats. First, it forced the Santa Clara County Board of Supervisors to approve the UAW's open housing plan; the alternative was for Milpitas and the county to lose considerable tax revenue and business stimulated by Ford and its workers. Second, it forced Ford to take a stand either in support of Local 560's seniority rights and its African American workforce or, for expediency purposes, to oppose open housing in favor of its short-term bottom line. Coercing Ford to take a stand on open housing came about in 1955, when Ben Gross led part of this coalition in a two-day boycott of San Lorenzo Homes, "asking Ford not to make purchases in the all-white development."[49] Ford's refusal to make purchases in San Lorenzo Homes immediately resulted in an alarming number of vacancies that threatened to become even greater. More important, Ford's participation would have undermined Agua Caliente, strengthened Sunnyhills under San Lorenzo Homes, and undermined Ford's financial interests and working relationship with the UAW. Wisely, Ford chose the UAW coalition, which contributed heavily to San Lorenzo Homes' losing this battle in the Santa Clara Valley housing market by the summer of 1955. Agua Caliente's development proceeded according to schedule, and Sunnyhills sales hit a severe slump because of the high rent for co-op housing, negative publicity over attempts to block an open-occupancy tract from being built, and efforts of the UAW coalition. San Lorenzo Homes sold Sunnyhills to the UAW in 1956, which canceled its litigation over sewage lines and extended the UAW tract to one hundred acres—fifty-five of which were under construction. Ironically, Local 560 also adopted the Sunnyhills name to assume a fresh beginning. In 1957, Sunnyhills opened and became the first planned interracial community west of the Mississippi.[50] In the 1950s and '60s, Sunnyhills represented an alternative notion of democracy grounded in cultural differences that found common ground in union solidarity, homeownership, and middle-class consumption in the latest form of American urbanization, the suburbs. From its inception, Sunnyhills projected itself as a model working-class community with a standard of open housing imbued with middle-class values.[51] It boasted of diverse demographic and spacious living accommodations at a good price.

By 1962, however, only 15 percent of the five-hundred-plus Sunnyhills residences were occupied by African Americans, and even as Ford added workers, the percentage never climbed much higher.[52] Virtually all of the black occupants were well-paid senior members of Local 560 who were hardcore Reuther supporters and were within a few years of retirement at Ford. Outside of Sunnyhills, African Americans remained residentially locked out of most parts of the Santa Clara Valley. For the few blacks working at Ford with lower seniority, living in the Santa Clara Valley was too expensive and racially restrictive because of homeowner prejudice, state and federal government policies, and real estate and bank lending practices.[53] Throughout the 1960s, African Americans suffered from customary and institutionalized forms of residential apartheid; for the most part they were generally limited to living in deteriorating housing in East Palo Alto, North Richmond, East Oakland, and northern and eastern parts of downtown San Jose. Most Sunnyhills occupants following the initial wave in the late 1950s were white workers with and without seniority. Most of these latter workers never fully embraced the concept of living in an integrated community; rather, it was something they tolerated because of convenience and inexpensive housing.[54]

What kept Sunnyhills together in its early years was its core of race and working-class liberals. Many of these individuals were senior members of Local 560 who were fiercely unyielding about making Milpitas into a "model community." Many were opposed to what historian Thomas Sugrue calls "the politics of home" or what historian Robert Self calls "white power in the suburbs." Crucial to Sunnyhills unity were its activists and institutions.[55] In 1957, progressive alliances evolved into lifelong commitments to race and class diversity at UAW functions at both its union hall and the Sunnyhills United Methodist Church. Goodwill between the UAW and the church was constantly expressed through members of both organizations attending one another's functions. Walter Reuther and Bill Oliver attended whenever they were in town, and twenty-three UAW members including Ben Gross became Sunnyhills United Methodist Church members. The church also had the support of UAW management and quickly grew as a consequence.[56] In this capacity, Ben Gross and his wife, Clara, proved highly instrumental in establishing the solidarity principle in the church and community. In spring 1959, Clara co-organized the church's women's group. Within the same period the Grosses became counselors to the church's youth fellowship group. Finally, Ben was instrumental in forming a men's club, and he served as its chairman during its period of growth from 1960 to 1961. Once this group became established, its members founded a neighborhood association and what became its locally famous institutions, the Democratic Club and the Sunnyhills Community Breakfast (1966), both of which continue to function today as vital organizations in Milpitas.[57]

Finally, black participation in the UAW and local Methodist church also brought Milpitas's African American community closer to the city—especially after Sunnyhills became central to the defeat of San Jose's attempts to annex Milpitas in an attempt to acquire Ford and its tax base in 1960.[58] Success in Milpitas's independence movement propelled Ben Gross onto San Jose NAACP's executive board and into city politics as a five-term member of the city council (1962–1970), two-term mayor (1966–1970), and vice mayor (1970–1972).[59] Gross's political career is historically significant because he is one of only a handful of black mayors in the United States who have held the reins of a city or town with a white majority, and he was the first African American mayor in California.[60] These feats, along with Sunnyhills's open occupancy and UAW's open shop, soothed race relations during a turbulent period fueled by urgency for social change and competing visions of democracy and freedom. For instance, following the assassination of Dr. Martin Luther King, Jr., in 1968, Milpitas was one of the few Bay Area communities to easily defuse high tensions with an open dialogue on race and to come together to publicly mourn his passing—an event that was held at Sunnyhills United Methodist Church.[61]

DURING THIS PERIOD, three narratives, told or untold, acknowledged or unrecognized, intertwined race and labor in Santa Clara Valley's history. In the first, the region's economy became dominated by the military-industrial complex and electronics industry from around 1953 to 1975, and blacks were almost entirely excluded from both workforces. African American workers endured stereotyping, residential apartheid, and the exclusionary hiring policies of high-tech companies. At the same time, policies in higher education steered them away from the engineering and business fields that might have made them valuable employees in these industries. For the few African Americans hired into the early high-tech industry, most were factory workers in the less affluent East Santa Clara County. And the handful of blacks fortunate enough to work in semi-skilled to skilled positions felt isolated and alienated.[62]

Second, the UAW under Walter Reuther kept its promise to honor the seniority rights of all members in Local 560 and relocate them from Richmond to Milpitas, with open occupancy and affordable housing awaiting their arrival. Meanwhile, Ford had to be threatened with the potential loss of an experienced workforce before the company placed its full support behind those workers. Within Ford, Local 560's old guard started to retire after 1965, and a new workforce that was typical of national labor trends since 1946 emerged to undo some of the racial liberalism established by older members. This new group was predominantly European American, with some Mexican Americans and a few African Americans. When these lower-seniority African Americans were hired, they often took the worst jobs, those that featured the nastiest aspects of production speed-ups, which coincided with the rise of automation and new managerial techniques in the automotive industry designed to increase productivity at minimal cost in the 1950s and 1960s. Nonetheless, the emergence of blacks within Local 560 created one of the few paths for African Americans to elevate themselves into the contemporary middle class and secure an acknowledged foothold in the high-tech-dominated and very white Santa Clara Valley before 1975.

Third, Sunnyhills brought racial liberalism to a town whose last acknowledged black presence was in the 1850s. Though blacks had been in the area before statehood, a formerly enslaved African American named James Williams would be erroneously reported more than a century later as being, in 1852, the first black presence in the Santa Clara Valley.[63] Sunnyhills of the 1950s and 1960s was an anomaly in postwar suburban America. While the neighborhood provided an alternative notion of democracy grounded in racial liberalism, union solidarity, and homeownership, its model for community development failed to spread beyond North Milpitas other than a few white working-class communities that were open to black families. In the next chapter, I show how the rise and the demise of the Santa Clara County civil rights movement took shape both in relation to the urban formation of the South Bay and to the local fair housing movement.

Chapter Six
The Santa Clara County Civil Rights Movement, 1949–1966

AS IMPORTANT AS THE CIVIL RIGHTS movement was to the American experience, almost no discussion has directly connected it to late-blooming cities in the West and their suburbs. Most histories discuss the movement in relation to cities in the North and South (such as Chicago and Birmingham) and southern Black Belt counties (such as Sunflower County in Mississippi).[1] When the West is mentioned at all, the traditional narrative is of African Americans forming a successful movement in early-twentieth-century cities through coalition politics in Los Angeles, Oklahoma City, San Francisco, and Topeka, to name a few. It is important to also place the modern civil rights movement in the context of late-blooming metropolitan areas that later take on the character of suburban metropolises, such as San Jose and Phoenix, because black suburbanization uncovers a complex of overlooked histories and political strategies.[2]

This chapter explores the Santa Clara County civil rights movement as it evolved from a few small sympathy strikes in 1960 in support of southern blacks to spirited efforts to address local racism and its attendant social injustices. After 1964, the movement lost momentum and then collapsed with the success of Proposition 14's repeal of the Rumford Act. What makes this experience unique is that the Santa Clara Valley civil rights movement was a metropolitan suburban movement that took place in San Jose and Palo Alto on several fronts often disconnected from one another, in large part because of the region's relatively small black community and the geographically sprawling nature of suburbs.

The origin of the movement goes back to the Santa Clara County NAACP's successful efforts to institutionalize a Negro History Week in 1947 and the South Bay fair housing movement in 1951. Both happened around the same time that direct-action civil rights activity was occurring in Albuquerque; Denver; Lawrence, Kansas; Omaha; and other western cities.[3] Also, similar to social justice movements throughout the West, the South Bay campaign against segregated neighborhoods consumed the local black population's energies through most of the post–World War II period.[4] In 1954, the movement was bolstered by the UAW Local 560 fight for worker solidarity and racial inclusion at the San Jose Ford assembly plant and fair housing at the Sunnyhills cooperative in Milpitas. By 1959, elements that would form the Santa Clara Valley civil rights movement of the 1960s made considerable headway in persuading San Jose homeowners to sign an "open housing covenant" despite the fact that the NAACP chapter in San Jose and Palo Alto had split and was losing members because many black and white liberals were not ready to commit to the local and statewide fair employment and fair housing movements. Still, the fair housing movement, buttressed by the California Committee for Fair Employment Practices and liberal Democrats, organized the passage of a fair employment practices bill and two fair housing bills in the Hawkins Act and Unruh Act.

Although the civil rights movement elsewhere was galvanized by the *Brown v. Board of Education* ruling in 1954, mandating desegregated public schools, residential segregation was by far a greater issue than fair education in Santa Clara Valley. Santa Clara County blacks had been attending integrated schools since 1890, following the California Supreme Court decision in *Wysinger v. Crookshank*.[5] Although, six years later, the U.S. Supreme Court ruling in *Plessy v. Ferguson* federally imposed "separate but equal," legal segregation was never reimposed on black students in the Santa Clara Valley because building schools for such a minute population would have been too expensive. Instead, black students went to schools in their neighborhoods, which were segregated because of restrictions on where their families could live. Here they suffered the same inequities as the neighborhood's Italian and Chinese immigrants and Mexican Americans, and all coexisted peacefully, according to elders like Mattie Berry.[6] However, in the 1950s the strain of a rapidly growing population within both the newly incorporated white suburbs such as Cupertino (est.

1955) and the diverse East San Jose led to the hardening of Santa Clara County's color line among adults, most readily seen in housing, racial profiling, and hiring practices. As for the youths, integrated education in diverse South Bay communities led to a racial intermingling that by the late 1960s was forging complex, complementary, and often politically contentious relationships.[7]

In 1955 Orvella Stubbs and her family migrated from Earlsboro, Oklahoma, to San Jose to reunite with their family the Dollarhydes. At that time, she was nine years old and her parents were separated. Her mother, who could pass for white, initially had a hard time finding an affordable home to rent in overcrowded downtown San Jose. She eventually found a house to rent in San Jose's Southside at Ninth and Margaret Streets, which was a white neighborhood. Everything in the negotiations went fine until she brought her brown-skinned children to the home. Then white adults attempted to intimidate the Stubbs family to prevent them from moving in, calling them "niggers" and other hateful epithets. The neighbors also interrogated the white woman who owned the house as to whether she knew that the family was black, then demanded that she make the Stubbses move. She refused because she was sympathetic to Orvella's mother. Consequently, the Stubbs lived in that house until 1961, when the family reunited with Orvella's father in Detroit, Michigan. But until then the Stubbses had to endure a continual barrage of insults and slights from their white adult neighbors.[8]

In the Southside, Orvella attended Lowell Elementary and Roosevelt Junior High, which had far better reputations and more resources than did the Northside schools. Both schools were segregated by custom, and Orvella was one of the few children of color to penetrate what essentially was an integrated school in a segregated community. Similar to children in the Northside, kids of all cultural backgrounds in the downtown were friends in most public places and walked to school together until they "hit the corner" of their own block, Orvella said many decades later. Then "everybody had to go their separate ways."[9] The pretense of these children not interacting with one another in the same geographical location, under the gaze of their parents, took its most dramatic form on the live televised dance party *Record Hop* (1959–1964), which aired on KNTV Channel 11 every weekend from its studio at 645 Park Avenue in San Jose. It was patterned on Dick Clark's *American Bandstand,* with teenagers dancing to rock-and-roll and soul music to win pizzas and movie tickets.[10] Though the show drew youths of various ethnicities, the dance floor on which these black, white, and brown youths danced was segregated. African Americans usually won the prizes. After the show, everybody left in separate cars.[11]

Living in a community of customary segregation was an odd experience for Orvella, because in Oklahoma she had been raised in a community undergoing legal desegregation. She and her African American friends played with white children at school, but as they were bused to the black side of town at the end of the school day, the white children would yell out, "niggers, niggers." The next day, this behavior would start all over again. In contrast, California communities had been legally desegregated since the 1890s, when most racially discriminatory codes were written out of the state constitution.[12] However, prior to the Second Great Migration, California's movement toward integration was never fully tested in communities with relatively small African American populations, such as San Jose. What has been discovered is that de facto racial discrimination is a barrier that prevents black suburbanites from feeling that they will ever achieve the American dream in housing, employment, or education. In Orvella Stubbs's world, the local color line of the 1950s was hardening because it was visibly exposed as practiced by established residents, white and black alike, who saw the new African American migrants as outsiders. Although she was surrounded by white neighbors (and a few Mexican Americans) and interacted with diverse young people away from their block, she never went into their homes except as a house cleaner.[13]

Sociologist and human rights activist Harry Edwards says that experiences such as Stubbs's placed most South Bay blacks on the defensive and in a perpetual mode of socioeconomic survival in the 1950s and 1960s.[14] It appears that most were not prepared to challenge the system. They saw what happened to those who did. As mentioned earlier, Emmit Dollarhyde lost most of his customers and was forced to temporarily close his auto-detailing business following the Santa Clara County NAACP's failed attempt in 1951 to end minstrelsy in the South Bay. This white backlash against one of the county's most visible black members succeeded not only in retarding an emerging civil rights movement but in arresting the development of a freedom rights consciousness until the late 1960s. In the final analysis, during the South Bay's hasty transition from the Valley of Heart's Delight to Silicon Valley, black exclusion became the logical conclusion to a postwar color line that hardened, driven by white flight and the movement of white middle-class professionals into new single-family subdivisions that had been federally subsidized and reserved for them.

IN 1960, THE SOUTH BAY'S BATTLE over segregated housing expanded into the realm of fair employment and higher education. It was sparked by the lunch counter sit-ins in Oklahoma City and Greensboro, North Carolina, and by a few socially conscious citizens like Inez Jackson and students at San Jose State College and Stanford University. Their first direct-action protest occurred on April 14, 1960, when a handful of people from the Women's International League for Peace and Freedom and the San Jose State free speech group Toward an Active Student Community picketed in front of the Woolworth and Kress stores in downtown San Jose.[15] Their actions were in support of African American sit-in demonstrations occurring throughout the South and coincided with a national effort to boycott stores with segregated lunch counters.[16] Demonstrators carried placards, handed out literature, and sought signatures for petitions asking the department chains to stop discriminating against blacks in the South. According to a manager of one of the stores, the picketing appeared to have little effect on either local store's volume of business during the day.[17] Neither Woolworth nor Kress in San Jose had segregated lunch counters, and both employed blacks in nonpublic positions such as custodian. Legal segregation in both stores occurred only in the South, where it was required by state laws. In San Jose, segregation in public accommodations was most pronounced in high-end establishments—not in department stores, where discrimination was subtle and regulated by social custom and individual bias.[18]

Nonetheless, sympathy demonstrations in front of department stores occurred throughout 1960. Five days after the San Jose demonstration an unrelated march occurred in front of stores in downtown Palo Alto and the Stanford Shopping Center. Twenty-five white Stanford students carried signs reading, "We are Stanford students. We demonstrate in support of the southern student movement."[19] Their main target was Woolworth in downtown Palo Alto at Stanford Shopping Center. Perhaps the most interesting question raised by the Stanford activists as they passed out literature concerning the southern desegregation campaign was "Why have African Americans been virtually restricted to living in East Palo Alto?"[20] This was the first of many similar questions that South Bay activists began asking which, by 1963, redirected the focus of their activism toward concerns more relevant and local, such as fair housing and fair employment. In the meantime, the third notable demonstration in 1960 occurred on July 13, as a rejuvenated San Jose NAACP boycotted Woolworth and Kress stores. The organization's goal was twofold: first, to apply enough economic pressure on the local chain stores to effect a change in policy at each one's national headquarters regarding legal segregation at the lunch counters in the South; and, second, to pressure lawmakers into adopting a national fair labor policy similar to California's Fair Employment Practice Commission. For Leo English, president of the San Jose NAACP in 1960, his group "has no fight with the stores [in the Santa Clara Valley]. Their record is commendable." Congress of Racial Equality (CORE) activists from national and Bay Area chapters did not agree with English's assessment.[21] CORE pushed not just for southern reforms, but also local reforms at the stores. This ruffled upper management in both department chains. Spokesmen for Woolworth and Kress in San Jose responded to the demonstrations by telling demonstrators and the *San Jose Mercury News* that "the companies would not be intimidated and coerced into efforts to change segregation policies of the chains in the South."[22] Then S. V. Herring, a public relations executive for Woolworth's in San Francisco, asked, "What justification do you have to attack friends?"[23] He continued, "If you are going to attack the southern whites, why don't you do it down there and they will accommodate you. You attack friends because you know it's safe."[24] Then Herring claimed to be a friend of "the Negro," helping many get jobs since 1940. He said he agreed with the motives of the demonstrators, but like many Bay Area residents he saw the problem of segregation as a southern one. In the end, Herring debunked the demonstration by discounting the influence that Woolworth might have on national policy in fair labor practices. He also saw the San Jose demonstrations as "reverse discrimination" against whites, who he claimed had always been friends of African Americans.[25]

As months passed, the demonstrations covered new ground, starting with protests that brought together white liberals at San Jose State College and blacks in the Northside. With each succeeding demonstration, participants became more critical of racial inequities in South Bay.

One of the most active organizations in the Santa Clara Valley civil rights movement was CORE, which on September 19, 1960, established a local chapter to channel the local youths' exuberance and to pressure San Jose State College into admitting St. John Dixon, who was expelled from Alabama State Teachers College for civil rights activity. On March 2, Dixon was one of nine demonstrators expelled by the Alabama State Board of Education (chaired by segregationist governor John Patterson) for participating in a sit-in demonstration in a basement snack bar in the Montgomery County Courthouse. Twenty other students were placed on probation. This made national headlines because, according to the *San Jose Mercury News*, "it was the sharpest action to be taken against student demonstrators since the current Southwide wave of protests against segregated eating facilities began over a month ago."[26] Dixon, a junior, was encouraged to apply to San Jose State College by non–tenure track economics professors William Stanton and Bud Hutchinson, who were sympathetic to the southern civil rights movement. Both professors said that they approached the college's vice president, William J. Dusel, on September 15 about waiving the August 12 registration deadline "to permit entrance of the Alabama student expelled for participation in sit ins." Dusel thought this was a good idea because dishonorable discharge did not apply in

Dixon's case. According to the professors, he assured them that Dixon would be more than welcome to attend San Jose State College. News of this meeting and the professors' intent was expressed in a letter sent to the famous civil rights leader the Reverend Ralph Abernathy, minister of First Baptist Church in Montgomery. He in turn relayed the message to Dixon in Alabama.

In San Jose, CORE sponsored Dixon's visit to San Jose on the day it was founded, September 19, with the promise that (to Dixon's surprise) the organization would help finance his education. But two days later the president of San Jose State College, John T. Wahiquist, denied Dixon entrance into the school for the fall semester because his transcript from Alabama State College was held up and he applied five weeks late. News of Dixon's rejection sparked protests in San Jose's downtown and the Eastside communities. Tempers boiled even hotter when the *Mercury News* wrote of allegations that the fourteen California State College presidents had over the summer of 1960 arrived at a "gentleman's agreement" that entailed not admitting "any student expelled because of taking part in sit-in demonstrations, against racial barriers in the South."[27]

Investigating the allegation was State Attorney General Stanley Mosk. President Wahiquist publicly admitted that there was such an agreement, but he said that it concerned the admission of students who had been dishonorably dismissed from other schools.[28] This contradicted and invalidated the testimony of Superintendent of Public Instruction Roy E. Simpson, who denied that a gentleman's agreement among college presidents existed. He insisted that Dixon was ruled ineligible because he did not apply before the August 12 deadline. Mosk discovered, however, that students expelled over sit-in activity were admitted to schools in New York and Georgia, and he saw Wahiquist's hands-off position as consistent with the allegations.

Beyond the gentleman's agreement and what exactly was agreed upon, top administrators at San Jose State College undoubtedly made a major mess of the Dixon affair. The president's office was at odds with the vice president's office over procedures for enrollment, and San Jose State was at odds with Sacramento over policy. Despite the controversy and preliminary rejection, Dixon publicly announced that he intended to stay in the San Jose area to find a job and to start taking classes at San Jose State in the spring.

Within San Jose, CORE mobilized to support both Dixon and Mosk's efforts to expose the racism within the California Department of Education and to denounce San Jose State's act "as myopic and as making California identifiable with the racists in southern states."[29] On Sunday, September 25, six days after the San Jose CORE officially unveiled itself to the public and brought Dixon to San Jose, Dixon's transcripts, which his former Alabama school had purposely delayed so as to punish Dixon, finally arrived, and he was put on file for evaluation. The major problem with Dixon's transcripts was that the grading system was different from San Jose State's, which could take some time to sort out. Not a problem at all, as it turned out. The Reverend C. W. Washington, Antioch Baptist Church's minister, joined the youth-led CORE to apply intense pressure on the college's administration to rush its evaluation of Dixon and proxy his acceptance through with the help of President Wahlquist. Finally, on December 19, 1960, Dixon enrolled as a junior majoring in accounting and finance and needing forty-four units to graduate.[30] Antioch Baptist started a scholarship fund, and its immediate goal was to raise $900 per semester for Dixon.[31]

During all this struggle, Dixon said that he was "surprised and embarrassed that there should have been so much trouble over [my] coming here."[32] But for San Jose civil rights activists, Dixon's transfer to San Jose State was a victory that directly linked their activism into the national freedom rights struggle and further legitimized the decentralized civil rights movement brewing in Santa Clara Valley.

WITH DIXON ENROLLED IN COLLEGE during winter break, the campus climate cooled a bit. However, during the spring semester new civil rights challenges emerged on San Jose State's horizon—some directly linked to Dixon and others to freedom of speech issues, such as bringing in controversial speakers, among them white civil rights activist Anne Braden. She was invited to talk on the subject of racial discrimination in the South on February 23. Her talk was sponsored by the progressive white student group Toward an Active Student Community, which thought this open forum advocating integration would fit nicely as one of several events held during Black History Month and would contribute to the intellectual and cultural life of San Jose State.

Immediately after this speaking engagement was advertised to the public on February 20, it was protested by another group, Students against Communism, and an engineering professor, Edward S. Carmick, who somehow invoked a Senate Internal Security Committee report from 1957 in Memphis alleging that Braden and her husband, Carl, were members of the Communist Party—a claim that she refused to refute, by invoking the First and Fifth Amendments.[33] Soon angry telephone calls, driven by a mixture of anticommunist hysteria and racism, bombarded President Wahiquist's office. Wahiquist, however, took no action to prevent Braden from speaking, citing the First Amendment's protection of free speech. "I think the topic of which she is to speak should be of interest to the students and faculty," he said. "I believe our students are sufficiently mature to hear all sides of such public questions and to evaluate for themselves what they hear."[34]

When February 23 came, Braden spoke to a standing-room audience of four hundred in the college cafeteria.[35] She opened her talk with a comment that she was accustomed to being called a communist in the South because "a lot of people [there] believe that integration is the same as communism."[36] After clearing away the communist/integrationist rhetorical fallacy used by segregationists, Braden insisted that "nonviolent revolution is coming about because Negroes have made up their minds that they are not going to put up with things as they have been."[37] She also acknowledged that white students were becoming more active in the civil rights movement, and she encouraged the school's white majority to get involved.

SEVERAL WEEKS AFTER BRADEN'S TALK, Jefferson Poland, a student activist at Florida State University who had been expelled for participating in sit-in demonstrations, applied for entrance to San Jose State College. For his sit-in activities, Poland had been locked up in a Tallahassee jail for sixty days because he couldn't post his $300 bail.

Transferring to San Jose State was attractive to Poland because of Dixon's experience there. When student activists at the school found out that Poland was interested in transferring, they collected money to bring him to San Jose. Sixty professors signed a statement endorsing their support for Poland, calling his activism "a courageous step in the direction of changing the pattern of segregation in the South."[38] Following Poland's acceptance, many more expelled student activists transferred to the school. According to Harry Edwards, who was then a San Jose student athlete, their presence had an immeasurable effect on the school's student body in terms of social justice consciousness.[39] Outside of San Jose State, many black youths native to San Jose got involved in the school's activities, but they were sluggish about it. Some were already activists with the blacker and more established San Jose NAACP centered in the Northside. Others lived in collective survival mode and were devoted to maintaining and strengthening neighborhood institutions such as Prayer Garden Church of God in Christ. And most were leery because of the historical sundown town relationship blacks had with the Southside and their relative exclusion from attending the college as students and not student athletes.[40]

While black youth contemplated participating in the civil rights movement beyond the Northside, behind the scenes at San Jose State, academic deans were making examples out of faculty who supported Dixon and Poland by systematically firing them. Out of twenty professors fired, the two non–tenure track professors who recruited Dixon, William Stanton and Bud Hutchinson, were said to be the only ones not given a month's notice—release notices normally occurred a week or two before final exams. After the final examination period, news of Stanton's and Hutchinson's firing sparked student protests led by an ad hoc group calling itself the Emergency Committee for Academic Freedom. The group circulated a petition and gathered more than two hundred signatures. The plan was to get one thousand and then submit the petition to the president's office with the demand that the professors' contracts be renewed on the basis of academic freedom and that the college administration clarify its procedures for releasing professors. Meanwhile, a petition circulated to confirm the firings, and *San Jose Mercury News* editorials supported them, arguing that the professors had not matched academic freedom with academic responsibility and competence.[41] As for the sixty professors who endorsed supporting Poland and an end to segregation in the South, they were silent on the subject of the firing of their colleagues.[42] Ultimately, with the summer break coming and many students leaving San Jose, their zeal to either retain or release the professors died out.[43]

IN LATE MAY 1961, AROUND the same time as the firing controversy, a couple of Freedom Riders arrived for speaking engagements in the Santa Clara Valley. The Freedom Riders were mostly black and white college students affiliated with CORE and the Student Nonviolent Coordinating Committee (SNCC) who rode in public buses throughout the South to test the enforcement of *Boynton v. Virginia* (1960), a U.S. Supreme Court decision that outlawed racial segregation in interstate passenger transportation.[44] The first Freedom Rider to arrive in the South Bay was James Farmer, national director of CORE, who spoke at San Jose's Unitarian church one week after leading one of the first Freedom Rider buses into Alabama. He was in San Jose to address the California CORE and to discuss political strategy while holding a workshop on fair housing. Farmer's visit also was an official gesture recognizing the South Bay as an important cog in the national fight for civil rights.[45]

Several days after Farmer's visit, CORE field secretary Edward Blankenheim arrived in San Jose to speak at the Cambrian Park Methodist Church about the Freedom Rides, nonviolent direct action, and his experience as a white civil rights activist.[46] On Sunday, Blankenheim attended services at Antioch Baptist Church as a special guest of Reverend Washington, who called on his parishioners "to pray for the success of such demonstrations."[47] Blankenheim's visit to San Jose had come at the request of Wester Sweet, a black lawyer who was the president of the San Jose CORE. Sweet used the occasion of the visit to strongly criticize local politicians and businessmen who preyed on the ignorance and prejudices of the white majority and the poor to perpetuate customary apartheid and race violence in the South Bay.

PALO ALTO'S FRAGMENTED CIVIL rights activity was led by white students, black and white professionals, and Stanford professors until 1966, when the Palo Alto–Stanford University chapter of the NAACP, Palo Alto SNCC, and Mid-Peninsula CORE became Black Power organizations and moved their operations from white and affluent Stanford University to black and impoverished East Palo Alto. Prior to 1966 the Palo Alto NAACP was run by professionals and students such as black computer programmer Stan "Muata" Puryear.[48]

In 1962, Puryear moved to the area from New Jersey to work on a doctorate in symbolic logic at the University of California at Berkeley. To support himself, he worked full time at Lockheed Missiles and Space Company in Sunnyvale, and he was able to find temporary housing in Los Altos with the help of the Peninsula Quakers. Puryear became a member and leader in all of the civil rights organizations in the western part of the county, including the Palo Alto–Stanford University branch of the NAACP. After the move toward Black Power politics, Puryear became the chapter's president, and the organization's focus shifted to empowering working-class blacks in East Palo Alto. Up to then, almost all of Puryear's Palo Alto colleagues had been affiliated with Stanford University and took an elite liberal approach to activism: they were reform agents, detached from the streets. They worked behind the scenes to desegregate the valley mostly for people like Puryear—black professionals who could afford to live in the western part of the county and who refused to be restricted to developing ghettos such as East Palo Alto.[49]

According to Jean Libby, a white Mid-Peninsula black empowerment activist and NAACP publicist, Palo Alto's approach to liberal reform was not necessarily a bad thing, as professors and students were the reason the NAACP branch grew to about a thousand members in the early 1960s and had the resources to be one of the national organization's top donors in assisting arrested freedom fighters in the South. The Palo Alto SNCC and Mid-Peninsula CORE were more radical and attracted a wider cross-section of people who worked in the streets as nonviolent-direct-action activists to desegregate the area. Through these groups, white students formed interracial coalitions with East Palo Alto blacks, such as future city council member

Gertrude Wilkes, much in the same way that Greater Palo Alto blacks worked with professional whites to residentially desegregate the western half of Highway 101 through the local NAACP.[50] Through CORE, grassroots activists in the area desegregated pockets of the community using various nonviolent methods. They negotiated with employers for black jobs in major stores and strip malls. They warned fair housing activists about white bread deliverymen creating a panic in housing sales by informing white residents about black families moving in, which ultimately segregated and divested East Palo Alto through white flight. They also secured plum educational opportunities for black children through the "sneak out system," whereby black youths would stay with a white family in Palo Alto during the week and be registered by the white family as surrogate parents for the child to attend high-quality secondary schools like Palo Alto High School.[51]

By the summer of 1963, political strategies within the San Jose and Palo Alto civil rights movements had expanded notably. Demonstrations were more sharply focused and better organized, and San Jose State and Stanford students were going to the Black Belt South to register disenfranchised voters. Civil rights demonstrations noticeably increased after San Jose's silent march on June 1, in which one thousand people walked through the downtown to protest racial bias.[52] The march was jointly sponsored by grassroots activists in Santa Clara County, and the lead organizer was the San Jose NAACP. Bowing to pressure, San Jose Mayor Robert Welch and the San Jose City Council endorsed the march at the eleventh hour and proclaimed June 1 to be Human Rights Day in the city. However, it is important to note that neither the mayor nor any city council members participated in the march. San Jose officials' support of the demonstration nonetheless reinforced what local social reformers had been publicly saying since 1951: that racial discrimination was not confined to the South and that in the urban North and West, segregation was administered more by subtleties in social custom than by obvious legal barriers.[53] The only elected official who participated in the march was state Assemblyman William F. Stanton (D-San Jose).

The march went from St. James Park on Second Street to East William Street, up to First Street, and finally back to the park. The

Dr. James Blackwell, outgoing president of the San Jose chapter of the NAACP, leads a freedom march through downtown San Jose, 1963. Courtesy *San Jose Mercury News*.

only reported incident was racially derogatory catcalls from several youths driving by in a car. The march was led by nine Catholic and Protestant clergy. According to a professor at San Jose State College, about forty faculty members participated. The professor also recognized a member of the local ultraconservative John Birch Society driving by and filming the event. Only one significant outburst of singing occurred—soon quieted when San Jose NAACP President James Blackwell reminded supporters that the march was a silent one. People carried small American flags and signs emblazoned "Job service not

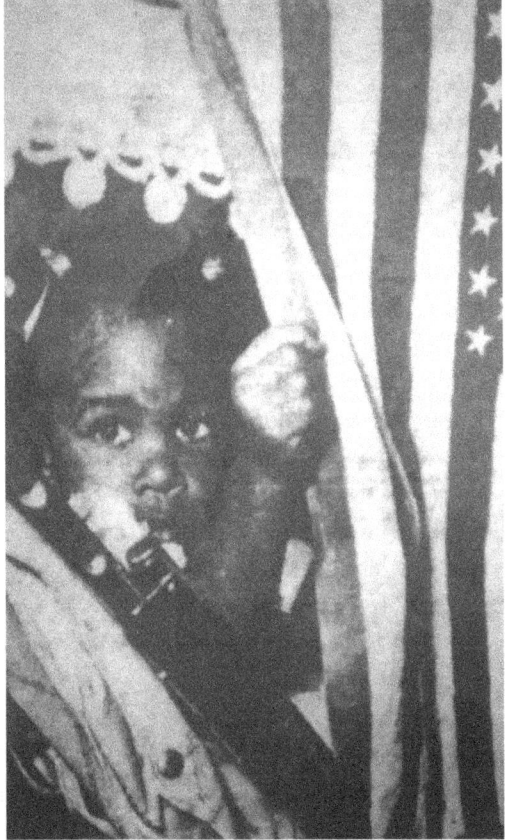

A child peering from behind an American flag at a rally at St. James Park following San Jose's March on Washington sympathy demonstration, 1963. Courtesy *San Jose Mercury News*.

lip service," "Freedom's call at City Hall," "JFK get off your rocker," and "JFK more courage and less profile." According to Catholic priest Thomas Fry, "There was no hostility [to the march] . . . just an awful lot of indifference."[54] The keynote speaker at the event was Terry Francois, a black San Francisco attorney who was in Birmingham in May when segregationists violently responded to "The Birmingham Truce Agreement" between the city and the Alabama Christian Movement for Human Rights and Southern Christian Leadership Conference. The truce led to the removal of "'Whites Only' and 'Blacks Only' signs in restrooms and on drinking fountains, [and created] a plan to desegregate lunch counters, an ongoing 'program of upgrading Negro employment,' the formation of a biracial committee to monitor the progress of the agreement, and the release of jailed protestors on bond."[55] "The Southern Negro's message to the Negro here was: 'You do something about the City Council of San Jose. We'll take care of lunch counters. You take care of fair housing,'" Francois said. "Voices of gradualism will no longer be heard. . . . There can be no peace in our country unless there is a recognition that inequalities must be corrected."[56] His speech was followed by a fund drive to bail demonstrators out of Birmingham and Jackson, Mississippi, jails. In spite of the apparent success of the march, city officials and Sacramento policymakers still displayed indifference. This set up the summer of 1963 as a critical period in which the local civil rights movement was forced to step up its activities from gradualism to more of a "Freedom Now" posture, or risk losing the nonviolent direct-action momentum that had been building since 1960.

Several weeks after the St. James Park march, a racially mixed group students attending San Jose State and Stanford University joined the effort to register black southerners to vote.[57] This was not the first time that college students from the South Bay had ventured into the South. During the winter break of 1960–1961, students from Stanford took two-week tours throughout the South and came back to describe the despicable and unequal conditions that African Americans had to endure. The lone person of African descent partaking in these tours was James Maina, a Stanford graduate in economics from Kenya, who said he perceived Alabama as a police state.[58] It is worth noting that this activity predated any mention of the Freedom Riders in the South Bay by three months, and the physical appearance of a Freedom Rider by almost half a year.[59]

On June 12, 1963, in San Jose, white student activist and Quaker Dick Frey rekindled the local press's interest in covering the participation by suggesting that the media follow local students in the southern civil rights movement. Frey, a student at Yale, was considering transferring to San Jose State.[60] Politically, he was a member of the Santa Clara Valley Friends of SNCC. A white professor and fair housing activist at the college, Florence Bryant, was the group's chair, and Norman Goerlich of the American Friends Service Committee was its treasurer. In this context, the Friends of SNCC raised money for voter registration drives and acquired a donated car to register black voters in the South. Moreover, the Friends of SNCC simultaneously campaigned in the Santa Clara Valley for fair housing legislation and participated in the pro–Rumford Act sit-in demonstrations at Sacramento. Frey said he wanted to work directly with SNCC because "it represents a chance to do something."[61] On June 12, Frey drove the donated car to Atlanta and assisted SNCC and its voter registration drives in Georgia and Greenwood, Mississippi, throughout the summer.[62]

Just as important were Stanford students taking temporary leaves during the 1963 fall semester and going to the South to participate in voter registration drives, which continued to the summer of 1965.[63] On one notable occasion on October 29, 1963, fourteen Stanford students traveled to Jackson, Mississippi, to register African Americans to vote. Simultaneously, another group of Stanford students in Palo Alto held fundraisers and solicited funds from campus living groups, professors, and people throughout the city. The money they raised was used to bail students out of jail when they were arrested, with the remaining proceeds given to organizations conducting a "freedom ballot" in Mississippi. Joining the Stanford students were sixty students from other predominantly white private institutions, including Yale.[64] Stanford University officials took no responsibility for the trip, leaving discretion with individual professors.[65] At the time, blacks made up half of the population of Mississippi, yet only 8 percent were registered to vote for the November 5 gubernatorial election.[66] By South Bay students' participation in southern registration drives, sympathy for the civil rights struggle immeasurably increased in the Santa Clara Valley. This gradually gave rise to student activists in the county becoming more vocal in addressing local racism and social injustices, especially after students came back with firsthand accounts of black poverty and segregation.[67]

Events like the St. James Park march, the Mississippi voter registration drive, and the fair housing battle to maintain the Rumford Act sparked a powerful surge of fair employment and fair housing civil rights activity in Santa Clara County during the latter half of 1963.[68] The marches on department stores in the South Bay expanded from protesting Woolworth and Kress stores to boycotting shopping centers and grocery chain stores that racially discriminated. In July 1963, a huge protest was launched in front of downtown San Jose stores and flea markets with the intent of pressuring national department chains with branches in the South to end their racial discrimination. This occurred almost two months before the national CORE began a nationwide boycott of major department and grocery chain stores immediately after the March on Washington on August 28.[69] According to James Blackwell, an estimated ten thousand people marched, which was by far the largest demonstration in the Santa Clara Valley up to that time.[70]

Behind the scenes, civil rights leaders such as black real estate agent and activist Andrew Montgomery translated the ten-thousand-person march into action by leading the San Jose CORE in negotiations with seven major chain stores and department stores.[71] According to Montgomery, CORE's strategy was "to point out those persons who recognize our problem and want to do something about it. If we find some who say 'No,' then we want to point them out, too."[72] CORE's major breakthrough happened during talks with Safeway. Montgomery pointed out that fifteen of the company's stores existed in Santa Clara County, and among the 350 clerks in the division, only one was black. Moreover, unemployment among blacks in the Santa Clara Valley was double that of any other racial group.[73] Prior to the talks, CORE tried to strengthen its claims by forming a coalition with Mexican American groups and was successful in getting the support of Rudy Belluomini, a top officer in the United Latin American Counsel of Santa Clara County. However, this group declined to get officially involved because most members either did not understand the civil rights movement or saw it as fighting solely for black people's rights.[74] Regardless, CORE continued to remind Safeway upper management that to cultivate fair employment and resolve the employment gap, the work environment had to become friendlier to persons of all cultural backgrounds, and the company would have to be more forthright about being the equal opportunity employer that it claimed to be. Out of these discussions emerged Safeway's promise to make its hiring policy more transparent to blacks and to publicly advertise itself as an equal employment employer. On August 21, CORE made similar arrangements with Hart's department store and the grocery store Purity. As for black employees working in more visible jobs, that issue had to wait for another day to be squared away, specifically, during the next round of discussions in September 1963.

Refuting San Jose CORE's claim that stores refused to hire blacks in visible positions was James McLoughlin, secretary of San Jose Local 492 of the Clerks Union. He told the *San Jose Mercury News* that the problem was not so much discrimination as it was one of inexperience. According to McLoughlin, all union stores hire through the local, which in August 1963 had two thousand members. He said that for the 150 to 200 people who applied for work every day at the hiring hall, the Clerks Union received ten calls a week from employers seeking labor. For McLoughlin the blame for job discrimination, if any, rested with the grocery chains, which were supplanting local grocers, did not have job-training programs, and usually did not hire inexperienced workers. So how did workers get experience as a clerk? Clearly, this was a catch-22 for prospective black grocers: no job without experience, but no experience without a job. And yet it was a catch-22 that young white men seemed to surmount regularly, as even the most casual shoppers in the many grocery stores in the county might have attested. If the bar marked "experience" could be lowered for young white men, why couldn't it be lowered for women and persons of color? In an attempt to mollify the situation McLoughlin said that the Clerks Union had been fighting a lonely battle against discrimination since 1959, and Local 492 has taken three cases of alleged discrimination to the Fair Employment Practices Commission. Finally, McLoughlin implicitly acknowledged that, in August 1963, Local 492 was pressured by the state under its Fair Employment Practices Act (1959) into training blacks who were on its waiting list and into placing five inexperienced African Americans in grocery chains.[75] However, for a conflicted McLoughlin, Local 492's actions had nothing to do with the local CORE campaign. "It's just a reaction to the whole pattern of things," he said. "Every time you pick up a newspaper this is what you read about."[76]

It was true that in the South Bay, civil rights coverage was a hot topic for news outlets like the *San Jose Mercury News* from the Greensboro lunch counter sit-ins in 1960 to the launch of the California Real Estate Association's anti–fair housing movement in 1964.[77] However, as successful as the county civil rights movement was becoming heading into the fall of 1963, it was no match for the white backlash following the passage of the Rumford Fair Housing Act in late September 1963. Still, the month before Rumford became law, the county civil rights movement launched one of its most successful and last notable nonviolent-direct-action demonstrations for African American equality. It was another silent march, a one-thousand-person march through downtown San Jose on August 27 in support of the March on Washington for Jobs and Freedom. The latter drew 250,000 marchers, who gathered at the National Mall in Washington, D.C., and well over 200,000 of those were black. It was one of many important events in the national civil rights movement on the path to the passage of the Civil Rights Act of 1964 and the Voting Rights Act of 1965.[78]

After the March on Washington sympathy demonstration, three hundred people stayed around for a rally at St. James Park that started at 2 P.M. Civil rights demonstrators listened to speeches by several local leaders in the African American and Mexican American communities, and they signed a petition with numerous proposals on how to improve race relations in the Santa Clara Valley. These proposals included policies promoting an end to segregation and racial exclusion in employment, job-training programs, housing, and education. Concerning fair employment, San Jose NAACP executive board member Roosevelt Walker said that many "businessmen are advertising for typists and other clerical help but are [letting these] positions stay vacant rather than hire qualified Negro help."[79] In housing, civil rights activists called for support of the Rumford Act, which the Senate had passed several months earlier and was already under attack by such powerful groups as the California Real Estate Association even before it became law. Moreover, marchers demanded an end to cronyism in the San Jose Unified School District and the hiring of qualified teachers regardless of their racial heritage.

Finally, activists demanded that San Jose officials take civil rights seriously. These demands included the hiring of an independent officer who would have enforcement powers over nondiscriminatory clauses in city contracts; the human relations commission being given subpoena and enforcement powers to combat discrimination; and both the city and county making public declarations against racial segregation.

The petition was read to San Jose Mayor Robert Welch at the rally by the president of the San Jose NAACP, James E. Blackwell, and by the vice president of the Mexican American Political Association of San Jose, Isaias Aguilera. The mayor promised to immediately present the proposals to the city council. He then attempted to mollify the crowd by describing the steps that city hall had taken in eradicating racial discrimination over the previous year. The majority of the marchers carried signs dismissing Welch's statements as double-talk: "Double talk is all at City Hall," "Mexican Americans are many—at City Hall few if any," and "Don't teach our kids to hate—let them integrate."[80]

In October, the petition was expanded to include affirmative action measures such as nurseries for children of women with paid jobs, action to encourage minority group hiring and training in private business, appointment of minority group members to county and city advisory boards, and the establishment of an office of public defender for indigent defendants in criminal cases.[81] This extended petition was presented to the San Jose Board of Supervisors in October 1963.

Before the demonstration held in sympathy with the March on Washington, several delegates from the South Bay had intended to travel to the actual march until the groups sponsoring the trip pulled out. The only Santa Clara Valley resident recorded by the local press as attending the actual March on Washington was nineteen-year-old Dana W. Reed of Palo Alto, who went to Washington to participate as a concerned individual. According to Reed, who viewed the march from the steps of the Capitol building, the event had the "air of the Stanford-California football game." She was especially impressed by how orderly, "well-dressed and well mannered" the marchers were.[82] However, Reed was troubled by what she perceived as congressional indifference. Members of the U.S. Congress excused themselves from participating in the march by claiming to take the day off out of fear of potential race violence.[83] The only other public interpretation of the national and local March on Washington came from the *San Jose Mercury News*, which had initially expressed grave concerns similar to those expressed by Congress—that is, fear that racial violence and disorder could erupt—but these concerns proved unfounded. As a result, just as President Kennedy was impressed with what he saw in Washington, the *San Jose Mercury News* was swept up in the moment, inspired to rhetoric that challenged racial discrimination, in effect combating the California Real Estate Association's closed housing campaign. In this transitory moment, the *San Jose Mercury News* informed readers that the hard task of implementing an equal rights program at all levels of American life remained ahead. Central to its implementation was the U.S. Congress and local city halls. Crucial to the paper's editorial was that the nation "is not only caught up in a new social revolution, [but it] is facing a crisis of conscience as well. [How our elected officials respond] will determine what kind of country this is going to be."[84]

For the county civil rights movement, 1963 closed with groups holding church memorial services for the four girls killed on September 15 in a bombing at the Sixteenth Street Baptist Church in Birmingham, Alabama.[85] Eight days later, memorial services throughout the nation were held. Then on September 29 at San Jose's Civic Auditorium, a memorial rally titled "That these dead shall not die in vain" was held. The theme brilliantly connected the 1960s civil rights movement to the 1860s abolitionist movement.[86] At the memorial rally, local civil rights activists assaulted Santa Clara Valley's record on discrimination and demanded countywide reforms of segregation and fair access in housing, employment, and education. This was one of the few times that local activism made front-page news in the local press. Perhaps the most piercing criticism aimed at local elected officials came from incoming San Jose NAACP President Richard Thomas, who said, "There is no city or county leader who is outspokenly in favor of strong civil rights legislation—no one who can be identified with the movement."[87] Thomas also stressed that that "most of these local leaders take the position that we have no serious problem here. But the freedom to enjoy unrestricted access to housing in accordance with financial means continues to be denied. Such ghetto living sustains *de facto* segregation in the schools, which is an undeniable fact here, and jeopardizes all efforts to broaden employment opportunities."[88]

Thomas took aim at the local clergy for supporting the movement only when asked to do so and seldom taking the lead; the exceptions were Reverend Washington of Antioch Baptist Church and the Reverend George Arthur Casaday of the Palo Alto First Congregational Church, who was white.[89] Thomas, like many local civil rights activists, essentially felt that the greatest threats to social justice and integration in the Santa Clara Valley were apathy and indifference.[90]

BY 1964 THE SANTA CLARA COUNTY civil rights movement had created a white backlash that became a conservative political movement within the South Bay. The foundations of this backlash were laid in May 1960 when the term "civil defense," which the civil rights movement popularized, was appropriated by local white people to address their personal anxieties in a constitutional rights context through major media outlets including the *San Jose Mercury News*.[91] With the meaning of democracy in the balance, 1964 became a very important year in Santa Clara County. It represented, on the one hand, the birth of a new Reconstruction era through the civil rights movement and, on the other hand, the rebirth of the rebel yell and home rule through suburban kitchen table activists and Barry Goldwater–Ronald Reagan conservatives (i.e., the New Right) mobilizing mass support to maintain the culturally intolerant makeup of their communities behind the curtain of homeowner rights, Christian evangelicalism, and anti-communism.[92] In California, this emerging form of conservatism linked to white suburbanization was successful in making racial apartheid housing in the private market legal from 1965 to spring 1966.

It also had a direct effect on racial uprisings in Watts in 1965 and Hunter's Point (San Francisco) in 1966.[93] Most important, it led to a massive loss of momentum in the California and Santa Clara County civil rights movements.

In the valley, local civil rights coverage became replaced in local media outlets by the fair housing battle in Sacramento from 1964 to 1967, until a group of racially conscious blacks at San Jose State made it their prerogative to rekindle the coals that made the earlier black freedom movement newsworthy. This new movement, popularly referred to as the "revolt of the black athlete," focused on black empowerment, higher education, amateur athletic boycotts, and transformative politics that went national after the first cancellation of a major college sporting event, and quickly expanded internationally, highlighted by Tommie Smith and John Carlos protesting U.S. oppression on the winner's podium at the 1968 Olympics.

Chapter Seven
The Revolt of the Black Athlete and Its Accomplishments, 1956–1987

> *Of all of the places it wasn't Michigan. It wasn't Ohio State. It wasn't USC or Notre Dame or University of Oklahoma or Texas. It was San Jose State [where the revolt of the black athlete began]. . . . From my era, I think that strand of liberality; the bringing of those students from those black schools on to the campus during my time there on scholarship [1961–1964] . . . that liberal group bringing in people such as Maya Angelou and Lewis Lomax to speak, had a phenomenal impact on where my generation went.*[1]
>
> Harry Edwards, 2012

IN 1968, BEFORE THE TRAUMATIC assassinations that changed America that year, desegregation had already made notable progress in the Santa Clara Valley. Although the assassination of Dr. Martin Luther King, Jr., triggered uprisings in most major cities, San Jose was set on a path to come out of this period without loss of life or property. Because of Dionne Warwick's recording of "Do You Know the Way to San Jose?" (1968), the city had become identified as a place where tourists could get "some peace of mind"—even though racial tensions based on white supremacy and the speed with which the valley was developing into an expanse of white suburbs betrayed the lyrics of the song, which implied that San Jose was another Monterey rather than another L.A.[2] At the center of the Santa Clara Valley's peculiar calm was a fragmented freedom rights movement rooted in earlier local civil rights, fair housing, and labor union movements dating back to 1947.[3] Black student athlete activism of the '60s—which linked the exploitation of black amateur athletes with the general exploitation of African Americans in U.S. society—became another essential component in the desegregation of late-blooming suburbanizing communities such as San Jose.

This movement, often referred to as the "revolt of the black athlete," was launched at San Jose State College on September 18, 1967, when sociology instructor Harry Edwards and Kenneth Noel, cofounders of United Black Students for Action (UBSA), addressed racism at the college in no uncertain terms. Their action led to the cancellation of the school's first football game of the season, against the University of Texas at El Paso, and university hearings. At San Jose State, the revolt desegregated rental housing in and around campus, integrated fraternities and sororities, opened up campus job opportunities for minorities, and set in motion the systematic growth in numbers of students and faculty of color. But the most momentous effect was the movement's reverberation all over the United States. Immediately after the revolt at San Jose State, similar black student athlete movements emerged across the country. Amateur athletics became inculcated with black consciousness and freedom rights politics, and the passion of the movement was dramatically highlighted at the 1968 Summer Olympic Games. Medal-winning African American athletes Tommie Smith and John Carlos, standing on the winner's podium and turning to face the American flag as "The Star-Spangled Banner" played, shocked the world by lowering their heads and raising black-gloved fists, holding that position through the national anthem's last measure.[4]

This chapter examines the revolt's effects on and beyond the Santa Clara Valley from the late 1960s to the present. It argues that the movement had far broader implications than most scholars have portrayed and had monumental effects on integration in the area. Though scholars and documentarians identify San Jose as the place where the revolt originated, their understanding of the area's history of race relations is meager, and thus they give short shrift to the city's significance. They never ask *why* the movement began at San Jose State, how the area was affected, or what the revolt ultimately achieved.

This chapter addresses all of these questions and will expand understanding of the revolt by centering the movement's narrative on black political expression and community formation in Greater San

Jose. It will treat key instigators of the revolt, most notably Harry Edwards, at the hub of events as they play out.

THE LEGACY OF EXPLOITATION OF black student athletes that led to the athletes' revolt in the late 1960s traces back to the Good Brothers in the mid-1950s. This was the first group of African Americans invited into the South Bay to improve their opportunities and living standards as student athletes at San Jose State College, and Dorothy Hines dubbed them the "Good Brothers." Hines was a black San Jose resident and a sister of Steve McKinney, a former Chicago Bear defensive end who played on the team when it won the 1985 Super Bowl.[5] The Good Brothers included Charles Alexander, Joe Barrington, Herb Boyer, Willie Bronson, George Cobb, Al Conley, Jack Crawford, Charley Hardy, Melvin Newton (Huey P. Newton's older brother), "Rapid Ray" Norton (Olympic participant), "Bullet Bob" Pointer, Art Powell, and Mel Powell. According to Alexander, who came from a small town in East Texas, most of the Good Brothers came from small towns in central California and were standouts in football and track and field. Altogether, San Jose State recruited about thirty-five black student athletes during the 1950s.[6] They were different from the few black student athletes who preceded them, such as football All-American Lloyd Thomas (1938) because they came to the college in groups as opposed to being the only black on a team. The advantage to this was that the Good Brothers used sports to gain a college education as a collective, bound by common struggle and mutual concern, assisting, uplifting, and advocating for one another's educational and professional success. They also saw the South Bay as a place that was rapidly transitioning from farms to suburbs, industrial parks, and shopping centers.[7] They saw opportunity there, the possibility of achieving their dreams. Alexander said that they "all ended up graduating and becoming doctors, judges, lawyers, dentists, coaches."[8] For San Jose native Cass Jackson, this high success rate was nearly unbelievable, just as it was to many other local African Americans who knew the Good Brothers through Cass and his mother, Inez Jackson. The Good Brothers had overcome long odds both as first-generation college students and

The Good Brothers, ca. 1960. Charles Alexander Collection.

as student athletes who had been exploited by the college athletics department. Their achievements gradually opened doors for other blacks in housing and professional employment in the eastern part of the county and, after 1968, in coaching.[9]

Alexander's premise for the Good Brothers' success was simple: they were trying to get out of their small towns and get to a place where they could access educational and economic opportunities. They found that in the South Bay. Their foundation for succeeding was working together in family, school, and church—a traditional African American survival tactic that the students applied to getting a college education at a predominantly white institution. Their models on how to achieve their goals were Joe Louis, Jackie Robinson, and Dr. Martin Luther King, Jr.—U.S. icons in the forefront of proving that African Americans were capable of impeccable integrity and determination in their efforts to excel in the boxing ring, professional baseball, or civil rights leadership. Unlike the revolt generation, the Good Brothers did not challenge San Jose State's athletic department and its treatment of student athletes, because they had approved housing, and they did not want to jeopardize this unprecedented opportunity to get a college education and evolve beyond living in survival mode. Although none graduated within the period of their scholarships, most Good Brothers graduated from fields that they were most passionate about, in which their greatest cost was time. In the example of Charles Alexander, he was given the necessary space at San Jose State to discover that he did not want to be a medical doctor, which is what he initially intended. Instead he earned an administration of justice degree. Immediately after graduating, he became the first African American hired in the San Jose Probation Department (from which he retired). Similar to other Good Brothers, Alexander's politics revolved around good character, education, and transferring the work-together ethos into professional employment, opening doors for African American hires like San Jose native Kenneth Blackwell and others from the late 1960s to the 1990s.[10]

Whatever their character or intent to get a good education, however, before 1969 the black student athletes at San Jose State were confronted with unfair housing in the rental market—an area marginal to the early fair housing struggle. None of the Good Brothers could get dormitory housing or find homes to rent around the college, as their white counterparts could. So they collectively pressured their coaches into finding them approved campus housing in a home that became known as the "Good Brothers' Pad" on Fifth and St. John Streets, located in a middle-class white community near San Jose State. This home was managed by Charles Alexander and his father, David Alexander, providing living space for black students and African Americans new to the region who would sometimes stay for a night while they discovered where black people could stay in San Jose.[11]

Together they paid the rent with their financial aid during the college year, and, during the off-season, they paid it by working on farms and doing odd jobs. The Good Brothers in one case earned their rent by loading, at night, what they at least thought was no fewer than ten thousand live chickens for a friend of the landlord. For Alexander, having a strong work ethic made the difference: "You see, I said [to his peers], 'We can't write home to Momma.' If your scholarship runs out (which mine did), you still gotta make it. You'll make it if there's a job that nobody else wants. . . . Nobody wants to wade in chicken shit. But them greenbacks still spend the same."[12]

The Good Brothers' Pad was one of the few places where people of racially different backgrounds freely intermingled in the Santa Clara Valley before the 1960s. Because of strict restrictions in town, 1960 Olympian "Rapid Ray" Norton, and three other blacks were housed in an equipment shed on the football field during their first six weeks at the college in 1956.[13] According to Alexander, the Good Brothers' Pad was the unwritten mecca of San Jose State's social scene in the 1950s. As a result, it received regular visits from future Hollywood legends such as the Smothers Brothers and Coach Bill Walsh, who would later end up in the National Football League Hall of Fame. The Good Brothers had to work together to make the most out of their situation by creating their own after-hours entertainment because they were excluded from most mainstream venues, and whatever activities they planned were confined to their home.[14]

FOR SOCIOLOGIST AND HUMAN RIGHTS activist Harry Edwards, seeds for his role as co-organizer in the revolt were planted when he was a student at San Jose in the early 1960s and discovered that race relations at the college and South Bay were similar to, if not worse than, his native East St. Louis.[15]

East St. Louis was a ghetto that in 1917 experienced one of the worse race riots in U.S. history.[16] For Edwards, the fallout from the riots permeated East St. Louis with tensions that were still tangible to him. His understanding of equality and justice had been shattered in 1955 at the age of twelve when he saw Emmitt Till's mutilated face in an open coffin pictured in an issue of *Jet* magazine that was passed around at his school, Dunbar Elementary. This was Edwards's "first real sense that there was something rotten at the core of human relations in America."[17]

He had not understood racism a year earlier when he and his mother made a rare trip into downtown St. Louis to shop for school clothes and bought a hotdog at Woolworth's lunch counter. A young and excited Harry Edwards saw other children eating at the counter and asked his mother if they could do the same. To avoid humiliation for a child who did not fully understand St. Louis's color line, Edwards's mother took him outside to eat before a white waitress could impolitely ask them to leave. What was strange to Edwards, when he looked through a window at the lunch counter, was a white woman sitting at the lunch counter and feeding her dog. The dog could eat at the lunch counter, but Edwards and his mother could not.

At the end of the day that the *Jet* magazine was circulated at school, Edwards brought it home to ask his father what was happening and where Till's dad had been. Edwards's father was an ex-con who carried himself as a "man's man," but on this occasion he talked around the issue rather than directly. For Edwards, the cautiousness of his father's response was an epiphany. "For the first time, [I understood] that there were some things that even my daddy cannot protect me against."[18]

Edwards was part of the first generation of African Americans who attended integrated high schools in St. Louis, and it was in that context that his understanding of race and sports developed. In his school, he felt that white educators did not know what to do with black students, except for the athletes, whose tasks were to "go play sports and get the hell out of Dodge." On the field he discovered that the motto, "It's not the color of your skin or the circumstances, only how well you play the game" was "a bunch of nonsense; that if you were black you weren't going to play quarterback. . . . You were going to have only so many [African Americans] playing on the basketball floor . . . [and black women] were not going to be on the cheerleading squad."[19] This was the background that Harry Edwards brought to San Jose State College.

Edwards came to California as a star high school athlete, and, at six foot, eight and 250 pounds, he had the potential for greatness. Before arriving at San Jose State, he had briefly attended Fresno City College as a four-sports student athlete, throwing the discus in track and field and playing football, basketball, and baseball. Edwards dreamed of going to the Olympics, and in 1961 he transferred to San Jose State on an athletic scholarship in track and field. On the surface, the college was, for a number of reasons, an ideal place for a young black man with great athletic potential coming out of the rough world of East St. Louis. First, world-class athletes such as "Rapid Ray" Norton and "Bullet Bob" Pointer attended San Jose State when Edwards transferred.[20] Second, slightly before Edward's arrival, the college hired Vern Wolf as its new track and field assistant coach. Wolf brought with him a reputation for cultivating world-class track and field talent at the high school level. Third, the school had one of the strongest social work programs on the West Coast, which was Edwards's interest at the time. Finally, Edwards anticipated no racial problems in the Santa Clara Valley because he had always been told that California was an interracial promised land.[21]

As a San Jose State student, however, Edwards immediately encountered roadblocks in academics and his athletics department. In 1961, the college had a minuscule African American population, and it consisted primarily of student athletes who rarely graduated within the period of their athletic eligibility. Of the more than fifteen thousand full-time students attending, only seventy were black; almost all (sixty) were male athletes, and three were women. The Good Brothers were graduating with relatively good college experiences and breaking new ground as African Americans working in professional employment; some even lived in suburban communities often off-limits to black occupancy. Edwards attributed the failure of black student athletes to graduate within the period of their athletic eligibility largely to the Eurocentric curriculum, shortage of mentors, and lack of support services geared toward dealing with African American concerns.[22]

However, it could be argued that the greatest barrier to blacks graduating from the school was its system of governance and academics. San Jose State and its athletic department systematically directed student athletes away from the sciences and humanities and funneled them into an easy curriculum of social work, probation and parole, and physical education designed to keep them eligible to compete in intercollegiate sports.[23] According to Edwards, the popular thought of the day "was that blacks were natural athletes so we could cut it in physical education."[24] Although most black student athletes were technically being prepared to work as assistant coaches or recreation directors, almost no African Americans majoring in physical education ever graduated from San Jose State before their scholarships ended. There were too many black student athletes taking units on the "techniques of teaching" any given sport in their fourth year, who academically speaking were still sophomores who had never taken biology, kinesiology, and chemistry, all of them requirements for graduation with the physical education major. As a student Edwards had no interest in coaching or being a recreation director. Nor was he interested in being labeled a "dumb jock." He knew he was smart and had a valuable voice to articulate something about black people to the world, and he actively pursued developing it.[25] In his sophomore year he convinced sociology chair Milt Rendall to let him provisionally major in sociology. To do so, he carried around a blue 3x5 notecard that had to be signed by each sociology professor every Friday saying that he was doing at least grade B work; under school policy, student athletes needed a C average for athletic eligibility. The policy did not change in this particular case until March 1964, when the sociology department discovered that Edwards had been awarded a Woodrow Wilson Fellowship and would be attending Cornell University in its doctorate program in sociology in the fall.[26]

Socially, Edwards found San Jose State and the Santa Clara Valley to be hostile toward African Americans. The most obvious issue confronting blacks living south of Santa Clara Street (where the college is located) was restrictive housing, which made most housing rentals off-limits to black students. According to Edwards, "The landlord's argument was that if off-campus housing were open to minority students, the majority of white students would move out, leaving apartment house owners with massive vacancies that they would be unlikely to fill given the negligible number of minority students enrolled at San Jose State."[27] San Jose State's housing office brochure assured that every student would have access to housing conducive to his or her education both on and off campus.

On campus, black students had a hard time living in dormitories operated by the school unless they found a black roommate or were able to find a white person willing to room with them.[28] Tommie Smith and Lee Evans, track stars at the college in the late 1960s, often found themselves living in motel rooms or sleeping in dormitory lobbies.

Housing discrimination around the campus was especially transparent during school breaks when dormitories closed, students went home, and the black students who couldn't afford to go home were stuck with few housing options. Such an arrangement usually forced black student athletes into severely cramped quarters. In one instance during Edward's senior year in 1964, sixteen people roomed in a two-bedroom apartment.[29]

Other problems African American students encountered at San Jose State involved its nightlife. In the 1960s, the college had a well-earned reputation of being a "party school." Even so, fraternity and sorority systems and campus social life at student-oriented events were segregated and often exclusionary.[30] From the Good Brothers era to the Speed City era (late 1960s) the only black fraternity at the school was Omega Psi Phi (established in the late 1950s). Unlike the Good Brothers, whose socializing was confined to their home but included a diverse range of people, black students in the 1960s were often steered into socializing in segregated conditions in the African American section at the school's cafeteria and off-campus in clustered communities and segregated areas at San Jose, San Francisco, Vallejo, Los Angeles, and the East Bay.[31] As for socializing on campus, if black students were stopped after dark by a campus police officer, a longstanding joke on campus went like this: "When campus police find a Negro on campus after dark, they throw him a football. If he fumbles it, they throw him a basketball. If he fumbles that, they throw him into their squad car—unless he can outrun them, in which case they just assume that he is one of (track coach) Bud Winter's boys."[32]

In several cases, the racism in and around the school's campus trained black students to accommodate the South Bay's color line, which was obvious in housing, employment, and education but seemed subtle in comparison with what people were reading in print media and seeing on television in the American South and cities in the North. The result of this media coverage led to the widespread belief that racism was a southern and urban issue and not a problem in a suburban metropolis like the Santa Clara Valley. The effect of this denial of the South Bay's racial problems was seen not only in racial indifference and complacency among many white people; black people were also affected, as most seemed more comfortable living in survival mode than in directly challenging the South Bay's structural injustices on race and poverty. As for Edwards, he tried to challenge the color line within San Jose State; outside of the campus his freedom rights consciousness was further developed under the tutelage of local civil rights legend Inez Jackson in San Jose's Northside.[33] His first attempt to challenge the exploitation of black student athletes at his college occurred during his sophomore year, 1962, as the co-captain of the track and field team. He felt strongly that the school was becoming renowned in football, basketball, and in track and field through the gross exploitation of first-generation black students living on a shoestring budget. "San Jose State was not Notre Dame or USC [University of Southern California]" in terms of resources, he said.[34] Edwards first saw how this exploitation functioned under famed track and field coach Lloyd C. "Bud" Winter, who annually recruited more than ten black sprinters from inner-city and small-town America on the promise that they would have a place on the team as scholarship athletes. However, once they got to the school they found they had to compete in a runoff for the only scholarship and half scholarship that Winter had to offer. While awaiting the outcome, "guys were sleeping at the track storage room, piling in with folks, and were at the Good Brother's house." Once the scholarships were awarded, "Bud would wash his hands" of the losers of the runoff.[35] Edwards eventually cornered Winter and urged him to stop treating black athletic prospects like this—at the time "white kids didn't have to worry about that, because what Bud couldn't give them, their parents could."[36] This request was a total break with how previous athletes dealt with the exploitation, and Winter met it with bewilderment and elusive responses about team unity, track and field practice, Edwards's studies, and his diet.[37] It also ended Edwards's Olympic dreams as a sophomore. It was this instance that prompted him to articulate the difference between racism in different regions of the United States: "The major difference between the Midwest and California, other than climate, was that in the Midwest racism was right up front. Blacks always knew where they

Student and Faculty Civil Rights Rally, San Jose State College, February 28, 1964. Courtesy San Jose State University Archives.

stood. In California the bright sun, the ready hello's and big smiles, and the false liberalism blinded unwary Blacks so that they couldn't see the racist steamroller until it crushed them flat."[38]

After Edwards's oral altercation with Winter, he was released from the track and field team and lost his scholarship.[39] Because he still played on the basketball team, however, he was able to work out a new scholarship arrangement that gave him the time to better commit to his academic studies and to fully discover what San Jose State had to offer. What he discovered was that the college provided a fertile environment for challenging the status quo, partly because "there was a nest of liberalism within the social sciences and humanities division of the school that taught about the sordid back history of America."[40] As a result, many student athletes signed up for classes in which the material covered was in conjunction with the courses that they were required to take, such as social work majors taking a literature course that examined the poems of Langston Hughes. In the end, "This created a fertile ground to think beyond what [students] saw."[41] Adding to this trend were expelled student activists transferring to San Jose State from colleges that were historically black and the school's social sciences division's invitations to guest speakers such as Lewis Lomax and Maya Angelou to address American race relations on the hundredth anniversary of the Emancipation Proclamation. Yet for such advances in human relations, San Jose State's liberal tradition was as fragmented as the Santa Clara County civil rights movement that paralleled it outside the walls of the campus. Nonetheless, the college had all of the ingredients: "The abuse, exploitation, racism, institutionalized and personal, right there on the campus" were critically addressed in many courses as an intellectual exercise, but as a whole the community never saw the revolt coming. Edwards found himself in the "backwaters of swirling interactions that fed into this funnel of burgeoning activism that exploded in the fall of 1967."[42]

AFTER GRADUATING FROM San Jose State in 1964, Edwards became a doctoral student at Cornell University in sociology. Here his black consciousness was enhanced by weekend pilgrimages into Harlem to hear Malcolm X (aka Malik el Hajj Shabazz) speak on black identity, black empowerment, and the state of black America.[43] Malcolm X profoundly influenced Edwards's outlook on life, the African American community, and his political approach to race and American institutions. From this experience, Edwards wrote his master's thesis on the Black Muslim family.[44] In 1966, after receiving his M.A. and completing his doctoral coursework, Edwards began writing his dissertation on the pioneering subject of the sociology of sports. He did this during a part-time lecturer appointment, teaching two classes a semester through the 1966–1968 academic years at San Jose State.[45]

Edwards's first brush with racism occurred soon after he returned to San Jose, in seeking housing around the college.[46] Landlords with rentals near the college did not care that Edwards was a faculty member at San Jose State or had an Ivy League master's degree, or had the money to pay several months' rent in advance. The housing customs within walking distance of the school dictated that he settle where vacancies opened up for black people, which in this instance, he said, was a "cold cement-floor garage, costing [the local premium of] $75 a month."[47] Tommie Smith, world-class sprinter and record holder, activist and protégé, responded to his mentor's situation with the comment that his situation was even worse: "I have you beat. . . . My wife's pregnant. We have no decent house. So far 13 lovely people have turned us down."[48]

As the 1966–1967 school year proceeded, more incidents of customary racism made Edwards realize that the racism and segregation in and around San Jose State had actually increased from the time he left the campus in 1964.[49] In this period, there were only two African American professors on the campus: Edwards and a tenured biologist. In intercollegiate sports, the athletic department coaching staff was still all white. The college was recruiting more black male athletes to play football and to run track, which developed into what had become the legendary "Speed City." As for black women, their population was minuscule because they were admitted into San Jose State only as transfer students, and only a few African American transfers were students who weren't athletes. Prior to admissions reform in the fall of 1968, many transfers came into the school under the 2 percent rule, which was used to make academic enrollment exceptions for athletes only and not to diversify the campus with qualified students of color.[50] Even foreign students were admitted in numbers far exceeding the black student population, by a ratio of 20:1.[51] The significance of this was that on the eve of the revolt in September 1967, of San Jose State's twenty-four thousand students, seventy-two were African Americans, and sixty of those were athletes.[52]

Still, the increase of black students and Black Power gripping their consciousness placed more pressure on segregated fraternities and sororities, segregated housing, and segregated majors.[53] In this environment it was no longer fashionable for African American students to get a college education in pursuit of living comfortably beyond the ghetto. By January 1967 socially conscious students, such as Bruce McCullough, Beverly Taylor, and James Shaw, were thinking seriously about black identity, black empowerment through institution

Speed City, San Jose, March 1968. First row *(left to right)*: Tommie Smith, Ronnie Ray Smith, John Carlos. Second row *(left to right)*: Kirk Clayton, Jerry Williams, Sam Davis, Bill Gaines, Lee Evans, Bob Griffin, Frank Slaton. Jeff Kroot Collection.

building and protest, and their significance in a region with a black population less than 2 percent.

THE UBSA WAS ESTABLISHED after Edwards reunited with former San Jose State track star and graduate student Ken Noel, shortly before the fall semester of 1967. According to Cass Jackson, Noel was nicknamed "Dad" because he was older than his peers, including Edwards, who was five years younger.[54] Noel was crucial to the revolt because he had extensive background in organizing black student athletes at San Jose City College. In 1962, he was suspended from that college "for attempting to organize a rebellion among out-of-state black basketball players," Edwards said.[55] He was also credited "for a demonstration at the State junior college basketball championship tournament involving a black SJCC basketball player who sat down in the center jump circle and had to be carried from the floor."[56] At San Jose State, Noel was working on his master's degree in sociology. The two got back together when Noel enrolled to take a course Edwards was teaching, titled "Racial and Cultural Minorities." After an hourlong casual conversation about "the old and the new aspects of life at San Jose for black students," Edwards later wrote, "it suddenly dawned on us that the same social and racial injustices and discrimination that had dogged our footsteps as freshmen at San Jose were still rampant on campus—racism in the fraternities and sororities, racism in housing, racism and out-and-out mistreatment in athletics, and a general lack of understanding of the problems of Afro-Americans by the college administration."[57] They also found themselves asking such questions as "Why should blacks play where they can't work?" "Why are there no Negro coaches at San Jose State?" and "If we can't be head coach, how could we ever be head of state?"[58] Together, Edwards and Noel turned their questions into a commitment to change negative circumstances confronting African American students at San Jose, a commitment that broke sharply with the politics of survival that gripped most blacks in the valley. At the core of what Edwards and Noel thought was a necessary action was for them to connect the fragments within San Jose State's liberal tradition and incorporate that tradition within a Black Power politic that moved African Americans beyond mere access to human dignity and respect, centered on arguably the most exploited people in the college: its black student athletes.[59]

Shortly before the fall semester, Edwards and Noel compiled a sweeping petition addressing the racist treatment at the college in "fraternities and sororities, intercollegiate athletics, student admission policies, housing, on-campus job opportunities, academic counseling, and campus social life."[60] After names for the petition were collected, they went to President Robert D. Clark's office to address the racism on campus with documented complaints in hand. He was not in the office, and they were sent to administrators in charge in areas that they were concerned about. The academic vice president was not in. No one would tell them when he would come in. Then they went to Vice President of Housing Stanley Benz to discuss opening approved housing to black students. Shocked that they were referring to themselves as "Black" rather than "Negro," Benz thought what they were asking for was ludicrous and gave them the runaround. Finally, they went to Athletic Director Walt McPherson about needing black coaches, black administrators, and black counselors for black athletes. McPherson responded, "You graduated, what business is it of yours?" For Edwards it was in this moment that he started to understand that San Jose State had no clue what was at stake: that the fertile environment of liberality critically addressed in many courses as an intellectual exercise was about to become a vehicle that students could rally around, starting with the organization of fifty-nine African American students, most of whom were athletes who "weren't graduating, just being exploited, used up, and dumped."[61] From this, the UBSA considered picketing the college, with a backup plan to demonstrate at its first football game of the season, organize a sit-in on fraternity lawns with tents, and block the entrances to the administration building. Ultimately, Edwards and Noel decided to meet with President Clark to address campus racism and the exploitation of black student athletes.

A meeting with Clark made sense at the time because he was reputedly an enlightened leader who supported free expression of student opinion on campus.[62] He also had his own problems with the school's athletic department.[63] During the meeting, Edwards and Noel told Clark that they were going to hold a public rally at noon of the opening day of classes on Monday, September 18, 1967, and asked Clark if he would attend, to which he replied that he would.[64] They also invited all faculty members and administration officials and publicized the event throughout the Bay Area as titled "The Rally on Racism at San Jose State." Seven hundred people attended the rally, including Clark and the dean of students. Edwards spoke to the crowd while Noel passed out leaflets describing UBSA's mission and orally delivered charges of institutional racism at San Jose State, which Clark said were true.[65] Edwards said that if UBSA's demands were not met, "we will mount a movement on campus to prevent the opening football game of the season from being played—by any means necessary."[66]

These demands included: an end to all forms of racial discrimination in housing, the athletic department, fraternity system, and student government as they pertain to San Jose State; public deliberation and proposed solutions on these demands; the systematic recruitment of minority faculty, students, and administrators through the creation of a permanent commission; and expanding the 2 percent rule to nonathlete students of color.[67]

The potential losses for San Jose State and the local community for failure to comply with the UBSA's demands were initially estimated at $15,000 to $30,000, in addition to the loss of revenue to businesses and damage to San Jose's reputation as a racially tolerant community.[68] Immediately after the rally, Edwards and Noel were attacked by critics for proposing to disrupt the season's opening football game. As for support, the UBSA stood alone at the college, with a small circle of San Jose freedom rights activists within Inez Jackson's circle offering support from the Northside.[69] Several former coaches said that they agreed with UBSA's goals but not its tactics. Most telling to Edwards was the response that sociology professor Mervyn Cadwallader gave him as to why UBSA members would not get any San Jose State liberal to stand with them in their attempt to transform the campus. Cadwallader was one of several professors who had arranged for black student activists to transfer into San Jose State from the South in the early 1960s. According to Edwards, Cadwallader agreed with what the UBSA was fighting for but thought that the revolt's leaders had underestimated the institutional relationships "with peers, the administration, [and] the athletic department that they did not want disturbed. They were not going to put the problems of a handful of blacks before their [own] concerns."[70] As Edwards noted, Cadwallader was right: "We stood alone."[71] The Good Brothers, still closely connected to the school's athletic department, were more concerned about Speed City–era students losing their athletic scholarships and being expelled. And student activists such as James Shaw were closely connected to professors and former sponsors, including Cadwallader.[72] Similar to Shaw, most critics of the revolt argued that sports provided the one arena in which black people competed against white people on an equal playing field. The viewpoint, Edwards said, was that in college athletics "you have more Negroes than anything else, and they have a scholarship, and you are going to rebel over that?"[73]

Many critics thought that the UBSA was doomed to failure if it followed through on its threat. Edwards and Noel realized, however, that intercollegiate sports was the one area in campus life in which African Americans had leverage. The threat was the UBSA's best shot at success, they thought, because it was a fresh strategy aimed toward disturbing an important American ritual to cast light on issues that sorely needed to be addressed in the county: fair housing, institutional racism in higher education, and the exploitation of amateur athletes in college sports.[74]

Within a week of the rally leading up to the game on September 23, an atmosphere of excitement and anxiety permeated the campus. While San Jose State officials sought to resolve the situation, controversies and tensions reverberated throughout Santa Clara County. A noncampus group calling itself the "Soul Brothers" contacted Edwards and proposed to take drastic measures at the game if needed.[75] On the other end of the spectrum, the white supremacist motorcycle group Hell's Angels publicly announced intentions to attend the football game to resist and counter the proposed demonstration. Within two days of the rally, black players at San Jose State and the University of Texas at El Paso (aka Texas Western College) systematically took themselves out of the game—some in support of the boycott and others fearing crowd violence.[76] San Jose officials feared the boycott as the spark that could trigger race violence in a region that, until then, had settled racial problems through negotiation. According to President Clark, there were threats of arson aimed at fraternity and sorority houses, and burning torches were thrown on their lawns. Athletic Director Bob Bronzan had "a firebomb tossed on his lawn" as a warning.[77] The dean of women advised female students to move out, which resulted in some houses being fully evacuated leading up to the game. Simultaneously, a critical mass of students reportedly left the campus several days after the rally, either at the request of their parents or in fear of race riots. Moreover, officials in the athletics department, including Coach Winter, felt attacked by picket signs that read "Stop exploitation of Negro athletes now."[78] Finally, rumors that the college's football stadium would be burned to the ground by outside agitators forced President Clark to respond to the situation with a public announcement.

Before making the announcement, Clark consulted Bronzan on the boycott and the effects it could have on the college. Bronzan had known Edwards and Noel for six years. He knew they were serious and that the UBSA was growing in members—in one week the group grew from two (Edwards and Noel) to fifty-nine members.[79] Bronzan also heard San Jose Police Department reports in which an Oakland informant urged that the football game be canceled because there was a threat of violence coming from Oakland. At San Jose State, Bronzan was the first official to ask Clark to cancel the football game. Clark said later that he "thought it was a mistake to cancel. One of the reasons I thought that was because I felt that the blacks wanted some public event as a point of resistance, and if I suddenly cancelled the game I removed that resistance."[80] As Clark considered cancelling the game, he talked to Edwards. The professor gave him no insight as to his thinking until after he talked it over with the UBSA and came back favoring the cancellation. Bronzan then spoke with the athletics director at the University of Texas at El Paso, who wanted the game transferred there. Bronzan was opposed, fearing that the change in venue would enrage the South Bay public, focus unwanted attention on the university community, "and invite the kind of violence that . . . was expressive all over this country at the time."[81] So on September 20, 1967, Clark cancelled the game in an attempt to "drain off the emotion," making San Jose State the first major college in the United States to cancel an athletic event under the threat of racial protest. At a news conference that sent shock waves throughout California, President Clark said:

> In view of disturbing threats from outside our college community to the peaceful conduct of Saturday night's football game, I have in consultation with the director of athletics, ordered cancellation of the game. I considered the action necessary to protect our students, their parents and friends, from the possibility of violence in Spartan Stadium. I wish to emphasize that this danger is not from San Jose State

students. Our own students and faculty have been seeking a resolution of differences through a week-long series of open hearings. The danger comes from the possible involvement of off-campus persons and groups, who by Saturday night, may be unaware of our progress towards a solution. We regret this disappointment to the community and our students. We feel that we don't have the right to take chances with people lives.[82]

The cancellation of the football game cost the college $100,000 and split people into two distinct camps—either supporting the decision or opposing it—with little middle ground. For President Clark the situation was laced with explosive racial and political connotations. In Sacramento, incoming governor Ronald Reagan wanted the game to be played with a heavy National Guard presence surrounding Spartan Stadium.[83] Campus officials and community groups balked at this proposal, fearing that a police presence would make matters worse. After Clark's announcement, Reagan charged him and other administrators with political "appeasement."[84] State Senator Clark L. Bradley (R–San Jose) wanted the attorney general's office to investigate and accused Clark of giving in to "coercion and blackmail."[85] Max Rafferty, the state superintendent of public instruction and ex-officio member of the California State University Board of Trustees, also said that Clark had submitted to "blackmail": "San Jose administrators should have been aware of any racial discrimination on campus long before last week's events and should have tried to solve the problem."[86]

Local residents wrote thousands of hate letters to both Clark and Edwards. Most wanted Clark either put on probation or fired for not taking a stand against, as one put it, "a handful of militant Negroes on your campus, [which] set a very bad example for your students of how an administration should act." Some suggested that he fire Edwards for blackmail. Clark lost the respect of many white taxpayers because, they said, he set himself up "as an easy target for future demands" from a handful of professors and students advocating what California State University Chancellor Glenn S. Dumke called in a report to the Board of Trustees "inexcusable violence and lawlessness."[87] As for

Edwards, his intelligence and character were attacked in a multitude of ways. The most reactionary letters came from San Jose State alumni who attended the college in the 1940s and '50s and lived in suburbs racially reserved for whites by redlining, Proposition 14, and discriminatory real estate practices. They wanted Edwards immediately discharged from either his tenure or tenure track appointment on San Jose State's faculty.[88]

Supporters of the cancellation included San Jose Mayor Ronald James, San Jose State faculty members, students of diverse backgrounds, University of Oregon administrators and faculty, and church leaders who approved of the way Clark handled race relations at his institution.[89] Many of the white supporters "admitted to the media that large-scale racial discrimination was widely practiced. Fraternity and sorority members at press conferences and meetings admitted that they discriminated against African Americans and asked for time to fix the problem."[90] Black students, including track star and UBSA member Lee Evans, informed the media that racism often manifested itself in the stereotypical presentation of black athletes as capable of fast running and long jumping but as unsuitable for such positions as coach or quarterback. He told a *Los Angeles Times* reporter, "Like all Negroes got rhythm and eat watermelon and chicken. You find a lot of [covert] discrimination here."[91] In an interview, sprinter Tommie Smith described feeling dehumanized because Coach Winter always referred to him as a world-class athlete, never as a man.[92] There were also voices of white resistance, with one defiant fraternity alumnus telling the media, "Yes, we discriminate. . . . We discriminate in favor of who we want to live with."[93]

The disagreement included the California State College Board of Trustees, which was sharply divided on how to investigate the issue. African American trustee Edward O. Lee wanted an outside investigator commissioned by the chancellor's office to look into the racial climate and institutional integrity at San Jose State, just as the chancellor's office had done at San Francisco State in 1966–1967. In the case of the latter school, the chancellor's office found the racial climate to be explosive because of the charge of reverse discrimination against white students in campus activities. Lee maintained that the atmosphere at San Jose State was similarly explosive. After hearing Lee, however, the board chose not to act, maintaining that President Clark had the situation under control.[94]

What they meant was that one day after the game's cancellation, Clark organized a weeklong public hearing to address San Jose State's racial climate. It was attended by faculty, administrators, and alumni. Edwards, representing the UBSA, attended two meetings, and according to Clark he "acted responsibly": there were "never any threats of violence on the part of students."[95] During the hearing, the main items addressed were the exploitation of black student athletes, fair campus housing, racism in the fraternity and sorority systems, and African American admissions. On fraternity and sorority discrimination, Edwards drew from his own experience and discussions with blacks around San Jose State and informed Clark of his findings. For Clark the most dramatic example involved Valerie Dickerson, a communications major and San Jose State's first black homecoming queen (in 1968), who was raised on military bases in remote areas with few African Americans. Hanging out with black students in their section of San Jose State's cafeteria was her first exposure to a concentration of African Americans her age. Further, she was raised to see people as individuals and not according to color. Clark goes on to state, "So when rush came from the sororities, some of her friends encouraged her to go for it. . . . And so she did. She was blackballed. It was a crushing experience for her." After hearing this story, Executive Vice President William J. Dusel cried.[96] The African American student who saw life through color-blind lenses was set on a path of further disappointments, disillusionments, and understandings of race in America. Though Dickerson was a staunch supporter of Dr. King's vision of an integrated America, she temporarily gave up that dream after his assassination in 1968. She saw King's destruction as

> the destruction of the last bridge between white and black society. Those black people who were sitting on the fence before have now been forced to take a stand. King's theory was the epitome of what white society called the answer to racial unrest. . . . For the first time in my life, I resented

everything white. It wasn't individuals, just whiteness. . . . The real American tragedy is that his death will never really be understood by white society.[97]

Within the hearing, one testimony after another informed the faculty, administrators, and alumni that race reforms were sorely needed at the campus if they were to prevent an environment of white privilege and black alienation of the sort that James Baldwin described in *The Fire Next Time*, anger and disillusionment sparking an urban uprising in Greater San Jose.[98] After listening to all sides, Clark, in an unprecedented move, read a decision recorded in a statement from the meetings to the UBSA for its members' reaction.[99] What all delegates to the hearing tacitly agreed to was that President Clark would give all twenty-seven fraternities and sororities until November 1 to produce an acceptable antidiscrimination plan that did not violate board policy; otherwise they would be placed on "probation because of alleged racial discrimination."[100] San Jose State officials agreed to make college and city officials take a public pledge that they would not engage in racist activities involving the school's students. Property owners who listed vacancies with the college were also warned about the school's new policies. According to Edwards and Clark, part of the agreement, not usually listed in newspaper articles, included instituting majors specifically defined as "non-discriminatory" and using the 2 percent rule to recruit full-time students of color, who would also automatically qualify for approved housing.[101] Beginning in fall 1968, these programs were strengthened by federal programs such as affirmative action and the Educational Opportunity Program.[102] Finally, the closed-door meeting produced an innovation—the appointment of an ombudsman, campus minister J. B. White, who would monitor and contain adverse racial activities.[103] After hearing this, the UBSA accepted the statement, and San Jose State became a model for student protest and institutional resolution promoting fairness for all parties. Several officers in the city police department told Clark of reports that some "sorority and fraternity houses were going to burn down the campus."[104] This never happened. After October 1967 the momentum for challenging the system for social justice and human rights

Dr. Harry Edwards and President Robert Clark at September Hearings on Race Relations at San Jose State (1967). Courtesy San Jose State University Archives.

snowballed—moving from the revolt of the black athlete to anti–Vietnam War activism and the establishment of formal diversity programs.

The politicization of the black student athlete at the college forged the beginnings of a sophisticated freedom rights movement. The success of the UBSA in getting campus administrators to commit to changing the campus climate and institutional racism went beyond its organizers, Edwards and Noel. The black students understood the circumstances confronting them on the predominantly white campus, and they supported the incipient organization in good numbers. The UBSA had tapped into the unique strength of San Jose State's African American community: its athletes and white people's addiction to seeing them perform. For Edwards, "The revolt of the black athlete in

America as the phrase of the overall black liberation movement is as legitimate as the sit-ins, the Freedom rides, or any other manifestation of Afro-American efforts to gain freedom."[105] The revolt became a national phenomenon. Edwards received letters from black student athletes at campuses all over the country with similar problems who wanted UBSA materials to help them to form their own organic movements. The letters came from "Iowa, Washington, Wyoming, Indiana, University of California, Oregon State. . . . Even at high-standing places like University of Oklahoma, black athletes began to say 'Hey, if they can change it at San Jose State, we can change it here.' San Jose State sparked the revolt of the black athlete."[106]

In between teaching classes, Edwards went on a lecture tour on which he encountered firsthand the deplorable conditions described in letters from student athletes. From this, UBSAs were formed throughout the nation, in particular in the Midwest, as organizational vehicles at campuses that lacked strong black student organizations. Where strong black organizations existed, such as the CORE and SNCC, those became the vehicles for organizing the revolt around the unique circumstances confronting black student-athletes and black students on their campuses.[107] Through affiliation with "Speed City" and with the Summer Olympics occurring in less than a year, UBSA leaders discovered what Edwards called an "interlocking directorate" between the U.S. Olympic Committee and the NCAA, in which "the same people responsible for what we were dealing with at NCAA Division I schools, were responsible for what we were seeing with regards to the Olympics."[108] For Edwards, it was a connection that had stared at him since 1964, when comedian and black activist Dick Gregory stood in front of an Olympic trial with a sign that said, "Why should we run in the Olympics and crawl at home?"[109] Edwards's epiphany included his estimate that 96 percent of U.S. Olympic athletes came from NCAA programs, from segregated southern schools like Tennessee State to predominantly white colleges and universities like San Jose State and the University of Southern California.[110] The typical treatment experienced by most black college athletes was that while they were cheered for performing on the field, once off the field they came home to joblessness and sometimes homelessness. And even if they were the few who had jobs to go to, Edwards said, they "came home to all of the challenges and problems that Negroes more generally in American society were suffering."[111]

In addition, similar to NCAA football, which had no African American as head coach of a Division I football team before Willie Jeffries at Wichita State in 1979, the Olympics Committee had no black coaches or committee members, even though there were many well-qualified and willing candidates, including Jesse Owens, Ralph Metcalf, and Mal Whitfield. The connection became crystal clear when revolt organizers factored in Coach Bud Winter, whom Edwards regarded as a "recycled exploiter and racist" and who had been sprint coach for the 1960 U.S. track team that included Ray Norton—the Good Brother who lived in a shed for six weeks. Winter was reappointed coach of the 1968 track team. The last straw came when Edwards, representing a newly formed Olympic Committee for Human Rights, challenged the U.S. Olympic Committee to put into place racial reforms like those being introduced into the colleges and universities.[112] The committee chairman, Avery Brundage, responded to this by asking why African Americans would challenge the Olympic Games or the U.S. Olympic Committee "when the only place that Negroes and Communists can stand on the same level with other human beings is in the Olympic Games?" Edwards then thought to himself, "Well I'll be damned, this is the same challenge."[113] Out of that realization emerged the structure of the Olympic Project for Human Rights, which would make challenging the U.S. Olympic Committee its top priority.

THE OLYMPIC PROJECT LAUNCHED its attack on the committee on November 23, 1967, Thanksgiving Day, following the Western Regional Black Youth Conference held at Second Baptist Church in South-Central Los Angeles, which galvanized a critical mass within the African American sports community around the project. In the Olympic Project's session at the conference, revolt leaders discussed their ideas on blacks in American sports with the fifty to sixty black athletes there.[114] Major amateur athletes who were staunch supporters of the revolt were Olympic Project committee members Tommie Smith,

Lee Evans, and UCLA basketball star Lew Alcindor (better known as Kareem Adbul Jabbar). Others included track and field athletes primarily at San Jose State and UCLA and UCLA football players, and the group claimed to have been in nearly unanimous support of the boycott of the upcoming Olympic Games.[115] Superstar professional athletes in support of the movement included the Boston Celtics' Bill Russell, Cleveland Browns' Jim Brown, and heavyweight champion boxer Muhammad Ali. Ali said he supported the revolt because he realized that "giving up a chance at the Olympics and a gold medal is a big sacrifice. But anything [they] do that's designed to get freedom and equality for [black] people, I'm with 1,000 percent."[116]

In February 1968, the revolt movement successfully boycotted the New York Athletic Club Indoor Track Classic at Madison Square Garden in February 1968.[117] Then the revolt challenged the International Olympic Committee for its reinstatement of South Africa into the Summer Olympic Games; in response to that nation's apartheid policies, a United Nations resolution in 1962 had barred South Africa from participating. The obvious link was the U.S. Olympic Committee's chair, Avery Brundage, who was also the president of the International Olympics Committee. Brundage thought of himself as a staunch advocate of politics' having no place in sports, yet he was a Nazi sympathizer who had fought against the boycott of the 1936 Munich Games while on the U.S. committee, and in 1968 it was he who led the effort to reinstate South Africa. Opposing this move were black athletes and freedom rights activists under the leadership of Edwards in the United States, and the thirty-two-nation Organization of African Unity. On May 28, they succeeded in pressuring the International Olympic Committee to ban South Africa from the Olympics by a vote of 47 to 16.[118] On the downside, after South Africa was banned from the Olympics most black athletes who qualified to participate in the Summer Olympics began having second thoughts about participating in a boycott, which led to its cancellation on September 1, 1968.[119]

The revolt became international news on October 16, 1968, after Tommie Smith won an Olympic gold medal and John Carlos won the bronze in the 200-meter race. Prior to the race the two men had secretly planned a nonviolent protest.[120] During the awards ceremony,

The Olympic Project for Human Rights, 1968. Courtesy Michelle Vignes Collection, Bancroft Library, University of California, Berkeley.

Smith and Carlos stepped onto the podium shoeless in black socks to signify African American poverty in the United States, and wore black scarves to symbolize black pride. As the national anthem played, they stood on the victory podium with eyes closed and heads bowed, each with a black-gloved fist raised in the air to form an arc that represented a cry for freedom in the form of black unity, social power, and social equity.[121] This display sent shock waves throughout the world. Edwards said, "The protest demonstration symbolized the courage, commitment, and the growing political sophistication of an entire generation of young black people."[122]

The next day, Smith and Carlos were suspended from the U.S. Olympic team and expelled from Olympic Village by the International Olympic Committee for deliberately and "violently" breaching "the fundamental principles of the Olympic spirit."[123]

In Santa Clara County, most people's first exposure to the revolt was watching the "silent gesture" of Smith and Carlos on television.[124] As stated in the *Palo Alto Times*, their action left many television viewers in the West Bay Area pondering "what their gesture meant

John Carlos and Tommie Smith with public artist Rigo 23's scale model of the commemorative statue at San Jose State University, 2003. Charles Alexander Collection.

and what brought it about."[125] In Greater San Jose, the public was very bitter toward Smith, Carlos, and Edwards. According to Clark, everyone within his administration was surprised by the intensity of the reaction, which was made much more controversial because of the sports commentaries of Howard Cosell and twenty-two-year-old Brent Musburger, who nationally made a name for himself after referring to Smith and Carlos as "black-skinned storm troopers."[126] The interpretations given by these commentators framed the characters of both men in the mainstream public, which in decades to follow resulted in death threats, poverty, and the suicide of Carlos's ex-wife in 1977.

In a show of support, Clark publicly defended Smith and Carlos with the statement: "They do not return home disgraced but as the honorable young men they are, dedicated to the cause of justice for black people in our society."[127] He then criticized the U.S. Olympic

Committee for its "'non-political' moralistic posture . . . which refused to allow our team to dip the American flag as a mark of respect to the host nation." Finally, the president "called for an understanding of the meaning of the bowed heads and the raised, gloved fists."[128] Academic Vice President Hobert Burns followed up on this statement, citing both the International and U.S. Olympic Committees for "smallness of mind [which] illustrated the very problem our black athletes find intolerable."[129]

Both Clark and Burns also expressed how proud they and San Jose State were of their Olympians, which were many.[130] At the time, San Jose State sent more athletes to the Olympics than any other college, and the athletes won more medals than athletes from any other college. Aside from John Carlos and Tommie Smith, athletes at the school who participated in the 1968 Olympics included Edward Burke, Tom Dooley, Lee Evans, Ronnie Ray Smith, Chris Papanicolaou (Greece).[131] According to San Jose State professor Steve Millner, who was a student there in fall 1968, the school erupted with pride. The San Jose NAACP organized its Thirteenth Annual Banquet around the theme "Black Youth on the Move," which honored Olympic medal winners Tommie Smith, John Carlos, Lee Evans, and Ronnie Ray Smith. The banquet was open to NAACP members and the general public. The keynote address was given by Julian Bond, one of the founders of SNCC and of the Southern Poverty Law Center who by then was serving in the Georgia House of Representatives. Only four whites attended: President Clark; his wife, Opal; and another couple.[132]

THE REVOLT OF THE BLACK ATHLETE made an enduring contribution to the achievement of the South Bay and America. For a brief period it united a fragmented social justice movement whose separate segments intersected and often competed with one another in Santa Clara County. Within Greater San Jose, the organizing of black student athletes spilled over into South Bay communities because revolt leaders worked closely with the Clark administration to resolve racism on campus. By reforming the fraternity and sorority systems, transforming closed housing into open housing, and creating spaces for black students to increase their population and to build institutions to make education welcoming to diverse populations, San Jose State created a climate that expanded into surrounding communities through black professionals who attended the school during the revolt years.

One such person was a San Francisco State transfer and Milpitas resident, Professor Charles "Mr." Murray. According to Professor Steve Millner, Mr. Murray was a unifier at San Jose State during the decline of the school's Black Power movement, which began after Edwards left San Jose State for Cornell to pursue a doctorate.[133] From 1968 to 1970, Murray played a critical role (along with Professor Leonard Jeffries of the City University of New York) in developing San Jose State's black studies program. After graduating from San Jose State, Mr. Murray, who was infused with Black Panther Party, Speed City, and UAW political expression, took his particular outlook to San Jose City College and the East Bay Area, where he taught and developed diversity programs and challenged people in the eastern part of the county to always be conscious of their needs and the needs of others. Other African Americans from the revolt era who influenced the South Bay were De Anza College Professor Ed Hunter (in Cupertino), Professor Millner (in East San Jose), and former San Jose NAACP president and educator T. J. Owens (in South San Jose and in Gilroy).[134]

Before the revolt, racial inequities restricted African Americans to the Northside, East Side, Milpitas, East Palo Alto, and San Jose State's athletic department. After September 18, 1967, the eastern part of the county, including San Jose State, opened doors more quickly to people of color. Housing and employment became fairer, ethnicity was explored through specific academic courses and as a natural byproduct of integration, the Chicano/a movement grew, the United Farm Worker movement grew, and jobs and coaching positions for African Americans opened up.[135]

Cass Jackson became the first African American to be the head coach of a high school football team in the Santa Clara County. He served at San Jose High School in 1969, when he was twenty-four

Dr. Charles "Mr." Murray after African American history course at San Jose City College, fall 1997. Herbert G. Ruffin II Collection.

years old. Three years later he became one of the first African American coaches to break the college-level color barrier while at Oberlin College (Division III), coaching outside of black conferences like the Southwestern Athletic Conference. Crucial to bringing him onboard were Harry Edwards's protégés, Athletic Director Jack Scott, and Assistant Athletic Director Tommie Smith.[136] Three years later, Jackson was hired to coach at Historically Black Colleges and Universities Morris Brown College (Division II), and he did so from 1975 to 1977.[137] In 1978, Jackson had the opportunity to further chip away at breaking the color barrier by working as an assistant coach under Bill Walsh at Stanford University, but he ended up declining the offer. In a conversation with Walsh, he disclosed that he had been offered a head coaching job at Southern University in the Southwestern Athletic Conference—the division where the legendary head coach Eddie Robinson worked at Grambling State University—and Walsh told Jackson that he did not get his first head coaching job until age forty-six in 1977 at Stanford. After this disclosure, both men, close friends, agreed that coaching at Southern University was the best option for Jackson, who was then twenty-seven years old. In Jackson's place, Walsh hired Dennis Green, an African American who would later coach in the National Football League at the Minnesota Vikings and at the Arizona Cardinals.[138]

How the differences in political tactics and in generations between the Good Brothers and Speed City came around full circle to unity, or *Sankofa*—looking back to the past as a guide to proceed forward in life—was that there was an interlocking directorate, between the Jackie Robinson–era athletes and Muhammad Ali–era athletes and civil rights movement–era activists and Black Power–era activists. The Charles Alexanders and Harry Edwardses of the world respected one another but had dramatically different approaches to black liberation because of their circumstances. In an ironic twist, it was a white man with a radically liberal vision on life and sports in Bill Walsh, an honorary Good Brother, in which the two eras, difficult to piece together in the turbulent 1960s, came together in the space of coaching and race relations from the late 1970s to 2000. Both sides were crucial to this development. Walsh knew that most of the Good Brothers were well qualified and had great character—they just needed the opportunity to prove that this was the case, similar to how Jackie Robinson simply needed access to professional sports in the locker room and on the baseball field to prove himself. Through long association with Edwards, Walsh acquired a sociology of sports consciousness, which led him to understand that African Americans' access on the field was not enough and that more work had to be done in the ranks of coaching, the front office, and in ownership if sports as a microcosm of American society was to be truly integrated and equal. With the help of Edwards and the legendary John Wooten—former Cleveland Brown offensive lineman and the second African American executive in NFL history—Walsh, then the San Francisco 49ers' head coach, created the NFL Minority Fellowship Program in 1987 to systematically give promising black coaches the opportunity to intern with

League teams "with the goal of preparing them for higher-level positions on his staff or elsewhere in the League."[139] The first coach hired under this program was Cincinnati Bengals head coach Marvin Lewis, who after interning with the Kansas City Chiefs and the San Francisco 49ers was hired as linebackers coach for the Pittsburgh Steelers in 1992, then crafting Super Bowl–caliber defenses for the Baltimore Ravens as that team's defensive coordinator. These opportunities led to Lewis's becoming the eighth African American to head coach in the NFL in 2003. Alums from the program include ESPN football analyst and NFL head coach Herman Edwards and former Indianapolis Colts head coach Tony Dungy—who regularly hired outreach alums in Indy as assistant coaches. Some of these became head coaches and coached perennial championship contenders, such as the Chicago Bears' Lovie Smith and the Pittsburgh Steelers' Mike Tomlin.[140]

As for San Jose State, the school went from having a fragmented nest of liberality to being nationally seen as a place of higher consciousness in which Black Power politics cross-pollinated with antiwar politics, Chicano politics, civil rights politics, and women rights politics. After the cancellation of the football game, the Black Panther Party became a consistent mainstay around the campus. The organization recruited students and nonstudents in the area with the intent to establish a San Jose chapter, establish survival programs, and join in the "Free Huey" movement to pressure law enforcement officials into releasing Black Panther Party cofounder Huey P. Newton from prison.[141] Black radicals ranging from Kwame Toure (aka Stokely Carmichael) to Angela Davis made the lecture rounds, traveling from San Francisco to Berkeley to Oakland and San Jose.

To a young black person such as Millner, San Jose State had a reputation for being a safe sanctuary where inner-city youth could get a quality education and freely express who they were. San Jose was also seen as a great place to get away from the urban uprisings taking place throughout the nation in the late 1960s, as was the case for Millner, who escaped from Los Angeles County to the more serene San Jose, excited and carrying "$85 and a lot of hope."[142] Similar to student athletes, many black students across America were aware of San Jose State because of what the revolt was able to accomplish, and

Charles Alexander and Dr. Harry Edwards, ca. 2008. Charles Alexander Collection.

many wanted to attend a school where African Americans were being integrated and empowered within the system.

The revolt set in motion the high-priority, systematic recruitment of students and faculty of color. In fall 1968, changes were already felt as two hundred African American students enrolled in San Jose State. Most were nonathletes who easily moved into approved housing. The year before, only seventy-two black students were enrolled. Increases in enrollment numbers continued well into the 1970s, and fifteen hundred African American students were enrolled by 1975. Following close behind were Mexican Americans, who in 1967–1968 comprised about fifty students. According to President Clark, they were interested in organizing their own movement but never got around to it, so they joined the black movement.[143] Through Equal Opportunity and English as a Second Language programs, the Mexican population rapidly increased and, in the 1970s, began competing with blacks for control of the Equal Opportunity Program. In the middle of this competition, Vietnamese refugees started enrolling at the school by the droves, drawn by English as a Second Language programs and cheap rental housing around the college, which they bought up as established locals were moving into the suburbs. Altogether, the increase in the black, brown, and yellow populations transformed San Jose State from a 90-plus percent white campus in 1967 to one of the most diverse universities in the United States by 1980. Within this transition, improved conditions for African American students reflected a positive change for a fragmented South Bay black community, and the revolt of the black athlete made a major contribution to the region as it transformed into the Silicon Valley in the post–civil rights era. Still, more work had to be done.

THE LOCAL CIVIL RIGHTS, fair housing, and black athlete movements revealed the inconsistencies in the Santa Clara Valley's dedication to racial equality and social justice. Beyond the revolt, African Americans were still visibly marginalized in South Bay affairs. On the one hand, the air of pessimism and insurgency in response to the ghettoization of the urban West and hardening of the postwar ghetto in the urban North were minor factors in late-blooming suburbanizing areas such as the South Bay. The closest episode to that effect was the workup to the San Jose State–University of Texas at El Paso football game at which a rebellion could have occurred in San Jose similar to the massive anti–Vietnam War demonstrations that broke out elsewhere in November 1967. On the other hand, the rarefied air of optimism in black urban America with population percentages around 10 percent in western cities like Seattle did not emerge in Santa Clara County, either; blacks constituted more than 2 percent of the overall population only after 1970. Moreover, blacks had little sway with the valley's white public in voting for racial liberal policies such as the California Fair Housing Act. Despite setbacks closely related to de facto racial discrimination, many African Americans learned from the freedom rights movement and the previous Great Migrations and extended the traditions of voting with their feet by going where they could achieve, in suburban communities previously off-limits to mass black migration. Their combined efforts paved the way for future African American generations in the valley to expand from 4,187 in 1960 to 56,211 in 1990 and to pursue the socioeconomic opportunities and equality withheld from them in the post–World War II central city. In essence, the history of the black Santa Clara Valley in the postwar period ushered in a new phase of African American history that revolved around intraregional and inner-city migration to the suburb, which is called the Third Great Migration.

Chapter Eight
The Third Great Migration
Black Suburbanization in Silicon Valley, 1968–1990

IN THE 1970s AND 1980s, THE BLACK population of Santa Clara County grew phenomenally, largely as a result of the enactment of the National Housing Act of 1968. Most of the black newcomers came from central cities in search of social fairness, professional opportunities, better education for their children, single-family housing, safe neighborhoods, and mild weather. In short, they sought entrance to a pleasant middle-class lifestyle. Demographic data indicate that on most of these scores they succeeded. From 1970 to 1990, blacks in this region were better integrated spatially and were more prosperous and educated than African Americans in many parts of the country. The median income for African American households in San Jose in 1990 was about $43,500 compared with $46,200 for the general population.[1] More than 34 percent of South Bay blacks earned at least $50,000,[2] whereas in California as a whole, only around 21 percent of the black population was doing so. And in 1990 around 23.5 percent of blacks were college graduates in the Santa Clara Valley, compared with 9 percent nationwide and 15 percent in California as a whole.

Thus by many standard markers of success in the United States, blacks in Santa Clara County were thriving. Many had a good job, a good education, a home in the suburbs—the prosperity that people identify with the American dream. But the original meaning of "the American dream" had as much to do with equal opportunity and fairness as it did with prosperity. It was this sense of the term that Dr. Martin Luther King, Jr., had in mind when in "Letter from a Birmingham Jail" he praised the young people involved in the sit-in movement as "standing up for what is best in the American dream."[3] No amount of demographic data about Santa Clara County blacks can gauge their success in this sense. Nor can the data reliably poll the usual markers of a fulfilling life, which by any reasonable measure include a sense of belonging and feelings of self-worth. For this kind of knowledge, one must look at the lived experience of blacks in the county: their everyday experience of successes and failures, freedoms and constraints, opportunities and obstacles, fairness and unfairness. This chapter addresses all those aspects as a model for understanding the black experience as the county transformed into Silicon Valley.

AFRICAN AMERICAN MIGRATION to the suburbs contributed to a demographic revolution within American communities called the Third Great Migration.[4] After the National Housing Act of 1968 was enacted, black suburban populations grew from 2.5 million people in 1960 to 11.9 million people by 2000, or from 13 percent to 34 percent of the national African American population.[5]

To many people in the post–civil rights era, notable black movement into the middle class and the suburbs symbolized America living up to its political creed that "all men are created equal."[6] In the South Bay this included most African Americans taking part in an ongoing freedom rights struggle (whether or not they saw it this way) by desegregating residential, educational, and employment spaces in pursuit of homeownership in middle-class, relatively low density communities while attempting to acquire comfortable incomes and professional occupations. During the first wave of contemporary suburban growth, from 1950 to 1970, this type of freedom would have been off-limits to most African Americans even if they could afford the house and had the right occupational pedigree. In the mid- to late 1960s, the passage of several civil rights laws set the tone for many African Americans anticipating the American dream before they came to the Santa Clara Valley. They, like most people who came to the region, saw the Silicon Valley as the latest example of the California gold rush. But like the gold rush of the nineteenth century, participation in the job market confronted most prospectors with mixed results. Many African Americans had middle-class aspirations and consciously looked to supplant

TABLE 8   African Americans in Santa Clara County, by City, 1970–2010

	1970	1980	1990	2000	2010
County population	18,090	43,716	56,211	47,182	46,428
Percentage increase	1.7	3.3	3.5	2.8	2.6
Campbell	45	311	741	964	1,158
Cupertino	49	247	399	347	344
Gilroy	27	137	296	745	942
Los Altos	97	22	81	130	148
Los Altos Hills	29	6	18	47	37
Los Gatos	38	108	116	226	269
Milpitas	1,411	2,715	2,946	2,295	1,969
Monte Soreno	2	0	0	6	14
Morgan Hill	13	213	407	573	746
Mountain View	674	2,221	3,382	1,789	1,629
Palo Alto	1,469	1,260	1,658	1,184	1,197
San Jose	10,955	28,792	36,397	31,349	30,242
Santa Clara	687	1,617	2,316	2,341	3,154
Saratoga	56	49	92	115	94
Sunnyvale	750	2,434	3,956	2,927	2,735

SOURCES: Metropolitan Transportation Commission (MTA) and the Association of Bay Area Governments (ABAG), *Bay Area Census: Santa Clara County; Cities in Santa Clara County, 1970–2010,* http://www.bayareacensus.ca.gov/counties/SantaClaraCounty70.htm; U.S. Bureau of the Census, *U.S. Census of Population and Housing: 1980 Census Tracts* (Washington, D.C.: Government Printing Office, 1983), 215; U.S. Bureau of the Census, *1990 Census of Population: General Population Characteristics, California* (Washington, D.C.: Government Printing Office, 1992).

race with class as the determinant of their life chances. By 1980, black flight, or the exodus of potential African American leaders and role models into the suburbs from central cities, hastened the gulf between the black middle class and the black working poor and was a major contributor to the post-1970 rise of the "underclass." With the loss of their middle class, the central cities became the home of perpetually poor populations who were getting poorer. Black business owners in many cases had moved out, taking jobs with them. So had many blacks whose educational and professional successes might have led others to aspire to the same.[7] When so many of the high-achieving people moved out, it was as if they had taken with them a piece of the neighborhood, and the people who were left behind had to deal with the loss as best they could. But what they likely didn't realize is that the loss cut both ways; the people who left the neighborhood would feel the loss, too. They went from being part of a black community to representing a black community everywhere they went.

THE SANTA CLARA COUNTY that blacks came to during the Third Great Migration was an area of rapid urban and high-tech industrial development, which in most areas was not noticeable until the late 1970s, when the South Bay became the computer and microelectronics capital of the United States. High-tech start-ups such as Apple Computer were able to make this so by relying more on venture capitalists to finance their companies than on the industry's military contracts and government purchases—which in the 1960s accounted for half of the semiconductor shipments but were in notable decline in the 1970s.[8] This became an important factor in the local electronics industry's ability to surpass Boston as the most important chip-, hardware-, and software-producing area in the world.[9]

Many South Bay towns gradually adopted what historian Richard White called the Palo Alto–Stanford University industrial park model of urban growth. After 1951, Palo Alto rapidly transformed its rural acreage into neatly zoned industrial parks, strip malls, and single-family subdivisions. Key to this model was that unlike traditional bedroom communities whose residents lived in the suburbs and worked in the central city, by the late 1970s the high-tech suburb had its own economy and was retaining its workers. From this model emerged the Silicon Valley's version of postsuburbia.[10] By the mid-1990s, most of San Jose and the Santa Clara County became engulfed by this development, and soon the county had the largest population in the Bay Area and the fourth-largest population in California (behind Los Angeles, San Diego, and Orange Counties).[11] As recognition of this and the fact that top technology firms were moving their headquarters to San Jose, city and county officials began advertising San Jose as the "capital of Silicon Valley," even though most suburbanites in West Santa Clara County did not acknowledge San Jose as the capital of the region and saw their cities as independent towns traditionally linked to San Francisco.[12] With the rise of Silicon Valley, the South Bay emerged as one of the fastest-growing regions in the United States. Its population grew from less than 650,000 in 1960 to almost 1.5 million in 1990. In that stretch of time, most urban populations in the country went into notable decline, and more than half of all Americans lived in suburbs for the first time in American history.[13] In San Jose, even though only 27 percent of its population lived in suburbs physically adjacent to the city such as Cupertino, Milpitas, and Santa Clara, most of its population lived in suburbs within the city limits, or in "inburbs."

The phenomenal growth caught most people in the South Bay by surprise. Prior to the 1970s, the region was still physically marked by apricot and cherry orchards, canneries, old farms, ranches, and sleepy towns, according to Stanford historian and Bay Area native Gordon Chang. What stood out for him was that there was very little ethnic diversity, in particular Asian Americans, who since the 1990s have had a dominant presence in both the South Bay and Bay Area.[14] Mountain View resident Albert Jones said that the region's phenomenal physical transformation did not occur until 1977—a period that loosely aligns with the testimony of most observers who migrated to the region within five years.[15] Other natives, such as Cass Jackson, say the Santa Clara Valley grew exponentially from 1972 to 1980, which was the period he was gone from the area to coach college football teams. It had changed so much, in fact, that when he came back to the region he felt out of place because he did not physically recognize Santa Clara

County. But as much as the landscape had changed, other components did not, such as blacks being scattered and having a weak sense of black community, which he experienced in the 1950s and 1960s, when blacks started leaving clustered communities in the Northside for the suburbanizing East San Jose.[16]

I EXPERIENCED THIS WEAK sense of African American community and strong sense of social isolation in the South Bay when, in 1979, my parents, Herbert and Sadie Ruffin, moved our family into Milpitas. At the time, they were in the forefront of an intraregional movement from East Palo Alto. Unknowingly they gained access to the city's white and affluent side, around Lake Victoria Drive in the southeast section, after purchasing a single-family tract home through Robert Jackson, a real estate agent and distant relative. Jackson was desegregating this and similar areas by selling homes to qualified black and brown families throughout East County in places like San Jose's Piedmont Hills and East Foot Hills. My parents bought our house for about $100,000, and its value increased fourfold in fifteen years. The neighbors on the block were almost all middle-class white families in which the man worked a professional job and the woman was a homemaker. This family economic structure changed for new homeowners moving into the region after 1980. They had to have at least two household incomes to keep up with the ever-increasing cost of living. The young people I and my siblings associated with were a diverse crowd of whites, Asian Americans, Mexican Americans, and a small group of blacks. My initial response to this arrangement was culture shock and self-isolation, in large part because of my segregated upbringing in East Palo Alto. In the 1970s, as the South Bay was transforming into Silicon Valley, East Palo Alto was black and underdeveloped, and local Black Power activists were pushing for the town to be incorporated as "Little Nairobi."[17] The only whites who lived in East Palo Alto were those who could not afford to move to newly incorporating cities in neighboring Santa Clara and San Mateo Counties, and those who were married to blacks or who were taking a stand against white flight, such as several friends of Palo Alto activist Ralph Libby.[18]

In Milpitas, the Ruffins went from being part of a black community to representing that community almost everywhere they went. This interpretation somewhat contradicted the perspective of Cass Jackson, who saw Milpitas as having a strong black presence in comparison with San Jose, where he grew up.[19] However, by 1970 the UAW population that anchored Sunnyhills were getting older, passing away, and retiring or moving on to high senior positions at UAW International in Detroit, as was the case of Mayor Ben Gross after 1972.[20] The Ruffins had come to Milpitas for the same reason many of the Third Great Migration migrants came to California: they wanted their children raised in a safe, diverse, and drug-free neighborhood where the family could amass net worth through home equity and have access to good public schools. The trade-offs for these advantages were traffic, overcrowding, and a community that did not understand blackness. They had to create new meanings of community. I found my voice from 1988 to 1996 as an underground hip-hop performer and producer.[21]

Charles Gary found his voice in school administration. Charles's family came to Milpitas in 1960 from Richmond, California, to give him, then a teenager, a better education and better life opportunities. Richmond was a segregated city with a strong black culture in its northern side. In 1959, school district officials shocked Charles's parents with the news that "he will be working with his hands" and that his prospects for college were low. His mother responded, "He needs to work with his head." When ask to test his abilities, the school district declined; essentially it wrote him off. Recent black migrants to Milpitas told the Garys that the town had a racially liberal environment and that their son would have a better opportunity to excel there. After contemplating, the Garys moved into Sunnyhills tract #2 as part of a second wave of African American migration, whose distinction was that most were not affiliated with Local 560. They were pioneers migrating into the South Bay for other purposes.[22]

At Ayer High School, Charles was tested and qualified for college-prep classes. Similar to me, he felt like a minority for the first time in his life as he had to rapidly learn new cultures while associating with his small circle of black friends. As the only black student

Milpitas High School principal Charles Gary with student. Courtesy *Milpitas Post*.

in most college-prep classes or in student government, Charles was determined to be at his best. He understood that he was "a representative, and I came from some place, and there were certain expectations around what people expected of me because of my skin color." Ultimately he succeeded and became the first black vice principal (at Milpitas High, 1976), junior high principal (at Rancho Junior High, 1981), and high school principal (at Milpitas High, 1988) in Santa Clara County. Charles came of age during the Black Power years at Sacramento State College, and he understood clearly that his path was different from that of the white people who were encouraging him to succeed, such as the clergy at Sunnyhills United Methodist Church, Ayer principal Leo Murphy, and future Milpitas mayors Danny Weisberger and Joe House.[23] Central to the "black suburban spirit" that was crucial to people like Charles was black empowerment, driving a firm belief in fair opportunity, dignity, and respect of self and others. In addition, Charles, like most blacks who excelled after 1970, knew that "not only did I have to work twice as hard to succeed, but I also had to learn who [white people] were, and learn how to motivate them to care about me and my success."[24]

WHETHER THEY HAD LEFT RICHMOND, central cities in other parts of the country, East Palo Alto, or the Northside of San Jose, blacks almost invariably felt a sense of loss in the move to suburban California and its advantages. According to San Jose NAACP president, Tee Sweet, in the 1980s African Americans new to the area "might go two or three days without running into another black."[25] Irene and Ray Hardy, who came to San Jose from Paterson, New Jersey, in 1969 because "San Jose lacked skyscrapers, hard-core slums, and industrial pollution"[26] back then, quickly discovered that the city also lacked an identifiable black community. In the 1970s, Irene said, she sometimes went a month "without seeing any [other] black people. . . . It got to the point that whenever I saw another black person in a grocery store, I would go up and introduce myself."[27] For many South Bay blacks, this isolation led to feelings of seclusion and job burnout, because many people who came to the valley seeking economic freedom spent so much time working and socializing in the white professional world that they became disconnected from their own cultural identities. Family counselor Joseph Gill summed up the situation best as working and making money to "compensate for the lack of community. . . . Lots of blacks make the mistake of thinking that getting ahead means getting away from being who you are."[28]

The social isolation that blacks felt was rooted not in just being around a lot of white people much of the time, but in their having to learn new ethnic cultures and in having a hard time identifying definable ethnic markers such as churches, soul-food restaurants, and stores that said to new migrants "this is the black community." The exception to this for a long time was the Northside, but by the 1970s it was deteriorating, and its black population had been gradually declining since 1950. Rather than the black neighborhoods they were accustomed to, newcomers had to search out new places for community, such as clustered communities throughout East County where black families lived within close proximity of one another, businesses like

Giants barbershop, programs in local institutions such as black studies departments at San Jose State University and Stanford University, and interest-oriented groups such as the middle-class and gender-oriented 100 Black Men of Silicon Valley and the San Jose chapter of The Links Incorporated. African Americans who came to the area from places that were densely black had to adjust to a geographically fragmented community.

Many of the newcomers, especially black southerners, also had to get used to a new style of racism, one subtler and superficially kindlier than they were used to but perhaps more hurtful precisely because of that.

Several studies in the late 1970s and early 1980s have charted racism in the Santa Clara County housing market. Most of these studies focused on the rental market because most African Americans by the late 1970s were becoming renters. The most notable investigation was conducted in 1977 by *San Jose Mercury News* reporters Calvin Stovall and Bob Goligoski. Stovall was a black man from the South. His parents and grandparents pushed him to go to college to broaden his employment opportunities and life options. When he came to the Santa Clara Valley in 1973, he had lived in Arkansas, Mississippi, and Alabama, and he believed what he had been told back home about California: that people there don't judge other human beings by their race. This perspective changed for Stovall during his and Goligoski's research, the topic of which was racial discrimination in rental housing in the Santa Clara Valley.[29]

At first Stovall took the assignment lightly. That lasted until the first day he got on the streets and actually started reporting. The first landlord he approached politely declined to rent to him, saying that there were no vacancies. The same landlord, however, politely offered to rent an apartment to Goligoski, a white man, when he inquired about rentals thirty minutes later. This sort of switch went on throughout Stovall and Goligoski's reporting. Of the thirty-four apartments surveyed, thirteen landlords "politely" declined to rent to Stovall but rented to Goligoski. The excuse usually given to Stovall was that "there was a long 'waiting list,' and no apartments would be vacant soon."[30] By the end of the reporting, Stovall no longer felt casual about the assignment.

> Suddenly, I saw the California apartment managers who discriminate as Southerners in disguise.... I realized that I preferred the direct discrimination I have faced for years in the South where whites told you if they didn't like you. I would rather have some of the managers call me a dirty nigger, and tell me they didn't rent apartments to darkies.... Even those racial slurs would not have hurt as much as the subtle lies.... The racial slurs at least let me know who my friends were.[31]

The newspaper report stunned the Santa Clara region and set a precedent for subsequent surveys that found housing discrimination in apartment rentals to be widespread throughout the county up to 1990. Similar to Stovall, other black researchers such as Marvin Conley, a member of the San Jose Human Relations Commission, were furious. Conley said he was "ready to buy torches and start burning things" after several landlords turned him down and later offered rentals to white members of the commission.[32] The commission estimated that discrimination existed in 27 percent of leased apartments in San Jose. The discrimination didn't always mean barring someone from a rental; one white participant was told by an apartment manager "that she raises the rent when black persons inquire about apartments in order to keep black people out of her apartment."[33]

Local governments usually responded to these surveys with indifference or superficial concern. The most notable example occurred in 1982 when the Mid-Peninsula Citizens for Fair Housing surveyed and concluded that African Americans had a much harder time renting apartments in Sunnyvale than did any other group of people. City officials such as City Councilman Larry Stone, by then embarrassed by more than a decade of complaints about unfair housing, went through the motions of developing a program that addressed housing discrimination. After several months of half-hearted effort, Sunnyvale abruptly dropped its plan to write a fair housing law, saying that federal and state laws were sufficient and that the city could better assist through "enforcement mechanisms" such as seminars and mailings to discourage discriminatory behavior. Marcia Fein, part of the complaining group, addressed Sunnyvale's resolution as typical of what was happening nationwide. She was shocked, however, by how many people thought "because we have fair housing laws that the problem is solved."[34]

Although the enactment of state and federal fair housing laws had sparked the Third Great Migration, they were politically compromised and weakly enforced until the implementation of the National Housing Act of 1988. This law broadened the scope of fair housing coverage, gave HUD direct enforcement powers, and empowered administrative law judges to render judgment in unfair housing court cases.[35] Prior to the National Housing Act of 1988, enforcement and investigation on both the state and national levels were hampered by a lack of enforcement powers. This put the responsibility for enforcement on the private citizen, who assumed the cost of litigation in cases, which in some instances could last for several years. California fair housing law under the Rumford Act was just as ineffectual. During the 1970s–1980s, the law needed badly to be rewritten to fit the times and to omit the Proposition 14 compromises of the 1960s. Instead, as Dennis Keating writes in *The Suburban Racial Dilemma*, "Crowded dockets and less flexibility in the law [made] recourse to the Supreme Court, under California's Rumford Act . . . less attractive" to victims of housing discrimination.[36] Complainants usually bypassed government agencies and pursued lawsuits if they could afford to do so.

THE BEST WAY FOR BLACKS to avoid housing discrimination in the South Bay was to become homeowners. According to a 1979 HUD report, blacks stood a greater risk of being discriminated against in the rental market (85 percent) than in the homeownership market (48 percent).[37] Prior to the late 1970s, determination, rent discrimination, and the scarcity of rentals were the top contributing factors as to why more than 66 percent of African American families in Silicon Valley were homeowners.[38] Unlike the urban or suburban spaces that blacks moved into in other parts of the United States, the homes that Silicon Valley blacks moved into were relatively new (built from 1960 to 1980) in one of the youngest and fastest-urbanizing regions in America.[39] After 1970, home buying by African Americans depended on the national and local economies, public policy, and fair housing practices. In the 1980s, for example, black suburbanites were especially affected by the stagnation of the local housing market during economic recessions. Home buying by African Americans slumped in 1980–1984 and 1989–1990, whereas it increased by 66 percent in 1985–1988.[40] Still, by 1990 black homeownership had slipped to slightly less than a third of South Bay blacks in an increasingly expensive Silicon Valley. The median value of a home rose from $23,400 in 1970 to $107,700 in 1980 to $289,400 in 1990, and was exceeded only by prices in San Francisco County, the most expensive place in the United States.[41]

The ramifications of housing inflation over the decades has arguably made cost more of an inhibiting factor than race for blacks to live in most parts of the South Bay. And the decrease of homeownership has long-term effects on racial imbalances and on African Americans' chances to better themselves financially. Consider that although 66 percent of black households were homeowners before the late 1970s, that same percentage was renting housing by 1990, which means they were accumulating no land wealth, whereas 79 percent of whites (76 percent of the population) were homeowners earning equity and expanding their life chances.[42]

Traditionally, Silicon Valley blacks lived in the Northside of San Jose, East San Jose (after 1950), Northwest Milpitas (after 1957), downtown Palo Alto (in the 1920s), and unincorporated East Palo Alto (after 1950). During the Third Great Migration, much of this pattern held, but some African American households dispersed into most communities in the region. This included sprinkles of black people in formerly restricted communities in the very expensive and very white Mid-Peninsula area (i.e., Los Altos, Los Gatos, and Saratoga).[43] From 1970 to 1990, most Santa Clara County blacks lived in diverse lower-middle-class and working-class communities in East San Jose, but sizable numbers resided in middle-class communities in Milpitas,

Mountain View, Palo Alto, Santa Clara, and Sunnyvale.[44] In some of the richer communities, however, entrée was difficult for black people, even the most prominent ones.

In 1990, LaDoris Cordell, a Santa Clara County Superior Court judge, was looking to buy a home in Palo Alto. Or at least she was trying to look. "I became very frustrated because the racism was just so blatant," she said.

> I remember one instance I went to a home where a "For Sale" sign was up, and the person who answered the door was either a manager and/or a tenant, and I was told, immediately, that there was nothing available. And, of course, I checked, and it was actually available, and I went right back and confronted her. . . . I went into the house and was followed by the Realtor. She followed me everywhere, upstairs and downstairs. It was an open house, and there were a lot of other people there. The Realtor inquired what I was doing there and told me that this house was not for rent, it was for sale. The assumption was that I could not have been interested in buying a house. [This behavior] was a shock to me because I was in Palo Alto, and I'm thinking, "This is a somewhat enlightened city."[45]

A KEY GOAL OF MANY PARENTS who were part of the Third Great Migration was to secure a good education for their children. But in many cases, through no fault of their own, this didn't happen. Although California had a stellar public education system before 1970, academic gains plummeted in the 1980s, and in the 1990s California ranked among the bottom ten states in subjects such as math, reading, and science. The education that African American children received was a major factor in that decline. According to Kati Haycock, director of The Education Trust, "The data are deeply troubling. [They] suggest that [California's] educational system is so riddled with inequities, that we actually exacerbate the effects of race and poverty rather than ameliorate them."[46] The lowest-ranking districts in the county were Alum Rock, East Side, Luther Burbank, and San Jose Unified. What these districts had in common was that they were in working-poor communities, had high student-of-color enrollments, and had high student turnover. Their students stood far greater risk of facing problems with drugs, violence, and police harassment than did their South District and West County counterparts.[47] And they were at far greater risk of being utterly unprepared for jobs in the new economy being forged in Silicon Valley.

According to Maurice Hardeman, the first African American municipal court judge in Santa Clara County, "the biggest area of racial change" in the region from 1960 to 1980 was in employment opportunities for blacks.[48] Crucial to this process were civil rights legislation during the 1960s, the selective picketing of stores and businesses, and the revolt of the black athlete, all of which softened the local color line by opening unskilled and entry-level jobs to people of color. Hardeman recalled that prior to the 1970s, "There were no blacks [working] in department stores, the telephone or gas company."[49] The Reverend C. W. Washington of San Jose's Antioch Baptist Church, who came to the area in 1946, has similar memories. "There were no blacks working in any major grocery store or department stores or in municipal government, or in banks or hospitals . . . not even janitors."[50] By the 1970s, blacks were accessing these jobs. By 1980, however, most living-wage jobs being created in Silicon Valley were in highly specialized positions in the information and high-tech sector, which had very few training programs. Specialized skills were expected at the outset. As a result, unskilled and entry-level positions were in sharp decline in a rapidly changing economy that took many working- and lower-middle-class residents by surprise.[51] This change fundamentally altered both the region's economy and its urban space. It changed the type of people who could afford to live in Silicon Valley after the 1980s.

After the 1980s, the South Bay and San Francisco Bay Area became a magnet for educated people with technical skills. In 1992, U.S. Census Bureau chief Roderick Harrison called this mass movement of labor "selective migration, particularly for Santa Clara County," which

TABLE 9 Median Owner-Occupied Home Prices, by County, 1980–1990

	1980	1990	% increase
Alameda	$84,900	$227,200	168
Contra Costa	94,300	219,400	133
Los Angeles	87,400	226,400	159
Orange	106,800	252,700	137
Riverside	67,300	139,100	107
Sacramento	63,300	129,800	105
San Bernardino	63,000	129,200	105
San Diego	90,000	186,700	107
San Francisco	103,900	298,900	188
Santa Clara	107,700	289,400	169

SOURCE: County of Santa Clara, Advance Planning Office, "Home Prices: California's Largest Counties, 1980–1990," Issue 92-5.

was "attracting people from elsewhere in the country and even around the world."[52] The abundance of jobs kept South Bay residents working in the valley and attracted many workers from neighboring Alameda, San Mateo, and Santa Cruz Counties.

The valley's shift to an information age economy fundamentally altered the region, and the changes affected the black population especially. Though some African American workers were highly skilled and educated and had more annual income than their counterparts elsewhere, there were more un- and underemployed Silicon Valley blacks living paycheck to paycheck and barely surviving on credit cards, payday advance loans, unemployment insurance, and welfare.[53] Even by 1980 the economic gap in the South Bay black community was notably widening, according to Bob Watson, the assistant director of the County Welfare Recipients League, including the steady deterioration of the lower black middle class, who occupied jobs predominantly in the older manufacturing and service economies.[54]

Traditional patterns of African American underrepresentation exacerbated in high-tech occupations and in such professions as accounting and law. In 1988, African Americans were among the most unrepresented people in professional occupations within the high-tech industry. Much of this discrepancy was rooted in education and the hiring practices of an industry enormously dominated by white men. In higher education, African Americans made up less than 5 percent of engineering undergraduates, and in graduate school only 2 percent.[55] According to David Reyes-Guerra, the director of the Accreditation Board in Engineering and Technology, when "large companies hire blacks and other minority engineering students for entry-level engineering jobs, they move them out of engineering and into supervisory positions."[56] This prospect has been discouraging for many prospective high-tech professionals of color. Even more dispiriting was the change in who hired engineers. Prior to 1988, the federal government was reputed to be a fairly decent employer for the few qualified engineers of color. This dramatically changed during the Reagan administration, which promoted an ultraconservative free-market economy dominated by privatization, deregulation, low taxation on corporations and wealthy Americans, increased military spending, diminished welfare programs, and the encouragement of high-risk business practices designed to maximize the wealth of a few individuals, which theoretically would in turn trickle down to working Americans (aka Reaganomics).[57] In the high-tech industry, this economy dramatically transferred engineering jobs and hiring duties to private subcontractors, who were more overt in their discriminatory practices. The ramifications of extreme privatization and deregulation ensured that very few African Americans had the opportunity to affect the high-tech industry because they lacked access to engineering and programming jobs. The blacks who have had a notable influence in the high-tech industry have been those in executive positions, and they have filled these jobs only since 1995, when Michael Sears became the director of group marketing and chief of staff for the president of SunSoft, Sun Microsystems' software division. His counterparts were few: Howard Smith, who became the CEO and president of Clarity Software in 1997, and John W. Thompson, who became the CEO of Symantec Corporation in 1999.[58]

THE SIMPLEST WAY FOR Silicon Valley blacks to succeed financially during the Third Great Migration was to operate their own businesses. During the 1970s and early 1980s, black-owned businesses flourished in the United States, with California leading this trend. In the Santa Clara Valley, the number of black-owned businesses doubled from 711 in 1977 to 1,575 in 1982. Based on the percentage increase and population size, Silicon Valley had more dynamic black business growth than San Mateo, Monterey, Contra Costa, and Alameda Counties.[59] Crucial to this growth were the South Bay's economic and urban expansion, black population growth, and affirmative action programs. These businesses ranged from retail outlets, restaurants, and beauty shops to nonprofit agencies providing community services. After 1982, however, black businesses in the valley found it hard to survive. They often declined during the economic recessions of the early and late 1980s and climbed during brief economic recovery periods in between.

Black business instability in the South Bay sometimes occurred because of inexperience and disorganization. In some cases, the targeted populations the businesses were meant to serve were too small. Sometimes there was no target population, however, and the businesses just happened to be run by a black person. Such was the case with Herbert Ruffin, my father, who made and sold barbecues (Herb-B-Ques), steamer-smokers, and rotisseries out of his welding shop, the Magic Arc, in East Palo Alto. Ruffin, a native of New Berlin, Texas (near San Antonio), settled in the Bay Area in 1968 after serving in the U.S. Air Force, where he had been stationed in northern California. His targeted clientele were, as was the case with most South Bay black businesses, whoever could afford what he was selling, which ranged in price from several hundred dollars to $20,000 in the case of a large

National Parks and Services order. Before his retirement from Stanford University as a carpenter and welder, Ruffin's business was a part-time endeavor and was financially supplemented by his full-time job.[60]

Unlike Ruffin's business, most Third Great Migration–era black businesses in the South Bay were not supplemented by full-time jobs, however, and most were financially unstable because of insufficient capital. Discrimination in federal and private lending contributed to that insufficiency. In the 1980s and 1990s, African Americans in California received a small share of Small Business Administration loans, but a disproportionate amount went to European Americans and, after 1990, Asian Americans. A study by the California Reinvestment Committee in San Francisco examined Small Business Administration data from 1990 to 1992. Its findings quantified what people of color seeking small business loans already knew: that the agency's loans disproportionately went to whites, who comprised 57.2 percent of California's population but had obtained 70.5 percent of the loans. In the same period, African Americans received only 1.9 percent of Small Business Administration loans, even though they represented 7 percent of California's population.[61] Nationally this percentage was even worse. In 1990, 88 percent of all SBA loans went to white entrepreneurs.[62] Essentially this practice betrayed the agency's 1953 federal mandate of helping people get into business and stay in business. Instead of using federal loan guarantees to funnel dollars to qualified businesses that needed assistance the most, the loans primarily went to white-owned enterprises that, in many cases, would have qualified for traditional loans.

DURING THE THIRD GREAT MIGRATION, South Bay police officers notoriously harassed African Americans, especially in working-poor communities and when the people from those places drove through white affluent neighborhoods.[63] Police harassment, police brutality, and racial profiling increased with the valley's growth and escalating population of color. This was especially true in the 1980s as race, class, and cultural strife became national phenomena undermining liberal political and economic gains achieved since the New Deal and civil rights eras. The growing divisions between black and white, rich and poor, urban and suburban played themselves out in America's streets in altercations between police officers and the citizens they were assigned to protect and serve.

In San Jose during the 1970s and 1980s, the city police department had a notorious reputation among local blacks for, as attorney Constance Carpenter once stated, "harass[ing] anybody who doesn't look like a Saratoga housewife."[64] In the 1980s, this earned San Jose the reputation of having one of the worst police harassment records in the country. Police Chief Joseph McNamara said that he had seen an increase in violence, strife, and subtle forms of racism between the local police and black residents since 1976, which was the year he took the job. San Jose's black population, which was 5 percent of the total population in the late 1980s, was disproportionately arrested (at 13 percent), while an even more disproportionate 16 percent were suspected of crimes, and 6 percent were victims of crime.[65]

In the South Bay, police brutality reached its apex in 1987, when San Jose police officers murdered Anton Ward in his backyard for carrying a concealed weapon. The officers where quickly exonerated by a grand jury.[66] Two months after killing Ward, city police officers reportedly beat up at least three black men—at the time, the few victims to report such maltreatment. One of the men, Jerry Stevens, was beaten senseless while being arrested. When he reported the incident, his right eye was swollen nearly shut, and his face was puffy. Incidents such as these stretch back to at least 1972, when black motorist John Henry Smith was shot to death by three San Jose police officers.[67]

Nate Newman, an investigator for the San Jose District Attorney's Office, said that local police "overreact to black people."[68] Blacks in the city would agree. Shawn Luten, a well-groomed and well-spoken young black man, said that police have always harassed him, especially around the East San Jose apartment complex where he was raised.[69] Unsure about the area's subtle color line, Luten questioned some of the many instances of being followed, stopped, and questioned by San Jose police officers that felt like harassment: "I may be overdramatizing the situation. . . . I don't know. But it seems like any time there's a group of blacks that get together for a reason, they are somehow 'gang-affiliated.'"[70] In one instance, patrol officers strip-searched Luten in public, forcing him to drop his pants, saying they were looking for drugs on a suspected user or dealer.

According to white police officer Bruce Unger, who patrolled the Eastside in the 1980s, police officers normally made random stops of suspected drug users as an effort to reduce drug use and clean up the Eastside's streets. The reporter interviewing Unger on several patrols saw that almost all the people Unger stopped were Mexican American or black. In one instance, Unger created a situation in which it appeared that an African American woman who was pulled over was on drugs when answering him. She in fact was shocked and terrified. During these "random" stops, Unger commonly profiled his suspects with such questions as: "Are you on probation?" "When was the last time you were arrested?" "If so, what for?" "Do you have a gun?" "What's your name?" "Where do you live?" This behavior extended to the police randomly crashing parties at private homes. By the mid-1990s, police misconduct was so bad for young people of color that James A. Hudson, De Anza College's student body vice president, said that when he was in a car with a group of friends, they always expected the police to pull them over.[71]

Police misconduct was a major issue in the valley in large part because very few police officers were black. Since Inez Jackson in the 1950s, blacks have pressed South Bay police departments to increase the black presence on the local police forces. The first victory occurred in 1951, when the police department added Northsider Francis Tanner as traffic officer. Thirty-six years later (1987), the black presence on the police force had increased to thirty-one officers—by far the most in any South Bay police force. Seven years after that (1994), fifty-four African Americans were San Jose police officers on a force of twelve hundred. According to experts, this presence is minuscule and would have to increase at least 2.5 times for tensions in the black population to noticeably reduce.[72]

For black San Jose Police Sergeant Don Black, a large part of the police department's harassment of people of color was related to San

Jose's aspirations to be a big city but not becoming one because its people were not as cosmopolitan or as urban as they and city promoters presented them to be. In fact, he found San Jose to be

> closed, extremely cliquish, and unbelievably racist, but it's that subtle underhanded racism, not the kind that you would face if you were in the South, or that you would face in places like Boston or Chicago or New York. It's very, very disturbing and I think because there is a covert kind of racism people get deluded into really believing that they're about something. But there's nothing happening here for black folks.[73]

Customary discrimination occurred even in such simple everyday situations as shopping. Blacks were disproportionately placed under unwarranted surveillance by retailers and the private security officers they employed. In the South Bay, this situation was especially onerous in predominantly white, affluent communities in West County such as Palo Alto, where the prevailing assumption seemed to be that blacks did not belong there and were pathologically criminal. Similar to thousands of other South Bay blacks, Judge LaDoris Cordell and San Jose city councilwoman Alice Woody expected to be followed in retail stores, with the caveat that "people aren't as blatant as they used to be" when "Whites Only" signs were all over West County prior to 1970.[74] The situation was so bad for Cordell that she stopped shopping in retail stores in the early 1990s.

In East County, racial discrimination was just as rampant. Charles Gary's son's best friend was white, and both of the young men found out the hard way how differently black and white people can be treated. In Milpitas, many people said that the two boys, who grew up together, related to each other as if they were twins. As employees of Mervyns department store, they made the same wages and had similar credit scores. Their first notable brush with differences in treatment came around 1990, when both young men applied for credit cards. Gary's son was given a credit limit of $300, whereas his friend was given a credit limit of $1,000. Around this same time the "twins" went to Marriott Great America (in Santa Clara) wearing identical jackets.

Gary's son was denied entry because the park's employees and security guards said that he was wearing gang attire, whereas the best friend went in with no problem.[75]

Perhaps the most infamous incident of racial discrimination to confront South Bay blacks during the Third Great Migration occurred on December 31, 1991, at a Denny's restaurant on Blossom Hill Road in South San Jose. Following an annual Christmas party at the home of Black College tour guide Carl Ray, eighteen prospective college students from San Jose stopped at Denny's for a late-night meal. Before they were admitted, they were ordered to pay a cover charge and to pay for their meals before being served. The young people filed suit and talked to news reporters. In 1993 they joined a class-action suit after six African American Secret Service agents guarding President Clinton were refused service at a Denny's in Annapolis, Maryland. Soon after, a landslide of complaints bombarded the restaurant chain. Embarrassed, Denny's paid $54 million to 295,000 aggrieved customers and their lawyers, and the company was ordered to publicize its new nondiscriminatory policies and to train its employees in diversity issues. The restaurant chain was under scrutiny for seven subsequent years to investigate further claims of discrimination.[76] San Jose resident Reginald Braddock, a Tuskegee University alumnus and former civil rights activist in Selma and Montgomery, said, "Blacks have tried so hard to make everything OK for their children, to make them safe. Having achieved a certain level of middle-class comfort, we got complacent."[77] For his son Rodney, who later became a Tuskegee University student with double majors in aerospace and mechanical engineering, complacency was wiped away that December night at Denny's on Blossom Hill Road in San Jose. He was there.

Around the mid-1990s, Silicon Valley engulfed most of the South Bay and San Francisco Bay Area, just as the Third Great Migration peaked. During this massive transformation, the South Bay started challenging San Francisco for the crown of which county was the most unaffordable U.S. area in which to live.[78] At the same time this light-speed urban and industrial growth was taking place, San Jose developed a weak urban character. This has played a big role in why many Bay Area blacks who work in the South Bay live in and around San Francisco or Oakland. For African American residents like Alissa Owens, the daughter of locally renowned educator and activist T. J. Owens, San Jose is just a place where she once lived. Raised among whites in South San Jose, Alissa went to school with a handful of blacks in the early 1980s. While the public schools she attended were better than the San Jose schools in the northern section of the district, the trade-off was that she was culturally isolated from the people that her father was raised around in the Northside. Years later, after graduating from the University of California–Berkeley, she chose to stay in the East Bay near black culture and in a town that has what she calls "personality," Point Richmond near Richmond. Before the passing of her father in 2005, she often drove to South San Jose and Gilroy, where he lived. What pulled her to the region was family. Without family or a job there, the pull was weak because there was not that much happening for African Americans from a recognizable black community perspective. For Owens and former Dallas columnist and "Speed City" expert Urla Hill, what the region lacked was a strong character that felt familiar and organic.[79]

Since 1960, the City of San Jose has tried to create a strong character for the city.[80] This coincided with a couple of firsts: landing on the U.S. Census Bureau's "Population of the 100 Largest Cities" list at 57, and becoming designated an All-American City.[81] By 2005, San Jose was the tenth-most-populated U.S. city, surpassing Detroit.[82] Although San Jose calls itself the "capital of Silicon Valley," for many the nickname does not work, because what makes San Jose dynamic is its high-tech economy, which has fostered a work-and-commute culture with a limited nightlife. And though the downtown has been built up since the mid-1990s, the transplanted growth featuring chain stores and the gentrification and loss of shops organic to the area has arguably made San Jose into any convention city in America.

At the same time, however, Santa Clara County has become more ethnically diverse. During its hasty transformation into Silicon Valley, Mexican American and Asian American population growth has been much larger than that of the region's African American population.

Black communities in Northern California by 1990.

In 2000, Mexican Americans had the largest minority population in the region, mostly because of births. But in the 1990s, their rate of growth was far exceeded by that of persons of Asian descent, whose population nearly doubled from about 261,000 to 430,000, mostly because of immigration from China, India, Korea, the Pacific Islands, the Philippines, and Vietnam. This was a far cry from the 15,000 Asian Americans who lived in the South Bay in 1960.[83]

Most notable in the 1990s population growth was high-tech immigration from India and China.[84] This growth pattern has resulted in Silicon Valley becoming more international and sophisticated. Ethnicity changed the character of the valley, even as anti-immigrant sentiment seethed among non-immigrant residents who were increasingly living from paycheck to paycheck.[85]

As the black population declined in numbers and in percentage of population, the South Bay black community seemed to become even more fragmented. Blacks whom nurse and community activist Ellen Rollins (from Washington, D.C.) came into contact with after 1989 were becoming comfortable with surviving and living fragmented, increasingly individualistic lives without a stable sense of community and local historical legacy because they were socioeconomically dispersing every which way throughout the county.[86] In this metropolis without a black center, interested African Americans found black communities geographically scattered throughout Santa Clara County in black churches, professional organizations, barbershops, beauty shops, sociopolitical organizations, and night spots such as the jazz and dance bar Casablanca.[87] James C. Dennis, a black marketing communications director for Hewlett-Packard, found black community by making the extra effort to find black barbershops, ethnic grocery stores, and nightclubs playing familiar music that could not be found in white and affluent Saratoga, where he lives. Dennis's wife, Tonya, 38, said that meeting blacks in Silicon Valley required being bold about calling the friends of friends, inviting people to dinner, and introducing themselves to strangers.[88]

Most South Bay blacks encounter black community in the valley at annual events such as Juneteenth. Juneteenth is the largest annual African American event in the South Bay. It is a four-day celebration commemorating black emancipation from slavery in Texas on June 19, 1865, several months after the Civil War officially ended east of the Mississippi River.[89] Although Juneteenth was a tradition in many parts of the South for decades, in 1979 it was relatively new to California.[90] Juneteenth festivities showcase black tradition in arts, crafts, food,

San Jose NAACP Youth Group at 1992 Freedom Train. Charles Alexander Collection.

music, religion, and personal narrative through oral, performance, and written traditions. It started as a fund-raising activity for the Afro-American Community Service Agency in 1979.[91] Originally conceptualized as Emancipation Proclamation Day, as a counterpart to Cinco de Mayo, this ideal was replaced with Juneteenth after the festival was brought to the attention of agency's board by several members from Texas.[92] In subsequent decades, the Juneteenth festival was strengthened by black-culture advocates such as Lula Briggs Galloway, CEO of the National Association of Juneteenth Lineage, founder of the Juneteenth Creative Cultural Center and Museum (in Saginaw, Michigan), and founder of History San Jose's African American Heritage House at Kelley Park.[93] For many blacks, Juneteenth was a reminder of how important black community is. When Irene and Ray Hardy were thirsting for community, Juneteenth was one of the few local events that brought the black community together beyond going to a black church or attending black sociopolitical institutions that were sometimes more intent on building their constituencies than building the black community.[94]

In 1986, the Freedom Train commemorating Dr. Martin Luther King Day joined Juneteenth in providing Bay Area blacks a base for reaffirming their cultural identity and celebrating African American progress. This event was more political than Juneteenth, serving to remind and educate Bay Area residences about the black freedom struggle. The Freedom Train was a one-hour ride from San Jose to San Francisco, with stops at Sunnyvale, Palo Alto, and San Mateo. In 1986, three thousand people from the South Bay packed into ten two-tier railroad cars and joined more than fifty thousand people in San Francisco City Hall, which had formal ceremonies, celebratory marches, and many musical tributes that marked the federal holiday. Nearly all of the riders from the South Bay were black, and most (two thousand) came from San Jose. The few whites who came were young people who wanted to partake in the festivities.[95]

Since 1986, blacks have formed progressive political agendas centered on group interests and the needs of communities of color and their children. These priorities led to the creation of the recently opened African American Heritage House, the African American Parent Coalition, the Black Chamber of Commerce of Silicon Valley, and the Silicon Valley African American Cultural Center (still under way). Together with Juneteenth, these institutions are designed to build a stronger sense of black community in the area and to relieve some of the social isolation that African Americans have felt. Perhaps in the future they will bring South Bay blacks closer to feeling like *welcomed* neighbors.

Notes

Introduction

1. The incident described in this paragraph occurred almost a year after Dr. King spoke in the same auditorium on April 14, 1967, which briefly motivated Stanford administrators to contemplate racial reforms at the campus. See the *Stanford Daily*, "Martin Luther King Sets 'True Equality' as Goal," April 17, 1967; *San Francisco Examiner*, "King Links War, Racism," April 15, 1967; and "Correspondence Letters: Office of the President, 1967–1970," in Black Student Union files (Special Collections, Stanford University Libraries).

2. This account, including quotations, appeared in the *San Jose Mercury News*, January 21, 2002.

3. See Ruth Hammond, "Richard Lyman, 88, Stanford's 7th President," *Chronicle of Higher Education*, June 3, 2012 (http://chronicle.com/article/Richard-Lyman-Stanfords/132085/); Jeanne Friedman, "The Roots of the Stanford Peace Movement," in Stanford Historical Society, *Sandstone and Tile* 35, 1 (Winter 2011): 3–22; and Sarah Drake, "Current Protestors Worthy Successors to Stanford Student Activists of Past," in *Campus Report* (Special Collections, Stanford University Libraries).

4. See the *San Jose Mercury News*, January 21, 2002.

5. Ibid. Today the programs and student groups created by blacks at schools such as Stanford are in danger of becoming insignificant in comparison to the concerns of other racial-ethnic groups. This trend has occurred in the Silicon Valley since the 1970s. Stanford's student body president, Matt Brewster, who is black, summed up the situation this way: despite the fact that Stanford underfunds community centers, departments, and programs and maintains an overwhelmingly white faculty, it still ranked number seven in *Black Enterprise Magazine's* annual ranking of the fifty best colleges for African Americans in 2002 because of the school's high academic ranking, its huge endowment, small class size, location in the suburbs, and elite status as a private school. In 1967, about a hundred blacks were enrolled. The year before, only thirty-five blacks attended Stanford. In January 2002, black undergraduates at the university numbered 556, representing 9 percent of the undergraduate student body.

6. In this book I interchangeably use "Santa Clara Valley," "Santa Clara County," "South Bay," and the "Valley of Heart's Delight." I mention "Silicon Valley" only in relation to the Santa Clara Valley after 1971. Geographically, most of Santa Clara County is in the Santa Clara Valley. Prior to the 1950s, when the valley

was dominated by agricultural pursuits, it was commonly referred to as the Valley of Heart's Delight. Local residents also refer to the region as the South Bay or the Greater San Jose region (which is south of San Francisco and the East Bay).

7. See Stanford University Libraries, Department of Special Collections, SC 215, Box 4: Chicano Students; Black Students; Black Student Union 1968–1968; Activism (Stanford); and see the *San Jose Mercury News*, June 11, 1963, and January 21, 2002. In 1963, fifteen blacks were admitted and enrolled at Stanford—a record number. The admission of black students was initially pushed by alumni and white students who complained that the school did not try hard enough to attract qualified black students. The fifteen blacks were included in a freshman class of 1,275 students, making them 0.012 percent of the class.

8. For more on modern urban and postsuburban development in the West, see Lawrence de Graaf, "African American Suburbanization in California, 1960 through 1990," in *Seeking El Dorado: African Americans in California*, ed. Lawrence De Graaf, Kevin Mulroy, and Quintard Taylor (Seattle: University of Washington Press, 2001), 405–449; Allan A. Saxe, *Politics of Arlington, Texas: An Era of Continuity and Growth* (New York: Eakins Press, 2001); Hal K. Rothman, *Devil's Bargain: Tourism in the Twentieth-Century American West* (Lawrence: University Press of Kansas, 1998), 338–370; Matthew C. Whitaker, *Race Work: The Rise of Civil Rights in the Urban West* (Lincoln: University of Nebraska Press, 2007), 225–266; Adrian Florido, "Feeling a Different Pulse in the Heart of Black San Diego" (http://www.voiceofsandiego.org/survival/article_f78c10fc-4ddf-11e0-baaf-001cc4c002e0.html); and Albert S. Broussard, "Percy H. Steele, Jr., and the Urban League: Race Relations and the Struggle for Civil Rights in Post–World War II San Diego," *California History* 83 (Spring 2006): 7–23. Also see Robert E. Lang and Patrick A. Simmons, ""Boomburbs": The Emergence of Large, Fast-Growing Suburban Cities in the United States," Fannie Mae Foundation Census, Note 06, June 2001, 1–3.

9. See Joe William Trotter, *Black Milwaukee: The Making of an Industrial Proletariat, 1915–1945* (Urbana: University of Illinois Press, 1985); Joe William Trotter, *The Great Migration in Historical Perspective: New Dimensions of Race, Class, and Gender* (Bloomington: Indiana University Press, 1991); Albert S. Broussard, *Black San Francisco: The Struggle for Racial Equality in the West, 1900–1954* (Lawrence: University Press of Kansas, 1993); Albert S. Broussard, "In Search of a Promised Land: African American Migration to San Francisco, 1900–1945," in *Seeking El Dorado: African Americans in California*, ed. De Graaf et al., 181–209; Albert S. Broussard, "Strange Territory, Familiar Leadership: The Impact of World War II on San Francisco's Black Community," *California History* 65, 1 (1986): 18–25; Albert S. Broussard, "The Politics of Despair: Black San Franciscans and the Political Process, 1920–1940," *Journal of Negro History* 69, 1 (Winter 1984): 26–37; Gretchen Lemke Santangelo, "Deindustrialization, Urban Poverty, and African American Community Mobilization in Oakland, 1945

through the 1990s," in *Seeking El Dorado*, 343–376; Gretchen Lemke Santangelo, *Abiding Courage: African American Migrant Women and the East Bay Community* (Chapel Hill: University of North Carolina Press, 1996); Lawrence de Graaf, "Recognition, Racism, and Reflections on the Writing of Western Black History," *Pacific Historical Review* 44, 1 (February 1975): 22–51; Quintard Taylor, *In Search of the Racial Frontier: African Americans in the West, 1528–1990* (New York: W. W. Norton, 1998); Quintard Taylor, *The Forging of a Black Community: Seattle's Central District, from 1870 through the Civil Rights Era* (Seattle: University of Washington Press, 1994); Quintard Taylor, "Urban Black Labor in the West, 1849–1949: Reconceptualizing the Image of a Region," in *The African American Urban Experience: Perspectives from the Colonial Period to the Present*, ed. Joe William Trotter, Earl Lewis, and Tera W. Hunter (New York: Palgrave McMillan, 2004), 99–120; and Quintard Taylor and Shirley Ann Wilson Moore, eds., *African American Women Confront the West, 1600–2000* (Norman: University of Oklahoma Press, 2003).

10. De Graaf, "African American Suburbanization."

11. For more on this method see Taylor, *Forging of a Black Community*, 3–10.

12. For a rich discussion on the subjectification of Bay Area blacks during WWII and before the mid-1970s, see Jack B. Forbes, *Afro-Americans in the Far West: A Handbook for Educators* (Berkeley, Calif.: Far West Laboratory for Educational Research and Development, 1968); Edward E. France, *Some Aspects of the Migration of the Negro to the San Francisco Bay Area since 1940* (San Francisco: R and E Research Associates, 1974); Joseph James, "Profiles: San Francisco," *Journal of Educational Sociology* 19, 3, Race Relations on the Pacific Coast (November 1945): 166–178; and Charles S. Johnson, *The Negro War Worker in San Francisco, A Local Self-Survey* (San Francisco: privately printed, 1944). For early writings on racism in education and the black studies movement, see Dikran Karagueuzian, *Blow It Up! The Black Student Revolt at San Francisco State College and the Emergence of Dr. Hayakawa* (Boston: Gambit, 1971); James McEvoy and Abraham Miller, eds., *Black Power and Student Rebellion* (Belmont, Calif.: Wadsworth, 1969); Wilson Record, "Racial Integration in California Schools," *Journal of Negro Education* 27, 1 (Winter 1958): 17–23; Neil Vincent Sullivan and Evelyn S. Stewart, *Now Is the Time: Integration in the Berkeley Schools* (Bloomington: Indiana University Press, 1970); and Charles Wollenberg, *Ethnic Conflict in California History* (Los Angeles: Tinnon-Brown, 1970). For early studies on the Black Panthers see Earl Anthony, *Picking Up the Gun: A Report on the Black Panthers* (New York: Dial, 1970); Michael J. Arlen, *An American Verdict* (Garden City, N.Y.: Doubleday, 1973); Sara Blackburn, *White Justice; Black Experience Today in America's Courtrooms* (New York: Harper and Row, 1971); Paul Chevigny, *Cops and Rebels: A Study of Provocation* (New York: Pantheon, 1972); Eldridge Cleaver, *Soul on Ice* (New York: McGraw-Hill, 1968); Erik H. Erikson

and Huey P. Newton, *In Search of Common Ground* (New York: Norton, 1973); Donald Freed, *Agony in New Haven: The Trial of Bobby Seale, Ericka Huggins, and the Black Panther Party* (New York: Simon and Schuster, 1973); George Jackson, *Soledad Brother: The Prison Letters of George Jackson* (New York: Coward-McCann, 1970); Reginald Major, *A Panther Is a Black Cat* (New York: W. Morrow, 1971); Gene Marine, *The Black Panthers* (New York: New American Library, 1969); Gilbert Stuart Moore, *A Special Rage* (New York: Harper and Row, 1971); Huey P. Newton, *Revolutionary Suicide* (New York: Harcourt Brace Jovanovich, 1973) and *To Die for the People: The Writings of Huey P. Newton* (New York: Random House, 1972); Don A. Schanche, *The Panther Paradox, A Liberalism Dilemma* (New York: McKay, 1970); Bobby Seale, *Seize the Time: The Story of the Black Panther Party and Huey P. Newton* (New York: Random House, 1970); and Gail Sheehy, *Panthermania: The Clash of Black Against Black in One American City* (New York: Harper and Row, 1971).

13. Quote is from Taylor, *The Forging of a Black Community*, 5.

14. Walter Prescott Webb contends in "The American West: Perpetual Mirage," *Harper's Magazine* (May 1957), that "the scarcity of water, timber, cities, industry, labor, and Negroes in the desert" (western states such as Idaho, Nevada, Arizona, Montana, Wyoming, Utah, Colorado, and New Mexico) meant the absence of many problems that western historians had to discuss by the 1950s. In Webb's attacks on environmentalism, urbanization, industrialization, and social history, the "Negro problem" existed only in Texas and California.

15. Although there are surveys before 1980 that examine blacks in the West, written by historians such as Sherman Savage, Kenneth W. Porter, and William Loren Katz, their research centered solely on the western frontier in the nineteenth century. Ultimately, their discussions ignored twentieth-century developments and failed to challenge the traditional view of the black western experience in the post-1941 period. For instance, Porter's *The Negro on the American Frontier* (1971) was a compilation of writings based on nineteenth-century themes in the Southwest and Native American–black American relations. It supported the traditional western image of hardy white Americans conquering and civilizing the western frontier while reimagining their identities and communities as democratic and symbolically "American." Prior to 1980, *The Negro on the American Frontier* was the most scholarly survey of the black West. In this period, most surveys on blacks in the West were simplistic, acknowledging their presence and listing their achievements without scholastic analysis. The most notable text in this genre was William L. Katz's *The Black West* (Garden City, N.Y.: Doubleday, 1971). This was a pictorial and documentary history that offered laymen an introduction to black activity from Spanish America to the turn of the twentieth century. For more on this discussion, see also W. Sherman Savage, *Blacks in the West* (Westport, Conn.: Greenwood, 1976); and De Graaf, "Recognition, Racism, and Reflections," 33.

16. Broussard, "The Politics of Despair, 26–37.

17. This postwar period witnessed unprecedented demographic growth for African Americans, many of whom migrated to the West Coast from Texas, Oklahoma, Louisiana, Arkansas, and Mississippi. See Broussard, *Black San Francisco*, 138; and Taylor, *In Search of the Racial Frontier*, 256.

18. See Ingrid Banks, Gaye Johnson, George Lipsitz, Ula Taylor, Daniel Widener, and Clyde Woods, eds., *Black California Dreamin': The Crises of California's African-American Communities* (Santa Barbara, Calif.: U.C. Santa Barbara Center for Black Studies Research, December 2012); Broussard, *Black San Francisco*; Broussard, "In Search of a Promised Land," 181–209; Lawrence P. Crouchett, Lonnie G. Bunch III, and Martha Kendall Winnacker, *Visions toward Tomorrow: The History of the East Bay Afro-American Community, 1852–1977* (Oakland: Northern California Center for Afro-American History and Life, 1989); Jonathan Dembo, "The West Coast Teamsters' and Longshoremen's Unions in the Twentieth Century," *Journal of the West* 25, 2 (1986): 27–35; Delores Nason McBroome, *Parallel Communities: African Americans in California's East Bay 1850–1963* (New York: Garland, 1993); Shirley Ann Wilson Moore, *To Place Our Deeds: The African American Community in Richmond, California, 1910–1963* (Berkeley: University of California Press, 2000); Donna Jean Murch, *Living for the City: Migration, Education, and the Rise of the Black Panther Party in Oakland, California* (Chapel Hill: University of North Carolina Press, 2010); Bruce Nelson, "The Big Strike," in *Working People of California*, ed. Daniel Cornford (Berkeley: University of California Press, 1995), 225–264; Bruce Nelson, "The 'Lords of the Docks' Reconsidered: Race Relations among West Coast Longshoremen, 1933–61," in *Waterfront Workers: New Perspectives on Race and Class*, ed. Calvin Winslow (Urbana: University of Illinois Press, 1998), 155–192; Santangelo, *Abiding Courage*; Santangelo, "Deindustrialization"; Robert O. Self, *American Babylon: Race and the Struggle for Postwar Oakland* (Princeton, N.J.: Princeton University Press, 2003); Taylor, *In Search of the Racial Frontier*; and Taylor, "Urban Black Labor."

19. The tendency to interpret western urban centers such as San Francisco as the North is common among "traditional" African American historians who conceptualize U.S. history and its culture in reference to southern slavery, the Civil War, Jim Crow, and the civil rights movement, and who forget about the history of the West as a place and not a process of U.S. imperialism moving westward. For a short list of like treatment in surveys, see Lerone Bennett, *Before the Mayflower: A History of Black America* (New York: Penguin, 1993); John Hope Franklin and Alfred A. Moss, Jr., *From Slavery to Freedom: A History of African Americans* (New York: A. Knopf, 2000); Herbert H. Haines, *Black Radicals and the Civil Rights Mainstream, 1954–1970* (Knoxville: University of Tennessee Press, 1988); and August Meier and Elliott Rudwick, *CORE: A Study in the Civil Rights Movement, 1942–1968* (New York: Oxford University Press, 1973).

20. See De Graaf, "African American Suburbanization in California," 407.

21. Ibid., 405.

22. Notable social histories about the Santa Clara Valley emerging in recent memory include Glenna Matthews, *Silicon Valley, Women, and the California Dream: Gender, Class, and Opportunity in the Twentieth Century* (Stanford, Calif.: Stanford University Press, 2003); and Stephen J. Pitti, *The Devil in Silicon Valley: Northern California, Race, and Mexican Americans* (Princeton, N.J.: Princeton University Press, 2003). For a short list of the history of business and technology in the making of Silicon Valley, see AnnaLee Saxenian, *Regional Advantage: Culture and Competition in Silicon Valley and Route 128* (Cambridge, Mass.: Harvard University Press, 1996); AnnaLee Saxenian, *The New Argonauts: Regional Advantage in a Global Economy* (Cambridge, Mass.: Harvard University Press, 2007); Robert X. Cringely, *Accidental Empires: How the Boys of Silicon Valley Make Their Millions, Battle Foreign Competition, and Still Can't Get a Date* (New York: HarperBusiness, 1996); David A. Kaplan, *The Silicon Boys: And Their Valley of Dreams* (New York: William Morrow, 1999); Christophe Lecuyer, *Making Silicon Valley: Innovation and the Growth of High Tech, 1930–1970* (Cambridge, Mass.: MIT Press, 2007); and Stuart Leslie, *The Cold War and American Science: The Military-Industrial-Academic Complex at MIT and Stanford* (New York: Columbia University Press, 1994).

23. See the Garden City Women's Club, *History of Black Americans in Santa Clara Valley* (Sunnyvale, Calif.: Lockheed Missiles and Space Co., 1978). To my knowledge, this is the only Santa Clara County study aside from Harriett Arnold's *Antioch: A Place of Christians* (San Mateo, Calif.: Western Book Journal Press, 1993) that attempts to grapple with the local black experience after 1941.

24. Garden City Women's Club, *History of Black Americans in Santa Clara Valley*, 66.

25. U.S. Bureau of the Census, *1950 Census of Population*, Vol. 11, *Characteristics of the Population*, pt. 5, *California* (Washington, D.C.: GPO, 1952), 5–21; U.S. Bureau of the Census, *1970 Census of Housing*, Vol. 1, *Housing Characteristics for States, Cities, and Counties*, pt. 6, *California* (Washington, D.C.: GPO, 1972), 7–10, 14–15, 453; U.S. Bureau of the Census, *U.S. Census of Population and Housing, 1980 Census Tracts* (Washington, D.C.: GPO, 1983), 215; University of Virginia Library, *Historical Census Browser: County-Level Results for 1850–1960* (Charlottesville: University of Virginia Library Geospatial and Statistical Data Center, 2005), http://fisher.lib.virginia.edu/collections/stats/histcensus/; and U.S. Bureau of the Census, *1990 Census of Population: General Population Characteristics, California* (Washington, D.C.: GPO, 1992), 1920.

26. Garden City Women's Club, *History of Black Americans in Santa Clara Valley*, 68, 116.

27. For a rich discussion on black migration to California from 1940 to 1970, see Broussard, *Black San Francisco*, 133–142, 171; McBroome, *Parallel Communities*, 129–147; Moore, *To Place Our Deeds*, 127–146; and Santangelo,

Abiding Courage, 133–152. Between 1941 and 1970, the general narrative of the Black Bay Area canon indicates that southern blacks came to the Bay Area, and the West Coast generally, for economic opportunity, education, and the right to vote. According to the literature these black migrants were younger, more ambitious, and more educated than the blacks already settled in the area, and their new presence immediately challenged and replaced established residents' local customs and mores. Moreover, they brought with them the blues, gospel music, the black Baptist church, soul food, skills, Juneteenth, and a population determined to struggle for equality. Although they did not bring a watershed of black consciousness or radical evolution of political tactics, they did bring forth a demographic revolution that resulted in black nationalism grounded in grassroots politics. Ultimately, an urgency distinguished this new group from the older one, and this urgency is what produced a civil rights movement and Black Power movement in the 1950s and '60s.

Chapter 1

1. Hasan Kwame Jeffries conceptualizes freedom rights as "the assortment of civil and human rights that emancipated African Americans identified as freedom," an assortment that also "acknowledges the centrality of slavery and emancipation to conceptualizations of freedom." See Jeffries, *Bloody Lowndes: Civil Rights and Black Power in Alabama's Black Belt* (New York: New York University Press, 2009), 4.

2. See Seonaid McArthur, *Historias: The Spanish Heritage of Santa Clara Valley* (Cupertino: California History Center, De Anza College, 1976), 5–6. Also see Russell K. Skowronek, *Situating Mission Santa Clara de Asis: 1776–1851, Documentary and Material Evidence of Life on the Alta California Frontier: A Timeline* (Berkeley, Calif.: Academy of American Franciscan History, 2006), 4, 22, 379, 381; and Jack D. Forbes, "The Early Heritage of California," in *Seeking El Dorado: African Americans in California*, ed. Lawrence de Graaf et al. (Seattle: University of Washington Press, 2001), 78. According to this account, Spanish explorers and priests such as Gaspar de Portola had at least one mulatto soldier assist them on their excursions into Alta California from 1769 to 1776.

3. McArthur, *Historias*, 5; and Forbes, "The Early Heritage of California," 78.

4. See these four essays in *Telling the Santa Clara Story*, ed. Russell K. Skowronek (Santa Clara, Calif.: City of Santa Clara and Santa Clara University, 2002): Ann-Marie Sayers, "Today's Native American in the Santa Clara Area," 13–19; Robert M. Sekewicz, "The California Context," 20–25; Robert H. Jackson, "Demographic Patterns at Santa Clara Mission, 1777–1840"; and Lorie Garcia, The Immigrants Who Built Santa Clara," 94–98. Moreover, for an excellent discussion on Native American life and labor in the missions of California, see

Douglas Monroy, *Thrown among Strangers: The Making of Mexican Culture in Frontier California* (Berkeley: University of California Press, 1990), 63–96. Also see University of Virginia Library, *Historical Census Browser*, 1850–1960. For an excellent survey that examines San Jose Native Americans' forced removal from the San Jose frontier, see Albert L. Hurtado, *Indian Survival on the California Frontier* (New Haven, Conn.: Yale University Press, 1988), 40–45, 49, 52, 61, 62, 99.

    5. San Jose was the first European settlement in California.

    6. *San Jose Mercury News*, November 29, 1963; Sekewicz, "The California Context," 23; and Clyde Arbuckle, *Clyde Arbuckle's History of San Jose* (San Jose, Calif.: Smith McKay Printing Co., 1985), 10–12.

    7. See Skowronek, *Situating Mission Santa Clara de Asis*, 23.

    8. The census figure is taken from Oscar Osburn Winther, "The Story of San Jose, 1777–1869, California's First Pueblo, Part I," *California History* 14 (1935): 3; and Edith Smith, *Some Early African American Settlers in the Santa Clara Valley* (San Jose, Calif.: Sourisseau Academy, 1994), 2.

    9. R. Douglas Cope, *The Limits of Racial Domination: Plebeian Society in Colonial Mexico City, 1660–1720* (Madison: University of Wisconsin Press, 1994), 24.

    10. Ibid.

    11. Quoted in Jackie R. Booker, "Needed but Unwanted: Black Militiamen in Veracruz, Mexico, 1760–1810," *Historian* 55 (Winter 1993): 270.

    12. See Taylor, *In Search of the Racial Frontier*, 32.

    13. On Spanish intermarriage policy in Alta California, see B. Gordon Wheeler, *Black California: The History of African-Americans in the Golden State* (New York: Hippocrene, 1993), 31.

    14. See Forbes, "The Early Heritage of California," 82.

    15. Quoted from ibid., 75. Also see Wheeler, *Black California*, 31.

    16. For a rich discussion of the role of men of African descent in frontier colonial Spanish society, see Forbes, "The Early Heritage of California," 82. A criollo was usually a colonist born in Latin America who was part Spanish and part Native American claiming to be Spanish.

    17. See Taylor, *In Search of the Racial Frontier*, 36.

    18. Mark A. Burkholder and Lyman L. Johnson, *Colonial Latin America* (New York: Oxford University Press, 2001), 290–300, 314–323; Leslie B. Rout, *The African Experience in Spanish America: 1502 to the Present Day* (New York: Cambridge University Press, 1976), 162.

    19. For local census records, see H. H. Bancroft, *The Works of Hubert Howe Bancroft* (San Francisco, 1888), 371, 377 (archives at the Bancroft Library, University of California, Berkeley); and Skowronek, *Situating Mission Santa Clara de Asis*, 236, 238.

20. See years 1795, 1812, and 1815 in "Translations of Spanish/Mexican Archives: Pueblo of San Jose, 1792–1859" (California Room, Dr. Martin Luther King, Jr., Library, San Jose).

21. Forbes, "The Early Heritage of California," 82, 84, 89.

22. Quote is from Ted Vincent, "The Blacks Who Freed Mexico," *Journal of Negro History* 79, 3 (1994): 257–276.

23. Ibid.; Forbes, "The Early Heritage of California," 84–85; Ilona Katzew, *Casta Painting: Images of Race in Eighteenth–Century Mexico* (New Haven, Conn.: Yale University Press, 2004), 39–53; Monroy, *Thrown among Strangers*, 106–112, 134–148; and Rout, *The African Experience in Spanish America*, 180–182.

24. For a rich discussion on what Jack Forbes calls the "whitening" process, see Forbes, "The Early Heritage of California," 83–84, 87. Also see Rudolph M. Lapp, *Afro-Americans in California* (San Francisco: Boyd and Fraser, 1979), 9–11; and Ancestry.com "Jose Dolores Pico (1764–1827)" (http://records.ancestry.com/Jose_Dolores_Pico_records.ashx?pid=25473770). Jose was Antonio's father and Santiago and Maria's son.

25. "Translations of Spanish/Mexican Archives," 312, 485; "Election in El Pueblo de San Jose de Guadelupe, August 1, 1849" in "Translations of Spanish/Mexican Archives"; and "Antonio Maria Pico" (http://www.findagrave.com/cgi-bin/fg.cgi?page=gr&GRid=35879145).

26. "Translations of Spanish/Mexican Archives," 485.

27. See letter to the alcalde of San Jose from Monterey, May 7, 1832, in the H. H. Bancroft Collection (university archives at the Bancroft Library, University of California–Berkeley); and Rudolph M. Lapp, *Blacks in Gold Rush California* (New Haven, Conn.: Yale University Press, 1977), 4.

28. See Lapp, *Blacks in Gold Rush California*, 4.

29. Letter to the alcalde of San Jose from Monterey, May 7, 1832.

30. Quoted from Lapp, *Blacks in Gold Rush California*, 8.

31. See Taylor, *In Search of the Racial Frontier*, 47. Also see Michael S. Malone, "The Mission Bell's Toll," in *Telling the Santa Clara Story*, ed. Russell K. Skowronek (Santa Clara, Calif.: City of Santa Clara and Santa Clara University, 2002), 173; and "Treaty of Guadalupe Hildalgo" (http://www.blackpast.org/?q=primaryWEST/treaty-guadalupe-hidalgo).

32. See *San Jose Mercury News*, August 21, 1960; and University of Virginia Library, *Historical Census Browser*, 1850–1960. In 1850 San Jose's population boomed to four thousand people, and its infrastructure mirrored this growth (see Arbuckle, *Clyde Arbuckle's History of San Jose*, 65, 299). By California statehood (September 9, 1850) the population was nearing five thousand, then dipped after the capital was moved to Vallejo in February 1851, only to increase up to eight thousand by 1852. The black population of California in 1850 was 962

persons assumed to be free by census enumerators because of California's status as a free state. Of them, 872 were men, and 90 were women. The 1850 federal census for Santa Clara County was lost.

33. See the Garden City Women's Club, *History of Black Americans in Santa Clara Valley*, xvii; Linda S. Larson, *San Jose's Monument to Progress: The Electric Light Tower* (San Jose: San Jose Historical Association, 1989), 1, 15, 20; and the *San Jose Mercury News*, "'When San Jose Was Young': Scrapbooks" (California Room, Dr. Martin Luther King, Jr., Library). In 1849, San Jose laid out Market, First, and Santa Clara Streets. Also in this year, the U.S. Post Office replaced the Spanish courier system in San Jose. In 1853, an intraregional telegraph between San Francisco and San Jose was constructed. In 1861, gas lamps maintained by coal replaced oil lamps, which were used from 1820 to 1861. Prior to oil lighting, candles and fireplaces provided locals with heat and light.

34. See University of Virginia Library, *Historical Census Browser*, 1850–1860. Also see in the appendix "Blacks in the Santa Clara Valley, 1852" and "African American Population in California, 1860." In 1852 the Santa Clara Valley had a black population of forty-nine—forty-one men and eight women. Forty-one of them were free, and eight were enslaved. In 1860 the black South Bay population increased to eighty-seven—fifty-two men and thirty-five women—in a county with a total population of 7,309. All blacks in the 1860 census for California were assumed to be free by enumerators.

35. See J. S. Holiday, *Rush for Riches: Gold Fever and the Making of California* (Berkeley: University of California Press, 1999).

36. "Governor's Annual Message to the Legislature, January 7, 1851," in California Legislature, *Journals of the Legislature*, 2nd sess., 1851 (San Jose, Calif.: Eugene Cassidy, State Printer, 1851), 796–797.

37. See *National Park Service*, "Underground Railroad." Also see Eugene H. Berwanger, "Negrophobia in Northern Proslavery and Antislavery Thought," *Phylon* 33, 3 (1972): 266–275; Eugene H. Berwanger, "The 'Black Law' Question in Ante-Bellum California," *Journal of the West* 6, 2 (1967): 205–220; De Graaf, "Recognition, Racism, and Reflections," 36; Taylor, *In Search of the Racial Frontier*, 75–77; and Elizabeth McLagan, *A Peculiar Paradise: A History of Blacks in Oregon, 1778–1940* (Portland, Ore.: Georgian Press, 1980), 23–48.

38. See "Voting Regulations in Gold Rush California," California Constitution, art. 2, sec. 3; "Anti–Persons of Color Testimony against White People in California Court," in California Legislature, *Journals of the Senate and Assembly*, 3rd sess. (1852), 75; "Provisions for Separate Schools and State Normal Schools," in California Legislature, *Statutes of California*, 16th sess. (1865–56), sec. 63–77, 399–402; "Education of Black and Indian Children in California Restricted until 1872," in *California Political Code*, sec. 1669, 1872; "An Act to Enforce the Educational Rights of Children," in California Legislature, *Statutes of California*, 20th

sess., 751–753; "Homestead Act in California (1860)," in California Legislature, *Statutes of California*, 11th sess. (1860), 87–89; "Social and Political Restrictions on People of Color in Gold Rush California," in "Governor's Annual Message to the Legislature, January 7, 1851," in California Legislature, *Journals of the Legislature of the State of California*, 2nd sess. (1851), 796–797; and Connie Young Yu, *Chinatown San Jose, USA* (San Jose, Calif.: History San Jose, 2001), 11–38.

39. Quote appears in National Park Service, "The Underground Railroad." Also see Don Gagliardi, "Roots: The Northside Origins of San Jose's African American Community," *Northside* (Fall 2001): 16–19; and the *San Jose Mercury News*, November 24, 1963. By 1858 a slave could be held in bondage up to a year in California.

40. For more on fugitive slaves in California, see Wheeler, *Black California*, 63. Many African Americans liberated themselves in California by running away.

41. For more information see Lapp, *Blacks in Gold Rush California*, 194; and *People v. Hall*, 4 Cal. 399 (S. Ct. 1854), http://www.uchastings.edu/racism-race/people-hall.html). Anti–black testimony law occasionally functioned in unexpected ways in California courts. An enslaved African American woman caught in a grand larceny in the 1850s confessed her guilt before a Judge Redman. Contrary to using California law against black people, as was normally the case, the judge used anti–black testimony against itself by ruling that the African American woman's testimony was not permissible because she was a slave, and she was thus acquitted. Redman's action was the exception to the rule in gold rush California. More common for the courts and state law was to relegate "persons of color" to a status inferior to that of Anglo-Americans. This was fully experienced by California Mexicans of obvious African lineage. Augustus Negreto was part African and part Portuguese, and he lived in Santa Clara before American occupation and consolidation, and thus had full civil rights in Mexican California. In the early years of the gold rush, Negreto, working under the assumption of the Treaty of Guadalupe Hildalgo—which promised that property rights and first-class citizenship of former citizens of Mexico would remain intact—took a white man named George W. Vincent to court in San Jose for assault. To Negreto's astonishment the case was thrown out under the anti–black testimony laws.

42. The statement and account appear in Lapp, *Blacks in Gold Rush California*, 135–136.

43. See Wheeler, *Black California*, 63.

44. The theory that slavery had "natural limits" is addressed in Taylor, *In Search of the Racial Frontier*, 151–169; and in Charles Desmond Hart, "The Natural Limits of Slavery Expansion: Kansas-Nebraska, 1854," *Kansas Historical Quarterly* 34, 1 (1968): 32–50.

45. See Taylor, *In Search of the Racial Frontier*, 78.

46. See Lapp, *Blacks in Gold Rush California*, 133. In the Santa Clara Valley most African American bondsmen were either domestic servants or hired themselves out for monthly wages ranging from $150 to $300 a month.

47. Quoted from Gagliardi, "Roots," 17.

48. See Arbuckle, *Clyde Arbuckle's History of San Jose*, 315. According to Arbuckle, San Jose was a criminal society with a small police force of questionable legal status during its gold rush period.

49. Lapp, *Blacks in Gold Rush California*, 132; M. H. Field, "Grandma Bascom's Story of San Jose in '49," *Overland Monthly and Out West Magazine* 9, 53 (May 1887): 543–551; and Helen Arbuckle, "Anna Maria Bascom: San Jose's First Official Hostess," http://www.sanjose.com/history/bascom.html. According to Anna Maria Bascom (Dr. Bascom's wife), she informed the cook of California's free state status, and yet he chose to stay at the Bascom residence for four years. So far, legal documents have not been uncovered as to whether the cook, whose name is unknown, lived in the Bascom resident as a slave. What is certain from Anna's testimony is that she was peculiarly silent about the cook who lived under her family's roof for four years. With this said, the author agrees with historian Rudolph Lapp's assertion that the African American cook was enslaved until further evidence says otherwise.

50. Quoted in Eastbay Negro Historical Society, "Slavery in San Jose," *Chronicle of Black History* 1, 1 (October 1978): 6. Also see Ronald Takaki, *Strangers from a Different Shore: A History of Asian Americans* (Little, Brown and Company, 1989), 99–111. From 1849 to 1941, the Chinese were seen as an internal enemy to Anglo-Americans, who like African Americans "were viewed as antagonistic to republican and free-labor society." Further, whites' opposition to the Chinese in California was arguably greater than their opposition to blacks because of the former's much larger population, more intense economic competition with whites, permanent status as immigrants, and "unassimilable" status as non-Anglo and non-Christian.

51. See Delilah L. Beasley, *The Negro Trailblazers of California* (New York: Negro Universities Press, 1969), 71. Usually the head of household was responsible for purchasing his own and his family's freedom and resettling.

52. Quote is from the *San Jose Mercury News*, March 19, 1979. See James Williams, *Life and Adventures of James Williams, a Fugitive Slave, with a Full Description of the Underground Railroad*. This book, first published in 1873, has been reprinted by numerous presses and is available in an electronic edition through the University of North Carolina at http://docsouth.unc.edu/neh/williams/williams.html. See also Edith Smith, *Some Early African American Settlers*; California History Center, *Sunnyvale*, 62–63; and Arbuckle, *Clyde Arbuckle's History of San Jose*, 63.

53. See Edith Smith, *Some Early African American Settlers*, 3–5.

54. The Spanish-speaking black population was not counted in the census. The African American population, with the one-drop rule prevailing, probably was larger.

55. Quoted material is from Gagliardi, "Roots," 17. Also see the *San Jose Mercury News*, March 19, 1979; and Edith Smith, *Some Early African American Settlers*, 3–5.

56. Edith Smith, *Some Early African American Settlers*, 3–5. Information was taken from the California state census of 1852 for the Santa Clara Valley.

57. See "Anti–Persons of Color Testimony against White People in California Court," 75; "Foreign Miners Tax of 1852," in California Legislature, *Statutes of California*, 3rd sess., ch. 37, 84–87; and "Homestead Act in California (1860)," in California Legislature, *Statutes of California*, 11th sess., 1860, 87–89. For a discussion of the black economy in nineteenth-century California, see Wheeler, *Black California*, 55; and Beasley, *The Negro Trailblazers of California*, 60.

58. See the Garden City Women's Club, *History of Black Americans in Santa Clara Valley*, 10–12; and First AME Zion Church, San Jose, "About Us" (http://westernamezion.org/california/firstsanjose.html). The black church in late-nineteenth-century Santa Clara Valley was the central African American institution. Black churches in the nineteenth-century Bay Area received their greatest periods of growth during the Civil War years with the return of African Americans from Vancouver, British Columbia. In the 1890s the black population grew with an increase in childbirth, railroad travel, and social and economic opportunities in Oakland and the South Bay.

59. For a rich discussion on the black Baptist church and community formation from 1890 to 1970, see Arbuckle, *Clyde Arbuckle's History of San Jose*, 281; the Garden City Women's Club, *History of Black Americans in Santa Clara Valley*, 17; and Arnold, *Antioch*, 8.

60. See McBroome, *Parallel Communities*, 22.

61. Quoted from Ibid., 9.

62. Quoted from *Pacific Appeal*, February 6, 1864. Also see Taylor, *In Search of the Racial Frontier*. Blacks in California read the *Mirror of the Times* (1855–1862), *Pacific Appeal* (1862), and the *Elevator* (1865). According to Taylor, these papers were crucial for "providing information on protest struggles and leaders elsewhere, articulately expressing indignation, defending their small communities and the race, and encouraging responsible challenges to discrimination and exclusion" (196).

63. See "Anti–Persons of Color Testimony against White People in California Court," 75; Hudson, "When 'Mammy' Becomes a Millionaire," 74; and Beasley, *The Negro Trailblazers of California*, 59–60. The law barring minority testimony was repealed for blacks, but it continued to restrict American Indians, Mongolians, and Chinese after 1863. For black Californians, the repeal of the

testimony ban was more important than the Emancipation Proclamation because it had more of a direct effect on their lives.

64. Quote is from *Pacific Appeal*, April 18, 1863.

65. *San Jose Mercury News*, "When San Jose Was Young: No. 302 Oldest Janitor in San Jose," October 9, 1917; "Death of Owen," January 16. 1895; Santa Clara County Research Net, "Hon. J.J. Owen" (http://www.santaclararesearch.net/SCBIOS/jjowen.html); and Special Collections Research Center, Syracuse University Library, "That laboratory of abolitionism, libel, and treason: Syracuse and the Underground Railroad" (http://library.syr.edu/digital/exhibits/u/undergroundrr/index.html). Owen was born and raised in Auburn, New York, the home of abolitionists Harriet Tubman and New York Governor William H. Seward, and it was a central Underground Railroad station.

66. See *Mirror of the Times*, August 22, 1957, and December 12, 1857; and *Pacific Appeal*, April 12, 1862–May 31, 1873 (California State Archives, Sacramento).

67. *San Jose Mercury News*, February 6, 1996; and the National Park Service, "A History of Blacks in California: And Historic Sites—Phoenixonian Institute Site" (http://www.cr.nps.gov/history/online_books/5views/5views2h81.htm).

68. See Douglas Henry Daniels, *Pioneer Urbanites: A Social and Cultural History of Black San Francisco* (Berkeley: University of California Press, 1991), 112.

69. See *San Jose Mercury News*, December 10, 1977; Deborah LeFalle, "Peter Williams Cassey: The Man and His Mission" (1992 California Pioneer Paper, California Room, San Jose Public Library), 1; and Amy Johnson (daughter of Amy Cassey Thomas), "An Informal Family History of the Cassey Family" (California Room, San Jose Public Library), 4. Cassey's grandfather was from Martinique and was a French citizen with a fair complexion.

70. Bell is important to California history because he was the publisher of San Francisco's *Pacific Appeal* and later the *Elevator*.

71. *San Jose Mercury News*, December 10, 1977; LeFalle, "Peter Williams Cassey," 1; and Amy Johnson, "An Informal Family History of the Cassey Family," 4. For a brief overview of the Freedom's Journal see PBS, "Freedom's Journal," in *The Black Press: Soldiers Without Swords* (http://www.pbs.org/blackpress/news_bios/newbios/nwsppr/freedom/freedom.html).

72. National Park Service, "A History of Blacks in California."

73. Quoted from *San Jose Mercury News*, February 6, 1996.

74. See LeFalle, *Peter Williams Cassey*, 1. Also see *San Jose Mercury News*, December 10, 1977; and the Trinity Church brochure "The Rev. Peter Williams Cassey" (Research Library, History San Jose), 25.

75. Policy makers during the gold rush era were indifferent to education until a critical mass of women and children began arriving into the state in the mid-1850s. In 1855, a state school law went into effect organizing sixteen school

districts in the Santa Clara Valley. For more, see the *San Jose Mercury News*, November 24, 1963; *Ward v. Flood* (http://www.blackpast.org/?q=primarywest/ward-v-flood-1874); and Susan Bragg, "'Anxious Foot Soldiers': Sacramento's Black Women and Education in Nineteenth-Century California," in Quintard Taylor and Shirley Ann Wilson Moore, eds., *African American Women Confront the West, 1600–2000* (Norman: University of Oklahoma Press, 2003), 97–116.

76. Quoted in Lapp, *Blacks in Gold Rush California*, 166. In 1851 and 1852, education segregation in California was customary and was imposed by local school districts. From 1852 to 1854, the state was an accomplice by providing a percentage of funds to "whites only" public schools. In 1855, public education became legally segregated across the state.

77. Beasley, *The Negro Trailblazers of California*, 173–174; Charles Wollenberg, *All Deliberate Speed: Segregation and Exclusion in California Schools, 1855–1975* (Berkeley: University of California Press, 1976), 10–13; and National Park Service, "A History of Blacks in California."

78. See *San Jose Mercury News*, February 6, 1996; and Trinity Church brochure "The Rev. Peter Williams Cassey," 25.

79. Cassey as a philanthropist invested about $3,000 of his own money into St. Phillip's School.

80. *San Jose Mercury News*, February 6, 1996.

81. See *San Jose Mercury News*, February 6 1996; LeFalle, *Peter Williams Cassey*, 8; National Park Service, "A History of Blacks in California"; Beasley, *The Negro Trailblazers of California*, 63, 173–174. The December 22, 1863, date appears in Beasley (63). Throughout this chapter, St. Phillip's and the Phoenixonian Institute are used interchangeably.

82. *San Jose Mercury News*, December 10, 1977; and the Garden City Women's Club, *History of Black Americans in Santa Clara Valley*, 7.

83. *San Jose Mercury News*. February 6, 1996.

84. See advertisements in *Pacific Appeal,* July 14, 1866, and September 14, 1867.

85. Quoted from Trinity Church brochure, "The Rev. Peter Williams Cassey," 25.

86. *San Jose Mercury News*, February 6, 1996.

87. See LeFalle, "Peter Williams Cassey," 8.

88. Ibid., 9; National Park Service, "A History of Blacks in California"; and Daniels, *Pioneer Urbanites*, 121. Unlike most Episcopalian and Methodist churches in California, Phoenixonian Hall was sustained by blacks and unsupported by white Californian and eastern churches. Christ Episcopal Church was cofounded by Rev. Cassey and Reverend A. B. Smith of San Francisco's AME Zion Church.

89. Daniels, *Pioneer Urbanites*, 19. Also see Beasley, *The Negro Trailblazers of California*, 172–182; and Lapp, *Blacks in Gold Rush California*, 167.

90. For a discussion of education and equality in nineteenth-century California, see Beasley, *The Negro Trailblazers of California*, 185; and Wollenberg, *All Deliberate Speed*, 1.

91. Quoted from the National Park Service, "A History of Blacks in California."

92. "Provisions for Separate Schools and State Normal Schools," in California Legislature, *Statutes of California*, 16th sess. (1865–66), sec. 63–77, 399–402. The scientific racist term "Mongolian" applied to Chinese people.

93. See *San Jose Mercury News*, February 6, 1996; and National Park Service, "A History of Blacks in California." An opposing account of the Phoenixonian Institute's existence after 1866 is in Beasley, *The Negro Trailblazers of California*, 232. Beasley acknowledges Cassey's establishment of a seminary school but claims that when California legislators passed the law for public education, Cassey's school went into immediate decline.

94. National Park Service, *A History of Black Americans in California: Phoenixonian Institute Site* (http://www.cr.nps.gov/history/online_books/5views/5views2h81.htm).

95. Beasley, *The Negro Trailblazers of California*, 176; and National Park Service, *A History of Black Americans in California: Phoenixonian Institute Site* (http://www.cr.nps.gov/history/online_books/5views/5views2h81.htm). The unequal partnership between Cassey and the San Jose Board of Education peculiarly worked with Cassey's integrationist thought in the 1860s, which went along the lines of African American tax dollars being used to educate black children in a seemingly stable financial environment. Yet this was accomplished at the expense of the institute's survival, and there was no telling what would have happened to black children's education in San Jose if St. Phillip's closed—which it did in 1874.

96. See Jerry Drino, "Two Lives—Two Congregations—San Jose and the Civil War" (the Reverend Jerry Wm. Drino Files, Trinity Cathedral, San Jose, April 15, 2012). Christ Church Mission for Colored People was officially organized in December 1872.

97. See Wheeler, *Black California*, 109.

98. See the Garden City Women's Club, *History of Black Americans in Santa Clara Valley*, xx.

99. See "Reconstruction Amendments," http://www.blackpast.org/?q=primary/reconstruction-amendments; Territorial Suffrage Act (aka "Elective Franchise in the Territories"), *U.S. Statutes at Large*, 39th Cong., sess. 2, ch. 12, 15 (1867), 379–380; Taylor, *In Search of the Racial Frontier*, 123–129. Women received the vote in the western territories and states of Wyoming, Colorado, Utah, and Idaho in the 1890s, and universally through the Nineteenth Amendment to the U.S. Constitution in 1920.

NOTES TO PAGES 42–44   245

100. See *San Jose Mercury News*, "The Colored Voters," in *San Jose Historical Mercury News* Archive (1886–1922) Online (Santa Clara County Library: http://www.santaclaracountylib.org/database/). The judge's last name was King.

101. Quoted from archives, "Registration" (Fifteenth Amendment Ratification in San Jose Papers: Research Library, History San Jose); and "Registration of Citizens and Enrollment of Voters during Reconstruction Era," in California Legislature, *Statutes of California*, 17th sess. (1867–68), 647–655.

102. Quote is from "Registration," History San Jose archives.

103. *San Jose Mercury News*, February 14, 1995; and "Registration" and "Reconstruction Amendments," History San Jose archives.

104. See the *San Jose Mercury News*, February 14, 1995. Also see "Voting Regulations in Gold Rush California" in the California Constitution, art. 2, sec. 1; and "Registration of Citizens and Enrollment of Voters during Reconstruction Era."

105. In some areas, such as San Joaquin County, African Americans were not allowed to register. The county clerk contended that the black vote "wasn't legal until the Legislature met and changed the law in California," according to the *San Jose Mercury News*, February 14, 1995.

106. This account appears in the *San Jose Mercury News*, February 14, 1995; and "Fifteenth Amendment Ratification Celebrations" (Fifteenth Amendment Ratification in San Jose Papers: Research Library, History San Jose).

107. See "Fifteenth Amendment Ratification Celebrations," History San Jose archives; and *San Francisco Call*, April 8, 1970.

108. Anecdote appears in *San Jose Mercury News*, February 14, 1995; and archives, "California's First Black Voters under the 15th Amendment" (Fifteenth Amendment Ratification in San Jose Papers: Research Library, History San Jose).

109. "Fifteenth Amendment Ratification Celebrations," History San Jose archives.

110. Ibid., and *Nevada Daily National Gazette*, April 11, 1870.

111. During this election, 1,236 ballots were cast.

112. Sucheng Chan, *Asian Californians* (San Francisco: MTL/Boyd and Fraser, 1991), 46 (also see page 51); and the Burlingame Treaty, 18 Stat. 147 (1868). The Burlingame Treaty, which recognized the citizens from the United States and China who changed their residences, was undermined by a treaty in 1880 which, Chan stated, gave the United States "the right unilaterally to limit Chinese immigration, thereby enabling Congress to pass the 1882 exclusion law . . . which was to have a life of ten years."

113. Quoted in "California's First Black Voters under the 15th Amendment," History San Jose archives.

114. Quoted from *San Jose Mercury News*, February 14, 1995.

115. See "P.F. Collins Letter—Black San Jose and 1870 Vote" (University Archives at the Bancroft Library, U.C.–Berkeley).

116. The Port of Alviso is the South Bay's most natural harbor. From 1849 to 1968, it never developed into the deepwater seaport and major railroad terminus that county investors and officials imagined. Its failure to develop stunted Santa Clara Valley's industrial and urban growth in favor of agricultural industrial pursuits. This story is further discussed in chapter 2.

117. To get a sense of Jacob Overton's life, see *San Jose Mercury News*, "Overton Dies," in *San Jose Historical Mercury News* archive (1886–1922); *San Jose Mercury News*, "When San Jose Was Young: No. 302 Oldest Janitor" and City Hall Exhibits Committee, "Hidden Heritages: Six African American Families, San Jose 1860–1920" (San Jose City Hall, 2009–2010). In San Jose, Jacob Overton settled and immediately found steady employment as a porter at Knox-block, a commercial building owned by Dr. Knox's widow, Sarah L. Knox-Goodrich. Sarah Knox-Goodrich was a racial liberal and suffragist whose working relationship with Jacob lasted until her passing in 1903. Around 1873, in gratitude for his work at Knox-block she gave him her greatest treasure: a bust of freedom fighter John Brown. In addition, Jacob Overton was the only black member of California Pioneers of Santa Clara County, which was the first organization to preserve, promote, and celebrate the history of the county.

118. City Hall Exhibits Committee, "Hidden Heritages."

119. See Myra Lynn Wysinger, "African American Pioneer of California: Edmond Edward Wysinger (1816–1891)," at http://wysinger.homestead.com/courtcase.html; and *"Wysinger v. Crookshank* (1890)," at http://www.blackpast.org/?q=primarywest/wysinger-v-crookshank-1890. Also see *Plessy v. Ferguson*, 163 U.S. 537 (1896). Segregation was never legally imposed in South Bay because the cost of separate facilities for such a minute black population would have been prohibitive.

120. PBS, and New York Life, "Jim Crow Laws: California—1893: Barred Public Accommodation Segregation," in *The History of Jim Crow* (http://www.jimcrowhistory.org/scripts/jimcrow/lawsoutside.cgi?state=California).

121. Ancestry.com, "African Americans in Santa Clara County," in the 1870 U.S. census and 1880 U.S. census. The 1890 U.S. census for California was destroyed by a fire at the Commerce Department in Washington, D.C., on January 10, 1921.

122. See Gagliardi, "Roots," 16.

Chapter 2

1. Quote is from Albert Broussard, "Civil Rights Leader in San Francisco, 1940s," in *Peoples of Color in the American West*, ed. Sucheng Chan et al. (Lexington, Mass.: D. C. Heath, 1994), 489.

2. Ibid., 495. For histories that suggest passive, subdued behavior and exclude Bay Area blacks, see Richard M. Dalfiume, "The 'Forgotten Years' of

the Negro Revolution," *Journal of American History* 55, 1 (June 1968): 90–106; Gerald D. Nash, *The American West Transformed: The Impact of the Second World War* (Bloomington: Indiana University Press, 1985); Michael P. Malone and Richard W. Etulain, *The American West: A Twentieth-Century History* (Lincoln: University of Nebraska Press, 1989), 146; and Douglas Henry Daniels, *Pioneer Urbanites: A Social and Cultural History of Black San Francisco* (Berkeley: University of California Press, 1991), xiv, 165–175. Dalfiume's basic argument is that black activism developed from 1939 to 1945, from which there was the Great Migration, which sparked a sense of urgency that catapulted blacks into political activism. Nash's work is best seen as caught between the transitional shift in western writing from interpreting the West as a frontier to attempting to chart the region's social developments, including race, in the twentieth century.

3. Clyde Arbuckle Ephemera Collection. "The Valley of Heart's Delight Pamphlet" (ca. 1922), San Jose Public Library California Room (http://digitalcollections.sjlibrary.org/cdm/compoundobject/collection/sjplephemer/id/174).

4. For a rich discussion on the construction of race and whiteness, see Matthew Frye Jacobson, *Whiteness of a Different Color: European Immigrants and the Alchemy of Race* (Cambridge, Mass.: Harvard University Press, 1998), 1–14.

5. "California Alien Land Laws of 1913," in California Legislature, *Statutes of California, and Amendments to the Codes,* 40th sess. (1913), 206–208; "Naturalization Act of 1790," in the Library of Congress, "A Century of Lawmaking for a New Nation: U.S. Congressional Documents and Debates, 1774–1875" (http://rs6.loc.gov/cgi-bin/ampage?collId=llsl&fileName=001/llsl001.db&recNum=226); "Page Law," 43rd Cong., 2nd sess. 2, ch. 141 (March 3, 1875); *Chinese Exclusion Act of 1882,* in *U.S. Statutes at Large* 22 (December 1881–March 1883), 58–62; *Cable Act of 1922,* in *Prologue Magazine* 30, 2 (Summer 1998), http://www.archives.gov/publications/prologue/1998/summer/women-and-naturalization-1.html; *Immigration Act of 1924* (aka *National Origins Act* or the *Johnson-Reed Act*), in *U.S. Statutes at Large* 42, pt. 1 (December 1923–March 1925), 153–169; *Immigration and Nationality Act of 1952* (*McCarran-Walter Act*), in Public Law 82-414, 66 Stat. 163; *Immigration and Naturalization Services Act of 1965* (aka *Hart-Celler Act* or the *INS Act of 1965*), in Public Law 89-236. For a rich discussion of European Americans' discriminatory practices toward Japanese and Japanese Americans see Takaki, *Strangers from a Different Shore,* 179–229; and Leslie G. Kelen, ed., *Missing Stories: An Oral History of Ethnic and Minority Groups in Utah* (Salt Lake City: University of Utah Press, 1996), 313.

6. See Pitti, *The Devil in Silicon Valley,* 78–127; California History Center, *Sunnyvale: City of Destiny* (Cupertino: California History Center, De Anza College, 1974), 68, 90–91; and George J. Sanchez, *Becoming Mexican American: Ethnicity, Culture, and Identity in Chicano Los Angeles, 1900–1945* (New York: Oxford University Press, 1993), 17–62, 87–107, 129–150, 188–226. The early

twentieth century was a tumultuous period for persons of Mexican ancestry whose citizenship was always in question. From 1910 to the early 1930s, most Mexicans temporarily migrated to the Southwest United States as refugees from Revolutionary Mexico or for economic opportunities as sojourners. At Libby, McNeil & Libby the canning season ran from early June to December. The company furnished housing for its laborers on the grounds. Migrant workers were also fed at the company's restaurant.

7. See Ancestry.com, "African Americans in Santa Clara County," in 1900 U.S. census; 1910 U.S. census; 1920 U.S. census; and 1930 U.S. census.

8. University of Virginia Library, *Historical Census Browser*, 1920–1940. In 1920, farms operated by blacks and other nonwhites in Santa Clara County numbered 202; minority tenant farmers totaled 133. Forty out of the 5,016 farms in the county were operated by blacks and other nonwhites. In 1930 blacks and nonwhites operated 262 of 5,975 farms in Santa Clara County. People of color operated 9,671 acres of farmland in the county out of 516,974 farm acres available. In 1940, farms operated by nonwhites in the South Bay were 415 out of 5,608. People of color operated 12,108 farm acres in the county out of 516,974. In final sum, although persons of color were operating more farms by 1940, their average farm acreage decreased. Also see *San Jose Mercury News*, August 11, 1977, and May 20, 1962.

9. See *Los Angeles Times*, March 14, 1896; and Joseph A. Rodriguez, *City against Suburb: The Culture Wars in an American Metropolis* (Westport, Conn.: Praeger, 1999), 80. San Jose city officials and boosters from the 1890s to 1950s have either attempted to mirror Los Angeles' unexpected and phenomenal growth in this period or rival "the City of Angels." According to the *Los Angeles Times* article, San Jose dominated one of the most enterprising agricultural regions in the world; its downtown was being modernized; and its sense of importance traces back to 1777, as a Spanish pueblo and mission city and, in the statehood period, as California's first state capital. To demonstrate the city's rise in status as the center of the valley in the 1890s, city officials built in the center of the downtown (Market and Santa Clara Streets) a two-hundred-foot-tall iron electrical tower nicknamed the "Tower of Jewels," a giant beacon lighting the entire length and breadth of the valley until 1915, when it was destroyed by a storm.

10. The county's black population was less only that that of San Francisco County, with 1,847 black residents, and that of Los Angeles County, with 1,817. See University of Virginia Library, *Historical Census Browser*, 1890; and the Garden City Women's Club, *History of Black Americans in Santa Clara Valley*, 66.

11. According to the voting register of Santa Clara County, African American residents came from states such as Missouri, Kentucky, Georgia, Arkansas, and Virginia. The 1900 figure is from the *Historical Census Browser*, 1940. University of Virginia Library, *Historical Census Browser*, 1900; and Ancestry.com, 1900–1930 U.S. census.

12. U.S. Bureau of the Census, *1950 Census of Population*, Vol. 11, *Characteristics of the Population*, pt. 5, *California*, 5–164; *Historical Census Browser*, 1910–1950. In 1910, the African American population was 262; in 1920, 335; in 1930, 536. In 1950, 1,718 (830 were males, and 888 were females; 591 lived in San Jose, 14 in Santa Clara, 542 in Palo Alto, 410 in Redwood City, and 161 scattered in other cities). The gender ratio was always been balanced in the early twentieth century.

13. The "end of the line" notion of black migration to the urban West is taken from Taylor, *The Forging of a Black Community*, 9–10.

13. See Taylor, "Urban Black Labor in the West, 1849–1949," 114.

14. Quoted in Gretchen Lemke Santangelo, *Abiding Courage*, 54.

15. For more information on early-twentieth-century black families see Ancestry.com, 1900–1930 U.S. census; and City Hall Exhibits Committee, "Hidden Heritages."

16. Garden City Women's Club, *History of Black Americans in Santa Clara Valley*, 129.

17. See Heather Ribbs, "What's in a Name: A Family Chronicle: The Ribbs Family—An Eastside Plumbing Dynasty" (http://www.nnvesj.org/Y04/Ed13/Edition1352.htm). Henry, born in 1899, was Felix and Eliza Beck's youngest child. The Becks amassed a fortune from oil royalties on their land in Louisiana. Felix in turn opened a mortgage holding company for black families. This success and domestic tensions within the United States connected to World War I and the postwar period prompted a white backlash against the Becks around 1920. After returning from military duty in Paris, France, during the war, Henry's older brother Benjamin bought a farm. He was determined to not work for anyone, especially not a white man. Local whites did not respond well to Benjamin's attitude and economic empowerment. Following an altercation with a white neighbor, Benjamin was shot, and the neighbor was either blinded or killed. Immediately a mob formed to lynch Benjamin and put the Becks in their place. Benjamin, fleeing bounty hunters and white posses, left Louisiana for California (via Oklahoma) in haste after bounty hunters and white posses were formed. After this incident, the Becks were forced to change their names for protection from bounty hunters. Henry Beck became Henry William Ribbs (Heather calls him William), Benjamin Beck became Charlie Carter, and Philip Beck became Clyde Ribbs.

18. Ibid., 130.

19. For the full account of Henry Ribbs's oral testimony, see the Garden City Women's Club, *History of Black Americans in Santa Clara Valley*, 125–136.

20. Quote is from Gagliardi, "Roots," 17. Also see *San Jose Mercury News*, March 19, 1979; and Edith Smith, *Some Early African American Settlers*, 3–5.

21. See the Garden City Women's Club, *History of Black Americans in Santa Clara Valley*, 66; "AME Zion Church files," Palo Alto Historical Society; and Ancestry.com, 1900–1930 U.S. census.

22. Garden City Women's Club, *History of Black Americans in Santa Clara Valley*, 123.

23. Ancestry.com, 1900–1930 U.S. census.

24. Ibid.

25. See Garden City Women's Club, *History of Black Americans in Santa Clara Valley*, 125.

26. Ibid., 132–136.

27. *Shelley v. Kraemer*, 334 U.S. 1 (1948); Gagliardi, "Roots," 16; Testbed for the Redlining Archives of California's Exclusionary Spaces (T-RACES), "San Jose, Santa Clara, and Vicinity Redlining Map" (1937) at http://salt.unc.edu/T-RACES/mosaic.html; George Lipsitz, *The Possessive Investment in Whiteness* (Philadelphia: Temple University Press, 2006), 1–23; and Eduardo Bonilla-Silva, *Racism without Racists: Color-Blind Racism and the Persistence of Racial Inequality in America* (New York: Rowman and Littlefield, 2009).

28. Santa Clara County Office of the Clerk Recorder, Archives, "Declaration of Restrictions, Conditions, Covenants, Charges and Agreements Affecting the Real Property." Author examined deeds from 1915 to 1947.

29. See Gagliardi, "Roots," 16; and University of Virginia Library, *Historical Census Browser*, 1940. According to longtime San Jose resident Joyce Ellington, "A black man building a house on the north side of Santa Clara Street was not that unusual" in the early twentieth century. In 1940 Santa Clara Valley had a total of 51,916 occupied dwellings. Of them, 50,654 were occupied by whites, 214 by blacks, and 1,048 by other people of color—a 2.4 percent occupancy rate by nonwhites. Eighty-three dwellings were owned by blacks, and 131 rentals were home to African Americans; their homeownership rate in 1940 was 39 percent, which was comparable to African American homeownership rates in Seattle and Los Angeles (see Taylor, *Forging of a Black Community*, 85).

30. See Gagliardi, "Roots," 17.

31. Ancestry.com, "African Americans in Santa Clara County," in the 1930 U.S. census; and William T. Ribbs, Sr., phone interview by the author, July 22, 2013. In San Jose, the Sallie L. Brown household included four seamstresses who co-owned a dressmaking shop. All dressmakers were her daughters. Like most local African Americans, the Browns lived in the Northside, on North Eleventh Street.

32. The Garden City Women's Club, *History of Black Americans in Santa Clara Valley*, 16–17. The Overtons were one of the few black families to own a home south of Santa Clara Street before the 1970s. According to Boyer, the home was paid for with the husband's salary as an independent photographer. The only black photographer in early San Jose was Charles Overton, son of Jacob and Sarah Massey Overton.

33. Social Explorer Professional, "1940 Census Tract–% Black Population, in Santa Clara County" (2011 Social Explorer). Social mapping correlates with

the testimony of people I interviewed in San Jose, Los Altos, Mountain View, and Palo Alto in August 2010 and October 2011: Helen Anderson Gaffin, Orvella Stubbs, Patricia Perkins, Kenneth Blackwell, Gloria Anderson, Charles Alexander, Mattie Briggs, Cazetta Gray, Jean Libby, the staff at Mountain View Historical Society, and Steve Staiger at Palo Alto Historical Society. Also see the Garden City Women's Club, *History of Black Americans in Santa Clara Valley*.

34. See Social Explorer Professional, "1940 Census Tract"; Ancestry.com, 1900–1930 U.S. census; and "AME Zion Church files," Palo Alto Historical Society.

35. Quote from Octavia Jones appears in D. Cassandra Fletcher's "The History of Palo Alto: The Minorities Point of View," 1987 ("AME Zion Church files," Palo Alto Historical Society).

36. Ancestry.com, 1900–1930 U.S. census; and "Palo Alto City Council Public Hearing of July 22, 1996: Reclassification to category one of the former University AME Zion Church located at 819 Ramona Street, Palo Alto" ("AME Zion Church files," Palo Alto Historical Society).

37. Ancestry.com, "African Americans in Santa Clara County," in 1930 U.S. census.

38. Based on people I interviewed in San Jose in August 2010: Patricia Perkins, Kenneth Blackwell, and Gloria Anderson; and on Ancestry.com, "African Americans in Santa Clara County," in 1930 U.S. census.

39. See Fletcher, "The History of Palo Alto," 13.

40. Ancestry.com, 1900–1930 U.S. census; and a documentary on African Americans in Mountain View titled "We Were There Too" (Mountain View History Center, Mountain View Library).

41. "Palo Alto City Council Public Hearing of July 22, 1996"; and "University AME Zion Church, 1925–1964 Pamphlet" ("AME Zion Church files," Palo Alto Historical Society).

42. "Palo Alto City Council Public Hearing of July 22, 1996."

43. Urban historians and sociologists have called this time period "the beginning of an era of family disintegration and social disorientation in the black urban North." For more information on this subject see Taylor, *The Forging of a Black Community*, 146.

44. See Gagliardi, "Roots," 16–19, 18.

45. Garden City Women's Club, *History of Black Americans in Santa Clara Valley*, 116–117.

46. Ibid.

47. See Glenna Matthews, "A California Middletown: The Social History of San Jose in the Depression" (Ph.D. diss., Stanford University, 1977), 79. Parts of the county—Sunnyvale, West San Jose, and Palo Alto—were saved from severe economic hardship. Crucial to economic solvency was passage of a public works bill in 1931 that injected about $5 million and 150,000 jobs into the South Bay

Peninsula and San Francisco Bay Area economies called Airbase Sunnyvale (aka Moffett Field).

48. Ibid., 98–99. St. James Park had a history of being a forum for free speech, and so it was ideal for congregating and rallying for civil liberties and labor rights. It was one of the few spaces in California where the inclusive International Workers of the World was allowed to make speeches and hold rallies in the 1910s. During the 1920s the American Civil Liberties Union protected free speech at St. James Park from San Jose's city hall, which wanted political and labor rallies banned. Progressive rallies at St. James Park in the 1930s brought together people ranging from farmworkers and union leaders to Stanford University professors and San Francisco's literary and artistic intelligentsia. Half of these activists were blue-collar Italian Americans. Most activists from 1931 to 1935 were cannery and agricultural workers protesting their wages being slashed by 20 to 25 percent while being mandated to work more hours in deteriorating work conditions. In 1931 about fifteen hundred Cannery and Agricultural Workers Industrial Union members rioted after a rally at St. James Park when police stopped them from marching on city hall; the police chief swore in 178 "special officers" for the occasion. Twenty people, all labor leaders, were arrested. The riot and arrests caught the attention of the Communist Party, which sent its legal arm, the International Labor Defense, to represent the labor leaders. From then until 1935, the Communist Party had a presence of eight or nine members who provided leadership in cannery labor organizing. It was a period of great agricultural organizing and strikes after almost two decades of such activity being dormant in the valley. In 1934, the Cannery and Agricultural Workers Industrial Union, which had set up its headquarters at San Jose only months before, turned its attention toward organizing cotton workers in a protracted strike at the San Joaquin Valley. The union moved it headquarters to Sacramento for statewide organizing, and in 1935 it aborted its attempts to organize cannery workers and left the South Bay.

49. See Matthews, "A California Middletown," 58. Racially segregated neighborhoods within San Jose were Little Italy (Italian American, working class), Little Tijuana (Mexican American, working class), Goose Town (Eastern European American, working class), Tar Flats (Black American, working class), and South of the Tracks (European American, middle to upper class).

50. The Northside borders on St. James Park.

51. Matthews, "A California Middletown," 138.

52. Ibid., 99. The South Bay had the largest canneries and packing plants in the world. Its main agricultural products were prunes, apricots, pears, and cherries.

53. Agricultural workers in the 1930s wanted restoration of 1920s wages, time and a half after eight hours, union recognition from the AFL, equal work regardless of age or sex, and free transportation to work for women.

54. See Loomis, *Milpitas*, 100. Also see Matthews, "A California Middletown," 125–139.

55. Kidnappers John Holmes and Thomas Thurmond could have been tried in San Francisco. See Matthews, "A California Middletown," 125–139.

56. Matthews, "A California Middletown," 128; and Banana Peel Entertainment, *Valley of the Heart's Delight* (San Francisco: Banana Peel Entertainment, 2006).

57. Quote appears in the Garden City Women's Club, *History of Black Americans in Santa Clara Valley*, 120. Also see *San Jose Mercury News*, August 11, 1977; and Matthews, "A California Middletown," 125–139. California Governor Jim Rolph refused to call out troops to bring order before the lynching. He publicly praised the lynch mob—many of whom were outsiders—with the politically utilitarian belief that "the people make the laws, don't they." In addition, the local police department was slow to have hearings to investigate itself. Ultimately, the lynching at St. James Park was the nadir in citizens' respect for law and order, and civil liberties completely broke down until they were forced to comply after 1935. Vigilantism was a hot topic in the South Bay from 1931 to 1935.

58. Matthews, "A California Middletown," 143.

59. For a rich discussion on the Great Strike of 1934, see Albert S. Broussard, *Black San Francisco*, 129; Mike Davis, *Prisoners of the American Dream: Politics and Economy in the History of the U.S. Working Class* (London: Verso, 1986), 9–13; Dembo, "The West Coast Teamsters' and Longshoremen's Unions," 27–35; Paul Eliel, *The Waterfront and General Strikes, San Francisco, 1934* (San Francisco: Hooper Printing Co., 1934), 166; McBroome, *Parallel Communities*, 73–75; Nelson, "The 'Lords of the Docks' Reconsidered," 157, 163, 181; and Art Preis, *Labor's Giant Step; Twenty Years of the CIO* (New York: Pathfinder, 1972), 12, 19–33. The Great Strike of 1934, which is often called "the Big Strike," began on May 9 after months of tensions between the AFL's International Longshoreman Association and the Industrial Association of San Francisco. Ten thousand to fifteen thousand members of the longshoreman association on the West Coast went on an unauthorized strike to address better wages, fewer work hours, control over their conditions, and the right to organize in unions free from the control of company agents. Their numbers escalated to twenty-five thousand with ten thousand sympathetic seamen joining the cause. The strike was led by rank-and-file union member Harry Bridges. Bridges was a progressive socialist, symbolic of the new labor movement's leadership in that he believed in racial equality, whereas most white workers saw the average African American as competition and as someone who occupied dock positions traditionally held by their own family members. Bridges was sympathetic to the history and the position of black workers and knew that they were essential to the strike's success. "In San Francisco, principle, practical necessity, and political expediency merged in a way that reinforced Bridge's commitment to the union's black members," Nelson wrote

(181). Prior to 1934, blacks functioned as strikebreakers, undermining the gains of the local labor movement in the general strikes of 1916 and 1919. In 1934, the Brotherhood of Sleeping Car Porters' Dellums and Bridges had several meetings, which culminated in the tentative stipulation that African Americans, through merit, could join the International Longshoreman Association and take part in waterfront employment if they did not break the lines and become scabs. In the African American community, Dellums was reinforced by growing support for labor radicalism that was in turn fueled by worsening dislocations in the local economy and social life. Opponents of the general strike in the African American community were found within its professional classes and well-educated elites, such as doctors, lawyers, and teachers—the ones who lived in prestigious Bay Area places such as South Berkeley. Overall, Bay Area blacks were very cautious and well aware that "union labor never seems to need the loyalty of black workers until it calls a strike" (Broussard, 129). With the tentative understanding that African Americans would not break the strike, the union eventually closed all Bay Area ports. The strike dissolved from July 20 to July 31 with an arbitrated settlement favoring the industrialists. Perhaps the best part of the agreement for the workers was that they earned the right to exist on the waterfront as an organized body for the first time since 1919. Gains included winning union recognition, union control of hiring on the West Coast, somewhat better race relations, and improved relationships between dock workers and employers. African American workers earned a limited inclusion arrangement with the union by being placed in auxiliary units and getting two blacks—Dellums and Ishmael Flory of the Dining Car Cooks and Waiters Union—on the Alameda County Central Labor Council to serve as representatives. For eligible African American dockworkers, the auxiliary scheme was a progressive half-step forward from near-absolute exclusion at the strike's outset.

60. For a rich discussion on the black Baptist church and community formation from 1890 to 1970, see Arbuckle, *Clyde Arbuckle's History of San Jose*, 281; Garden City Women's Club, *History of Black Americans in Santa Clara Valley*, 17; and Arnold, *Antioch*, 8.

61. For more information on the black women club movement see the Garden City Women's Club, *History of Black Americans in Santa Clara Valley*, 56–66; and Paula Giddings, *When and Where I Enter: The Impact of Black Women on Race and Sex in America* (New York: William and Morrow, 1984), 94–117.

62. Josephine St. Pierre Ruffin, "Address to the First National Conference of Colored Women," in *Lift Every Voice: African American Oratory, 1787–1900*, ed. Philip S. Foner and Robert James Branham (Tuscaloosa: University of Alabama Press, 1998), 797–800.

63. Giddings, *When and Where I Enter*, 94–117. See Sharon Harley, "Mary Church Terrell: Genteel Militant," in *Black Leaders of the Nineteenth Century*,

ed. Leon Litwack and August Meier (Urbana: University of Illinois Press, 1991), 307–321; and Moore, "Your Life Is Really Not Just Your Own, 211–212.

64. See Arnold, *Antioch*, 37. Also see Loomis, *Milpitas*, 69–71; and the *San Jose Mercury News*, August 11, 1977. The earthquake of 1906 rocked the Bay Area. According to Mattie Berry, "that was a disaster that brought many people together. . . . I remember we went to live in a small shack my father found at the edge of town. The rest of the city [San Jose] was in tents."

65. See the Garden City Women's Club, *History of Black Americans in Santa Clara Valley*, 56–66. San Jose has always had a strong black women club presence. Boyer demonstrated this by becoming the third president of the State Federation of Colored Women's Clubs of California in 1911–1912. Out of the twenty-nine clubs at the state convention, San Jose had three, whereas San Francisco had one, and Oakland had five. The bulk of women club activity in California occurred in Southern California. For Marcus Garvey's visit, see Garden City Women's Club, History of the Garden City Women's Club (http://gardencitywomensclub.org/history.html).

66. For more on the Prince Hall Grand Lodge tradition, see William A. Muraskin, *Middle-Class Blacks in a White Society: Prince Hall Freemasonry in America* (Berkeley: University of California Press, 1975); PBS, "Prince Hall 1735–1807," in *Africans in America* (http://www.pbs.org/wgbh/aia/part2/2p37.html); and Raymond T. Coleman, "Prince Hall History Education Class" (http://www.princehall.org/History/Ray%20Colemans%20History.pdf). See the Garden City Women's Club, *History of Black Americans in Santa Clara Valley*, 89; and "Prowler," *Palo Alto Times*, September 6, 1934 ("AME Zion Church files," Palo Alto Historical Association). History has been more open to charting Theodore Moss, who apparently came to the South Bay with the initial intent of establishing the black lodge tradition. From 1930 to 1939 Moss was the grand master of the Free and Accepted Masons. Later he became the grand master of the Prince Hall Grand Lodge of California. The Free and Accepted Masons was the umbrella organization for all black lodges from 1912 to 1975. During Moss's heyday he was a member of at least ten Mason organizations in California and authorized the extension of the institution on the West Coast and Hawaii in the 1930s and 1940s. In Palo Alto, black men were socially active in the black freemason group, Community Lodge 43, Free and Accepted Masons (Prince Hall affiliation), founded in 1927.

67. Garden City Women's Club, *History of Black Americans in Santa Clara Valley*, 89; and William T. Ribbs, interviewed by the author.

68. Douglas Flamming, "Becoming Democrats: Liberal Politics and the African American Community in Los Angeles, 1930–1965," in *Seeking El Dorado: African Americans in California*, ed. Lawrence de Graaf et al. (Seattle: University of Washington Press, 2001), 279.

69. See Edith Smith, *Some Early African American Settlers*, 2, 8–10; University of Virginia Library, *Historical Census Browser*, 1850–1960; County of Santa Clara, Advance Planning Office, "Issue 89-1A" (January 1989); and U.S. Bureau of the Census, *Census of Housing*, Vol. 1, *1970, Housing Characteristics for States, Cities, and Counties*, pt. 6, *California*, 7–10, 14–15, 453.

70. For a rich discussion concerning voting patterns in the 1930s South Bay, see Matthews, "A California Middletown," 27. In 1920s California, "of 555 electoral contests . . . Democrats won only 25."

71. Ibid., 227.

72. Paraphrased from B. Gordon Wheeler, *Black California: The History of African-Americans in the Golden State* (New York: Hippocrene, 1993), 209.

Chapter 3

1. Broussard, "In Search of a Promised Land," 189.

2. See Taylor, *In Search of the Racial Frontier*, 251; and University of Virginia Library, *Historical Census Browser*, 1930–1950.

3. Taylor, *In Search of the Racial Frontier*, 251.

4. An excellent understanding of the San Francisco–Bay Area Great Migration narrative can be read in Broussard, *Black San Francisco*; Crouchett et al., *Visions toward Tomorrow*; Marilynn S. Johnson, *The Second Gold Rush: Oakland and the East Bay in World War II* (Berkeley: University of California Press, 1993); McBroome, *Parallel Communities*; Moore, *To Place Our Deeds*; Donna Jean Murch, *Living for the City: Migration, Education, and the Rise of the Black Panther Party in Oakland, California* (Chapel Hill: University of North Carolina Press, 2010); Herbert G. Ruffin, "The Search for Significance in Interstitial Space: San Jose and its Great Black Migration, 1941–1968," in *Black California Dreamin': The Crises of California's African-American Communities* (http://www.escholarship.org/uc/item/63g6128j), 19–56; Santangelo, *Abiding Courage*; and Self, *American Babylon*.

5. To get a better understanding of the traditional Great Migration narrative, see Trotter et al., *The African American Urban Experience*; Trotter, *The Great Migration in Historical Perspective*; Trotter, *Black Milwaukee*; Kenneth W. Goings and Raymond A. Mohl, eds., *The New African American Urban History* (Thousand Oaks, Calif.: Sage, 1996); and James R. Grossman, *Land of Hope: Chicago, Black Southerners, and the Great Migration* (Chicago: University of Chicago Press, 1991).

6. See Albert Broussard, "Black San Francisco as a Model for Examining the Urban West" (filmed presentation), in Program in African American Culture Archives (National Museum of American History), *A Quest for Freedom: The Black Experience in the American West* (Washington, D.C.: Smithsonian Institution, 2001); Douglas Flamming, *Bound for Freedom: Black Los Angeles in Jim*

Crow America (Berkeley: University of California Press, 2005), 350–353; and Josh Sides, *L.A. City Limits: African American Los Angeles from the Great Depression to the Present* (Berkeley: University of California Press, 2006), 11–35.

7. Walter Prescott Webb, "The American West: Perpetual Mirage," *Harper's Magazine*, May 1957, 25–31.

8. See chap. 2.

9. T-RACES, "San Jose, Santa Clara, and Vicinity Redlining Map"; California Newsreel, and Independent Television Service, "The House We Live In," in *Race: The Power of an Illusion* (San Francisco: California Newsreel, 2003); Robert A. Beauregard, *When America Became Suburban* (Minneapolis: University of Minnesota Press, 2006), 83.

10. David M. P. Freund, *Colored Property: State Policy and White Racial Politics in Suburban America* (Chicago: University of Chicago Press, 2007), 99–139; Kenneth T. Jackson, *Crabgrass Frontier: The Suburbanization of the United States* (New York: Oxford University Press, 1985), 195–230; California Newsreel, "The House We Live In"; Lipsitz, *The Possessive Investment in Whiteness*, 1–23; and Beauregard, *When America Became Suburban*, 83.

11. See Jackson, *Crabgrass Frontier*, 202; and Oliver Gillham, *The Limitless City: A Primer on the Urban Sprawl Debate* (Washington, D.C.: Island Press, 2002), 37.

12. Gillham, *The Limitless City*, 37; and Dolores Hayden, *Building Suburbia: Green Fields and Urban Growth, 1820–2000* (New York: Vintage, 2003), 123. The FHA supplied funds for new home mortgages on favorable terms that included an extension of the loan period from five years and a down payment of 50 percent. Buyers were allowed to pay off the mortgage up to thirty years with a down payment of 10 percent with fixed interest rates ranging from 4 to 4.5 percent. By doing this, Gillham wrote, "interest charges and a portion of the principal were paid off with each loan payment, eliminating the huge balloon payments at the end of the loan" (37). The FHA also reduced the risk to the lender by insuring "banks so that they could provide 80 percent production advances to developers who would purchase land, capital," Hayden wrote. "In return, developers had to submit site plans and housing plans for review by the FHA" (123).

13. See James T. Patterson, *Grand Expectations: The United States, 1945–1974* (New York: Oxford University Press, 1996), 27. The aim of property ratings was to guarantee at any time during the term of a home mortgage that the market value of the dwelling would exceed the outstanding debt. The lower the valuation placed on properties, the less government risk and the less generous the aid to the potential buyers (and sellers).

14. T-RACES, "San Jose, Santa Clara, and Vicinity Redlining Map"; Hayden, *Building Suburbia*, 124–125; Freund, *Colored Property*, 99–139; California Newsreel, "The House We Live In"; Lipsitz, *The Possessive Investment in Whiteness*, 1–23; and Beauregard, *When America Became Suburban*, 83. The

FHA favored single-family homes over multifamily apartments and public housing with the belief that an economically stable community had to be spacious and sparsely populated. The agency also gave smaller loans with shorter durations for repairing existing homes such as the ones in Northside San Jose than for newer built single-family dwellings constructed in a city such as Saratoga, California.

15. For more on Japanese internment, see Asian Women United of California, eds., *Making Waves: An Anthology of Writings by and about Asian American Women* (Boston: Beacon, 1989), 116; Stephanie Cope, "The Effect World War II Had on the Japanese Living in Santa Clara County" (California Pioneer Paper: San Jose Public Library), 7, 16, 22; Roger Daniels, *Prisoners without Trial: Japanese Americans in World War II* (New York: Hill and Wang, 2004); Patricia Loomis, *Milpitas: The Century of "Little Cornfields," 1852–1952* (Cupertino: California History Center, 1986); Ralph M. Pearce, *From Asahi to Zebras: Japanese American Baseball in San Jose, California* (Japanese American Museum of San Jose, 2005); Takaki, *Strangers from a Different Shore*, 209–212; James J. Rawls and Walton Bean, *California: An Interpretive History* (New York: McGraw Hill, 2003), 361–367; and David K. Yoo, *Growing Up Nisei: Race, Generation, and Culture among Japanese Americans of California, 1924–49* (Urbana: University of Illinois Press, 2000), 1–16.

16. *San Jose Mercury News*, "Blacks Make Solid Leap," January 30, 1972; and *San Jose Mercury News*, "NAACP Chieftain Sees Pendulum Swing towards New Racism," March 31, 1979.

17. Kenneth Blackwell, interviewed by the author, San Jose, August 2010.

18. People interviewed by the author at San Jose in August 2010: Helen Anderson Gaffin, Orvella Stubbs, Patricia Perkins, Kenneth Blackwell, Gloria Anderson, and Charles Alexander. People interviewed by the author and Patricia Perkins at San Jose in 2005: Gladys Anderson, Gloria I. Ellington, Bertha Stafford, Frank Sypert, Jr., Grace Sypert, and Lenora Sypert. Also see the Garden City Women's Club, *History of Black Americans in Santa Clara Valley.*

19. University of Virginia Library, *Historical Census Browser*, 1940–1960; and U.S. Bureau of the Census, *1950 Census of Population,* Vol. 11, *Characteristics of the Population,* pt. 5, *California,* 5–21.

20. Helen Anderson Gaffin, interviewed by the author, San Jose, August 2010.

21. For more on the black migration to Oklahoma, see Taylor, *In Search of the Racial Frontier*, 143–151.

22. Based on people interviewed by author at San Jose in August 2010: Helen Anderson Gaffin, Orvella Stubbs, Patricia Perkins, Kenneth Blackwell, Gloria Anderson, and Charles Alexander.

23. David P. Lee, "Forest Anderson: The Black Oklahoma Millionaire," Anderson Family Reunion Documentary (San Jose: Pat Perkins Collection); and *Ebony* magazine, "The Ten Richest Negroes in America," April 1949, 13–18.

24. Pat Perkins, interviewed by the author, San Jose, February 2011.

25. Helen Anderson Gaffin, interviewed by the author; and Orvella Stubbs, interviewed by the author; Taylor, *In Search of the Racial Frontier*, 272–273; and Thelma Thurston Gorham, "Negroes and Japanese Evacuees," *Crisis* 52, 11 (November 1945), 314–316, 330–331.

26. See Broussard, *Black San Francisco*; Broussard, "In Search of a Promised Land," 181–209; Dembo, "The West Coast Teamsters' and Longshoremen's Unions," 27–35; McBroome, *Parallel Communities*; Moore, *To Place Our Deeds*; Bruce Nelson, "The Big Strike"; Winslow, *Waterfront Workers*; Santangelo, *Abiding Courage*; Taylor, *In Search of the Racial Frontier*, 251–277; and Taylor, "Urban Black Labor in the West," 99–120.

27. Based on people interviewed by the author: Helen Anderson Gaffin, Gloria Anderson, and Orvella Stubbs. Also see *James et al. v. Marinship Corporation*, 25, 2d *California Reports*, 721 (1944); and Taylor, *In Search of the Racial Frontier*, 258–260.

28. Helen Anderson Gaffin, interviewed by the author; and Gloria Anderson, interviewed by the author.

29. Helen Anderson Gaffin, interviewed by the author.

30. Santangelo, *Abiding Courage*, 50.

31. Helen Anderson Gaffin, interviewed by the author.

32. Taylor, *In Search of the Racial Frontier*, 255.

33. Ibid., 257–260; Broussard, *Black San Francisco*, 158–165; McBroome, *Parallel Communities*, 106–112.

34. "Executive Order 8802" (http://www.blackpast.org/?q=primary/executive-order-8802-1941).

35. See *James et al. v. Marinship Corporation*.

36. Julia and Daisy Dollarhyde's letter to President Roosevelt appears in Philip S. Foner and Ronald L. Lewis, *The Black Worker: From the Founding of the CIO to the AFL-CIO Merger, 1936–1955* (Philadelphia: Temple University Press, 1978), 290–291.

37. Based on Mattie Tinsley, interviewed by the author, San Jose, August 2010; Helen Anderson Gaffin, interviewed by the author; and Steve Millner, interviewed by the author, San Jose, October 2011.

38. See Pitti, *The Devil in Silicon Valley*, 136–138.

39. California History Center, *Sunnyvale: City of Destiny*, 63, 85. During WWII Hendy manufactured engines for Liberty ships "and built ship propulsion steam turbines and gears under license from Westinghouse."

40. Ibid., 60.

41. Taylor, "Urban Black Labor in the West," 110.

42. Kenneth Blackwell, interviewed by the author.

43. Based on interviews by the author with Patricia Perkins, Kenneth Blackwell, and Gloria Anderson.

44. Patricia Perkins, interviewed by the author, San Jose.

45. For a rich discussion on black migration to California from 1941 to 1970, see Broussard, *Black San Francisco*, 133–142, 171; McBroome, *Parallel Communities*, 129–147; Moore, *To Place Our Deeds*, 127–146; and Santangelo, *Abiding Courage*, 133–152.

46. Interviews are from the Garden City Women's Club, *History of Black American in Santa Clara Valley*, 68, 116.

47. Cass Jackson, phone interview by the author, June 25, 2012.

48. Based on the interviews by the author with Patricia Perkins, Gloria Anderson, and Kenneth Blackwell.

49. Gagliardi, "Roots," 17.

50. *San Jose Mercury News*, November 20, 1993. Also see Harry Edwards, *The Struggle That Must Be: An Autobiography* (New York: Macmillan, 1980), 112; and *San Jose Mercury News*, "Black Apartment Hunter Encounters Waiting List," July 17, 1977.

51. The home was at 386 North Twelfth Street.

52. See the Garden City Women's Club, *History of Black Americans in Santa Clara Valley*, 148; Helen Anderson Gaffin, interviewed by the author; and Orvella Stubbs, interviewed by the author. According to the *History of Black Americans in Santa Clara Valley*, Dollarhyde came to San Jose in 1933, whereas my interviews suggest 1940.

53. Helen Gaffin, interviewed by the author; and Orvella Stubbs, interviewed by the author.

54. Garden City Women's Club, *History of Black Americans in Santa Clara Valley*, 148.

55. Ibid., 94.

56. See NAACP West Coast Region Files, "NAACP Membership Report, San Jose Branch, 1948–1976" (Bancroft Library, U.C.–Berkeley).

57. Garden City Women's Club, *History of Black Americans in Santa Clara Valley*, 94.

58. Patricia Loomis, *Milpitas: The Century of "Little Cornfields," 1852–1952* (Cupertino: California History Center, 1986), 51; *San Jose Mercury News*, April 19, 1965; and Pitti, *The Devil in Silicon Valley*, 224.

59. Quoted from Pitti, *The Devil in Silicon Valley*, 84.

60. Quoted from the Garden City Women's Club, *History of Black Americans in Santa Clara Valley*, 94, 148.

61. See the Garden City Women's Club, *History of Black Americans in Santa Clara Valley*, 94.

62. See Joe William Trotter, *The Great Migration in Historical Perspective: New Dimensions of Race, Class, and Gender* (Bloomington: Indiana University Press, 1991), 14.

Chapter 4

The epigraph to this chapter is from the position paper "The Fair Housing Act" by Rumford in defending the California Fair Housing Act against efforts to repeal it via Proposition 14. The text can be found online in *William Byron Rumford: Legislator for Fair Employment, Fair Housing, and Public Health* (Berkeley: Regents of the University of California, 1973), an oral history taken from interviews conducted by Joyce A. Henderson, at http://www.oac.cdlib.org/view?docId=hb8n39 p2g3;NAAN=13030&doc.view=frames&chunk.id=div00041&toc.depth=1&toc .id=&brand=oac4, 144.

 1. For background on restrictive covenants and racial steering see *Shelley v. Kramer*, 334 U.S. 1 (1948); W. Dennis Keating, *The Suburban Racial Dilemma: Housing and Neighborhoods* (Philadelphia: Temple University Press, 1994), 195, 214; Self, *American Babylon*, 116; John H. Denton, *Apartheid American Style* (Berkeley, Calif.: Diablo, 1968), 4; and Gerald Lee Klein, "Housing Discrimination in California: The Case of Proposition 14" (M.A. thesis, San Jose State College, 1968), 10.

 2. See "Trail Blazers in Open Housing, 1949–64" in "The San Jose Chapter of The Links, Incorporated files" (Research Library, History San Jose).

 3. Ibid.

 4. Ibid.

 5. For more information on Milpitas see Herbert Ruffin, "Sunnyhills: Race and Working Class Politics in Postwar Silicon Valley, 1945–1968," *Journal of the West* 48, 4 (Fall 2009): 113–123. The San Jose movement for a fair housing ordinance is discussed later in the chapter.

 6. *Los Angeles Times*, February 17, 1964.

 7. Keating, *The Suburban Racial Dilemma*, 8. Most experts have said that the new housing market was a sellers' market from 1945 to around 1960, based on a high demand fueled by federal government subsidies to the buyer (i.e., FHA, VA), and the weak bargaining power of the buyer because of the scarce availability of private loan money. In the 1960s, the housing market favored the buyer because of the relatively low demand for homes and the federal government becoming less intent on meeting housing demands to stabilize the national economy. This retreat by the federal government hastened the housing industries' move toward privatization.

 8. *San Jose Mercury News*, May 1, 1961. Most U.S. black homeowners in 1960 lived in the Northeast.

 9. See Self, *American Babylon*, 116.

 10. Pitti, *The Devil in Silicon Valley*, 90–91. According to Pitti, East San Jose was a rural backwater that most white farmers, with the exception of the Portuguese, abandoned by 1915 because of the area's poor soils. The first groups to

replace the white farmers were Puerto Ricans, who arrived "during World War I from Hawaiian cane fields," he writes. "Mexicans settled there by the early 1920s in part to be near Spanish-speakers." After 1950, African Americans outgrew the Northside and began migrating to an urbanizing Eastside.

11. *San Jose Mercury News*, April 29, 1962. According to the U.S. Savings and Loan League, Americans purchased homes based on the house and community. Important to the buyer, the league said, were community services such as paved streets, proper sewage and storm drainage systems, garbage pickup, mail delivery, police and fire protection; community taxes consistent with the services rendered; affordability; proximity to schools, playgrounds, stores, entertainment, and church; public transportation; and employment opportunities. And the touchy question concerned congeniality with your neighbors. Most people tended to live in neighborhoods where people had similar educational and social background: income, age, race, family size. The more homogenous, the better the chemistry within a community was the popular thought.

12. *San Jose Mercury News*, June 1, 1989.

13. For a better understanding of the South Bay's housing market in the postwar era see *San Jose Mercury News*, September 8, 1963; and *Valley Journal*, October 10, 1990. The median price of a single-family home in the South Bay in 1963 went from $17,200 to $18,100. Overall, the cost of housing went from $12,000 around 1947–1953 to $75,000 in 1972 (*Valley Journal*, October 10, 1990, 9).

14. Gagliardi, "Roots," 19. Discriminatory real estate practices in the South Bay prior to the 1970s also hampered Mexican Americans, Japanese Americans, and Chinese Americans.

15. University of Virginia Library, *Historical Census Browser*, 1850–1960; U.S. Bureau of the Census, *1950 Census of Population*, Vol. 11, *Characteristics of the Population*, pt. 5, *California*, "Population of Urbanized Areas: 1950," 5–21; U.S. Bureau of the Census, *1970 Census of Housing*, Vol. 1, *Housing Characteristics for States, Cities, and Counties*, pt. 6, *California*, 7–10, 14–15, 453.

16. U.S. Bureau of the Census, *1970 Census of Housing*, Vol. 1, *Housing Characteristics for States, Cities, and Counties*, pt. 6, *California*, 7–10, 14–15, 453; and *U.S. Census of Population and Housing, 1970 Census Tracts*, table P-1. Homes with black heads of household in the Santa Clara Valley were 1.5 percent, which was well below the state average of 6.5 percent. However, blacks in this area had a homeownership rate of 62 percent, significantly higher than the state average of 55 percent. Possible exclusive areas were Campbell, Cupertino, Fremont, Los Altos, Los Gatos, Santa Clara, Sunnyvale, and Saratoga—where rates of homes with black heads of household were less than 0.7 percent. Milpitas, at 4.6 percent, was close to the state average, 6.5 percent. San Jose and Palo Alto had a small black presence in their downtown areas at 1.3 percent to 2.4 percent. Santa Clara County and San Mateo County areas East Palo Alto and Menlo Park had

black homeowner populations well above the state average at 47.3 percent and 13 percent; however, blacks were a mix of renters and owners. In Santa Clara County, blacks were mostly owners, especially at Fremont, 75 percent; Los Altos, 84 percent; Milpitas, 79 percent; and Saratoga, 91 percent. The exception was Mountain View (34 percent), which was becoming an apartment city. Most Santa Clara County areas ranged between 55 percent and 66 percent owner occupancy. Palo Alto and Santa Clara were 55 percent—perhaps expensive areas, and many blacks in this population were students and staff at Stanford and Santa Clara University. All-white areas in the county and surrounding areas were Campbell, Cupertino, Los Altos, Los Gatos, Santa Clara, Saratoga, Sunnyvale, and Fremont. Moreover, the owner–median value is higher in Santa Clara County by at least 5,000, or 20 percent—Orange County is off the charts and very exclusive. Renting an apartment seems to be more expensive in the suburbs than in metropolitan areas.

17. See Keating, *The Suburban Racial Dilemma*, 9; and Andrew Wiese, *Places of Their Own: African American Suburbanization in the Twentieth Century* (Chicago: University of Chicago Press, 2004), 254.

18. Ibid.

19. De Graaf, "African American Suburbanization," 407; Bruce D. Haynes, *Red Lines, Black Spaces: The Politics of Race and Space in a Black Middle-Class Suburb* (New Haven, Conn.: Yale University Press, 2001), 60; Mark Gottdiener and Ray Hutchison, *The New Urban Sociology* (New York: Westview, 2006), 205; and Sheryll Cashin, *The Failures of Integration: How Race and Class Are Undermining the American Dream* (New York: PublicAffairs, 2005), 43.

20. For a rich discussion on ring suburbs or what many scholars call black suburban boomtowns in areas such as Warrensville Heights, Ohio; Wellston, Missouri; Harvey, Illinois; East Palo Alto, California; Suitland, Maryland; and Roosevelt, New York, see Wiese, *Places of Their Own*, 215–217.

21. See Rhonda Rigenhagen, *A History of Palo Alto* (Romic Environmental Technologies, 1993 and 1997: http://www.romic.com/epahistory/index.htm); Vicky Anning, "Reversal of Misfortune" (*Stanford Magazine*: January–February 1998, http://www.stanfordalumni.org/news/magazine/1998/janfeb/articles/epa.html); and Herbert Ruffin I, interviewed by the author, East Palo Alto, 2002.

22. *San Jose Mercury News*, January 15, 1989. Jackson stressed responsibility and community work of San Jose's citizenry. In an effort to continue her legacy she put together numerous scrapbooks, and she taped and archived her thoughts and her many battles. From the 1940s to her death in 1993, Inez Jackson was one of the pillars of black South Bay community.

23. Ibid. Jackson lived within a half block of Antioch Baptist Church and the Afro-American Community Cultural Center. Her home was central to at least three or four activist meetings a week.

24. "Trail Blazers in Open Housing, 1949–64" (Research Library, History San Jose). Berthina Nelson, working as a real estate agent, helped desegregate the

Santa Clara Valley in the 1960s and '70s. Like Smith, Nelson was encouraged by Williams to become a licensed broker, and she was the second black to be hired into his firm. Her specialty was defeating redlining "by filling out clients' loan applications herself to make certain there would be no excuse for rejection because of 'faulty paperwork.'"

25. See *San Jose Mercury News*, January 15, 1989. Mary Anne Smith said that her parents were the key to her success as a broker. They taught her and her siblings not to hate anyone. As adults, Smith and her siblings migrated to larger towns and cities for better work and educational opportunities.

26. Ibid. Immediately after the incident, the Portuguese woman told Mary of her conversation with the white real estate broker. From the late 1940s to Mary's passing in 1989, she and the Portuguese woman were very good friends.

27. *San Jose Mercury News*, October 29, 1986.

28. See ibid., January 15, 1989.

29. Quote is from "Trail Blazers in Open Housing, 1949–64."

30. See ibid.; and Ned Eichler, *Eichler Insights* 2, 4 (Late Summer 1993): 5.

31. Ibid.

32. Gagliardi, "Roots," 16.

33. *San Jose Mercury News*, October 29, 1986.

34. Quoted in Gagliardi, "Roots," 18.

35. See *San Jose Mercury News*, October 29, 1986.

36. Ibid.

37. Ibid., January 15, 1989.

38. For more information on the CCU, see Garden City Women's Club, *History of Black Americans in Santa Clara Valley*, 153.

39. "Trail Blazers in Open Housing, 1949–64."

40. Garden City Women's Club, *History of Black Americans in Santa Clara Valley*, 153.

41. Ibid., 154.

42. Ibid., 152.

43. Church coalitions addressing race, religion, and housing started to form in Santa Clara County after the area held its first Interfaith Conference on Religion and Race in October 30, 1963. This well-publicized local event attempted to answer pleas made by local civil rights activists who had asked the clergy to become active in the fair housing battle because at that time the moral rhetoric was being dominated by residential segregationists. More than five hundred Catholic, Protestant, and Jewish clergy and laymen attended. However, the only minority presence consisted of several Antioch Baptist church members. Questions could appropriately be raised about how effective the discussions and resolutions on religion and race were, given the low minority turnout. Nonetheless, the delegates left the conference vowing full support for fair housing and racial integration

within white churches and temples throughout the valley. They also suggested that minority congregations such as Antioch should invite whites to their church services—an option that has always existed in South Bay black churches stemming back to the days of the Reverend Peter Williams Cassey and the racial interchange between his San Jose AME church and the white Unitarian church. What this suggestion indicates is the critical disconnect in communication between the white and black churches. With the exception of the Sunnyhills Methodist Church in Milpitas, which was integrated since its founding in the mid-1950s, almost all churches in the Santa Clara Valley were segregated well into the 1970s and 1980s. Ultimately the supportive role taken by most Interfaith Conference delegates as supporters was common for most religious groups throughout California. They were not what Dr. King called the "headlights" on race and religion matters, and they certainly were not in the forefront of the fair housing campaign.

44. For a discussion of freedom rights, see Hasan Kwame Jeffries, *Bloody Lowndes: Civil Rights and Black Power in Alabama's Black Belt* (New York: New York University Press, 2009), 4. Jeffries conceptualizes freedom rights as "the assortment of civil and human rights that emancipated African Americans identified as freedom." It also "acknowledges the centrality of slavery and emancipation to conceptualizations of freedom."

45. Jean Libby, interviewed by the author in Palo Alto, October 2011.

46. *San Jose Mercury News*, October 24, 1963.

47. The cost of living in 1960s Palo Alto was discussed in interviews by the author in October 2012 with Jean Libby and Clayborne Carson, respectively.

48. Ibid.

49. Jean Libby, interviewed by the author in Palo Alto, October 2011.

50. *New York Times*, February 7, 1999. Eichler Homes was one of the largest builders in the United States in the 1960s. In 1964, sales volume from residential development was $19 million. In the 1950s and 1960s the firm built more than twelve thousand houses.

51. See Edward P. Eichler, "Race and Housing: An Interview with Edward P. Eichler, President, Eichler Homes, Inc." (1964), 16–17, 21.

52. The husband taught science and conducted research at Stanford's laboratory.

53. Ibid., 4.

54. Wiese, *Places of Their Own*, 223.

55. See Ned Eichler, *Eichler Insights* 2, 4 (Late Summer 1993): 5.

56. Ibid., 6.

57. Ibid., 19.

58. See Ibid., 5, 17, 22. According to Edward, the common threshold for a white backlash was when more than one or two African American families moved into a community with ten homes. A number of tactics used to combat African Americans from moving into suburbia have been implemented to keep others

from following or to artificially change the cultural and economic composition of the community to encourage white flight. The range of possibilities go from violence to white homeowner associations to block busting.

59. See Ned Eichler, *Eichler Insights* 2, 4 (Late Summer 1993), 7; and *Valley Journal*, October 10, 1990. According to Steve Eichler, grandson of Joseph, by 1970 there was no such thing as affordable housing in the valley.

60. See Gagliardi, "Roots," 19; and *San Jose Mercury News*, August 8, 1988.

61. *San Jose Mercury News*, January 15, 1989.

62. Ibid.

63. Quote in *San Jose Mercury News*, June 24, 1963.

64. Joyce Henderson, *C. L. Dellums: International President of the Brotherhood of Sleeping Car Porters and Civil Rights Leader* (Berkeley: Regents of the University of California, 1973), 115; Klein, "Housing Discrimination in California," 48; Flamming, "Becoming Democrats: Liberal Politics and the African American Community in Los Angeles, 1930–1965," 279–308; and Henderson, *C. L. Dellums*, 116. The California FEPC evolved from the national March on Washington Movement headed by A. P. Randolph, who in 1945 led a committee that selected five states for FEPC bills in that year. California was one of them. The initial objective of the FEPC was to stop whites from using their demographic majority and power to prevent blacks from exercising their civil rights, or human rights as C. L. Dellums put it. Moreover, Dellums did not initially support the California FEPC initiative movement, because he did not trust the will of a white majority that had "been using their majority and their control of the law of the enforcing agencies and firearms to prevent" blacks from exercising their civil rights. He also did not want to set a precedent in the use of the initiative process (115).

65. See Henderson, *C. L. Dellums*, 115; Klein, "Housing Discrimination in California," 48.

66. Klein, "Housing Discrimination in California," 48–49; and Mark Brilliant, *The Color of America Has Changed: How Racial Diversity Shaped Civil Rights* (Oxford: Oxford University Press, 2010), 130–132. The NAACP became active in the FEPC movement in 1951. Christian church groups became active in 1953.

67. Henderson, *C. L. Dellums*, 113. The Hawkins Act passed by a vote of 88 to 1.

68. See *San Jose Mercury News*, May 17, 1961; and Klein, "Housing Discrimination in California," 49. The Hawkins Act brought California up to speed with Connecticut, Massachusetts, and New York, which had some form of open housing by 1963, but they were enacted in separate bills, which often confused lawmakers and the public as to what open housing was. See Klein (49) for a good definition of public-assisted housing.

69. Klein, "Housing Discrimination in California," 53.

70. Henderson, *C. L. Dellums*, 113; and Klein, "Housing Discrimination in California," 46.

71. Quote is taken from the *San Jose Mercury News*, January 25, 1960.

72. Ibid., March 22, 1960.

73. *San Jose Mercury News*, May 25, 1961. Commissioner John Thorne's public agenda was get people to live together so that "they will learn to get along together."

74. Ibid., May 5, 1961.

75. Ibid., November 30, 1963.

76. Ibid., April 26, 1962. Under the Uhruh ordinance a private property owner caught discriminating could be forced to pay for damages, $250; attorney fees; and for enforcement through civil or criminal proceedings or both.

77. *San Jose Mercury News*, May 24, 1962.

78. Ibid.

79. Ibid.

80. Ibid.

81. Other California policy makers supporting the California Fair Housing Act of 1963 included Gov. Brown, the NAACP, the Democratic Party; and specifically Augustus Hawkins and Jesse Unruh, who had bills addressing fair housing. To make matters simple, supporters called it the Rumford Act.

82. See U.S. Commission on Civil Rights. *Civil Rights: 1963 Report of U.S. Commission on Civil Rights* (Washington, D.C.: U.S. Government Printing Office, 1963). The federal government began addressing the closed housing issue around 1962 during the Kennedy administration. In the 1963 U.S. Civil Rights Commission report the federal government publicly announced that "housing discrimination is perhaps the most ubiquitous and deeply rooted Civil Rights problem in America."

83. Quote from *San Jose Mercury News*, June 20, 1963.

84. See Henderson, *William Byron Rumford*, 119; and Klein, "Housing Discrimination in California," 57.

85. For a good understanding of how the Rumford Act passed through the Senate see Herbert G. Ruffin, *Uninvited Neighbors: Black Life and the Racial Quest for Freedom in the Santa Clara Valley, 1777–1968* (Ann Arbor, Mich.: UMI Dissertation, 2007), 284–307. Also see Fair Employment and Housing Act (Rumford Act), sec. 12955; *San Jose Mercury News*, June 6, 1963, and June 20, 1963; Henderson, *C. L. Dellums*, 124; Henderson, *William Byron Rumford*, 116–120.

86. Quote from Denton, *Apartheid American Style*, 2.

87. *Los Angeles Times*, January 5, 1964; and Klein, "Housing Discrimination in California," 48.

88. *San Jose Mercury News*, March 22, 1964.

89. Ibid.

90. See *San Jose Mercury News*, March 23, 1964; *San Jose Mercury News*, November 30, 1963; *Los Angeles Times*, October 24, 1964; *Los Angeles Times*, June 25, 1964; *Los Angeles Times*, August 5, 1964; and *Los Angeles Times*, August 6, 1964.

91. *San Jose Mercury News*, March 23, 1964, and November 30, 1963.

92. Ibid., September 10, 1964.

93. Ibid., November 30, 1963.

94. Ibid., March 14, 1964.

95. Ibid., November 30, 1963. Most lawyers and religious groups throughout Santa Clara Valley opposed Proposition 14 on legal and moral grounds. This included the Palo Alto Bar Association and San Jose Bar Association. The California State Bar Association did not oppose Proposition 14 until September 30, 1964—several weeks to several months after the Santa Clara Valley bar associations declared their stand. Most lawyers felt that the bill added little to the substantial law already established by the Hawkins and Unruh Acts except for the fact that a prospective buyer with strong evidence of discrimination could apply to the FEPC for investigation.

96. In Sunnyvale, the Citizens Committee against CREA, and the Sunnyvale-Cupertino branch of the American Association of University Women distributed pamphlets, protested, and opened debates on fair housing throughout the city.

97. *San Jose Mercury News*, October 16, 1964, and April 6, 1965. The *San Jose Mercury News* also publicly denounced the Ku Klux Klan.

98. See *Los Angeles Times*, June 15, 1964; July 5, 1964; August 13, 1964; August 19, 1964; and August 30, 1964. In Southern California, Rumford supporters had a harder time getting the support of Mexican Americans. Based on a poll conducted at UCLA, many Mexican Americans in Southern California felt they were being neglected by state agencies (such as the FEPC) favoring black interests (*Los Angeles Times*, July 5, 1964). As a result, many who were polled were mixed in their support of Rumford. This started with African American and Mexican American groups forming a tentative coalition around July 1964 in Los Angeles, San Francisco, San Diego, Fresno and Pico Rivera, and San Jose. The lead critic of the California civil rights movement was the Mexican American Political Association, an avid supporter of liberal causes and grassroots politics in California. Much of the its criticism was geared toward the FEPC, which, according to Eduardo Quevedo, the state chairman of the Mexican American group, had done "a fine job for the Negroes but a dismal one for the Mexican Americans." Based on the UCLA survey, most Mexican Americans did not know about the housing discrimination controversy. This movement was not being really discussed and supported in Mexican American neighborhoods until the Mexican Chamber of Commerce of Los Angeles decided to take on the issue. It at first favored Proposition 14 on the

basis that it would protect voting members' property rights. After an uproar in the Mexican American community, however, the chamber switched sides, opposing the initiative in August 1964.

99. Denton, *Apartheid American Style*, 40, 115. According to Denton the common theme promoted by the California Real Estate Association to fair housing supporters was that "you cannot legislate morality" (40).

100. *Los Angeles Times*, March 18, 1964.

101. *Los Angeles Times*, December 4, 1964; and De Graaf, "African American Suburbanization," 415.

102. *San Jose Mercury News*, October 14, 1964.

103. *Los Angeles Times*, November 12, 1964.

104. See Denton, *Apartheid American Style*, 59. According to the author the federal Kerner Commission in March 1968 "firmly concluded that the riots stemmed from the persistence of racial discrimination and a historical legacy of disadvantages in employment, education, and welfare; but one additional factor was clearly identified by the commissioners as underlying all other social and economic problems: segregation." One of the remedies the commission came up with to resolve the issue was expanding federal housing or low and moderate income housing outside of the central city to break the pattern of residential segregation.

105. *San Jose Mercury News*, April 17, 1965.

106. Klein, "Housing Discrimination in California," 86. Also see California Supreme Court decision *Mulkey v Reitman*, 64 Cal 2d 529 (1966); and the U.S. Supreme Court decision *Reitman v. Mulkey*, 387 U.S. 369 (1967). Section 1 of the Fourteenth Amendment states: "No state shall make or enforce any law which abridges the privileges or immunities of citizens of the United States; nor shall any state deprive any person of life, liberty, or property without due process of law; nor deny any person within its jurisdiction the equal protection of the laws."

107. *Mulkey v Reitman*, 64 Cal 2d 529 (1966); *1866 Civil Rights Act*, 14 Stat. 27–30, April 9, 1866 A.D.; "1866 Civil Rights Act," in PBS, *Reconstruction: The Second Civil War* (http://www.pbs.org/wgbh/amex/reconstruction/activism/ps_1866.html); and *Los Angeles Times*, June 18, 1968.

108. Ibid.

109. See "Civil Rights Act of 1968, Title 8 (Fair Housing Act of 1968)" at http://www.usdoj.gov/crt/housing/title8.htm.

110. De Graaf, "African American Suburbanization," 415.

111. *Stanford Encyclopedia of Philosophy*, s.v. "Affirmative Action," http://plato.stanford.edu/entries/affirmative-action/.

112. Ocie Tinsley, interviewed by the author, San Jose, August 2010.

113. Ibid. Today, Tinsley is a retired software engineer from Kaiser Electronics, and he lives in the formerly restricted Rose Garden community in West San Jose. Prior to living in Rose Garden, he and wife, Mattie Briggs, made the South Bay live up to their expectations in East San Jose.

114. U.S. Bureau of the Census, *1970 Census of Housing*, Vol. 1, *Housing Characteristics for States, Cities, and Counties*, pt. 6, *California*, 7–10, 14–15, 453; and U.S. Census, *U.S. Census of Population and Housing: 1970 Census Tracts*, table P-1.

115. University of Virginia Library, *Historical Census Browser*, 1850–1960; U.S. Census, *1970 Census of Housing*, Vol. 1, *Housing Characteristics for States, Cities, and Counties*, pt. 6, *California*, 7–10, 14–15, 453; U.S. Census, "General Characteristics of Black Persons: 1980," in *U.S. Census of Population and Housing: 1980 Census Tracts,* 109; and Santa Clara County Planning Office, "1990 Population and Ethnicity of Santa Clara County by City and CDP; County of Santa Clara," Advance Planning Office 89-1A (January 1989).

116. See Arnold, *Antioch*, 50; and *American Baptist of the West* (December 1970), 1. Antioch was in the forefront of building the San Juan Bautista Apartments (on Cunningham Street in the Tropicana Village area of San Jose). Antioch and HUD formed a partnership in which Antioch directors took the lead, called the San Juan Bautista Corporation, to provide low-income housing just outside of downtown San Jose in the late 1960s. Discussions of building the apartments began at a race relations conference in 1965, but funding for the complex was not available until 1970, when Congressmen Donald Edwards and Charles Gubner secured a $4 million loan at a low interest rate. Construction on the complex began in early 1970, and it opened on October 15 of that year. The complex had 192 apartments and rested on 13.5 acres just east of Highway 101 between Story Road and Tully Road. The price for a two-bedroom apartment with one full bath was $121 a month. The complex also had a day care center, swimming pool, and up-to-date facilities.

117. U.S. Bureau of the Census, *U.S. Census of Population and Housing, 1970*, 239–240, 321, 451, 456; U.S. Bureau of the Census, *1990 Census of Population and Housing, San Jose Primary Statistical Metropolitan Area (PMSA)*, 1288–1289. Forty-three percent of the black population in the San Jose Standard Metropolitan Statistical Area purchased single-family homes in 1969 and 1970. Most houses that blacks moved into were built after 1950, and slightly more than half (53.1 percent) were built from 1960 to 1970. Despite this trend in homeownership, blacks began renting apartments more than buying homes after 1965 because the cost of homes in the valley was rapidly rising. Black homeowners lived mostly in nuclear families (an average of 3.5 people per housing unit, according to the 1970 census). In addition, most blacks in the county in 1990 lived in residential units that had been built between 1960 and 1980. Buying a home after 1970 depended on the national and local economy, public policy, and fair housing practices. Still, after 1970 twice as many blacks became homeowners. After 1980 the national and state economy hit recessions and brief recovery periods. This affected black residential patterns and the local housing market. For example, low periods of black homeownership were in the years 1980–1984 and 1989–1990;

from 1985 to 1988, black homeownership increased by 66 percent over the prior four-year period, 1980–1984. Though the county had relatively few rental apartments prior to the 1970s, by the mid-1980s they were the predominant housing unit.

118. See De Graaf, "African American Suburbanization," 415.

Chapter 5

1. See U.S. Bureau of the Census, *1950 Census of Population,* Vol. 11, *Characteristics of the Population,* pt. 5, *California;* "Population of Urbanized Areas: 1950," 5–21; U.S. Bureau of the Census, *1960 U.S. Census of Population and Housing, General Characteristics of the Population, by Census Tracts,* 16–37; U.S. Bureau of the Census, *1970 Census of Housing,* Vol. 1, *Housing Characteristics for States, Cities, and Counties,* pt. 6, *California,* 7–10, 14–15, 453; U.S. Bureau of the Census, *1980 U.S. Census of Population and Housing, General Characteristics of Black Persons,* 109; Santa Clara County Planning Office, *1990 Population and Ethnicity of Santa Clara County by City and CDP;* County of Santa Clara, Advance Planning Office, 89-1A (January 1989); Robert J. Devincenzi et al., *Milpitas: Five Dynamic Decades* (Milpitas, Calif.: City of Milpitas, 2004), 26; De Graaf, "African American Suburbanization in California"; Emory J. Tolbert and Lawrence B. de Graaf, "'The Unseen Minority': Blacks in Orange County," *Journal of Orange County Studies* 3, 4 (Fall 1989/Spring 1990): 54–61; Lisa McGirr, *Suburban Warriors: The Origins of the New American Right* (Princeton, N.J.: Princeton University Press, 2001); Robert O. Self, *American Babylon: Race and the Struggle for Postwar Oakland* (Princeton, N.J.: Princeton University Press, 2003); and University of Virginia Library, *Historical Census Browser: County-Level Results for 1850–1960* (University of Virginia Library: Geospatial and Statistical Data Center, 2009).

2. Leon Fink, "American Labor History," in *The New American History,* ed. Eric Foner (Philadelphia: Temple University Press, 1997), 343.

3. David Brody, "The Old Labor History and the New: In Search of the American Working Class," *Labor History* 20 (Winter 1979): 111–126; Broussard, *Black San Francisco;* Mike Davis, *Prisoners of the American Dream;* Mario T. García, *Mexican Americans: Leadership, Ideology, and Identity, 1930–1960* (New Haven, Conn.: Yale University Press, 1989); Gilbert G. Gonzalez, *Labor and Community: Mexican Citrus Worker Villages in a Southern California County, 1900–1950* (Urbana: University of Illinois Press, 1994); William H. Harris, *The Harder We Run: Black Workers since the Civil War* (New York: Oxford University Press, 1982); McBroome, *Parallel Communities;* Moore, *To Place Our Deeds;* Bruce Nelson, "The Big Strike"; Nelson, "The 'Lords of the Docks' Reconsidered"; Vicki Ruíz, *Cannery Women, Cannery Lives: Mexican Women, Unionization, and the California Food Processing Industry, 1930–1950* (Albuquerque:

University of New Mexico Press, 1987); George J. Sanchez, *Becoming Mexican American: Ethnicity, Culture, and Identity in Chicano Los Angeles, 1900–1945* (New York: Oxford University Press, 1993); Thomas J. Sugrue, *The Origins of the Urban Crisis: Race and Inequality in Postwar Detroit* (Princeton, N.J.: Princeton University Press, 1996); Ronald Takaki, *Pau Hana: Plantation Life and Labor in Hawaii, 1835–1920* (Honolulu: University of Hawaii Press, 1983); Taylor, *In Search of the Racial Frontier*; and Trotter, *Black Milwaukee*.

4. Kevin Boyle, *The UAW and the Heyday of American Liberalism, 1945–1968* (Ithaca, N.Y.: Cornell University Press, 1995), 2–34; and Nelson, "The 'Lords of the Docks' Reconsidered, 155–184; Jacqueline Jones, *American Work: Four Centuries of Black and White Labor* (New York: W.W. Norton, 1998), 339–366; and David M. Kennedy, *Freedom from Fear: The American People in Depression and War, 1929–1945* (New York: Oxford University Press, 1999), 288–322.

5. Boyle, *The UAW and the Heyday of American Liberalism*, 2–34; Nelson, "The 'Lords of the Docks' Reconsidered," 155–184; Jones, *American Work*, 339–366; Kennedy, *Freedom from Fear*, 288–322, 363–380; and Patterson, *Grand Expectations*, 10–60.

6. See Boyle, *The UAW and the Heyday of American Liberalism*; and Fink, "American Labor History," 333–352.

7. Ben Gross, interviewed by the author, Detroit, December 11, 2008.

8. See Devincenzi, *Milpitas*, 26; Sunnyhills United Methodist Church, *Sunnyhills United Methodist Church: A History, 1957–1982* (Milpitas: Sunnyhills United Methodist Church, from the Ben Gross Collection, Detroit), 3; and Sunnyhills United Methodist Church, *Sunnyhills United Methodist Church*, http://www.gbgm-umc.org/sunnyhills/history.htm.

9. See *San Jose Mercury News*, August 14, 1963; Boyle, *The UAW and the Heyday of American Liberalism*; *Color*, January 1956 (William Oliver Collection, William P. Reuther Library, Wayne State University, Detroit); Harris, *The Harder We Run*, 139, 141; Ben Gross, interviewed by the author; Manning Marable, *How Capitalism Underdeveloped Black America: Problems in Race, Political Economy, and Society* (Cambridge, Mass.: South End Press, 2000), 23–51; and Joseph Szczesny, "African Americans and the UAW: A Rocky but Fruitful Union," *AAOW Magazine*, February–March 2000.

10. *Argonaut*, May 13, 1955; and *Los Angeles Times*, May 22, 1955.

11. Devincenzi, *Milpitas*, 20.

12. See *Argonaut*, May 13, 1955; *Los Angeles Times*, May 22, 1955; and Devincenzi, *Milpitas*, 20.

13. *East San Jose SUN*, January 5, 1966, 14; Devincenzi, *Milpitas*, 19; and *Mercury News*, November 6, 2008.

14. See *East San Jose SUN*, January 5, 1966, 14; and Devincenzi, *Milpitas*, 37.

15. *Los Angeles Times*, May 22, 1955, July 26, 1960, July 11, 1964, and November 21, 1964; *East San Jose SUN*, January 5, 1966; Devincenzi, *Milpitas*, 37; and *San Jose Mercury News*, March 14, 1961, and March 19, 1961.

16. See Devincenzi, *Milpitas*, 26; and Sunnyhills United Methodist Church, *Sunnyhills United Methodist Church*, 3.

17. University of Virginia Library, *Historical Census Browser*; and U.S. Bureau of the Census, *1950 Census of Population*, 5–21.

18. U.S. Bureau of the Census, *U.S. Census of Population and Housing, Characteristics of the Population, by Census Tracts: 1950*; U.S. Bureau of the Census, *U.S. Census of Population and Housing, San Jose SMA: 1960 U.S. Census of Population and Housing, General Characteristics of the Population, by Census Tracts*, 16–37; and U.S. Bureau of the Census, *U.S. Census of Population and Housing; 1970 Census Tracts*, table P-1.

19. U.S. Bureau of the Census, *1970 Census of Housing*, Vol. 1, *Housing Characteristics for States, Cities, and Counties*, pt. 6, *California*, 7–10, 14–15, 453.

20. University of Virginia Library, *Historical Census Browser*; *1950 Census of Population*, Vol. 11, *Characteristics of the Population*, pt. 5, *California*, 5–21; U.S. Bureau of the Census, *U.S. Census of Population and Housing, Characteristics of the Population, by Census Tracts: 1950*, 7–10; U.S. Bureau of the Census, *U.S. Census of Population and Housing, San Jose SMA: 1960 U.S. Census of Population and Housing, General Characteristics of the Population, by Census Tracts*, 16–37; U.S. Bureau of the Census, *1970 Census of Housing*, Vol. 1, *Housing Characteristics for States, Cities, and Counties*, pt. 6, *California*, 7–10, 14–15, 453; U.S. Bureau of the Census, *U.S. Census of Population and Housing, 1970 Census Tracts*, table P-1; U.S. Bureau of the Census, *U.S. Census of Population and Housing, 1980 Census Tracts*, "General Characteristics of Black Persons: 1980," 109; and Santa Clara County Planning Office, "1990 Population and Ethnicity of Santa Clara County by City and CDP."

21. Ocie Tinsley, interviewed by the author, San Jose, August 2010; and Stanford Encyclopedia of Philosophy, s.v. "Affirmative Action."

22. See John Frederick Keller, "The Production Worker in Electronics: Industrialization and Labor Development in California's Santa Clara Valley" (diss., University of Michigan, 1984), 201, 208.

23. Ibid., 205.

24. Sunnyhills United Methodist Church, *Sunnyhills United Methodist Church*, 3; and Ben Gross, interviewed by the author.

25. Devincenzi, *Milpitas*, 26.

26. Ben Gross, interviewed by the author.

27. See De Graaf, "African American Suburbanization in California," 405.

28. Self, *American Babylon*, 116.

29. Bennett M. Berger, *Working-Class Suburb: A Study of Auto Workers in Suburbia* (Berkeley: University of California Press, 1968), xvi, xviii.

30. Ibid.

31. See Devincenzi, *Milpitas*, 26; Ben Gross, interviewed by the author; and Sunnyhills United Methodist Church, *Sunnyhills United Methodist Church: A History, 1957–1982*, 3.

32. *Planted Slants*, December 1954 (William Oliver Collection, William P. Reuther Library, Wayne State University, Detroit).

33. Ben Gross, interviewed by the author.

34. Quoted from Tanisha Davis-Perez, "DC's African Americans Build a Network for Success" (UAW–DaimlerChrysler National Training Center Communications, http://www.uadcx.com/ resources/news.cfm?NewsID=309).

35. Devincenzi, *Milpitas*, 26; and Sunnyhills United Methodist Church, *Sunnyhills United Methodist Church*, 3.

36. Sunnyhills United Methodist Church, *Sunnyhills United Methodist Church*, 5.

37. Ben Gross, interviewed by the author.

38. See Devincenzi, *Milpitas*, 26; Sunnyhills Brochure (William Oliver Collection); and Sunnyhills United Methodist Church, *Sunnyhills United Methodist Church*, 7.

39. See Devincenzi, *Milpitas*, 25–26; and Sunnyhills United Methodist Church, *Sunnyhills United Methodist Church*, 10.

40. Ben Gross, interviewed by the author.

41. Tanisha Davis-Perez, "DC's African Americans Build a Network for Success."

42. Sunnyhills United Methodist Church, *Sunnyhills United Methodist Church*, 5–7.

43. Ben Gross, interviewed by the author.

44. *Housing Act of 1950*, sec. 203 and sec. 213, in U.S. Congress, 81st Cong., 2nd sess. (1950), *U.S. Code Congressional Service*, Vol. 2, *Legislative History* (Brooklyn, N.Y.: Edward Thompson Co., 1951), 2033–2037 and 2039–2041; and "Information Bulletin: Sunnyhills Cooperative no. 3 Inc." (William Oliver Collection).

45. Quoted in Sunnyhills United Methodist Church, *Sunnyhills United Methodist Church*, 12. See Department of Housing and Urban Development, "Federal Housing Administration: Mortgage and Loan Insurance Programs," http://www.hud.gov/offices/cfo/repots/04estimates/fhafund.pdf, 4. Also see *Housing Act of 1950*, sec. 203 and 213.

46. Self, *American Babylon*, 115.

47. Ben Gross, interviewed by the author; and Sunnyhills Brochure.

48. See Sunnyhills United Methodist Church, *Sunnyhills United Methodist Church*, 8–9; and Self, *American Babylon*, 114.

49. Ben Gross, interviewed by the author; and Sunnyhills United Methodist Church, *Sunnyhills United Methodist Church*, 8–11.

50. Sunnyhills United Methodist Church, *Sunnyhills United Methodist Church*, 10–11.

51. *Oakland Tribune*, August 30, 1959; and "Cablegram to Nikita Khrushchev" (UAW Fair Practices Collection, William P. Reuther Library, Wayne State University, Detroit).

52. Quoted in Self, *American Babylon*, 116; and *Oakland Tribune*, August 30, 1959.

53. Gagliardi, "Roots," 19.

54. Sunnyhills United Methodist Church, *Sunnyhills United Methodist Church*, 14–19.

55. See Sugrue, *The Origins of the Urban Crisis*, 209–229; and Robert Self, "Black Power City, White Power Suburb" (paper given at Unimagined Futures Conference, May 19, 1999, Stanford University).

56. Ben Gross, interviewed by the author.

57. *Milpitas Post*, January 17, 2002.

58. Devincenzi, *Milpitas*, 19.

59. Ben Gross was appointed mayor and vice mayor by the Milpitas City Council.

60. *Los Angeles Times*, April 20, 1966; and Devincenzi, *Milpitas*, 35.

61. See Sunnyhills United Methodist Church, *Sunnyhills United Methodist Church*, 32; and Devincenzi, 32.

62. Ocie Tinsley, interviewed by the author; and Charles Murray, Charles Murray Oral History Project: Santa Clara County African Americans (ca. 1979). Ocie Tinsley, a Kansas City, Missouri, native, was one of about fifty African American engineers recruited to work in the high-tech industry in the late 1960s. Like many of this new generation of black newcomers, Tinsley initially failed to understand the South Bay's color line and figure out where most African Americans lived. This early experience of social isolation and difficult adjustment almost persuaded Tinsley to leave the Bay Area.

63. See *San Jose Mercury News*, March 19, 1979; James Williams, *Life and Adventures of James Williams*; Oscar Osburn Winther, "The Story of San Jose, 1777–1869"; Edith Smith, *Some Early African American Settlers*; California History Center, *Sunnyvale*, 62–63; and Arbuckle, *Clyde Arbuckle's History of San Jose*, 63.

Chapter 6

1. For texts examining the traditional civil rights movement narrative, see Susan Youngblood Ashmore, *Carry It On: The War on Poverty and the Civil Rights Movement in Alabama, 1964–1972* (Athens: University of Georgia Press,

2008); Martha Biondi, *To Stand and Fight: The Struggle for Civil Rights in Postwar New York City* (Cambridge, Mass.: Harvard University Press, 2003); Stewart Burns, ed., *Daybreak of Freedom: The Montgomery Bus Boycott* (Chapel Hill: University of North Carolina Press, 1997); Clayborne Carson et al., *The Eyes on the Prize Civil Rights Reader* (New York: Penguin, 1991); Clayborne Carson, *In Struggle: SNCC and the Black Awakening of the 1960s* (Cambridge, Mass.: Harvard University Press, 1981); Matthew Countryman, *Up South: Civil Rights and Black Power in Philadelphia* (Philadelphia: University of Pennsylvania Press, 2006); Emilye Crosby, *A Little Taste of Freedom: The Black Freedom Struggle in Claiborne County, Mississippi* (Chapel Hill: University of North Carolina Press, 2005); Greta de Jong, *A Different Day: African American Struggles for Justice in Rural Louisiana, 1900–1970* (Chapel Hill: University of North Carolina Press, 2002); John Dittmer, *Local People: The Struggle for Civil Rights in Mississippi* (Urbana: University of Illinois Press, 1995); Glenn T. Eskew, *But for Birmingham: The Local and National Movements in the Civil Rights Struggle* (Chapel Hill: University of North Carolina Press, 1997); Cynthia Griggs Fleming, *In the Shadow of Selma: The Continuing Struggle for Civil Rights in the Rural South* (Lanham, Md.: Rowan and Littlefield, 2004); Frye Gaillard, *Alabama's Civil Rights Trail: An Illustrated Guide to the Cradle of Freedom* (Tuscaloosa: University of Alabama Press, 2004); Winston A. Grady-Willis, *Challenging U.S. Apartheid: Atlanta and Black Struggles for Human Rights, 1960–1977* (Durham, N.C.: Duke University Press, 2006); Christina Greene, *Our Separate Ways: Women and the Black Freedom Movement in Durham, North Carolina* (Chapel Hill: University of North Carolina Press, 2005); Herbert H. Haines, *Black Radicals and the Civil Rights Mainstream, 1954–1970* (Knoxville: University of Tennessee Press, 1988); Jeffries, *Bloody Lowndes*; Nicholas Lemann, *The Promised Land: The Great Black Migration and How It Changed America* (New York: Vintage, 1992); Manning Marable, *Race, Reform, and Rebellion: The Second Reconstruction in Black America, 1945–1980* (Jackson: University of Mississippi Press, 1991); Meier and Rudwick, *CORE*; Kay Mills, *This Little Light of Mine: The Life of Fannie Lou Hamer* (New York: Plume, 1994); J. Todd Moye, *Let the People Decide: Black Freedom and White Resistance Movements in Sunflower County, Mississippi, 1945–1986* (Chapel Hill: University of North Carolina Press, 2004); Barbara Ransby, *Ella Baker and the Black Freedom Movement: A Radical Democratic Vision* (Chapel Hill: University of North Carolina Press, 2005); Christopher B. Strain, *Pure Fire: Self-Defense as Activism in the Civil Rights Era* (Athens: University of Georgia Press, 2005); Thomas Sugrue, *Sweet Land of Liberty: The Forgotten Struggle for Civil Rights in the North* (New York: Random House, 2008); Jeanne Theoharis and Komozi Woodard, *Freedom North: Black Freedom Struggles Outside the South, 1940–1980* (New York: New York University Press, 2003); Rhonda Williams, *The Politics of Public Housing: Black Women's Struggles against Urban Inequality* (New York: Oxford University Press, 2004).

2. For histories on the civil rights movement in suburban metropolises in the West, see Matthew C. Whitaker, *Race Work: The Rise of Civil Rights in the Urban West* (Lincoln: University of Nebraska Press, 2007); and Broussard, "Percy H. Steele, Jr., and the Urban League."

3. Sit-ins and boycotts in the immediate postwar West are discussed in George Long, "How Albuquerque Got Its Civil Rights Ordinance," *Crisis* 60, 1 (November 1953): 521–524; Meier and Rudwick, *CORE*, 27, 56–57, 60; and Taylor, *In Search of the Racial Frontier*, 278–284.

4. See Taylor, *In Search of the Racial Frontier*, 236.

5. Myra Lynn Wysinger, "African American Pioneer of California: Edmond Edward Wysinger (1816–1891)," http://wysinger.homestead.com/courtcase.html, and http://www.blackpast.org/?q=primarywest/wysinger-v-crookshank-1890.

6. See Gagliardi, "Roots," 17.

7. Based on people interviewed by the author in October 2011: Charles Alexander, Gloria Anderson, Kenneth Blackwell, Albert Camarillo, Helen Anderson Gaffin, Steve Millner, Patricia Perkins, Monica Ramos of Mexican Heritage Corporation, and Orvella Stubbs of San Jose and Palo Alto. Also see the Garden City Women's Club, *History of Black Americans in Santa Clara Valley*; Pitti, *The Devil in Silicon Valley*, 178–197; and the *San Jose Mercury News*, May 24, 1962, August 1, 1963, and August 22, 1963. As momentous as the civil rights movement in the county was, the relative lack of black and brown collaboration on civil rights projects hurt the movement. According to Charles Alexander, of all the groups of color, blacks were "probably closer to Mexicans. Politically, Mexican American were following the Black Freedom Movement and developing their own struggle. "They were basically work, big families, like we were in the South. Like our folk, their goal for their youth was to move up through education." However, prior to March 1968, when Cesar Chavez fasted for twenty-five days to rededicate the United Farm Workers and its grape boycott to the principles of nonviolence, African Americans and Mexican Americans approached coalition politics in relation to one another more as political competitors than as allies. Historian Albert Camarillo said that political conflict in cities of color like East Palo Alto and East San Jose were common in the 1960s and '70s. However, beyond the organizations and within diverse communities, conversations occurred and coalitions developed.

8. Orvella Stubbs, interviewed by the author.

9. Ibid.

10. For an idea how Record Hop functioned see World News Network, *KNTV Record Hop* (San Jose: KNTV, 1964; URL: http://wn.com/KNTV_Record_Hop).

11. Orvella Stubbs, interviewed by the author.

12. See Lawrence B. De Graaf and Quintard Taylor, "Introduction: African Americans in California History, California in African American History," in De Graaf et al., *Seeking El Dorado*, 20–53.

13. Orvella Stubbs, interviewed by the author.

14. Harry Edwards, interviewed by the author, Fremont, California, June 13, 2012; and by phone on June 21, 2012.

15. For more on the Women's International League for Peace and Freedom, see "What Is the Women's International League for Peace and Freedom?" in *Reaching Critical Will: Reaching for a Critical Mass of Political Will for Nuclear Disarmament* (http://www.reachingcriticalwill.org/about/ aboutindex.html). The league was a progressive peace organization interested in the civil rights movement for the purposes of forming an interracial coalition and establishing a socio-economic system in the United States "in which political equality and social justice for all could be attained."

16. For more information on the national effort to boycott stores with segregated lunch counters, see Jeffrey A. Turner, *Sitting In and Speaking Out: Student Movements in the American South, 1960–1970* (Athens: University of Georgia Press, 2010); Linda Williams Reese, "Clara Luper and the Civil Rights Movement in Oklahoma City, 1958–1964," in *African American Women Confront the West, 1600–2000*, ed. Quintard Taylor and Shirley Ann Wilson Moore (Norman: University of Oklahoma Press, 2008), 328–343; and Meier and Rudwick, *CORE*, 101–134.

17. See *San Jose Mercury News*, April 15, 1960.

18. *San Jose Mercury News*, April 15, 1960; and based on the testimony of Harry Edwards.

19. Quote from *San Jose Mercury News*, April 20, 1960.

20. Ibid.

21. Meier and Rudwick, *CORE*, 110. According to this text it was possible that San Jose had a CORE chapter by June 1960. After the NAACP national office urged its members to give full support to the CORE movement in mid-March 1963, a competition between CORE and the NAACP, which was larger and had better resources, overshadowed most CORE chapters. In San Jose, historians Meier and Rudwick wrote, the problem resolved "when the NAACP agreed to sponsor the picketing on alternate weekends" (110). The emergence of the San Jose CORE, as told in the *San Jose Mercury News*, took place in September 1963, during the St. John Dixon affair. My interpretation adheres to when the group was mentioned in the local media, because Meier and Rudwick's interpretation is limited to a sentence in their survey on the San Jose CORE, and when the group was formed is left unclear.

22. *San Jose Mercury News*, July 14, 1960.

23. Ibid.

24. Ibid.

25. Ibid.

26. Ibid., March 3, 1960.

27. Ibid., September 23, 1960, and December 27, 1960.

28. Ibid.

29. Ibid., September 26, 1960.

30. After fifty years, Alabama State finally reinstated the nine expelled student protesters, but by then six were believed to have passed away. See *HBCU Digest.com*, "50 Years Later, Alabama State Reinstates Expelled Student Protesters," February 26, 2010, http://www.hbcudigest.com/50-years-later-alabama-state-reinstates-expelled-student-protesters/. The official court decision on Dixon's being expelled can be found at *St. John Dixon v. Alabama State Board of Education*, No. 18641, United States Court of Appeals Fifth Circuit (August 4, 1961).

31. *San Jose Mercury News*, December 27, 1960. The Antioch Baptist Church scholarship fund was financed by the church; businessman Alden B. Campen; Reverend G. L. Collins, the chaplain at San Jose State; attorney Marice H. Hardeman; Professor George C. Hoyt of San Jose State; and attorney Wester Sweet, who represented the local NAACP and CORE.

32. Quoted in the *San Jose Mercury News*, October 4, 1960.

33. For more on Anne Braden in the Santa Clara Valley, see Catherine A. Fosl, *Subversive Southerner: Anne Braden and the Struggle for Racial Justice in the Cold War South* (Lexington: University of Kentucky Press, 2006), 267–268.

34. The quote is from the *San Jose Mercury News*, February 22, 1961. Also see the *Mercury News*, November 19, 1963. Harry Edwards, interviewed by the author. Under President Wahlquist, student organizations brought in controversial speakers regularly. In November 1963, he was commended by sixty-three members of the San Jose State College faculty for his open forum policy, which was not a public forum but was conducted through invitation for unrecognized college officials or organizations to contribute to the intellectual and cultural life of the college. Student groups at San Jose State in the early 1960s ranged from the ultraliberal to the Young Democrats and Young Republicans to the ultraconservative Students Against Communism.

35. *San Jose Mercury News*, February 24, 1961. Also see Fosl, *Subversive Southerner*, 268.

36. *San Jose Mercury News*, February 24, 1961.

37. Ibid. Statewide, anticommunist policymakers such as State Senator Jack F. Thompson (R-Evergreen) had been stirring public anxieties for almost a year—he was the author of Senate Bill 706, which would prohibit communists from speaking on state school property. In the Santa Clara Valley of the 1960s, anticommunism was growing, but when invoked it was usually a strawman attack to contain discussions on civil rights and integration, which were increasing in the region.

38. *San Jose Mercury News*, March 24, 1961.

39. Harry Edwards, interviewed by the author.

40. Harry Edwards and Charles Alexander, interviewed by the author; NAACP West Coast Region Files, "NAACP Membership Report, San Jose

Branch, 1948–1976" (Bancroft Library, University of California, Berkeley); *San Jose Mercury News*, July 24, 1963; Garden City Women's Club, *History of Black Americans in Santa Clara Valley*; and Ruffin, *Uninvited Neighbors*, diss., 300–344. According to Edwards, most South Bay blacks lacked a social consciousness from 1960 to 1964, when he attended San Jose State. They were just surviving. The exception to this was Inez Jackson. Jackson was said to be frustrated with black youths not picking up on the civil rights struggle, even when it was happening around them. By 1963, San Jose black youth were slowly coming of age and making demands on adults in the local NAACP, and they were aggressively resisting their elders' attempts to stem the tide of a youth rebellion. In the end, a youth chapter was formed within the San Jose NAACP during the summer of 1963.

41. See *San Jose Mercury News*, June 3, 1961, and June 7, 1961.

42. Ibid., March 24, 1961.

43. Apparently both Stanton and Hutchinson, who were under contract, were released by San Jose State.

44. For more on the Freedom Riders, see Raymond Arsenault, *Freedom Riders: 1961 and the Struggle for Racial Justice* (New York: Oxford University Press, 2007); *Boynton v. Virginia*, 364 U.S. 454 (1960); Carson et al., *The Eyes on the Prize Civil Rights Reader*, 108–109, 124–141; Carson, *In Struggle*, 1, 31–38, 43–44, 73; Meier and Rudwick, *CORE*, 39, 72, 119, 135–200; and NPR, "Get On the Bus: The Freedom Riders of 1961," broadcast on *Fresh Air from WHYY*, January 12, 2006 (http://www.npr.org/templates/story/ story.php?storyId=5149667).

45. Meier and Rudwick, *CORE*, 135–158.

46. *San Jose Mercury News*, June 1, 1961, and June 30, 1961. For more on Edward Blankenheim, see Office of Continuing Education at University of Illinois at Urbana-Champaign, "About the Freedom Riders" (http://civilrights.continuinged.uiuc.edu/about.html); NPR, "Freedom Riders," *Weekend Edition Saturday*, April 7, 2001 (http://www.npr.org/ templates/story/story.php?storyId=1121173). Blankenheim was on one of the first Freedom Rider buses to be set on fire, in Anniston, Alabama.

47. *San Jose Mercury News*, May 30, 1961.

48. I thank Jean and Ralph Libby, whom I interviewed in Palo Alto in October 2011, for enhancing my understanding of the Mid-Peninsula civil rights movement.

49. Puryear's vignette can be seen at "Muata Weusi-Puryear—Class of 1953," in Asbury Park High School: Distinguished Alumni Hall of Fame (http://aphshalloffame.com/Inductees/MuataWeusiPuryear.html). Jean Libby, interviewed by the author. Libby began her freedom rights career with Mid-Peninsula CORE in 1961. She was unusual in that she was not affiliated with Stanford and was considered to be "unemployed" as a homemaker raising several children in a low-income household in East Palo Alto and Palo Alto. In fact, she did not start college until she was 40, and she graduated from the University of California–Berkeley in

the same year her daughter graduated. In the late 1960s, she also had the unusual distinction of being a Black Power activist with CORE and the Palo Alto NAACP, which had shifted its operations from Stanford to East Palo Alto.

50. See "Lifecycles: Honoring Mrs. Gertrude Wilkes," *East Palo Alto Today*, February–March 2008 (http://www.epatoday.org/pdf/February_March2008_EPA _Today_pgs1_8.pdf).

51. Jean Libby, interviewed by the author; *San Jose Mercury News*, August 22, 1963, and September 19, 1963.

52. *San Jose Mercury News*, June 2, 1963.

53. For a good understanding of the black freedom movement in the postwar West see Alwyn Barr, *Black Texans: A History of African Americans* (Norman: University of Oklahoma Press, 1996); Brilliant, *The Color of America Has Changed*; Broussard, *Black San Francisco*, 239–245; Crouchett et al., *Visions toward Tomorrow*; Santangelo, "Deindustrialization"; De Graaf, "African American Suburbanization in California"; McBroome, *Parallel Communities*, 129–156; Moore, *To Place Our Deeds*, 94–151; Murch, *Living for the City*; Santangelo, *Abiding Courage*, 153–182; Self, *American Babylon*, 133-214; Sides, *L.A. City Limits*; Taylor, *In Search of the Racial Frontier*, 278–310; Taylor, *The Forging of a Black Community*, 185–233; Taylor and Moore, *African American Women Confront the West, 1600–2000*; and Whitaker, *Race Work*.

54. *San Jose Mercury News*, June 2, 1963.

55. Martin Luther King, Jr., Research and Education Institute, "Birmingham Campaign (1963)" (http://mlk-kpp01.stanford.edu/index.php/encyclopedia/encyclopedia/enc_birmingham_campaign/).

56. *San Jose Mercury News*, June 2, 1963.

57. The black registration drive is discussed in Carson, *The Eyes on the Prize Civil Rights Reader*, 107–132; Meier and Rudwick, *CORE*, 159–181; Dittmer, *Local People*, 116–169; Jeffries, *Bloody Lowndes*; and Mills, *This Little Light of Mine*, 34, 43–56, 78–104, 115, 139, 158.

58. *San Jose Mercury News*, January 5, 1961.

59. See ibid., May 15, 1961, and June 13, 1963. Freedom rides were first mentioned in the *San Jose Mercury News* on May 15, 1961.

60. Like many students attending predominantly white private institutions of higher learning, Frey was an idealist motivated to changing America in a racially liberal manner and could financially afford his efforts to do so.

61. *San Jose Mercury News*, June 13, 1963.

62. Ibid., August 11, 1963. Also see Carson, *In Struggle*, 77–87.

63. See "KZSU Project South Interviews" (Stanford University Archives, Palo Alto, California).

64. Student participation in the voter registration drive is discussed in Dittmer, *Local People*, 203–207, 232–234; Meier and Rudwick, *CORE*, 305; and Carson, *In Struggle*, 98–99.

65. *San Jose Mercury News*, October 30, 1963.

66. For a good discussion on the voter registration drive, see Carson et al., *Eyes on the Prize Civil Rights Reader*, 163, 204–206, 687–691, 262–268, 170–179, 209–211; Dittmer, *Local People*, 116–193; Jeffries, *Bloody Lowndes*; and Meier and Rudwick, *CORE*, 85–91, 122, 143–145, 163–182, 209–213, 242.

67. See *San Jose Mercury News*, November 5, 1963, November 7, 1963, and November 8, 1963.

68. Ibid., June 1, 1963, and June 12, 1963.

69. Ibid., July 15, 1963. On July 14, James L. Farmer, national director of CORE, announced that the organization would launch a nationwide boycott of major department stores and grocery chain stores in an effort to pressure the management into hiring blacks and other minority groups. This was to occur immediately after the March on Washington on August 28, 1963.

70. *San Jose Mercury News*, October 22, 1963.

71. Ibid., August 22, 1963, and September 19, 1963. Civil rights activists protesting and boycotting national grocery chains and department stores was a national phenomenon during the summer of 1963. In the proximity of Palo Alto, a protest of supermarkets similar to that in San Jose occurred. These protests were led by the South San Mateo County NAACP and Mid-Peninsula CORE, who were meeting in unsuspected places with large halls such as Kavanaugh Oaks Elementary School in East Palo Alto. Their purpose was to get their strategy together and directly protest East Palo Alto supermarket chains in an effort to pressure management into entering negotiations with them over fair employment practices. Though Lucky, Safeway, and Purity stores were heavily frequented by black customers, their staffs and managers were exclusively white. The big breakthrough for both civil rights organizations occurred between August 21 and September 18, during which all of the stores except one contacted the NAACP and CORE and agreed to take steps to eliminate job discrimination on good faith, not quotas.

72. *San Jose Mercury News*, August 1, 1963.

73. Ibid.; and ibid., August 22, 1963.

74. Ibid., August 21, 1963. Rudy Belluomini of the United Latin American Counsel of Santa Clara County publicly supported CORE's fight for black people's rights as individuals, even though his group declined to get involved.

75. *San Jose Mercury News*, August 21, 1963.

76. Ibid.

77. Assessment is based on the author's microfilm research of every *San Jose Mercury* newspaper from 1945 to 1980 at Honnold-Mudd Library, Claremont University Colleges, Claremont, California; Dr. Martin Luther King, Jr., Library, San Jose, California; and San Diego State University Library, San Diego, California.

78. The March on Washington movement is further discussed in Carson, *The Eyes on the Prize Civil Rights Reader*, 32, 138, 163–165, 201, 258–260, 403–408, 425, 485, 593, 720–721; and PBS, "The March on Washington for Jobs and Freedom," aired on NewsHour, August 27, 2003 (http://www.pbs.org/newshour/extra/features/july-dec03/march_8-27.html).

79. *San Jose Mercury News*, August 28, 1963.

80. Ibid. Sponsors of the San Jose March on Washington sympathy demonstration were the local chapters of the NAACP, CORE, UAW, Anti-Defamation League, Catholic Interracial Council, Community Service Organization, Council for Civic Unity, Japanese Americans Citizens League, Santa Clara County Council of Churches, American Jewish Congress, the 25th Assembly District Council of Democratic Clubs, and activists with other causes. Featured speakers at the rally included Richard Thomas, a black nuclear physicist and incoming president of the San Jose NAACP; Faye Morton, vice president of San Jose CORE; and James Blackwell, a San Jose State sociology professor and outgoing NAACP president.

81. Ibid., October 22, 1963.

82. Ibid., September 5, 1963.

83. See ibid., June 10, 1963, and September 5, 1963.

84. Ibid., August 30, 1963.

85. For a good discussion on the Birmingham church bombing see NPR, "16th Street Baptist Church Bombing: Forty Years Later, Birmingham Still Struggles with Violent Past," aired on *All Things Considered*, September 15, 2003 (http://www.npr.org/templates/story/story.php?storyId=1431932); Martin Luther King Papers, "Birmingham Campaign" (http://www.npr.org/templates/story/story.php?storyId=1431932).

86. *San Jose Mercury News*, September 29, 1963. "That these dead shall not die in vain" was a statement borrowed from President Abraham Lincoln's "Gettysburg Address."

87. Quote from *San Jose Mercury News*, September 29, 1963.

88. Ibid.

89. Ibid., October 2, 1960. Dr. George Arthur Casaday gave one of the public addresses on civil rights in the Santa Clara Valley that was covered by the mainstream press to delegates of seventy-two churches from sixteen Protestant denominations in the Santa Clara Valley on October 1, 1960. He told this group that the Santa Clara Valley's racial lines should not be as hard to change as those in the South; though integration existed there, he said, racism existed as well, especially institutionally and economically, a situation that locals ought to be able to change. "About 70 percent of our Negro workforce is employed below its level of skill," he said. To combat this, he urged the delegates to support peaceful sit-in and kneel-in demonstrations by blacks in the South, and he called for more positive government action. Any less than that, he argued, would be "an escape from needed action."

90. *San Jose Mercury News*, September 30, 1963.

91. Ibid., December 11, 1960. This appropriation's impact was amplified by the fact that it regularly made the headlines in the local press, several months after the Greensboro sit-ins on February 7 popularized the term. May 19, 1960, was the first time "civil defense" was used in non–civil rights related articles in the *San Jose Mercury News*. The subject on that day addressed Santa Clara County creating a coordinator of a Civil Defense Department, which was to help residents cope with any type of disaster, natural or foreign. This type of civil rights for the individual not connected to race also occurred at Los Gatos high school to protect the constitutional rights of students arrested or questioned on the campus by police officers.

92. McGirr, *Suburban Warriors*, 3–19, 133, 147–216; Self, *American Babylon*, 256–290; and Sugrue, *The Origins of the Urban Crisis*, 209–258.

93. See *San Jose Mercury News*, May 15, 1962; and Edwards, *The Struggle That Must Be*, 170; Horne, "Black Fire," 377–404; and Broussard, *Black San Francisco*, 242.

Chapter 7

1. Harry Edwards, interviewed by the author, Fremont, California, June 13, 2012; and by phone, June 21, 2012.

2. Dionne Warwick, "Do You Know the Way to San Jose," New York: Scepter, 1968, http://www.elyrics.net/read/b/burt-bacharach-lyrics/do-you-know-the-way-to-san-jose-lyrics.html.

3. Jeffries, *Bloody Lowndes*, 4.

4. See also Amy Bass, *Not the Triumph but the Struggle: 1968 Olympics and the Making of the Black Athlete* (Minneapolis: University of Minnesota Press, 2004); CBS, *The Early Show*, "'Silent Gesture' Still Speaks Volumes: Tommie Smith on His '68 Olympics Raised-Fist Protest" (http://www.cbsnews.com/stories/2007/02/08/earlyshow/leisure/books/main2446168.shtml); John Carlos, Dave Zirin, and Amy Goodman interview, "John Carlos, 1968 Olympic U.S. Medalist, on the Revolutionary Sports Moment That Changed the World," *Democracy Now* (October 12, 2011), available at http://www.democracynow.org/2011/10/12/john_carlos_1968_olympic_us_medalist; David Davis, "Olympic Athletes Who Took a Stand: For 40 Years, Olympians Tommie Smith and John Carlos Have Lived with the Consequences of Their Fateful Protest," *Smithsonian Magazine*, August 2008, available at http://www.smithsonianmag.com/people-places/indelible-olympics-200808.html#ixzz21kRHEbra; Douglas Hartmann, *Race, Culture, and the Revolt of the Black Athlete: The 1968 Olympic Protests and Their Aftermath* (Chicago: University of Chicago Press, 2004); Michael E. Lomax, "Bedazzle Them with Brilliance, Bamboozle Them with Bull: Harry Edwards, Black Power, and the Revolt of the Black Athlete Revisited," in Michael E. Lomax, *Sports and the Racial*

Divide: African American and Latino Sport Experience in the Era of Change, 55–89 (Jackson: University Press of Mississippi, 2008); Donald Spivey, "Black Consciousness and Olympic Protest," in *Sport in America: New Historical Perspectives*, ed. Donald Spivey (Westport, Conn.: Greenwood Press, 1985); and David K. Wiggins and Patrick B. Miller, *The Unlevel Playing Field: A Documentary History of the African American Experience in Sport* (Urbana: University of Illinois Press, 2003).

5. Cass Jackson, interviewed by the author by phone, June 25, 2012.

6. Charles Alexander, interviewed by the author, San Jose, August 2010.

7. Some discussions on the transformation of the South Bay include Clyde Arbuckle, *Clyde Arbuckle's History of San Jose*; Lecuyer, *Making Silicon Valley*; Matthews, *Silicon Valley, Women, and the California Dream*; Pitti, *The Devil in Silicon Valley*; and Richard White, *It's Your Misfortune and None of My Own* (Norman: University of Oklahoma Press, 1991), 541–574.

8. Charles Alexander, interviewed by the author.

9. Cass Jackson, interviewed by the author.

10. Charles Alexander, interviewed by the author.

11. Based on the testimony of Charles Alexander and Harry Edwards with the author.

12. Charles Alexander and Cass Jackson, interviewed by the author.

13. Ray Norton, interviewed by the author by phone, San Jose, October 2011; and "Speed City" exhibit curator, Urla Hill, interviewed by the author, San Jose, October 2011.

14. Charles Alexander, interviewed by the author; and *Sparta Life*, "No Place for the Negro," Winter 1967, 10. According to Alexander, the only black fraternity of San Jose State from the late 1950s to the late 1960s was Omega Psi Phi. In 1967, social affairs chairman Glen Vaughn said the frat was "generally accepted at SJS [San Jose State] as long as [it didn't] interfere with [the Pan-Hellenic Council's] decision making." This council was the coordinating body for the school's fraternities and sororities and also ran student government, which was supported by student fees. Yet despite the council's good standing, it had "no Negroes" and "no Jews" clauses filed with the university.

15. Harry Edwards, interviewed by the author.

16. See Harper Barnes, *Never Been a Time: The 1917 Race Riot That Sparked the Civil Rights Movement* (New York: Walker and Company, 2008); Charles Lumpkins, *American Pogrom: The East St. Louis Race Riot and Black Politics* (Athens: Ohio University Press, 2008); and Elliott Rudwick, *Race Riot at East St. Louis, July 2, 1917* (Champaign: University of Illinois Press, 1982).

17. Harry Edwards, interviewed by the author.

18. Ibid.

19. Ibid.

20. For an overview on the evolution of the college's track team, see Urla Hill, "Speed City: The Civil Rights Years" (M.A. thesis, San Francisco State

University, 2005); Urla Hill's exhibit, *Speed City: From Civil Rights to Black Power (1956–1969)*.

21. Edwards, *The Struggle That Must Be*, 106–107, 112.

22. See David Leonard, "What Happened to the Revolt of the Black Athlete? A Look Back Thirty Years Later—An Interview with Harry Edwards," *Colorlines* (Summer 1998). Available at http://www.arc.org/C_lines/CLArchive/story1_1_01.html.

23. Harry Edwards, interviewed by the author; and Edwards, *The Struggle That Must Be*, 107.

24. Harry Edwards, interviewed by the author; and Leonard, "What Happened to the Revolt of the Black Athlete?"

25. Edwards, *The Struggle That Must Be*, 130, 134.

26. Harry Edwards, interviewed by the author

27. Ibid. Also see Edwards, *The Struggle That Must Be*, 111; and Leonard, "What Happened to the Revolt of the Black Athlete?" 2.

28. Edwards, *The Struggle That Must Be*, 111; and Hill, *Speed City*.

29. See Edwards, *The Struggle That Must Be*, 130–131; and Hill, *Speed City*.

30. For a better idea of how San Jose State social culture functioned, see Edwards, *The Struggle That Must Be*, 108; Edwards, *The Revolt of the Black Athlete*, 75–76, 108; and *Sparta Life*, "No Place for the Negro," 8–10.

31. See Edwards, *The Struggle That Must Be*, 108–111.

32. Ibid., 108.

33. Based on oral testimony from Harry Edwards and Cass Jackson.

34. Quoted from Harry Edwards, interviewed by the author.

35. Ibid.

36. Ibid.

37. Edwards, *The Struggle That Must Be*, 113–115; and Harry Edwards, interviewed by the author.

38. Quote appears in Edwards, *The Struggle That Must Be*, 112.

39. Ibid., 124–127.

40. Harry Edwards, interviewed by the author.

41. Ibid.

42. Ibid., June 2012.

43. Edwards, *The Struggle That Must Be*, 145. This is also discussed in Lomax, "Bedazzle Them with Brilliance."

44. Edwards, *The Struggle That Must Be*, 144–145.

45. Harry Edwards, interviewed by the author; and "Correspondence Files with Hobert W. Burns on Harry Edwards' Teaching Appointment at San Jose State" (December 21, 1967), in Robert D. Clark Files at San Jose State University Archives, Dr. Martin Luther King, Jr., Library, San Jose.

46. "Correspondence Files," 157.

47. Harry Edwards, interviewed by the author; and ibid., 158.
48. Edwards, *The Revolt of the Black Athlete*, 40–47 and 75–76.
49. There is a rich discussion on Edwards's rearrival into the South Bay in Leonard, "What Happened to the Revolt of the Black Athlete?" 2. Also Harry Edwards, interviewed by the author.
50. See "President Emeritus Robert D. Clark Interviews," in H. Brent Melendy Files at San Jose State University Archives (Dr. Martin Luther King, Jr., Library, San Jose), 23.
51. Edwards, *The Struggle That Must Be*, 158.
52. Harry Edwards, "Mounting the Protest," in David K. Wiggins and Patrick B. Miller, *The Unlevel Playing Field: A Documentary History of the African American Experience in Sport* (Urbana: University of Illinois Press, 2003), 288.
53. Harry Edwards, interviewed by the author; and *Sparta Life*, "No Place for the Negro," 8–10.
54. Cass Jackson, interviewed by the author.
55. Edwards, *The Struggle That Must Be*, 159.
56. Ibid.
57. Edwards, "Mounting the Protest," 288.
58. Harry Edwards, interviewed by the author. At the time, Edwards's idea of this form of black progress was getting a black person elected governor of California.
59. See Harry Edwards, interviewed by the author; and Roger Allen, "Harry Edwards: We Get What's Ours or Burn It Down," *Sparta Life*, Winter 1968, 7–9.
60. Quote from Edwards, *The Struggle That Must Be*, 159.
61. The narrative is based on Harry Edwards, interviews with the author.
62. See "Richard Clark's Administration," *San Leandro News*, November 8, 1967. The article was also circulated in the Fremont *News-Register* and *Alameda Time Star*. Also see the boxes of "Support Letters for President Clark" in the Robert D. Clark files at San Jose State Archives, at San Jose State University Archives (Dr. Martin Luther King, Jr., Library, San Jose).
63. "President Emeritus Robert D. Clark Interviews," 23.
64. Ibid., 27.
65. Ibid.
66. The quote is from Edwards, *The Struggle That Must Be*, 160.
67. Ibid., 160–161.
68. *San Jose Mercury News*, September 22, 1967.
69. Harry Edwards, interviewed by the author.
70. Ibid.
71. Ibid.
72. Ibid.
73. Quoted from Harry Edwards, interviewed by the author.

74. And later in the Olympics. See Leonard, "What Happened to the Revolt of the Black Athlete?" 3.

75. Themis Chronopoulos, "Racial Turmoil at San Jose State: The Incident of the 1967 University of Texas at El Paso vs. San Jose State Football Game," 1994 California Pioneer Paper (California Room, Dr. Martin Luther King, Jr., Library, San Jose), 6; and Hobart W. Burns, "Why Cancel the Game: Hobart W. Burns Letter to Paul Castoro," December 19, 1967, in Robert D. Clark files, San Jose State University Archives (Dr. Martin Luther King, Jr., Library, San Jose).

76. Harry Edwards, interviewed by the author. The University of Texas at El Paso changed its name in 1967 from Texas Western College.

77. "President Emeritus Robert D. Clark Interviews," 87.

78. *Los Angeles Times*, September 24, 1967.

79. Edwards, *The Struggle That Must Be*, 129.

80. "President Emeritus Robert D. Clark Interviews," 29.

81. Narrative is based on Clark's recollections in "President Emeritus Robert D. Clark Interviews," 30; and Ruffin, *Uninvited Neighbors*, PhD diss., 416–417.

82. *San Jose Mercury News*, September 21, 1967; and "President Emeritus Robert D. Clark Interviews," 30.

83. *Los Angeles Times*, September 27, 1967; and Leonard, "What Happened to the Revolt of the Black Athlete?" 3.

84. *Los Angeles Times*, September 27, 1967.

85. *San Jose Mercury News*, September 22, 1967.

86. "President Emeritus Robert D. Clark Interviews," 29–31; *San Jose Mercury News*, September 10, 1963; and *Los Angeles Times*, September 27, 1967.

87. See "Letters" in Robert D. Clark and Harry Edward files at San Jose State University Archives, Dr. Martin Luther King, Jr., Library, San Jose; and "Special Report by Chancellor Glenn S. Dumke to the Board of Trustees of the California State Colleges, November 30, 1967," in Robert D. Clark files.

88. See "Letters" in Robert D. Clark files and Harry Edward files.

89. *San Jose Mercury News*, September 21, 1967; "Support Letters" in Robert D. Clark files; and "President Clark Has Been Fair to All. And Isn't That What America Is All About?" *San Leandro News*, November 8, 1967.

90. Quote is from Chronopoulos, "Racial Turmoil at San Jose State," 5.

91. *Los Angeles Times*, September 23, 1967.

92. Ibid., September 24, 1967.

93. Chronopoulos, "Racial Turmoil at San Jose State," 5.

94. *Los Angeles Times*, September 22, 1967.

95. "President Emeritus Robert D. Clark Interviews," 30.

96. See *Sparta Life*, "No Place for the Negro," 10; and "President Emeritus Robert D. Clark Interviews," 26–28.

97. *Sparta Life*, "Valerie Dickerson: Beyond Stereotypes" (Winter 1968).

98. James Baldwin, *The Fire Next Time* (New York: Dial Press, 1963; reprint, New York: Vintage, 1992).

99. "President Emeritus Robert D. Clark Interviews," 27.

100. Quote is in Chronopoulos, "Racial Turmoil at San Jose State," 7. Also see *Los Angeles Times*, September 23, 1967; and Edwards, *The Struggle That Must Be*, 178–179.

101. Harry Edwards, interviewed by the author; and "President Emeritus Robert D. Clark Interviews," 36.

102. Based on Steve Millner, interviewed by the author, San Jose, October 2012.

103. See Edwards, *The Struggle That Must Be*, 178–179; "President Emeritus Robert D. Clark Interviews," 36; and *Los Angeles Times*, October 3, 1967, and December 18, 1967.

104. "President Emeritus Robert D. Clark Interviews," 28.

105. See quote in Edwards, *The Revolt of the Black Athlete*, 38.

106. Harry Edwards, interviewed by the author.

107. Allen, "Harry Edwards," 8.

108. Harry Edwards, interviewed by the author.

109. Harry Edwards, interviewed by the author. Also see Mal Whitfield, "Let's Boycott the Olympics," *Ebony*, December 1964, 66; and Douglas Hartmann, *Race, Culture and the Revolt of the Black Athlete: The 1968 Olympic Protests* (Chicago: University of Chicago Press, 2003), 50–51.

110. Harry Edwards, interviewed by the author.

111. Ibid.

112. The Olympic Committee for Human Rights was the predecessor to the Olympic Project for Human Rights.

113. All quotes are from Harry Edwards, interviewed by the author.

114. *Los Angeles Times*, November 24, 1967; Edwards, *The Struggle That Must Be*, 179–180.

115. *Los Angeles Times*, November 24, 1967, and November 25, 1967.

116. Ibid., December 14, 1967.

117. Ibid., September 22, 1968; and "President Emeritus Robert D. Clark Interviews," 32.

118. Allen Guttmann, *The Games Must Go On: Avery Brundage and the Olympic Movement* (New York: Columbia University Press, 1984), 62–81; 82–109; 228–240.

119. Harry Edwards, interviewed by the author.

120. See Temple University Press, "Interview with Tommie Smith (http://www.temple.edu/tempress/authors/1916_qa.html); and Carlos, Zirin, and Goodman interview, "John Carlos, 1968 Olympic U.S. Medalist."

121. CBS, *The Early Show*, "'Silent Gesture'"; and Carlos, interview, "John Carlos, 1968 Olympic U.S. Medalist, on the Revolutionary Sports Moment That Changed the World," *Democracy Now*.

122. Quote from Edwards, *The Struggle That Must Be*, 203. Also Harry Edwards, interviewed by the author; Cass Jackson, interviewed by the author; and *Track and Field News*, "More Boycott Reaction," letters to the editor, January 1968.

123. BBC, "1968: Black Athletes Make Silent Protest," http://news.bbc.co.uk/onthisday/hi/dates/stories/october/17/newsid_3535000/3535348.stm.

124. Tommie Smith, with David Steele, *Silent Gesture: The Autobiography of Tommie Smith* (Philadelphia: Temple University Press, 2007), 138–140.

125. *Palo Alto Times*, November 8, 1968.

126. "President Emeritus Robert D. Clark Interviews," 32. Also see D. Davis, "Olympic Athletes Who Took a Stand."

127. *Eugene Register-Guard*, "Upon Return to the U.S.: Carlos, Smith Mum," October 22, 1968.

128. Ibid.

129. Hobert Burns, "Hobert Burns Letter to *Washington Post* Editor, October 23, 1968," in Robert D. Clark Files at San Jose State University Archives, Dr. Martin Luther King, Jr., Library, San Jose.

130. See Hobert Burns, letter to James Noah, San Jose State director of communications, October 18, 1968, in Robert D. Clark Files. In the letter Burns said, "Personally I am proud that athletes such as Tommie Smith, John Carlos, and Lee Evans are from San Jose State College, and that they have a moral courage to match their athletic ability."

131. Hobert Burns, letter to the editor, *Washington Post*, October 23, 1968; and Burns, letter to Arthur Suguitan, special assistant to the chancellor, August 5, 1968, San Jose State University, Special Collections, Dr. Martin Luther King, Jr., Library, San Jose.

132. "President Emeritus Robert D. Clark Interviews," 33. Also see "13th Annual Banquet: San Jose Branch NAACP—Honoring San Jose's Black Olympic Athletes," in "NAACP West Coast Region Files" (Bancroft Library, University of California, Berkeley).

133. Steve Millner, interviewed by the author.

134. Based on people interviewed by the author: Steve Millner; Harry Edwards; Cass Jackson; Patricia Perkins (in San Jose, August 2010); Kenneth Blackwell (in San Jose, August 2010); and Alisa Owens (in Oakland, October 2011).

135. Cass Jackson, interviewed by the author.

136. Madeleine O'Meara, "When 'Radical Athletics' Meets Patty Hearst," *Oberlin Review* (July 28, 2012; http://oberlinreview.org/article/when-radical-athletics-meets-patty-hearst/); and Anne Trubek, "The Oberlin Experiment: Why the Failed Revolution of Radical Athleticism May Be the Great Unwritten Chapter

in American Sports History," *Smart Set* (Drexel University; http://thesmartset .com/article/article12140702.aspx).

137. Wire report, "Football," *Spartanburg (S.C.) Herald*, January 6, 1978.

138. Harry Edwards, interviewed by the author; and Cass Jackson, interviewed by the author.

139. NFL Communications, "43 Former NFL Players Participated in 2010 Bill Walsh Minority Coaching Fellowship"; and N. Jeremi Duru, and Tony Dungy, *Advancing the Ball: Race, Reformation, and the Quest for Equal Coaching Opportunity in the NFL* (New York: Oxford University Press, 2011), 59, 61–86. Prior to Bill Walsh's program, African American front office pioneers John Wooten, Paul "Tank" Younger, and Frank Gilliam pressured NFL Commissioner Pete Rozelle into implementing the Black Coaches Visitation Program, which was designed for HBCU coaches to get exposure for coaching through interning with an NFL team. In 2002, the league owners took partial ownership of discriminatory hiring in the head coaching ranks implementing the Rooney Rule.

140. Harry Edwards, interviewed by the author; and N. Jeremi Duru and Tony Dungy, *Advancing the Ball: Race, Reformation, and the Quest for Equal Coaching Opportunity in the NFL* (New York: Oxford University Press, 2011), 1–14.

141. Steve Millner, interviewed by the author; Patricia Perkins, interviewed by the author; Kenneth Blackwell interviewed by the author; and Ocie Tinsley, interviewed by the author, San Jose, August 2010.

142. Steve Millner, interviewed by the author.

143. Ibid.; and "President Emeritus Robert D. Clark Interviews, 34–36."

Chapter 8

1. *San Jose Mercury News*, "Blacks Make Solid Leap," January 30, 1992.

2. See *San Jose Mercury News*, "San Jose Upstages Nation's Other Melting Pots," June 11, 1993; and *San Jose Mercury News*, "Minorities Fare Better in County Than Nation: Income, Education Statistics Analyzed," October 28, 1992.

3. Martin Luther King, Jr., "Letter from a Birmingham Jail." Full text available at abacus.bates.edu/admin/offices/dos/mlk/letter.html.

4. For rich discussions that imply another Great African American Migration see De Graaf, "African American Suburbanization in California," 436–437; and Wiese, *Places of Their Own*, 255–292.

5. Weise, *Places of Their Own*, 255.

6. For more on the black middle class and their movement to the suburbs and the American symbolism involved, see De Graaf, "African American Suburbanization in California"; Karyn R. Lacy, *Blue-Chip Black: Race, Class, and Status in the New Black Middle Class* (Berkeley: University of California Press, 2007); Weise, *Places of Their Own*, 257–258; and Whitaker, *Race Work*.

7. For more on bifurcation in the black community, see *San Francisco Chronicle*, "Prosperity Still Out of Reach for Many Blacks," March 28, 1998; and *San Jose Mercury News*, "Urban Racial Isolation Persists," April 9, 1991. Also see William Julius Wilson, *The Ghetto Underclass: Social Science Perspectives* (Newbury Park, Calif.: Sage, 1993); Carl Husemoller Nightingale, "The Global Inner City: Toward a Historical Analysis," in *W. E. B. Du Bois, Race, and the City*, ed. Michael B. Katz and Thomas J. Sugrue (Philadelphia: University of Pennsylvania Press, 1998); WGBH Educational Foundation, *The Two Nations of Black America* (http://www.pbs.org/wgbh/pages/frontline/shows/race/economics/; http://www.pbs.org/wgbh/pages/frontline/shows/race/interviews/wilson.html); James J. Rawls and Walton Bean, *California: An Interpretive History* (Boston: McGraw-Hill, 2003), 463–467, 536; NPR, "Special Series: California in Crisis" (http://www.npr.org/templates/story/story.php?storyId=106486189); *Los Angeles Times*, "Fixing California" (http://theenvelope.latimes.com/la-me-state-budget-sg,0,6845417.storygallery); Grandmaster Flash and the Furious Five, "The Message" (12-inch single produced in Englewood, N.J. by Sugar Hill Records, 1982); the Stop the Violence Movement, "Self Destruction" (12-inch single and video, produced by Jive in New York, 1989); West Coast All Stars, "We're All in the Same Gang," video (Burbank, Calif.: Warner Brothers, 1990); John Singleton, *Boyz 'N the Hood*, film (Culver City, Calif.: Sony Pictures, 1991); and Randy Holland, *The Fire This Time: Why Los Angeles Burned*, film (Los Angeles: Rhino/Wea International, 1994).

8. Sucheng Chan and Spencer Olin, eds., *Major Problems in California History* (London: Wadsworth, 1996), 392. Also see Rawls, *California*, 511–514.

9. Chan and Olin, *Major Problems in California History*, 393.

10. Richard White, *It's Your Misfortune and None of My Own: A New History of the American West* (Norman: University of Oklahoma Press, 1991), 547.

11. Social Explorer Dataset (SE), Census 1990, Social Explorer; U.S. Census Bureau, "County Populations in California, 1990" (http://www.socialexplorer.com/pub/reportdata/htmlresults.aspx?ReportId=R10291770&Page=); and *San Jose Mercury News*, "Silicon Valley Exodus: Thousands Leave Congested County as Others Move In," April 29, 1989.

12. Based on the testimony of people interviewed by the author in October 2011: in Palo Alto, Albert Camarillo (at Stanford University), Clayborne Carson (at Stanford University), Gordon Chang (at Stanford University), Jean Libby (at home and driven around the peninsula), Ken Lowe (at his home), Steve Staiger (at Palo Alto Historical Association, Palo Alto City Library), and the staff at the Stanford University Special Collections. In Mountain View, Barbara Kinchen (Mountain View Historical Association, Mountain View Public Library) and Monica Ramos (Mexican Heritage Corporation, San Jose). In Los Altos, Cazetta Gray (at her home). At Cupertino, the staff at the California History Center at De Anza College.

13. Quoted from De Graaf, "African American Suburbanization in California," 405.

14. Gordon Chang, interviewed by the author.

15. See Rosiland Bivings, *We Were Here, Too!* (Black History Month documentary; Mountain View, Calif.: Mountain View Public Library History Center, 1997).

16. Cass Jackson, interviewed by the author by phone, June 25, 2012.

17. See Herbert G. Ruffin, "East Palo Alto, California (1925–)," http://www.blackpast.org/?q=aaw/east-palo-alto-1925.

18. Jean Libby (and Ralph Libby), interviewed by the author.

19. Cass Jackson, interviewed by the author.

20. Ben Gross, interviewed by the author at UAW International, Detroit, December 11, 2008.

21. In this period I produced several records copyrighted with the Library of Congress under the name RUFF. The most notable album was Herbert G. Ruffin, "The Ruff Experience . . . Songs from the G-Hype Experience" (Washington, D.C.: Library of Congress, 1991).

22. Charles Gary, interviewed by the author.

23. Ibid.

24. Quoted in ibid.

25. *San Jose Mercury News*, "In Silicon Valley, Blacks Are Reaching Out to Create Their Community Feeling at Home, January 20, 1986.

26. *San Jose Mercury News*, "Juneteenth Brings Blacks Together," June 19, 1982.

27. Ibid.

28. *San Jose Mercury News*, "In Silicon Valley, Blacks Are Reaching Out."

29. *San Jose Mercury News*, "Black Apartment Hunter Encounters Waiting List," July 17, 1977.

30. Ibid.

31. Quoted from ibid.

32. *San Jose Mercury News*, "San Jose Race Bias Noted in Rentals," March 28, 1978.

33. Ibid.

34. *San Jose Mercury News*, "Apartment Bias in Sunnyvale," June 17, 1982.

35. Dennis Keating, *The Suburban Racial Dilemma: Housing and Neighborhoods* (Philadelphia: Temple University Press, 1994), 196.

36. Ibid.

37. *San Jose Mercury News*, "Blacks Still Face Tremendous Discrimination in Housing," July 23, 1979; and "Discrimination in Housing Still Rife in U.S.," April 17, 1978.

38. *San Jose Mercury News*, "Landlords Rarely Gave Same Stories to Black, White Applicants," January 28, 1979.

39. County of Santa Clara, Advance Planning Office, "Home Prices: California's Largest Counties, 1980–1990," Issue 92-5.

40. U.S. Bureau of the Census, *1990 Census of Population and Housing, San Jose PMSA* (Washington, D.C.: U.S. Government Printing Office, 1992), 1288–1289. Findings are based on a sample tract with four hundred black people in the county.

41. U.S. Bureau of the Census, *1970 Census of Housing:* Vol. 1, *Housing Characteristics for States, Cities, and Counties;* pt. 6, *California* (Washington, D.C.: U.S. Government Printing Office, 1972), 7–10, 14–15, 453; and U.S. Bureau of the Census, *1990 Census of Population and Housing, San Jose PMSA,* 1288–1289.

42. ABAG Regional Datacenter, "1990 Census STF1A" (May 1991).

43. Cazetta Gray, resident of Palo Alto, interviewed by the author; and Jean Libby, interviewed by the author. The Palo Alto NAACP led by Muata Puryear was instrumental in getting hundreds of blacks residential access into the white-affluent Mid-Peninsula region in the late 1960s to the 1970s.

44. *San Jose Mercury News*, "Diversity Brings New Perspectives to Black Community," September 13, 1980.

45. Quoted in "Color Separations," *Metro*, March 9–15, 2000, 26–27. Also see page 10. Black Santa Clara University law professor Margalynne Armstrong mentions a similar incident in Palo Alto.

46. See *San Jose Metro*, "Community of Fear," April 23–29, 1987.

47. Ibid.

48. *San Jose Mercury News*, "NAACP Chieftain Sees Pendulum Swing Towards New Racism," March 31, 1979.

49. Ibid.

50. Quoted in the *San Jose Mercury News*, "Blacks Make Solid Leap," January 30, 1972.

51. *San Jose Mercury News*, "Diversity Brings New Perspectives."

52. Quoted in *San Jose Mercury News*, "Minorities Fare Better in County Than Nation," October 28, 1992.

53. *San Jose Mercury News*, "Diversity Brings New Perspectives," and "San Jose Upstages Nation's Other Melting Pots," June 11, 1993.

54. *San Jose Mercury News*, "Diversity Brings New Perspectives."

55. *San Jose Mercury News*, "Large Companies Look to Blacks, Hispanics," March 23, 1988.

56. Ibid.

57. Jacqueline Jones, Thomas Borstelmann, Elaine Tyler May, Peter H. Wood, and Vicki L. Ruiz, *Created Equal: A Social and Political History of the United States* (New York: Pearson Education, Inc., 2008), 640–644.

58. *San Jose Mercury News*, "Black High-Tech Executive," July 13, 1997; "African-American Gets Symantec Post," April 15, 1999; and the *West*, "Visible Man West," May 11, 1997.

59. *San Jose Mercury News*, "Black Businesses Increasing in California Leads Nation, Report Says," December 31, 1985.

60. Herbert Ruffin I, interviewed by the author at East Palo Alto, March 2002; and Andrew Thompson, "A Miracle in Metal: Welder Creates One-of-a-Kind Herb-B-Ques," *Palo Alto Online,* June 30, 2006 (http://www.paloaltoonline.com/weekly/story.php?story_id=1829).

61. *San Jose Mercury News*, "SBA Loans Go Disproportionately to Whites, Asian-Americans," February 14, 1994. Private lending practices were not disclosed because banks were not required to reveal their lending practices by ethnicity.

62. Jessie Carney Smith, Millicent Lownes Jackson, Linda T. Wynn, "Small Business Administration Loans to Small Businesses, 1990–2003," *Encyclopedia of African American Business* (Westport, Conn.: Greenwood, 2006), 56.

63. *San Jose Metro*, "Community of Fear," April 23–29, 1987; and Ellen Rollins, interviewed by the author at Dr. Martin Luther King, Jr., Library, San Jose, August 2010.

64. *San Jose Metro*, "Community of Fear."

65. Ibid. Also see Michelle Alexander, *The New Jim Crow: Mass Incarceration in the Age of Colorblindness* (New York: New Press, 2010).

66. Ibid.

67. See *San Jose Metro*, "Community of Fear"; and *San Jose Mercury News*, "Valley Blacks on Offense," March 23, 1972. In 1972, the shooting death of black motorist John Henry Smith by three white San Jose police officers mobilized San Jose's black community behind the efforts of the Ad Hoc Committee of Concerned Citizens. This group was led by Professors Charles "Mr." Murray and Leonard Jeffries, and Aaron Harris. They used the Smith case to address the escalating problem of police misconduct targeting race with San Jose Police Chief Robert Murphy and San Jose Mayor and future Congressman Norman Mineta.

68. Quote is from *San Jose Mercury News*, "Cops Pick On Us, Young Blacks Say," July 25, 1994. Also see *San Jose Metro*, "Community of Fear."

69. *San Jose Mercury News*, "Cops Pick On Us."

70. Ibid.

71. Ibid.

72. Ibid.

73. See *Metro*, "Color Separations." Don Black's interview was one of many interviews of South Bay Blacks in the weekly community paper *Metro*.

74. Ibid.

75. Charles Gary, interviewed by the author.

76. Crisis Communication Strategies and the University of Oklahoma, "Case Study: Denny's Class Action Lawsuit" (http://www.ou.edu/deptcomm/dod-jcc/groups/02C2/Denny's.htm).

77. Quoted in *West*, "Black Colleges," December 31, 1995.

78. Performance Urban Planning, "8th Annual *Demographia* International Housing Affordability Survey: 2012—Ratings for Metropolitan Markets" (http://www.demographia.com/dhi.pdf). According to this survey, San Jose is the most unaffordable place to live in the United States, and the fifth most unaffordable place to live in the world, behind Hong Kong, Vancouver, Sydney, and Melbourne.

79. Allisa Owens and Urla Hill, interviewed by the author.

80. County of Santa Clara Planning Department, *Facts and Forecasts: A Supplement to the General Plan of Santa Clara County* (1960; San Jose State University Archives, Martin Luther King, Jr., Library, San Jose). According to county planners, as early as 1960 "many people have been concerned with the loss of human values which result when mass production and mass living supplant individuality. In rapidly urbanizing areas, there is a loss of a sense of community . . . and a detachment of human beings from one another. . . . In the Santa Clara County this trend toward a lack of identity can be seen most clearly as the open space which once separated communities is filled in."

81. U.S. Census Bureau, "Population of the 100 Largest Cities and Other Urban Places in the United States: 1790–1990" (http://www.census.gov/population/www/documentation/twps0027/twps0027.html); and National Civic League, Past Winners of the All-America City Award: Winning Communities, 1960" (http://www.allamericacityaward.com/things-to-know-about-all-america-city-award/past-winners-of-the-all-america-city-award/past-winners-of-the-all-america-city-award-1960s/).

82. *San Francisco Chronicle*, "Silicon Valley Hub Knocks Off Detroit as 10th Largest City," July 1, 2005; Associated Press, "Do You Know the Way to America's 10th Largest City? Does Anyone?" July 1, 2005; and *New York Times*, "To the Chagrin of Detroit, Top 10 No Longer," June 29, 2005.

83. "Milpitas Experiences Increase in Percent Growth" (Reference, Milpitas Community Library, Milpitas—Population); *San Jose Mercury News*, "Whites Aren't Majority in Region, Figures Show Asian, Latino Percentages Rise," March 30, 2001.

84. Ken Lowe, interviewed by the author, Palo Alto, October 2011; Gordon Chang, interviewed by the author; Charles Gary, interviewed by the author; and Steven Millner, interviewed by the author. According to Chinese American physician and Palo Alto resident Ken Lowe, in 1986 when his family first moved into Palo Alto from Fremont (near Milpitas), the town was almost all white and affluent. In the 1990s, the racial composition gradually shifted as more Chinese moved in and many whites retired, died, or moved to more affordable places. In

the 2000s, Chinese and Asian Indians replaced affluent whites in a desirable place to live that had great public schools. In East County, San Jose State professor Steve Millner saw this process as early as 1975 with the Vietnamese in San Jose; and in Milpitas, according to Charles Gary, the city, 74 percent white when his family arrived in 1960, had by 2010 been turned upside down demographically; only 13 percent of the population was white by then, blacks had a 5 to 6 percent population, Latin Americans had a 16 percent population, and Asian Americans had a 62 percent population. These population figures were not isolated to the South Bay. In the Bay Area, Asian Americans have a dominant presence in most communities.

85. *San Jose Mercury News*, "Whites Aren't Majority," and "'Them' Must Become 'Us' to Meet Valley's Needs," September 18, 1989.

86. Ellen Rollins, interviewed by the author.

87. See *San Jose Mercury News*, "In Silicon Valley, Blacks Are Reaching Out."

88. Ibid.

89. Taylor, *In Search of the Racial Frontier*, 61.

90. *San Jose Mercury News*, "Juneteenth Brings Blacks Together," June 19, 1982. See similar stories published in the newspaper on June 14, 1992, and June 19, 1994.

91. Ellen Rollins, interviewed by the author. Rollins is a nurse, Service Employees International Union representative, national Juneteenth representative, and curator for History San Jose's African American Heritage House. Aside from hosting Juneteenth, the African American Community Service Agency also ran after-school programs and offered art classes, Christmas parties for kids, senior breakfasts, summer camps, and teaching seminars. The agency also was active in registering people of color and women to vote. In the 1970s and '80s, it annually brought in well-known speakers, such as Herbert Aptheker, to give a public lecture.

92. *San Jose Mercury News*, "Juneteenth Brings Blacks Together."

93. Ellen Rollins, interviewed by the author; and Ocie Tinsley and Mattie Briggs Tinsley, interviewed by the author at San Jose, August 2010.

94. *San Jose Mercury News*, "Juneteenth Brings Blacks Together."

95. Ibid., "Freedom Train," January 21, 1986.

Bibliography

Archival and Manuscript Collections

AME Zion Church Files. Palo Alto Historical Society, Palo Alto Library.

Black Student Union. Special Collections, Stanford University Libraries.

California Government Codes. Special Collections, Honnold-Mudd Library, Claremont Colleges, Claremont.

Campus Report. Special Collections, Stanford University Libraries.

Chicano Students Files. Special Collections, Stanford University Libraries.

Collection on Santa Clara County's Agricultural Past. California Room, Dr. Martin Luther King, Jr., Library, San Jose.

Harry Edwards Files. San Jose State University Archives, Dr. Martin Luther King, Jr., Library, San Jose.

H. Brent Melendy Files. San Jose State University Archives, Dr. Martin Luther King, Jr., Library, San Jose.

H. H. Bancroft Collection. Bancroft Library, University of California, Berkeley.

Historical Biographies of Santa Clara County. "Hon. J. J. Owen." In *Santa Clara County Research Net*. http://www.santaclararesearch.net/SCBIOS/jjowen.html.

Housing Deeds in the Santa Clara Valley. Santa Clara County Archives and County Clerk Office.

Inez C. Jackson Papers. Inez C. Jackson Historical Library. African American Community Service Agency, San Jose.

Local History Files. California History Center at De Anza College, Cupertino.

Local History Files. California Room, Dr. Martin Luther King, Jr., Library, San Jose.

Local History Files. Milpitas Library.

Local History Files. Mountain View Historical Society, Mountain View Library.

Local History Files. Palo Alto Historical Association, Palo Alto Library.

Local History Files. San Jose State University Archives, Dr. Martin Luther King, Jr., Library, San Jose.

Local History Files. Santa Clara City Library.

Local History Files. Sunnyvale Library.

Mission Santa Clara Files. University Archives, Santa Clara University Library, Santa Clara.

NAACP West Coast Region Files. "NAACP Membership Report, San Jose Branch, 1948–1976." Bancroft Library, University of California, Berkeley.

William Oliver Collection. William P. Reuther Library. Wayne State University, Detroit.
Reverend Jerry Wm. Drino Files. Trinity Cathedral, San Jose.
Reverend Peter Williams Cassey Papers. Research Library, History San Jose.
Robert D. Clark Files. San Jose State University Archives, Dr. Martin Luther King, Jr., Library, San Jose.
San Jose Chapter of The Links, Inc. , Files. Research Library, History San Jose.
Slavery in San Jose Papers. Research Library, History San Jose.
State History Files. California State Library, Sacramento.
Student Activism (Stanford). Special Collections, Stanford University Libraries.
Sunnyhills Papers. United Auto Workers (UAW) Ford Department Collection. Walter P. Reuther Library, Wayne State University, Detroit.
Sunnyhills Files. Ben Gross Personal Papers, Detroit.
Syracuse University Library. "That Laboratory of Abolitionism, Libel, and Treason: Syracuse and the Underground Railroad." http://library.syr.edu/digital/exhibits/u/undergroundrr/index.html.
Testbed for the Redlining Archives of California's Exclusionary Spaces (T-RACES). "San Jose, Santa Clara, and Vicinity Redlining Map" (1937). http://salt.unc.edu/T-RACES/mosaic.html.
UAW Fair Practices Collection. William P. Reuther Library. Wayne State University, Detroit.
UAW Local 560 Papers. United Auto Workers (UAW) Ford Department Collection. Walter P. Reuther Library. Wayne State University, Detroit.

Public Records

U.S. CENSUS

ABAG Regional Datacenter. "1990 Census STF1A" (May 1991).
Ancestry.com. "Jose Dolores Pico (1764–1827)." http://records.ancestry.com/Jose_Dolores_Pico_records.ashx?pid=25473770.
———. "United States Federal Census Collection, 1870–1930: African Americans in Santa Clara County." http://search.ancestrylibrary.com/search/category.aspx?cat=35.
FindaGrave.com. "Antonio Maria Pico." http://www.findagrave.com/cgi-bin/fg.cgi?page=gr&GRid=35879145.
Smith, Edith. *Some Early African American Settlers in the Santa Clara Valley.* Sourisseau Academy for California State and Local History, San Jose State University, 1994.
Social Explorer Dataset. Census 1990, Social Explorer; U.S. Census Bureau. "County Populations in California, 1990." http://www.socialexplorer.com/pub/reportdata/htmlresults.aspx?ReportId=R10291770&Page=1.

Social Explorer Professional. "Census Tract—% Black Population, in the Santa Clara County" (1940–2000). 2011 Social Explorer.
University of Virginia Library. *Historical Census Browser: County-Level Results for 1850–1960*. University of Virginia Library: Geospatial and Statistical Data Center, 2005. http://fisher.lib.virginia.edu/collections/stats/histcensus/.
U.S. Bureau of the Census. *1950 Census of Population*, Vol. 11, *Characteristics of the Population*, pt. 5, *California*. Washington, D.C.: U.S. Government Printing Office, 1952.
———. *1960 U.S. Census of Population and Housing, General Characteristics of the Population, by Census Tracts*. Washington, D.C.: Government Printing Office, 1963.
———. *1980 Census of Population and Housing, San Jose PMSA*. Washington, D.C.: U.S. Government Printing Office, 1983.
———. *American Fact Finder: Santa Clara County, California 2000 and 2005*. http://factfinder.census.gov/servlet/ACSSAFFFacts?_event=Search&geo_id=&_geoContext=&_street=&_county=santa+clara+county&_cityTown=santa+clara+county&_state=04000US06&_zip=&_lang=en&_sse=on&pctxt=fph&pgsl=010.
———. *Census of Housing, 1970*, Vol. 1, *Housing Characteristics for States, Cities, and Counties*, pt. 6, *California*. Washington, D.C.: U.S. Government Printing Office, 1972.
———. *Census of Population, 1960*, Vol. 1, *Characteristics of the Population*, pt. 6, *California*. Washington, D.C.: Government Printing Office, 1963.
———. *Census of Population, 1990, General Population Characteristics, United States Summary*. Washington, D.C.: Government Printing Office, 1992.
———. *Census of Population and Housing. Characteristics of the Population, by Census Tracts: 1950, SMSA San Jose, California*. Washington, D.C.: U.S. Government Printing Office, 1952.
———. "Population of the 100 Largest Cities and Other Urban Places in the United States: 1790–1990." http://www.census.gov/population/www/documentation/twps0027/twps0027.html.
———. *U.S. Census of Population and Housing*, San Jose SMSA: *1960 U.S. Census of Population and Housing, General Characteristics of the Population, by Census Tracts*. Washington, D.C.: Government Printing Office, 1963.
———. *U.S. Census of Population and Housing; 1970 Census Tracts*. Washington, D.C.: U.S. Government Printing Office, 1972. Table P-1. SMSA San Jose, California, Washington, D.C.: U.S. Government Printing Office, 1972.
———. *U.S. Census of Population and Housing; 1980 Census Tracts*. Washington, D.C.: U.S. Government Printing Office, 1983.

COURT CASES

Boynton v. Virginia, 364 U.S. 454 (1960).
Brown v. Board of Education of Topeka, 347 U.S. 483 (1954). Available at http://www.nationalcenter.org/brown.html.
Dred Scott v. Sanford, 60 U.S. 393 (1857).
Evans v. Newton, 382 U.S. 296 (1966).
James et al. v. Marinship Corporation, 25 Cal. 2d 721 (1944).
McKinney v. Southern White Knights: Forsyth County Marchers Case (1987). Available at http://www.splcenter.org/legal/docket/files.jsp?cdrID=20.
Mendez v. Westminster, 64 F. Supp. 544 (1946). Available at http://www.learncalifornia.org/doc.asp?id=1508.
Mulkey v. Reitman, 64 Cal 2d 529 (1966).
People v. Hall, 4 Cal. 399 (1854). Available at http://www.uchastings.edu/racism-race/people-hall.html.
Plessy v. Ferguson, 163 U.S. 537 (1896).
Reitman v. Mulkey, 387 U.S. 369 (1967).
Shelley v. Kramer, 334 U.S. 1 (1948).
St. John Dixon v. Alabama State Board of Education, 294 F.2d 150 (5th Cir. 1961).
Ward v. Flood, 48 Cal. 36 (1874). Available at http://www.blackpast.org/?q=primarywest/ward-v-flood-1874.
Westminster School Dist. of Orange County et al. v. Mendez et al., 161 F.2d 774 (1947).
Wysinger v. Crookshank, 82 Cal 588, 720 (1890). Available at http://www.blackpast.org/?q=primarywest/wysinger-v-crookshank-1890.

SURVEYS, REPORTS, AND OTHER GOVERNMENT DOCUMENTS

Anti–Persons of Color Testimony against White People in California Court. California Legislature, *Journals of the Senate and Assembly*, 3rd sess., 1852, 75.
Burlingame Treaty. 18 Stat. 147 (1868).
Cable Act of 1922 (ch. 411, 42 Stat. 1021, "Married Women's Independent Nationality Act").In *Prologue Magazine* 30, 2 (Summer 1998). Available at http://www.archives.gov/publications/prologue/1998/summer/women-and-naturalization-1.html.
California Alien Land Laws of 1913. California Legislature, *Statutes of California, and Amendments to the Codes,* 40th sess., 1913. Sacramento: Friend Wm. Richardson, Superintendent of State Printing, 1913, 206–208.
California Fair Employment Practices Act (1959). Lab. Code, sec. 1410 et seq. (current law is Gov. Code, sec. 12900 et seq.).
California Fugitive Slave Law of 1852. California Legislature, *Statutes of California*, 3rd sess., chap. 33. San Francisco: G. K. Fitch and Co., and V. E. Geiger and Co., State Printers, 1852, 67–69.

California Fugitive Slave Law Repealed (1867). California Legislature, *Statutes of California*, 17th sess, 1867–8. Sacramento: D. W. Gelwicks, State Printer, 1868, 13.
California Governor. McCone Commission Report: Complete and Unabridged Report by the Governor's Commission on the Los Angeles Riot. Los Angeles: Kimtex, 1965.
Chinese Exclusion Act of 1882. In *U.S. Statutes at Large* 22 (December 1881–March 1883), 58–62. Washington, D.C.: Government Printing Office, 1883.
City Hall Exhibits Committee. Hidden Heritages: Six African American Families, San Jose 1860–1920. Exhibit, San Jose City Hall, 2009–2010.
Civil Rights Act of 1866. Available at http://www.rent.com/company/legal/equal/.
Civil Rights Act of 1868. 42 U.S.C., sec. 1982.
Civil Rights Act of 1964. HR 7152, 88th Cong.
Civil Rights Act of 1968, Title 8 (Fair Housing Act of 1968). 42 U.S.C., sec. 3601. Available at U.S. Department of Justice, Civil Rights Division Housing and Civil Enforcement Section. http://www.usdoj.gov/crt/housing/title8.htm.
County of Santa Clara, Advance Planning Office. "Home Prices: California's Largest Counties, 1980–1990." Issue 92-5.
County of Santa Clara Planning Department. *Facts and Forecasts: A Supplement to the General Plan of Santa Clara County* (1960). San Jose State University Archives, Dr. Martin Luther King, Jr., Library, San Jose.
Department of Housing and Urban Development. "Federal Housing Administration: Mortgage and Loan Insurance Programs." http://www.hud.gov/offices/cfo/repots/04estimates/fhafund.pdf.
Devincenzi, Robert J., Thomas Gilsenan, and Morton Levine. *Milpitas: Five Dynamic Decades*. Milpitas, Calif.: City of Milpitas, 2004.
Discrimination in Public Assisted Housing Act of 1959 (aka Hawkins Act). California Legislature. *Statutes of California, General Laws, Amendments to the Codes, Resolutions, and Constitutional Amendments*. Vol. 2: 1958–1959, 4074–4077. Sacramento: State of California, 1959.
Dumke, Glenn S. "Special Report by Chancellor Glenn S. Dumke to the Board of Trustees of the California State Colleges, November 30, 1967." In the Robert D. Clark files at San Jose State University Archives, Dr. Martin Luther King, Jr., Library, San Jose.
Education of Black and Indian Children in California Restricted until 1872. *California Political Code,* Section 1669, 1872. Also see An Act to Enforce the Educational Rights of Children. In California Legislature, 20th sess., *Statutes of California*. Sacramento: G. H. Springer, State Printer, 1874, 751–753.
Executive Order 11063. 27 Federal Register 11527 (1962).
Executive Order 8802. Available at http://www.blackpast.org/?q=primary/executive-order-8802-1941. Fair Employment and Housing Act (Rumford Act). Gov. Code sec. 12955 et seq.

Foreign Miners Tax of 1852. In California Legislature, *Statutes of California*, 3rd sess., chap. 37. San Francisco: G. K. Fitch and Co., and V. E. Geiger and Co., State Printers, 1852, 84–87.

Homestead Act in California (1860). California Legislature, 11th sess.. Sacramento: Charles T. Botts, State Printer, 1860, 87–89.

House Committee on Un-American Activities. *Operation Abolition.* Washington, D.C.: U.S. Government Printing Office, 1960.

Housing Act of 1950. Sections 203 and 213. U.S. Congress, 81st Cong., 2nd sess. (1950). *U.S. Code Congressional Service*, Vol. 2, *Legislative History*. Brooklyn, N.Y.: Edward Thompson Co., 1951, 2033–2037 and 2039–2041.

Immigration Act of 1924 (aka National Origins Act or the Johnson-Reed Act). *U.S. Statutes at Large* 42, pt. 1 (December 1923–March 1925). Washington, D.C.: Government Printing Office, 1925, 153–169.

Immigration and Nationality Act of 1952 (McCarran-Walter Act). Public Law 82-414. *U.S. Statutes at Large* 66: Washington, D.C.: Government Printing Office, 1952, 163.

Immigration and Naturalization Services Act of 1965 (aka Hart-Celler Act or the INS Act of 1965). Public Law 89-236. Washington, D.C.: Government Printing Office, 1965.

The Library of Congress. *"With an Even Hand":* Brown v. Board *at Fifty*. Available at http://www.loc.gov/exhibits/brown/brown-brown.html.

McCone Commission Report. *Complete and Unabridged Report by the Governor's Commission on the Los Angeles Riot*. Los Angeles: Kimtex, 1965.

National Civic League. "Past Winners of the All-America City Award: Winning Communities, 1960." Available at http://www.allamericacityaward.com/things-to-know-about-all-america-city-award/past-winners-of-the-all-america-city-award/past-winners-of-the-all-america-city-award-1960s/.

Naturalization Act of 1790. Library of Congress. "A Century of Lawmaking for a New Nation: U.S. Congressional Documents and Debates, 1774–1875." Available at http://rs6.loc.gov/cgi-bin/ampage?collId=llsl&fileName=001/llsl001.db&recNum=226.

Page Law. 43rd Congress, sess. 2, ch. 141. March 3, 1875.

Performance Urban Planning. "Eighth Annual *Demographia* International Housing Affordability Survey: 2012—Ratings for Metropolitan Markets." Available at http://www.demographia.com/dhi.pdf.

Proposition 14. Cal. Const. Art 1, sec. 26.

Provisions for Separate Schools and State Normal Schools. In California Legislature, *Statutes of California*, 16th sess., 1865–56, sec. 63-77. Sacramento: C. M. Clayes, State Printer, 1866, 399–402.

Reconstruction Amendments. Available at http://www.blackpast.org/?q=primary/reconstruction-amendments.

Registration of Citizens and Enrollment of Voters during Reconstruction Era. California Legislature, *Statutes of California*, 17th sess., 1867–1868, 647–655. Sacramento: D. W. Gelwicks, State Printer, 1868.

Santa Clara County Office of the Clerk Recorder, Archives. "Declaration of Restrictions, Conditions, Covenants, Charges and Agreements affecting the Real Property" (deeds 1915–1947).

Santa Clara County Planning Office. "1990 Population and Ethnicity of Santa Clara County by City and CDP; County of Santa Clara." Advance Planning Office 89-1A (January 1989).

———. "Employment Growth, 1980–1990." Advance Planning Office 92-8 (1992).

———. "Home Prices: California's Largest Counties, 1980–1990." Advance Planning Office 92-5 (1992).

———. "Population Growth, 1980–1990." Advance Planning Office 92-7 (1992).

———. "Population Growth by County in Bay Area, 1990–2000." Advance Planning Office 90-7-A (1990).

Slavery and the Prospect of Restricting Free Persons of Color from Gold Rush California. Discussed in Governor's Annual Message to the Legislature, January 7, 1851. *Journals of the Legislature of the State of California*, 2nd sess., 1851, 789–790, 796–798. San Jose: Eugene Cassidy, State Printer, 1851.

Social and Political Restrictions on People of Color in Gold Rush California. Governor's Annual Message to the Legislature, January 7, 1851. California Legislature. *Journals of the Legislature of the State of California*, 2nd sess., 1851, 796–797. San Jose: Eugene Cassidy, State Printer, 1851.

Territorial Suffrage Act (aka "Elective Franchise in the Territories"). *Statutes at Large*, 39th Congress, sess. 2, chaps. 12 and 15, 1867, 379–380.

Testbed for the Redlining Archives of California's Exclusionary Spaces (T-RACES). "San Jose, Santa Clara, and Vicinity Redlining Map" (1937). Available at http://salt.unc.edu/T-RACES/mosaic.html.

Treaty of Guadalupe Hildago. Available at http://www.blackpast.org/?q=primary WEST/treaty-guadalupe-hidalgo.

UN Human Rights. "Universal Declarations of Human Rights." Available at http://www.un.org/Overview/rights.html.

Unruh Civil Rights Act. CC, sec. 51 et seq.

U.S. Commission on Civil Rights. *Civil Rights: 1963 Report of U.S. Commission on Civil Rights*. Washington, D.C.: U.S. Government Printing Office, 1963.

U.S. Department of Housing and Urban Development. *Housing and Home Finance Agency, Fair Housing Laws: 1966*. Washington, D.C.: U.S. Government Printing Office, 1966.

Voting Regulations in Gold Rush California. California Constitution, 1849, art. 2, sec. 1. San Jose: H. H. Robinson, State Printer, 1850.

Voting Rights Act. *U.S. National Archives and Records Administration*. Available at www.ourdocuments.gov/doc.php?doc=100&page=transcript.

Oral Sources

INTERVIEWS BY THE AUTHOR

Charles Alexander
Gloria Anderson
Kenneth Blackwell, Sr.
Mattie Briggs-Tinsley
Albert Camarillo
Claybourne Carson
Gordon Chang
Harry Edwards
Sofia Fojas
Helen Gaffin
Charles Gary
Cazetta Gray
Ben Gross
Urla Hill
Cass Jackson
Barbara Kinchen
Jean Libby
Ralph Libby
Ken Lowe
Steven Millner
Ray Norton, Sr.
Alissa Owens
Patricia Perkins
Clifford Price
Monica Ramos
William "Bunny" Ribbs, Sr.
Ellen Rollins
Herb Ruffin I
Talya Ruffin
Steve Staiger
Orvella Stubbs
Ocie Tinsley

The interviews listed below were organized by the author and conducted by Patricia Perkins. The transcripts are in the possession of Herbert G. Ruffin II.

Gladys Anderson
Helen Anderson
Patricia I. Anderson
Gloria I. Ellington
Bertha Stafford
Frank Sypert, Jr.
Grace Sypert
Lenora Sypert

INTERVIEWS BY CHARLES MURRAY (CA. 1979)
Interviews are in the possession of Herbert G. Ruffin II.

Ann Byrd
Joe Campbell
Marws Chatman
Aaron Harris
Martin Hudson
Henrietta Jefferson
Alvin McCollan
Douglass Robinson
T. Sweet
James Thomas
Boster Young
Pauline Young

PUBLISHED ORAL HISTORIES

Arbuckle, Helen. "Anna Maria Bascom: San Jose's First Official Hostess." In *SanJose.com.* http://www.sanjose.com/history/bascom.html.

Beasley, Delilah L. *The Negro Trailblazers of California.* A Compilation of Records from the California Archives in the Bancroft Library at the University of California, in Berkeley; and from the Diaries, Old Papers, and Conversations of Old Pioneers in the State of California. New York: Negro Universities Press, 1969.

Carlos, John, Dave Zirin, and Amy Goodman interview. "John Carlos, 1968 Olympic U.S. Medalist, on the Revolutionary Sports Moment That Changed the World." In *Democracy Now*, October 12, 2011. Available at http://www.democracynow.org/2011/10/12/john_carlos_1968_olympic_us_medalist.

Clark, Robert D. "President Emeritus Robert D. Clark Interviews." In H. Brent Melendy Files at San Jose State University Archives, Dr. Martin Luther King, Jr., Library, San Jose.

Eichler, Edward P. *Race and Housing: An Interview with Edward P. Eichler, President, Eichler Homes, Inc.*, 1964, 1–21.

Eichler, Ned. *Eichler Insights* 2, 4 (Late Summer 1993).

Foner, Philip S., and Ronald L. Lewis. *The Black Worker: From the Founding of the CIO to the AFL-CIO Merger, 1936–1955*. Philadelphia: Temple University Press, 1978.

Field, M. H. "Grandma Bascom's Story of San Jose in '49." In *Overland Monthly and Out West Magazine* 9, 53 (May 1887), 543–551.

Garden City Women's Club (San Jose, Calif.). *History of Black Americans in Santa Clara Valley*. Sunnyvale, Calif.: Lockheed Missiles and Space Co., 1978.

Henderson, Joyce. *C. L. Dellums: International President of the Brotherhood of the Sleeping Car Porters and Civil Rights Leader*. Berkeley: Regents of the University of California, 1973.

———. *William Byron Rumford: Legislator for Fair Employment, Fair Housing, and Public Health*. Berkeley: Regents of the University of California, 1973.

Kelen, Leslie G., and Eileen Hallet Stone, eds. *Missing Stories: An Oral History of Ethnic and Minority Groups in Utah*. Salt Lake City: University of Utah Press, 1996.

Ruffin, Josephine St. Pierre. "Address to the First National Conference of Colored Women." In *Lift Every Voice: African American Oratory, 1787–1900*, ed. Philip S. Foner and Robert James Branham. Tuscaloosa: University of Alabama Press, 1998.

San Jose Mercury News. "Who We Are: Voices of Diversity." In weekly section The West, December 4, 1994, 12–27.

San Jose Metro. "Color Separations." March 9–15, 2000.

Smith, Tommie. "Interview with Tommie Smith." http://www.temple.edu/tempress/authors/1916_qa.html.

———. "'Silent Gesture' Still Speaks Volumes: Tommie Smith on His '68 Olympics Raised-Fist Protest." *The Early Show*, CBS. http://www.cbsnews.com/stories/2007/02/08/earlyshow/leisure/books/main2446168.html.

Stanford University Archives. "KZSU Project South Interviews." Stanford University Archives, Palo Alto, California.

Newspapers

Alameda Time Star, 1967
The Argonaut, San Jose, 1955
The Atlanta Journal-Constitution, 2009
The Chronicle of Higher Education, 2012
Daily Finance, America Online, 2009
East San Jose SUN, 1966
The Elevator, San Francisco, 1865
Eugene Register-Guard, 1968
Los Angeles Times, 1896–2009
Milpitas Post, 1955–2010
Mirror of the Times, San Francisco, 1855–1862
Nevada Daily National Gazette, 1870
New York Times, 1999
News-Register, Fremont, 1967
Oakland Tribune, 1959
Palo Alto Online, 2006–2008
Palo Alto Times, 1920–1940
Peninsula Times Tribune, Palo Alto, 1991
Planted Slants, United Auto Workers Local 560, Milpitas, 1954
San Francisco Call, 1970
San Francisco Chronicle, 1993
San Francisco Examiner, 1967, 1994–2001
Pacific Appeal, San Francisco, 1862–1873
San Jose Mercury-Herald, 1860–1922, 1941
San Jose Mercury News, 1954–2009
San Jose Metro, 1987–2000
The Seattle Times, 2008
Sparta Life, San Jose State University Quarterly Magazine, 1967–1968
Spartan Daily, San Jose State University, 1960–1968
Spartanburg Herald, Spartanburg, South Carolina, 1978
St. Petersburg Times, Tampa Bay, 2003
Stanford Daily, 1967
Valley Journal, Sunnyvale, 1990
The West (Sunday Magazine in the *San Jose Mercury News*), 1993–1997

Histories from Manuscript Collections

Bancroft, H. H. *The Works of Hubert Howe Bancroft*. San Francisco, 1888. University archives at the Bancroft Library, University of California, Berkeley.

H. H. Bancroft Collection. "Letter to the Alcalde of San Jose from Monterey, May 7, 1832." University archives at the Bancroft Library, University of California, Berkeley.

H. H. Bancroft Collection. "P. F. Collins Letter—Black San Jose and 1870 Vote." University archives at the Bancroft Library, University of California, Berkeley.

Bivings, Rosiland. *We Were Here, Too!* (Black History Month documentary). Mountain View, Calif.: Mountain View Public Library History Center, 1997.

California History Center. *Historias: The Spanish Heritage of Santa Clara Valley.* Cupertino: California History Center, De Anza College, 1976.

———. *Sunnyvale: City of Destiny.* Cupertino: California History Center, De Anza College, 1974.

Chronopoulos, Themis. "Racial Turmoil at San Jose State: The Incident of the 1967 University of Texas at El Paso vs. San Jose State Football Game." 1994 California Pioneer Paper, California Room, San Jose Public Library.

Clyde Arbuckle Ephemera Collection. "The Valley of Heart's Delight Pamphlet" (ca. 1922). California Room, San Jose Public Library. http://digitalcollections.sjlibrary.org/cdm/compoundobject/collection/sjplephemer/id/174.

Cope, Stephanie. "The Effect World War II had on the Japanese Living in Santa Clara County." California Pioneer Paper, 1993 California Room, San Jose Public Library.

Drino, Jerry. "Two Lives—Two Congregations—San Jose and the Civil War." The Reverend Jerry Wm. Drino Files, Trinity Cathedral, San Jose, April 15, 2012.

Foothill Resource Associates, Murphy Ranch, California, 1990. Local History Files, Milpitas Library.

Johnson, Amy (daughter of Amy Cassey Thomas). "An Informal Family History of the Cassey Family." California Room, San Jose Public Library.

Lee, David P. "Forest Anderson: The Black Oklahoma Millionaire." Anderson family reunion documentary. Patricia Perkins Collection, San Jose.

LeFalle, Deborah. *Peter Williams Cassey: The Man and His Mission.* 1992 California Pioneer Paper, California Room, San Jose Public Library.

Marvin-Cunningham, Judith. "Historic Sites Inventory: Milpitas, California, 1990." Local History Files, Milpitas Library.

Nishino, Yuka. "The San Jose State College Anti-War Riots of November 1967." 1987 California Pioneer Paper, California Room, San Jose Public Library.

Rigenhagen, Rhonda. *A History of East Palo Alto.* Romic Environmental Technologies Corp, 1997: http://www.romic.com/epahistory/index.htm. Originally from Local History Files, Palo Alto Historical Association.

Staff of Dr. Martin Luther King, Jr., Library, San Jose. "Translations of Spanish/Mexican Archives: Pueblo of San Jose, 1792–1859." California Room, Dr. Martin Luther King, Jr., Library.

Sunnyhills United Methodist Church. "Sunnyhills United Methodist Church: A History, 1957–1982." Available at Global Ministries the United Methodist Church. http://www.gbgm-umc.org/sunnyhills/history.htm

Trinity Church brochure. Research Library, History San Jose.

Dissertations and Theses

Guyton, John Daniel, Jr. "Attitudes and Differences in the Concept of Work among Black Americans in the Southern San Francisco Bay Area." PhD diss., University of San Francisco, 1989.

Hill, Urla. "Speed City: The Civil Rights Years." M.A. thesis, San Francisco State University, 2005.

Hudson, Lynn M. "When 'Mammy' Becomes a Millionaire: Mary Ellen Pleasant, an African American Entrepreneur." PhD diss., Indiana University, 1996.

Keller, John Frederick. "The Production Worker in Electronics: Industrialization and Labor Development in California's Santa Clara Valley." PhD diss., University of Michigan, 1984.

Klein, Gerald Lee. "Housing Discrimination in California: The Case of Proposition 14." M.A. thesis, San Jose State College, 1968.

Matthews, Glenna. "A California Middletown: The Social History of San Jose in the Depression." PhD diss., Stanford University, 1977.

Novo, Marla. "The Indian Maiden Visits San Jose: Rediscovering Edmonia Lewis." M.A. thesis, San Jose State University, 1995.

Ruffin, Herbert G. "Uninvited Neighbors: Black Life and the Racial Quest for Freedom in the Santa Clara Valley, 1777–1968." PhD diss., Claremont Graduate University, 2007.

Books and Articles

Alexander, Michelle. *The New Jim Crow: Mass Incarceration in the Age of Colorblindness*. New York: New Press, 2010.

Allen, Roger. "Harry Edwards: We Get What's Ours or Burn It Down." *Sparta Life*, Winter 1968, 7–9.

American Baptist of the West, December 1970, 1.

Andrews, William L., Frances Smith Foster, and Trudier Harris, eds. *The Oxford Companion to African American Literature*. New York: Oxford University Press, 1997.

Anning, Vicky. "Reversal of Misfortune." *Stanford Magazine*, January/February 1998. Available at http://www.stanfordalumni.org/news/magazine/1998/janfeb/articles/epa.html.

Anthony, Earl. *Picking Up the Gun; A Report on the Black Panthers*. New York: Dial Press, 1970.

Appiah, Kwame Anthony, and Henry Louis Gates. *Africana: The Encyclopedia of the African American Experience.* New York: Perseus Books, 1999.

Arbuckle, Clyde. *Clyde Arbuckle's History of San Jose.* San Jose: Smith McKay Printing Co., 1985.

Arlen, Michael J. *An American Verdict.* Garden City, N.Y.: Doubleday, 1973.

Arnold, Harriet. *Antioch: A Place of Christians.* San Mateo, Calif.: Western Book Journal Press, 1993.

Arsenault, Raymond. *Freedom Riders: 1961 and the Struggle for Racial Justice.* New York: Oxford University Press, 2007.

Asbury Park High School: Distinguished Alumni Hall of Fame. "Muata Weusi-Puryear—Class of 1953." http://aphshalloffame.com/Inductees/MuataWeusi Puryear.html.

Ashmore, Susan Youngblood. *Carry It On: The War on Poverty and the Civil Rights Movement in Alabama, 1964–1972.* Athens: University of Georgia Press, 2008.

Asian Women United of California, eds. *Making Waves: An Anthology of Writings by and about Asian American Women.* Boston: Beacon Press, 1989.

Baldwin, James. *The Fire Next Time.* New York: Vintage, 1992.

Banana Peel Entertainment. *Valley of the Heart's Delight.* San Francisco: Banana Peel Entertainment, 2006.

Barnes, Harper. *Never Been a Time: The 1917 Race Riot That Sparked the Civil Rights Movement.* New York: Walker and Company, 2008.

Barr, Alwyn. *Black Texans: A History of African Americans.* Norman: University of Oklahoma Press, 1996.

Bass, Amy. *Not the Triumph but the Struggle: 1968 Olympics and the Making of the Black Athlete.* Minneapolis: University of Minnesota Press, 2004.

BBC. "1968: Black Athletes Make Silent Protest." Available at http://news.bbc.co.uk/ onthisday/hi/dates/stories/october/17/newsid_3535000/3535348.stm.

Beauregard, Robert A. *When America Became Suburban.* Minneapolis: University of Minnesota Press, 2006.

Benedetto, Richard. "GOP: 'We Were Wrong' to Play Racial Politics." *USA Today*, July 14, 2005. Available at http://www.usatoday.com/news/washington/2005-07-14-GOP-racial-politics_x.htm.

Bennett, Lerone. *Before the Mayflower: A History of Black America.* New York: Penguin Books, 1993.

Berger, Bennett M. *Working-Class Suburb: A Study of Auto Workers in Suburbia.* Berkeley: University of California Press, 1968.

Berwanger, Eugene H. "Negrophobia in Northern Proslavery and Antislavery Thought." *Phylon* 33, 3 (1972): 266–275.

———. "The 'Black Law' Question in Ante-Bellum California." *Journal of the West* 6, 2 (1967): 205–220.

Billington, Ray Allen, and Martin Ridge. *Westward Expansion: A History of the American Frontier.* Albuquerque: University of New Mexico Press, 2001.

Biondi, Martha. *To Stand and Fight: The Struggle for Civil Rights in Postwar New York City.* Cambridge, Mass.: Harvard University Press, 2003.

Blackburn, Sara. *White Justice: Black Experience Today in America's Courtrooms.* New York: Harper and Row, 1971.

Bonilla-Silva, Eduardo. *Racism Without Racists: Color-Blind Racism and the Persistence of Racial Inequality in the United States.* Lanham, Md.: Rowman and Littlefield, 2006.

Booker, Jackie R. "Needed but Unwanted: Black Militiamen in Veracruz, Mexico, 1760–1810." *Historian* 55 (Winter 1993): 270.

Boyle, Kevin. *The UAW and the Heyday of American Liberalism, 1945–1968.* Ithaca, N.Y.: Cornell University Press, 1995.

Bretchin, Gray. *Imperial San Francisco: Urban Power, Earthly Ruin.* Berkeley: University of California Press, 1999.

Brilliant, Mark. *The Color of America Has Changed: How Racial Diversity Shaped Civil Rights.* New York: Oxford University Press, 2010.

Bringhurst, Newell G. *Saints, Slaves, and Blacks: The Changing Place of Black People within Mormonism.* Westport, Conn.: Greenwood Press, 1981.

Brody, David. "The Old Labor History and the New: In Search of the American Working Class." *Labor History* 20 (Winter 1979), 11–26.

Broussard, Albert S. *Black San Francisco: The Struggle for Racial Equality in the West, 1900–1954.* Lawrence: University Press of Kansas, 1993.

———. "In Search of a Promised Land: African American Migration to San Francisco, 1900–1945." In *Seeking El Dorado: African Americans in California,* ed. Lawrence De Graaf et al., 181–209. Seattle: University of Washington Press, 2001.

———. "Percy H. Steele, Jr., and the Urban League: Race Relations and the Struggle for Civil Rights in Post–World War II San Diego." *California History* 83 (2006), 7–23.

———. "The Politics of Despair: Black San Franciscans and the Political Process, 1920–1940." *Journal of Negro History* 69, 1 (Winter, 1984): 26–37.

———. Strange Territory, Familiar Leadership: The Impact of World War II on San Francisco's Black Community." *California History* 65, 1 (1986): 18–25.

Burkholder, Mark A., and Lyman L. Johnson. *Colonial Latin America.* New York: Oxford University Press, 2001.

Burns, Stewart, ed. *Daybreak of Freedom: The Montgomery Bus Boycott.* Chapel Hill: University of North Carolina Press, 1997.

Calder, Lendol Glen. *Financing the American Dream: A Cultural History of Consumer Credit.* Princeton, N.J.: Princeton University Press, 1999.

California Newsreel, and Independent Television Service. "The House We Live In." In *Race: The Power of an Illusion.* San Francisco: California Newsreel, 2003.

Carson, Clayborne. *In Struggle: SNCC and the Black Awakening of the 1960s.* Cambridge, Mass.: Harvard University Press, 1981.
Carson, Clayborne, David J. Garrow, Gerald Gill, Vincent Harding, and Darlene Clark Hine. *The Eyes on the Prize Civil Rights Reader.* New York: Penguin, 1991.
Cashin, Sheryll. *The Failures of Integration: How Race and Class Are Undermining the American Dream.* New York: PublicAffairs, 2005.
Chan, Sucheng. *Asian Californians.* San Francisco: MTL/Boyd and Fraser.
Chan, Sucheng, Douglas Henry Daniels, Mario T. García, and Terry P. Wilson, eds. *Peoples of Color in the American West.* Lexington, Mass.: D. C. Heath and Co., 1994.
Chapman, Mark L. *Christianity on Trial: African-American Religious Thought Before and After Black Power.* Maryknoll, N.Y.: Orbis Books, 1996.
Chevigny, Paul. *Cops and Rebels: A Study of Provocation.* New York: Pantheon Books, 1972.
Cleaver, Eldridge. *Soul on Ice.* New York: McGraw-Hill, 1968.
Coleman, Raymond T. "Prince Hall History Education Class." http://www.princehall.org/History/Ray%20Colemans%20History.pdf.
Cone, James H. *Malcolm and Martin and America: A Dream or a Nightmare?* Maryknoll, N.Y.: Orbis Books, 1999.
Cope, R. Douglas. *The Limits of Racial Domination: Plebeian Society in Colonial Mexico City, 1660–1720.* Madison: University of Wisconsin Press, 1994.
Cornford, Daniel. *Working People of California.* Berkeley: University of California Press, 1995.
Countryman, Matthew. *Up South: Civil Rights and Black Power in Philadelphia.* Philadelphia: University of Pennsylvania Press, 2006.
Cozzens, Lisa. "School Integration in Boston." http://www.watson.org/~lisa/blackhistory/school-integration/boston/backgnd.html.
Cringely, Robert X. *Accidental Empires: How the Boys of Silicon Valley Make Their Millions, Battle Foreign Competition, and Still Can't Get a Date.* New York: HarperBusiness, 1996.
Crisis Communication Strategies and Oklahoma University. "Case Study: Denny's Class Action Lawsuit." http://www.ou.edu/deptcomm/dodjcc/groups/02C2/Denny's.htm.
Crosby, Emilye. *A Little Taste of Freedom: The Black Freedom Struggle in Claiborne County, Mississippi.* Chapel Hill: University of North Carolina Press, 2005.
Crouchett, Lawrence P., Lonnie G. Bunch III, and Martha Kendall Winnacker. *Visions toward Tomorrow: The History of the East Bay Afro-American Community, 1852–1977.* Oakland, Calif.: Northern California Center for Afro-American History and Life, 1989.
Cummins, Eric. *The Rise and Fall of California's Radical Prison Movement.* Stanford, Calif.: Stanford University Press, 1994.

Dalfiume, Richard M. "The "Forgotten Years" of the Negro Revolution," *Journal of American History* 55, 1 (June 1968): 90–106.
Daniels, Douglas Henry. *Pioneer Urbanites: A Social and Cultural History of Black San Francisco.* Berkeley: University of California Press, 1991.
Daniels, Roger. *Prisoners without Trial: Japanese Americans in World War II.* New York: Hill and Wang, 2004.
Darity, William A., and Samuel L. Myers. *Persistent Disparity: Race and Economic Inequality in the United States since 1945.* Northampton, Mass.: Edward Elgar, 1998.
Davidson, David M. "Negro Slave Control and Resistance in Colonial Mexico." In *Maroon Societies: Rebel Slave Communities in the Americas*, ed. Richard Price, 82–104. Baltimore: Johns Hopkins University Press, 1996.
Davis, David. "Olympic Athletes Who Took a Stand: For 40 years, Olympians Tommie Smith and John Carlos Have Lived with the Consequences of Their Fateful Protest." *Smithsonian Magazine,* August 2008. Available at http://www.smithsonianmag.com/people-places/indelible-olympics-200808.html#ixzz21kRHEbra.
Davis, Mike. *City of Quartz: Excavating the Future in Los Angeles.* New York: Verso, 1991.
———. *Dead Cities: And Other Tales.* New York: New Press, 2003.
———. *Prisoners of the American Dream: Politics and Economy in the History of the U.S. Working Class.* London: Verso, 1986.
Davis-Perez, Tanisha. "African Americans, UAW Forge Potent Alliance on Shared Goals." UAW–DaimlerChrysler National Training Center Communications. http://www.uaw-daimlerchrylerntc.org/resources/news.cfm?NewsID=303.
———. "D.C.'s African Americans Build a Network for Success." UAW–Daimler Chrysler National Training Center Communications. http://www.uadcx.com/resources/news.cfm?NewsID=309.
De Graaf, Lawrence B. "Recognition, Racism, and Reflections on the Writing of Western Black History." *Pacific Historical Review* 44, 1 (February 1975): 22–51.
De Graaf, Lawrence B., Kevin Mulroy, and Quintard Taylor, eds. *Seeking El Dorado: African Americans in California.* Seattle: University of Washington Press, 2001.
De Jong, Greta. *A Different Day: African American Struggles for Justice in Rural Louisiana, 1900–1970.* Chapel Hill: University of North Carolina Press, 2002.
Dembo, Jonathan. "The West Coast Teamsters' and Longshoremen's Unions in the Twentieth Century." *Journal of the West* 25, 2 (1986): 27–35.
Denton, John H. *Apartheid American Style.* Berkeley, Calif.: Diablo Press, 1968.
Dittmer, John. *Local People: The Struggle for Civil Rights in Mississippi.* Urbana: University of Illinois Press, 1995.

Djedje, Jacqueline Cogdell, and Eddie S. Meadows, eds. *California Soul: Music of African Americans in the West*. Berkeley: University of California Press, 1998.
Douglas, Jack. *Historical Footnotes of Santa Clara Valley*. San Jose: San Jose Museum Association, 1993.
Drake, Dick. "Tommie Smith and Lee Evans Discuss Potential Olympic Boycott." *Track and Field News*, November 1967. Available at http://www.trackandfieldnews.com/display_article.php?id=1605.
Duany, Andres, Elizabeth Plater-Zyberk, and Jeff Speck. *Suburban Nation: The Rise of Sprawl and the Decline of the American Dream*. New York: North Point Press, 2010.
Duru, N. Jeremi. *Advancing the Ball: Race, Reformation, and the Quest for Equal Coaching Opportunity in the NFL*. New York: Oxford University Press, 2011.
East Palo Alto Today. "Lifecycles: Honoring Mrs. Gertrude Wilkes." February–March 2008. http://www.epatoday.org/pdf/February_March2008_EPA_Today_pgs1_8.pdf.
Eastbay Negro Historical Society. "Slavery in San Jose." *Chronicle of Black History* 1, 1 (October 1978): 6.
Ebony. "The Ten Richest Negroes in America." April 1949, 13–18.
Edwards, Harry. "Mounting the Protest." In David K. Wiggins and Patrick B. Miller. *The Unlevel Playing Field: A Documentary History of the African American Experience in Sport*. Urbana: University of Illinois Press, 2003, 285–289.
———. *The Revolt of the Black Athlete*. New York: Free Press, 1970.
———. *The Struggle That Must Be: An Autobiography*. New York: Macmillan, 1980.
Edwards, Malcolm. "The War of Complexional Distinction: Blacks in Gold Rush California and British Columbia." *California Historical Quarterly* 56, 1 (Spring 1977): 34–45.
Eliel, Paul. *The Waterfront and General Strikes, San Francisco, 1934*. San Francisco: Hooper Printing Co., 1934.
Erikson, Erik H., and Huey P. Newton. *In Search of Common Ground*. New York: Norton, 1973.
Eskew, Glenn T. *But for Birmingham: The Local and National Movements in the Civil Rights Struggle*. Chapel Hill: University of North Carolina Press, 1997.
Faragher, John Mack, and Robert V. Hine. *The American West: A New Interpretive History*. New Haven, Conn.: Yale University Press, 2000.
Ferris State University, Jim Crow Museum of Racist Memorabilia. "Sapphire Caricature." http://www.ferris.edu/jimcrow/sapphire/.
Fink, Leon. "American Labor History." In *The New American History*, ed. Eric Foner., 333–352. Philadelphia: Temple University Press, 1997.

Fischer, James A. "Uncovering California Black History: Materials and Sources." In *California's Ethnic Minorities*. Sourisseau Academy for California State and Local History, San Jose State University, 1978, 28–31.

Flamming, Douglas. "Becoming Democrats: Liberal Politics and the African American Community in Los Angeles, 1930–1965." In *Seeking El Dorado: African Americans in California*, ed. Lawrence de Graaf et al., 279–308 Seattle: University of Washington Press, 2001.

Fleming, Cynthia Griggs. *In the Shadow of Selma: The Continuing Struggle for Civil Rights in the Rural South*. Lanham, Md.: Rowan and Littlefield, 2004.

Florido, Adrian. "Feeling a Different Pulse in the Heart of Black San Diego." http://www.voiceofsandiego.org/survival/article_f78c10fc-4ddf-11e0-baaf-001cc4c002e0.html.

Forbes, Jack B. *Afro-Americans in the Far West: A Handbook for Educators*. Berkeley, Calif.: Far West Laboratory for Educational Research and Development, 1968.

———. "The Early African Heritage of California." In *Seeking El Dorado: African Americans in California*, ed. Lawrence de Graaf et al., 73–97. Seattle: University of Washington Press, 2001.

Fosl, Catherine A. *Subversive Southerner: Anne Braden and the Struggle for Racial Justice in the Cold War South*. Lexington: University of Kentucky Press, 2006.

France, Edward E. *Some Aspects of the Migration of the Negro to the San Francisco Bay Area since 1940*. San Francisco: R and E Research Associates, 1974.

Franklin, John Hope, and Alfred A. Moss, Jr. *From Slavery to Freedom: A History of African Americans*. New York: A. A. Knopf, 2000.

Frazier, Edward Franklin, and C. Eric Lincoln. *The Negro Church in America. The Black Church since Frazier*. New York: Schocken Books, 1974.

Freed, Donald. *Agony in New Haven; The Trial of Bobby Seale, Ericka Huggins, and the Black Panther Party*. New York: Simon and Schuster, 1973.

Freire, Paulo. *Pedagogy of the Oppressed*. New York: Continuum, 1998.

Freund, David M. P. *Colored Property: State Policy and White Racial Politics in Suburban America*. Chicago: University of Chicago Press, 2007.

Frey, William H. "Melting Pot Suburbs: A Study of Suburban Diversity." In *Redefining Urban and Suburban America: Evidence from Census 2000*, ed. Bruce Katz and Robert E. Lang, 155–180. Washington, D.C.: Brookings Institution Press, 2003.

Friedman, Jeanne. "The Roots of the Stanford Peace Movement." In Stanford Historical Society, *Sandstone and Tile* 35, 1 (Winter 2011): 3–22.

Gagliardi, Don. "Roots: The Northside Origins of San Jose's African American Community." *Northside*, Fall 2001, 16–19.

Gaillard, Frye. *Alabama's Civil Rights Trail: An Illustrated Guide to the Cradle of Freedom.* Tuscaloosa: University of Alabama Press, 2004.

Gans, Herbert J. *The Levittowners: Ways of Life and Politics in a New Suburban Community.* New York: Columbia University Press, 1982.

García, Mario T. *Mexican Americans: Leadership, Ideology and Identity, 1930–1960.* New Haven, Conn.: Yale University Press, 1989.

Garden City Women's Club. *History of the Garden City Women's Club.* http://gardencitywomensclub.org/history.html.

Garreau, Joel. *Edge City: Life on the New Frontier.* Landover Hills, Md.: Anchor, 1992.

Gettings, John. "Civil Disobedience: Black Medalists Raise Fists for Civil Rights Movement." http://www.infoplease.com/spot/mm-mexicocity.html.

Giddings, Paula. *When and Where I Enter: The Impact of Black Women on Race and Sex in America.* New York: William and Morrow Co., 1984.

Gillham, Oliver. *The Limitless City: A Primer on the Urban Sprawl Debate.* Washington, D.C.: Island Press, 2002.

Goings, Kenneth W., and Raymond A. Mohl, eds. *The New African American Urban History.* Thousand Oaks, Calif.: Sage Publications, 1996.

Gonzalez, Gilbert G. *Labor and Community: Mexican Citrus Worker Villages in a Southern California County, 1900–1950.* Urbana: University of Illinois Press, 1994.

Gorham, Thelma Thurston. "Negroes and Japanese Evacuees." *Crisis* 52, 11 (November 1945).

Gottdiener, Mark, and Ray Hutchison. *The New Urban Sociology.* New York: Westview Press, 2006.

Grady-Willis, Winston A. *Challenging U.S. Apartheid: Atlanta and Black Struggles for Human Rights, 1960–1977.* Durham, N.C.: Duke University Press, 2006.

Greene, Christina. *Our Separate Ways: Women and the Black Freedom Movement in Durham, North Carolina.* Chapel Hill: University of North Carolina Press, 2005.

Grossman, Elizabeth. *High Tech Trash: Digital Devices, Hidden Toxics, and Human Health.* Washington, D.C.: Island Press, 2006.

Grossman, James R. *Land of Hope: Chicago, Black Southerners, and the Great Migration.* Chicago: University of Chicago Press, 1991.

Guttmann, Allen. *The Games Must Go On: Avery Brundage and the Olympic Movement.* New York: Columbia University Press, 1984.

Haddad, Yvonne Y. *The Muslims of America.* New York: Oxford University Press, 1993.

Haines, Herbert H. *Black Radicals and the Civil Rights Mainstream, 1954–1970.* Knoxville: University of Tennessee Press, 1988.

Harley, Sharon. "Mary Church Terrell: Genteel Militant." In *Black Leaders of the Nineteenth Century,* ed. Leon Litwack and August Meier, 307–322. Urbana: University of Illinois Press, 1991.

Harris, Cheryl. "Whiteness as a Property." In *Critical Race Theory: The Key Writings That Formed the Movement,* ed. Kimberly Crenshaw, Neil Gotanda, Gary Peller, and Kendall Thomas. New York: New Press, 1995.

Harris, William Hamilton. *The Harder We Run: Black Workers since the Civil War.* New York: Oxford University Press, 1982.

Hart, Charles Desmond. "The Natural Limits of Slavery Expansion: Kansas-Nebraska, 1854." *Kansas Historical Quarterly* 34, 1 (1968): 32–50.

Hartmann, Douglas. *Race, Culture, and the Revolt of the Black Athlete: The 1968 Olympic Protests and Their Aftermath.* Chicago: University Of Chicago Press, 2004.

Hayden, Dolores. *Building Suburbia: Green Fields and Urban Growth, 1820–2000.* New York: Vintage Books, 2003.

Haynes, Bruce D. *Red Lines, Black Spaces: The Politics of Race and Space in a Black Middle-Class Suburb.* New Haven, Conn.: Yale University Press, 2001.

HBCUDigest.com. "50 Years Later, Alabama State Reinstates Expelled Student Protesters." February 26, 2010. http://www.hbcudigest.com/50-years-later-alabama-state-reinstates-expelled-student-protesters/.

Higginbotham, Evelyn Brooks, *Righteous Discontent: The Women's Movement in the Black Baptist Church, 1880–1920.* Cambridge, Mass.: Harvard University Press, 1993.

Hine, Darlene Clark, William C. Hine, and Stanley Harrold. *The African-American Odyssey.* New York: Prentice Hall, 1999.

History San Jose. "Black Power: 1964–1969." http://www.speedcityera.com/blackpower.html.

Holiday, J. S. *Rush for Riches: Gold Fever and the Making of California.* Berkeley: University of California Press, 1999.

Horne, Gerald. "Black Fire: 'Riot' and 'Revolt' in Los Angeles, 1965 and 1992." In *Seeking El Dorado: African Americans in California,* ed. Lawrence B. de Graaf et al., 377–404. Seattle: University of Washington Press, 2001.

Hossfeld, Karen J. "Why Aren't High-Tech Workers Organized? Lessons in Gender, Race, and Nationality from Silicon Valley." In *Working People of California,* ed. Daniel Cornford. Berkeley: University of California Press, 1995.

Hudson, Lynn M. "A New Look, or 'I'm Not Mammy to Everybody in California.'" *Journal of the West* (July 1993): 35–40.

Hughes, Langston, C. Eric Lincoln, and Milton Meltzer. *The Pictorial History of the Negro.* New York: Crown Publishers, 1968.

Hurtado, Albert L. *Indian Survival on the California Frontier.* New Haven, Conn.: Yale University Press, 1988.

International Olympic Committee. "Olympic Games." http://www.olympic.org/uk/games/index_uk.asp "Moscow" and "Los Angeles."
Jackson, George. *Soledad Brother: The Prison Letters of George Jackson.* New York: Coward-McCann, 1970.
Jackson, Kenneth T. *Crabgrass Frontier: The Suburbanization of the United States.* New York: Oxford University Press, 1985.
Jacobson, Matthew Frye. *Whiteness of a Different Color: European Immigrants and the Alchemy of Race.* Cambridge, Mass.: Harvard University Press, 1998.
James, Joseph. "Profiles: San Francisco." *Journal of Educational Sociology* 19, 3. Race Relations on the Pacific Coast (November 1945): 166–178.
Jeffries, Hasan Kwame. *Bloody Lowndes: Civil Rights and Black Power in Alabama's Black Belt.* New York: New York University Press, 2009.
Johnson, Charles S. *The Negro War Worker in San Francisco: A Local Self-Survey.* San Francisco: privately printed, 1944.
Johnson, Marilynn S. "Mobilizing the Homefront: Labor and Politics in Oakland, 1941–1951." In Daniel Cornford, *Working People of California.* Berkeley: University of California Press, 1995.
———. *The Second Gold Rush: Oakland and the East Bay in World War II.* Berkeley: University of California Press, 1993.
Jones, Charles E., ed. *The Black Panther Party Reconsidered.* Baltimore: Black Classic Press, 1998.
Jones, Jacqueline. *American Work: Four Centuries of Black and White Labor.* New York: W. W. Norton and Company, 1998.
Jones, Jacqueline, Thomas Borstelmann, Elaine Tyler May, Peter H. Wood, and Vicki L. Ruiz. *Created Equal: A Social and Political History of the United States.* New York: Pearson Education, 2008.
Kaplan, David A. *The Silicon Boys: And Their Valley of Dreams.* New York: William Morrow, 1999.
Karagueuzian, Dikran. *Blow It Up! The Black Student Revolt at San Francisco State College and the Emergence of Dr. Hayakawa.* Boston: Gambit, 1971.
Katz, Michael B., and Thomas J. Sugrue, eds. *W. E. B. DuBois, Race, and the City: The Philadelphia Negro and Its Legacy.* Philadelphia: University of Pennsylvania Press, 1998.
Katz, William L. *The Black West.* Garden City, N.Y.: Doubleday, 1971.
Katzew, Ilona. *Casta Painting: Images of Race in Eighteenth-Century Mexico.* New Haven, Conn.: Yale University Press, 2004.
Keating, W. Dennis. *The Suburban Racial Dilemma: Housing and Neighborhoods.* Philadelphia: Temple University Press, 1994.
Kennedy, David M. *Freedom from Fear: The American People in Depression and War, 1929–1945.* New York: Oxford University Press, 1999.
Kozol, Jonathan. *Savage Inequalities: Children in America's Schools.* New York: Harper Perennial, 1992.

———. *The Shame of the Nation: The Restoration of Apartheid Schooling in America*. New York: Broadway, 2006.

Kusmer, Kenneth L. *A Ghetto Takes Shape: Black Cleveland, 1870–1930*. Urbana: University of Illinois Press, 1976.

Lacy, Karyn R. *Blue-Chip Black: Race, Class, and Status in the New Black Middle Class*. Berkeley: University of California Press, 2007.

Landry, Bart. *The New Black Middle Class*. Berkeley: University of California Press, 1987.

Lapp, Rudolph M. *Afro-Americans in California*. San Francisco: Boyd and Fraser Publishing Co., 1979.

———. *Blacks in Gold Rush California*. New Haven, Conn.: Yale University Press, 1977.

Larson, Linda S. *San Jose's Monument to Progress: The Electric Light Tower*. San Jose: San Jose Historical Association, 1989.

Leach, William. *Land of Desire: Merchants, Power, and the Rise of a New American Culture*. New York: Pantheon Books, 1993.

Lecuyer, Christophe. *Making Silicon Valley: Innovation and the Growth of High Tech, 1930–1970*. Cambridge, Mass.: MIT Press, 2007.

Lemann, Nicholas. *The Promised Land: The Great Black Migration and How It Changed America*. New York: Vintage Books, 1992.

Leonard, David. "What Happened to the Revolt of the Black Athlete?" Interview with Harry Edwards. *Colorlines* 1, 1 (Summer 1998). Available at http://colorlines.com/archives/1998/06/what_happened_to_the_revolt_of_the_black_athlete.html.

Library of Congress. "Colonization: The African-American Mosaic." http://www.loc.gov/exhibits/african/afam002.html.

Limerick, Patricia Nelson. *The Legacy of Conquest: The Unbroken Past of the American West*. New York: Norton, 1987.

Lincoln, C. Eric. *The Black Muslims in America*. Grand Rapids, Mich.: W. B. Eerdmans; Trenton, N.J.: Africa World Press, 1994.

Lipsitz, George. *The Possessive Investment in Whiteness: How White People Profit from Identity Politics*. Philadelphia: Temple University Press, 1998.

Litwack, Leon, and August Meier, eds. *Black Leaders of the Nineteenth Century*. Urbana: University of Illinois Press, 1991.

Lomax, Michael E. "Bedazzle Them with Brilliance, Bamboozle Them with Bull: Harry Edwards, Black Power, and the Revolt of the Black Athlete Revisited." In Michael E. Lomax, *Sports and the Racial Divide: African American and Latino Sport Experience in the Era of Change*. Jackson: University Press of Mississippi, 2008.

Long, George. "How Albuquerque Got Its Civil Rights Ordinance." *Crisis* 60, 11 (November 1953): 521–524.

Loomis, Patricia. *Milpitas: The Century of "Little Cornfields," 1852–1952*. Cupertino: California History Center, 1986.
Lumpkins, Charles. *American Pogrom: The East St. Louis Race Riot and Black Politics*. Athens: Ohio University Press, 2008.
Major, Reginald. *A Panther Is a Black Cat*. New York: W. Morrow, 1971.
Malone, Michael P., and Richard W. Etulain, *The American West: A Twentieth-Century History*. Lincoln: University of Nebraska Press, 1989.
Marable, Manning. *The Great Wells of Democracy: The Meaning of Race in American Life*. New York: BasicCivitas Books, 2002.
———. *How Capitalism Underdeveloped Black America: Problems in Race, Political Economy, and Society*. Cambridge, Mass.: South End Press, 2000.
———. *Race, Reform, and Rebellion: The Second Reconstruction in Black America, 1945–1980*. Jackson: University Press of Mississippi, 1991.
Marine, Gene. *The Black Panthers*. New York: New American Library, 1969.
Martin Luther King Papers. "Birmingham Campaign." http://mlk-kpp01.stanford.edu/index.php/encyclopedia/encyclopedia/enc_birmingham_campaign/.
Massey, Douglas S., and Nancy A. Denton. *American Apartheid: Segregation and the Making of the Underclass*. Cambridge, Mass.: Harvard University Press, 1993.
Matthews, Glenna. *Silicon Valley, Women, and the California Dream: Gender, Class, and Opportunity in the Twentieth Century*. Stanford, Calif.: Stanford University Press, 2003.
McBroome, Delores Nason. *Parallel Communities: African Americans in California's East Bay 1850–1963*. New York: Garland Publishing, 1993.
McCartney, John T. *Black Power Ideologies: An Essay in African-American Political Thought*. Philadelphia: Temple University Press, 1992.
McEntire, Davis. *Residents and Race*. Berkeley: University of California Press, 1960.
McEvoy, James, and Abraham Miller, eds. *Black Power and Student Rebellion*. Belmont, Calif.: Wadsworth Publishing Company, 1969.
McGirr, Lisa. *Suburban Warriors: The Origins of the New American Right*. Princeton, N.J.: Princeton University Press, 2001.
McLagan, Elizabeth. *A Peculiar Paradise: A History of Blacks in Oregon, 1778–1940*. Portland, Ore.: Georgian Press, 1980.
McWilliams, Carey. *California: The Great Exception*. Santa Barbara, Calif.: Peregrine Smith, 1979.
Meier, August, and Elliott Rudwick. *CORE: A Study in the Civil Rights Movement, 1942–1968*. New York: Oxford University Press, 1973.
Mills, Kay. *This Little Light of Mine: The Life of Fannie Lou Hamer*. New York: Plume Books, 1994.
Monroy, Douglas. *Thrown among Strangers: The Making of Mexican Culture in Frontier California*. Berkeley: University of California Press, 1990.

Moore, Gilbert Stuart. *A Special Rage*. New York: Harper and Row, 1971.
Moore, Shirley Ann Wilson. *To Place Our Deeds: The African American Community in Richmond, California, 1910–1963*. Berkeley: University of California Press, 2000.
———. "Your Life Is Really Not Just Your Own: African American Women in Twentieth-Century California." In *Seeking El Dorado: African Americans in California*, ed. Lawrence de Graaf et al., 210–248 Seattle: University of Washington Press, 2001.
Moye, J. Todd. *Let the People Decide: Black Freedom and White Resistance Movements in Sunflower County, Mississippi, 1945–1986*. Chapel Hill: University of North Carolina Press, 2004.
Muraskin, William A. *Middle-Class Blacks in a White Society: Prince Hall Freemasonry in America*. Berkeley: University of California Press, 1975.
Murch, Donna Jean. *Living for the City: Migration, Education, and the Rise of the Black Panther Party in Oakland, California*. Chapel Hill: University of North Carolina Press, 2010.
Nash, Gerald D. *The American West Transformed: The Impact of the Second World War*. Bloomington: Indiana University Press, 1985.
National Park Service. *A History of Blacks in California: Historic Sites: Phoenixonian Institute Site*. http://www.cr.nps.gov/history/online_books/5views/5views2h81.htm.
Nelson, Bruce. "The Big Strike." In *Working People of California*, ed. Daniel Cornford, 225–264. Berkeley: California University Press, 1995.
———. "The 'Lords of the Docks' Reconsidered: Race Relations among West Coast Longshoremen, 1933–61." In *Waterfront Workers: New Perspectives on Race and Class*, ed. Calvin Winslow, 155–192. Urbana: University of Illinois Press, 1998.
Newton, Huey P. *The Huey P. Newton Reader*. Edited by David Hilliard and Donald Weise. New York: Seven Stories Press.
———. *Revolutionary Suicide*. New York: Harcourt Brace Jovanovich, 1973.
———. *To Die for the People: The Writings of Huey P. Newton*. New York: Random House, 1972.
———. *War against the Panthers: A Study of Repression in America*. New York: Harlem River Press, 1996.
Nexus and the University of Minnesota. "Boston School Desegregation." http://nexus.umn.edu/Courses/pa8202/Case02.html#Boston_School_Desegregation.
NFL Communications. "43 former NFL players participated in 2010 Bill Walsh minority coaching fellowship." http://nflcommunications.com/2010/08/30/43-former-nfl-players-participated-in-2010-bill-walsh-minority-coaching-fellowship/.

NPR. "Freedom Riders." *Weekend Edition Saturday,* April 7, 2001. http://www.npr.org/templates/story/story.php?storyId=1121173.

———. "Get On the Bus: The Freedom Riders of 1961." *Fresh Air from WHYY,* January 12, 2006. http://www.npr.org/templates/story/story.php?storyId=5149667.

———. "16th Street Baptist Church Bombing: Forty Years Later, Birmingham Still Struggles with Violent Past." *All Things Considered,* September 15, 2003. http://www.npr.org/templates/story/story.php?storyId=1431932.

———. "Special Series: California in Crisis." http://www.npr.org/templates/story/story.php?storyId=106486189.

Office of Continuing Education at University of Illinois at Urbana-Champaign. "About the Freedom Riders." http://civilrights.continuinged.uiuc.edu/abou.html.

O'Meara, Madeleine. "When 'Radical Athletics' Meets Patty Hearst." *Oberlin Review,* February 27, 2012. Available at http://oberlinreview.org/article/when-radical-athletics-meets-patty-hearst/.

Patterson, James T. *Brown v. Board of Education: A Civil Rights Milestone and Its Troubled Legacy.* New York: Oxford University Press, 2002.

———. *Grand Expectations: The United States, 1945–1974.* New York: Oxford University Press, 1996.

Payne, Stephen. *Santa Clara County: An Illustrated History.* Sun Valley, Calif.: American Historical Press, 2008.

PBS. "COINTELPRO." In *A Huey P. Newton Story.* http://www.pbs.org/hueypnewton/actions/actions_cointelpro.html.

———. "Freedom's Journal." In *The Black Press: Soldiers Without Swords.* http://www.pbs.org/blackpress/news_bios/newbios/nwsppr/freedom/freedom.html.

———. "The March on Washington for Jobs and Freedom." *NewsHour,* August 27, 2003. http://www.pbs.org/newshour/extra/features/july-dec03/march_8-27.html.

———. "Prince Hall 1735–1807." In *Africans in America.* http://www.pbs.org/wgbh/aia/part2/2p37.html.

Pearce, Ralph M. *From Asahi to Zebras.* San Jose: Japanese American Museum of San Jose, 2005.

Pellow, David N., and Lisa Sun-Hee Park. *The Silicon Valley of Dreams: Environmental Injustice, Immigrant Workers, and the High-Tech Global Economy.* New York: New York University Press 2002.

Pitti, Stephen J. *The Devil in Silicon Valley: Northern California, Race, and Mexican Americans.* Princeton, N.J.: Princeton University Press, 2003.

Porter, Kenneth W. *The Negro on the American Frontier.* New York: Arno Press, 1971.

Preis, Art. *Labor's Giant Step: Twenty Years of the CIO.* New York: Pathfinder Press, 1972.

Raboteau, Albert J. *A Fire in the Bones: Reflections on African-American Religious History.* Boston: Beacon Press, 1995.

Ransby, Barbara. *Ella Baker and the Black Freedom Movement: A Radical Democratic Vision.* Chapel Hill: University of North Carolina Press, 2005.

Rawls, James J., and Walton Bean. *California: An Interpretive History.* Boston: McGraw-Hill, 2003.

Record, Wilson. "Racial Integration in California Schools." *Journal of Negro Education* 27, 1 (Winter 1958): 17–23.

Ribbs, Heather. "What's in a Name: A Family Chronicle: The Ribbs Family—An Eastside Plumbing Dynasty." 2004. http://www.nnvesj.org/Y04/Ed13/Edition1352.htm.

Robinson, Cedric J. *Black Marxism: The Making of the Black Radical Tradition.* Chapel Hill: University of North Carolina Press, 2000.

Rodriguez, Joseph A. *City against Suburb: The Culture Wars in an American Metropolis.* Westport, Conn.: Praeger Publishers, 1999.

Roediger, David R. *The Wages of Whiteness: Race and the Making of the American Working Class.* New York: Verso, 1991.

Rolle, Andrew. *California: A History.* Wheeling, Ill.: Harlan Davidson, 1998.

Rothman, Hal K. *Devil's Bargain: Tourism in the Twentieth-Century American West.* Lawrence: University Press of Kansas, 1998.

Rout, Leslie B. *The African Experience in Spanish America: 1502 to the Present Day.* New York: Cambridge University Press, 1976.

Rudwick, Elliott. *Race Riot at East St. Louis, July 2, 1917.* Champaign: University of Illinois Press, 1982.

Ruffin, Herbert. "Sunnyhills: Race and Working Class Politics in Postwar Silicon Valley, 1945–1968." *Journal of the West* 48, 4 (Fall 2009): 113–123.

———. "The Search for Significance in Interstitial Space: San Jose and its Great Black Migration, 1941–1968." In *Black California Dreamin': The Crises of California's African-American Communities.* Santa Barbara: U.C. Santa Barbara Center for Black Studies Research, December 2012.

———. "East Palo Alto, California (1925–)." http://www.blackpast.org/?q=aaw/east-palo-alto-1925.

Ruíz, Vicki. *Cannery Women, Cannery Lives: Mexican Women, Unionization, and the California Food Processing Industry, 1930–1950.* Albuquerque: University of New Mexico Press, 1987.

Sanchez, George J. *Becoming Mexican American: Ethnicity, Culture, and Identity in Chicano Los Angeles, 1900–1945.* New York: Oxford University Press, 1993.

Santangelo, Gretchen Lemke. *Abiding Courage: African American Migrant Women and the East Bay Community.* Chapel Hill: University of North Carolina Press, 1996.

———. "Deindustrialization, Urban Poverty, and African American Community Mobilization in Oakland, 1945 through the 1990s." In *Seeking El Dorado: African Americans in California,* ed. Lawrence De Graaf et al., 343–376. Seattle: University of Washington Press, 2001.

Santino, Jack. *Miles of Smiles, Years of Struggle: Stories of Black Pullman Porters.* Urbana: University of Illinois Press, 1989.

Savage, W. Sherman. *Blacks in the West.* Westport, Conn.: Greenwood Press, 1976.

Saxe, Allan A. *Politics of Arlington, Texas: An Era of Continuity and Growth.* New York: Eakins Press, 2001.

Saxenian, AnnaLee. *The New Argonauts: Regional Advantage in a Global Economy.* Cambridge, Mass.: Harvard University Press, 2007.

———. *Regional Advantage: Culture and Competition in Silicon Valley and Route 128.* Cambridge, Mass.: Harvard University Press, 1996.

Schanche, Don A. *The Panther Paradox: A Liberalism Dilemma.* New York: McKay, 1970.

Seale, Bobby. *Seize the Time: The Story of the Black Panther Party and Huey P. Newton.* Baltimore: Black Classic Press, 1970.

Self, Robert O. *America Babylon: Race and the Struggle for Postwar Oakland.* Princeton, N.J.: Princeton University Press, 2003.

———. "Black Power City, White Power Suburb: Rhetoric and Reality in Oakland and the East Bay." Paper delivered at Unimagined Futures Conference, May 19, 1999, Stanford University.

Sheehy, Gail. *Panthermania: The Clash of Black against Black in One American City.* New York: Harper and Row, 1971.

Sides, Josh. *L.A. City Limits: African American Los Angeles from the Great Depression to the Present.* Berkeley: University of California Press, 2006.

Skowronek, Russell K., with Elizabeth Thompson. *Situating Mission Santa Clara de Asis: 1776–1851, Documentary and Material Evidence of Life on the Alta California Frontier: A Timeline.* Berkeley, Calif., Academy of American Franciscan History.

———. *Telling The Santa Clara Story: Sesquicentennial Voices.* Santa Clara University, City of Santa Clara, 2002.

Smith, Jessie Carney, Millicent Lownes Jackson, and Linda T. Wynn. *Encyclopedia of African American Business.* Westport, Conn.: Greenwood, 2006.

Smith, Ted, David A. Sonnenfeld, and David Naguib Pellow, eds. *Challenging the Chip: Labor Rights and Environmental Justice in the Global Electronics Industry.* Philadelphia: Temple University Press, 2006.

Smith, Tommie, with David Steele. *Silent Gesture: The Autobiography of Tommie Smith.* Philadelphia: Temple University Press, 2007.

Sparta Life. "No Place for the Negro." Winter 1967, 8–10.

———. "Valerie Dickerson: Beyond Stereotypes." Winter 1968.

Spivey, Donald. "Black Consciousness and Olympic Protest." In *Sport in America: New Historical Perspectives,* ed. Donald Spivey. Westport, Conn.: Greenwood Press, 1985.

Stanford Encyclopedia of Philosophy, s.v. "Affirmative Action." http://plato.stanford.edu/entries/affirmative-action/.

Strain, Christopher B. *Pure Fire: Self-Defense as Activism in the Civil Rights Era.* Athens: University of Georgia Press, 2005.

Sugrue, Thomas J. *The Origins of the Urban Crisis: Race and Inequality in Postwar Detroit.* Princeton, N.J.: Princeton University Press, 1996.

———. *Sweet Land of Liberty: The Forgotten Struggle for Civil Rights in the North.* New York: Random House, 2008.

Szczesny, Joseph. "African Americans and the UAW: A Rocky but Fruitful Union." *AAOW Magazine,* February/March 2000.

Sullivan, Neil Vincent, and Evelyn S. Stewart. *Now Is the Time: Integration in the Berkeley Schools.* Bloomington: Indiana University Press, 1970.

Taeuber, Karl E., and Alma F. Taeuber. *Negroes in Cities: Residential Segregation and Neighborhood Change.* Chicago: Aldine Publishing, 1965.

Takaki, Ronald. *Pau Hana: Plantation Life and Labor in Hawaii, 1835–1920.* Honolulu: University of Hawaii Press, 1983.

———. *Strangers from a Different Shore: A History of Asian Americans.* Boston: Little, Brown, 1989.

Taylor, Quintard. *The Forging of a Black Community: Seattle's Central District, from 1870 through the Civil Rights Era.* Seattle: University of Washington Press, 1994.

———. *In Search of the Racial Frontier: African Americans in the West, 1528–1990.* New York: W. W. Norton, 1998.

———. "Urban Black Labor in the West, 1849–1949: Reconceptualizing the Image of a Region." In *The African American Urban Experience: Perspectives from the Colonial Period to the Present,* ed. Joe William Trotter, Earl Lewis, and Tera W. Hunter, 99–120. New York: Palgrave McMillan, 2004.

Taylor, Quintard, and Shirley Ann Wilson Moore, eds. *African American Women Confront the West, 1600–2000.* Norman: University of Oklahoma Press, 2003.

Theoharis, Jeanne, and Komozi Woodard. *Freedom North: Black Freedom Struggles Outside the South, 1940–1980.* New York: New York University Press, 2003.

Thurman, Sue Bailey. *Pioneers of Negro Origin in California.* San Francisco: ACME Publishing Co., 1949.

Tindall, George Brown, and David E. Shi. *America: A Narrative History.* New York: W. W. Norton, 1996.

Tolbert, Emory J., and Lawrence B. de Graaf. "'The Unseen Minority': Blacks in Orange County." *Journal of Orange County Studies* 3, 4 (Fall 1989/Spring 1990): 54–61.

Track and Field News. "More Boycott Reaction." Letters to the editor. (January 1968).

Trotter, Joe William. *Black Milwaukee: The Making of an Industrial Proletariat, 1915–1945.* Urbana: University of Illinois Press, 1985.

———. *The Great Migration in Historical Perspective: New Dimensions of Race, Class, and Gender.* Bloomington: Indiana University Press, 1991.

Trotter, Joe William, Earl Lewis, and Tera W. Hunter (eds.). *The African American Urban Experience: Perspectives from the Colonial Period to the Present.* New York: Palgrave McMillan, 2004.

Trubek, Anne. "The Oberlin Experiment: Why the Failed Revolution of Radical Athleticism May Be the Great Unwritten Chapter in American Sports History." *Smart Set* (Drexel University). http://thesmartset.com/article/article12140702.aspx.

Turner, Jeffrey A. *Sitting In and Speaking Out: Student Movements in the American South, 1960–1970.* Athens: University of Georgia Press, 2010.

"The Valley of Heart's Delight." Pamphlet. San Jose Public Library, California Room. http://content.cdlib.org/ark:/13030/kt4w1025s5/?order=3&brand=calisphere.

Van Deburg, William L. *Modern Black Nationalism: From Marcus Garvey to Louis Farrakhan.* New York: New York University Press, 1997.

Van den Berghe, Pierre L. "The African Diaspora in Mexico, Brazil and the United States." *Social Forces* 54, 3 (1976): 530–545.

Vincent, Ted. "The Blacks Who Freed Mexico." *Journal of Negro History* 79, 3 (1994): 257–276.

Washington, Guy M. "The Underground Railroad: The Quest for Freedom Moves West, 1848–1869." National Park Service. Brochure, 2000.

Webb, Walter Prescott. "The American West: Perpetual Mirage." *Harper's Magazine*, May 1957, 25–31.

WGBH Educational Foundation. *The Two Nations of Black America.* http://www.pbs.org/wgbh/pages/frontline/shows/race/economics/; http://www.pbs.org/wgbh/pages/frontline/shows/race/interviews/wilson.html.

Wheeler, B. Gordon. *Black California: The History of African-Americans in the Golden State.* New York: Hippocrene Books, 1993.

Whitaker, Matthew C. *Race Work: The Rise of Civil Rights in the Urban West.* Lincoln: University of Nebraska Press, 2007.

White, Richard. *It's Your Misfortune and None of My Own.* Norman: University of Oklahoma Press, 1991.

———. "Western History." In *The New American History*, ed. Eric Foner. Philadelphia: Temple University Press, 1997.

Whitfield, Mal. "Let's Boycott the Olympics." *Ebony*, December 1964, 66.

Wiese, Andrew. *Places of Their Own: African American Suburbanization in the Twentieth Century.* Chicago: University of Chicago Press, 2004.

Wiggins, David K., and Patrick B. Miller. *The Unlevel Playing Field: A Documentary History of the African American Experience in Sport.* Urbana: University of Illinois Press, 2003.

Wilkerson, Isabel. *The Warmth of Other Suns: The Epic Story of America's Great Migration.* New York: Vintage Books, 2011.

Williams, Iola. "Vice Mayor Iola Williams: A Study in Black Power." In *San Jose Metro*, April 23, 1987.

Williams, James. *Life and Adventures of James Williams, a Fugitive Slave, with a Full Description of the Underground Railroad: Electronic Edition.* University of North Carolina. Available at http://docsouth.unc.edu/neh/williams/williams.html.

Williams, Rhonda. *The Politics of Public Housing: Black Women's Struggles against Urban Inequality.* Oxford: Oxford University Press, 2004.

Wilmore, Gayraud S. *Black Religion and Black Radicalism: An Interpretation of the Religious History of African Americans.* Maryknoll, N.Y.: Orbis Books, 1998.

Wilson, William Julius. *The Ghetto Underclass: Social Science Perspectives.* Newbury Park, Calif.: Sage Publications, 1993.

Winther, Oscar Osburn. "The Story of San Jose, 1777–1869, California's First Pueblo, Part I." *California History Magazine* 14, San Francisco: California Historical Society, 1935, 3.

Wollenberg, Charles. *All Deliberate Speed: Segregation and Exclusion in California Schools, 1855–1975.* Berkeley: University of California Press, 1976.

———. *Ethnic Conflict in California History.* Los Angeles: Tinnon-Brown, 1970.

Women's International League for Peace and Freedom. "History." http://www.wilpfinternational.org/about-us/history/.

Woolfolk, George R. "Turner's Safety Valve and Free Negro Westward Migration." *Pacific Northwest Quarterly* 56, 3 (1965): 125–130.

Wysinger, Myra Lynn. "African American Pioneer of California: Edmond Edward Wysinger, 1816–1891." http://wysinger.homestead.com/courtcase.html.

Yoo, David K. *Growing Up Nisei: Race, Generation, and Culture among Japanese Americans of California, 1924–49.* Urbana: University of Illinois Press, 2000.

Yu, Connie Young. *Chinatown San Jose, USA.* San Jose: History San Jose, 2001.

Index

Abernathy, Ralph, 145
Abolition movement, 29, 33–34, 90, 160, 240n51
African American Heritage House, 227
African American West Logic. *See* U.S. West
Afro-American Community Service Agency, 86, 227
Alameda County, Calif., 131
Alexander, Charles. *See* Revolt of the black athlete
Alviso, Calif., 50–51, 246n116
American Dream, 201–202
American Friends Service Committee. *See* Sunnyhills, Milpitas, Calif.
Anderson, Forest, 79
Anderson, Lenora Sypert, 79
Antioch Baptist Church. *See under* Churches
Asian Americans: Asian Indians, 27; Chinese, 26, 28–29, 44, 49, 52, 139, 240n50, 241–42n63, 244n92; Filipinos, 52, 63; Japanese, 49, 52, 61, 68, 77, 80, 117; Vietnamese, 199; in Santa Clara County, Calif., 75, 105, 122, 206, 224–26, 296–97n84

Banks Bryant, Florence, 101, 103, 155
Beasley, Delilah, 8, 244n93
Bell, Peter, 33
Berry, Mattie, 10, 55–56, 58, 62, 64–65, 85, 139, 255n64
Black, Don, 221–22
Black California suffrage movement: California nativism, 41, 43–44; Democrats in Santa Clara Valley, 41, 42, 44; Hamilton Fish, 42, 245n105; Jacob Overton, 41; John E. Benton, 41; Peter Williams Cassey, 41–42; Reconstruction era, 41, 44; women, 244n99
Black middle class, 201–202, 204, 206, 210, 213, 223

Black Power movement: Black Panther Party, 5, 199; Black Studies Union (Stanford University), 1–3; Bruce McCullough, James Shaw, Beverly Taylor (San Jose State), 176–77; San Jose State, 176–77, 194, 197. *See also* Revolt of the black athlete
Black studies, 3, 194–95, 197, 229n5
Blackwell, Deelvin, 77
Blackwell, Kenneth, 77, 167
Blackwell, James, 152–53, 156, 159, 283n80
Black women's club movement: California State Association of Colored Women's Clubs, 67; 1895 Conference of Colored Women, 66, 255n65; Josephine St. Pierre Ruffin, 66; in San Jose, Calif., 45–46. *See also* Garden City Women's Club; Overton, Sarah Massey
Boyer, D. W., 55
Boyer, Elizabeth P., 66–67
Braddock, Reginald, 223
Braden, Anne, 146–47
Bremond, Ms., 108
Bronzan, Bob, 181
Brown, Edmund G., 105, 109, 115, 117, 132
Brown, Sallie L., 250n31
Bunch, Lucille, 81
Burnett, Calif., 50
Burton, John, 23

Caldwell, John, 22–23
California Fair Housing Act of 1963 (aka Rumford Act). *See* Housing legislation and reports
California gold rush, 22–24, 26–27, 29, 31, 35, 45, 202, 238n33
California nativism, 24–25, 41, 43–44, 88–89, 115; alien land law, 49; Peter H. Burnett, 24, 25; court testimony ban, 31, 33, 34, 239n41,

329

California nativism (*continued*)
241–42n63; fugitive slave law, 26, 34; homestead law, 31; "Negrophobia" concept, 25; scientific racism, 49
California Real Estate Association and the anti–fair housing movement. *See* Housing restrictions
California constitution, 2, 46–47, 141
California State College Board of Trustees, 183–84
Campbell, Calif., 262–63n16
Carlos, John. *See* Revolt of the black athlete
Cassey, Peter William, 24, 31, 34–42, 47, 264–65n43; abolitionism, 29; American Colonization Society, 35, 39; Joseph R. Cassey, 35; Mr. Higgins, 37; William Ingraham Kip, 40–41; Charles H. Mecier, 35; St. Phillips Episcopal Church, New York, N.Y., 35; St. Phillip's Mission School (aka Phoenixonian Hall and Phoenixonia Institute), 24, 32, 37–43, 45, 243n79, 243n88, 244n95; suffrage, 41–42; Peter H. Williams, 35
Catholic Interracial Council, 92, 103
Chico, Calif., 69
Churches: African Methodist Episcopal church (AME) in San Francisco and Sacramento, Calif., 32; AME in San Jose, Calif., 66; AME movement, 35, 66; Antioch Baptist Church, 65–66, 149, 270n116, 279n31; black religion, 241n58; Cambrian Park Methodist Church, 149; Christ Episcopal Church, 32, 39, 243n88; church coalitions, 264–65n43; First AME Zion Church, 24, 32, 39, 43; First Baptist Church, 32; Palo Alto African Methodist Episcopal Zion Church (aka University AME Zion Church), 60, 61, 86; Prayer Garden Church of God, 86; St. Cyprian's Church, New Bern, N.C., 41; St. Phillips Episcopal Church, 39; Trinity Episcopal Church, 37, 40; Unitarian Church, 149
Civic E. Social Club, 67
Civil rights movement: Isais Aguilar of, 159; antiwar movement, 187, 190; Edward Blankenheim, 149; Anne Braden, 146–47; Brother of Sleeping Car Porters, 92; California's Fair Employment Practice Commission, 143; Arthur Casaday, 161, 283n89; Chicano movement, 194, 197; Clerks Union, Local 492, 157–58; James Farmer, 149, 282n69; Terry Francois, 153–54; Freedom Riders, 149, 154; "Freedom rights" concept, 235n1, 265n44; Dick Frey, 154–55; Hart's department store, 157; S. V. Herring, 143–44; Human Rights Day in San Jose, 151; Bud Hutchinson, 144, 148; Kress, 142–43, 156; lunch counter sit-ins, 142, 284n91; March on Washington, 156, 158–59; March on Washington sympathy demonstration, 158, 283n80; memorial rally, 160; Andrew Montgomery, 156; as New Reconstruction movement, 161; Jefferson Poland, 147–49; Purity grocery store, 157; Dana W. Reed, 159–60; Safeway, 156–57; San Jose State College, 142, 144–45, 147–49, 154, 162; in Santa Clara County, Calif., 3, 90–92, 138–62, 168, 174–75, 197, 202; sneak out system, Palo Alto, Calif., 151; southern voter registration drives, 154–56; St. James Park March, 151–52, 156; St. John Dixon, 144–46, 148, 278n21, 279n30; Stanford University, 142–43, 150, 154; sympathy demonstrations, 143; William Stanton, 144, 148; Wester Sweet, 149; Richard Thomas, 161; United Farm Worker movement, 194; John T. Wahiquist, 145–47, 279n34; Woolworth's, 142–44, 156; in the U.S. West, 139. *See also* Civil rights organizations and Palo Alto–Stanford NAACP
Civil rights organizations: Afro-American League, 45; Congress of Racial Equality, 143–46, 149, 156, 188; Mid-Peninsula CORE, 150–51, 282n71; Palo Alto SNCC, 150; Palo Alto–Stanford NAACP, 89, 103–104, 139, 150–51; San Jose CORE, 149, 156–58; San Jose NAACP, 89, 117, 136, 139, 143–44; Santa Clara County CORE, 103, 112–13, 116; Santa Clara Valley Friends of SNCC, 155; South San Mateo County NAACP, 103, 282n71; Student Nonviolent Coordinating

INDEX 331

Committee, 149, 188; Toward an Active Student Community, 142, 147. *See also* Santa Clara County NAACP; Sunnyhills, Milpitas, Calif.
Civil War, 33, 41, 226
Clark, Robert D. *See* Revolt of the black athlete
Combs, Milton, 55
Community Lodge 43, Palo Alto, Calif., 255n66
Compromise of 1850, 26
Congress of Racial Equality (CORE). *See* Civil rights organizations
Conley, Marvin, 211
Convention of Colored Citizens of the State of California: annual convention in San Jose, Calif., 39–41; Peter Williams Cassey, 24, 29, 31, 34–42, 45–47, 90; colored schools, 37–40; *Mirror of the Times*, 35; *Pacific Appeal*, 33–35, 45, 59; Richard Shorter, 34–35; William A. Smith, 34–35; T. M. D. Ward, 34–35
Cordell, LaDoris, 214, 22
Council of Churches, 92, 103, 112
Cupertino, Calif., 106, 120, 139, 205, 262–63n16

Davis, Harriet, 29
De facto racial discrimination, 3, 62, 77, 86, 92, 107, 125, 140–41, 151, 161, 173–74, 214, 223. *See also* California nativism
Dellums, C. L., 109, 253–24n59, 266n64
Democrats: political realignment, 69–70; Santa Clara Valley, Calif., 41, 42, 44, 69–70, 105, 114
Dennis, James and Tonya, 226
Denny's, 223
Detroit, Mich., 66, 140, 207, 224
Dollarhyde family. *See* Migration
Dollarhyde, Emmitt. *See* Santa Clara County NAACP
Drake, St. Clair, 3
Dusel, William, 144, 185

Earthquake and fire of 1906, 83, 255n64
East Bay, Calif., 10, 73, 82, 121, 127, 172
East Palo Alto, Calif., 1, 4, 96–97, 105, 114, 120, 125–26, 135, 143, 150–51, 206, 209, 262–63n16, 282n71

Education: Ayer High School, Milpitas, Calif., 207–208; *Brown v. Board of Education*, 139; colored schools in California, 35–42; Minnie Darling and Negro Cultural class, 65; during Gold Rush era, 242n75, 243n76; Katie Haycock on the contemporary state of California's public education system, 214–15; Lowell Elementary School, San Jose, Calif., 140; Milpitas High School, 208; Frank and Pearl Moulden and the Excelsior Club, Palo Alto, Calif., 60; Palo Alto School District, 60, 151; Rancho Junior High, Milpitas, 208; Roosevelt Junior High School, San Jose, 140; San Jose Board of Education, 40, 159, 244n95; San Jose City College, 101, 177–78; San Jose High School, 194, 215; San Jose School for Coloreds, 40; San Jose State College, 142, 144–45, 147–49, 154, 162, 164–88, 193, 197–99, 210; San Jose Unified School District, 86, 215; sneak out system, Palo Alto, 151; St. Phillip's Mission School, San Jose, 24, 32, 37–43, 45; *Wysinger v. Crookshank*, 45, 139
Edwards, Harry, 141, 148, 163–65, 168–89, 191–92, 194–95, 197–98, 279–80n40; at Cornell University, Ithaca, N.Y., 171, 175; in East St. Louis, Mo., 68–169; epiphanies that led to the revolt, 169, 174–75, 178, 188–89; and Emmitt Till, 168. *See also* Revolt of the black athlete
Eichler Homes: Edward P. Eichler, 105–106; Joseph Eichler, 104–107, 265n50, 265–66n58
Electric light tower, 24
Elks Club, 56, 88
Ellington, Joyce, 58, 61, 250n29
Emeryville, Calif., 124
English, Leo, 143
Evans, Lee. *See* Revolt of the black athlete
European immigrants, 49; Italians, 63, 88, 139; Portuguese, 49, 88, 99, 101

Fair Employment Practices Act. *See* Labor
Fair Housing Act of 1968. *See* Housing legislation and reports

INDEX

Fair housing movements. *See* Housing activism
Ferguson, Jacob A., 55, 59, 84
First Great Migration, 10, 96. *See also* Migration
Freedom Train, 227
Freedom's Journal, 35
Fremont, Calif., 96, 116, 129–34, 262–63n16
Frey, Dick, 154–55, 281n60
Fry, Thomas, 153

Gaffin, Helen, 58, 78, 80–81, 85, 88
Galloway, Lula Briggs, 227
Garden City Women's Club, 8–9, 45, 66–68, 86, 90, 99, 116, 234n23; Marcus Garvey visit, 67
Gary, Charles, 207–208, 222–23, 296–97n84
General Motors, 96
Gilroy, Calif., 47, 50, 224
Good Brothers. *See* Revolt of the black athlete
Goodwin, Clarence, 57, 69
Gray, Benjamin, 55
Great Depression: Dust Bowl, 83, 87; and political realignment, 69–70; in South Bay, 251–52n47; St. James Park lynching, 62–65, 252n48, 253n57
Gross, Ben. *See* Sunnyhills, Milpitas, Calif.

Hamann, Anthony P., 89
Hardeman, Maurice, 215
Hardy, Irene and Ray, 209, 217
Harrison, Roderick, 215–16
Hill, Urla, 224
Housing: African American homeownership, 250n29, 262–63n16, 270–71n117; contemporary housing trends, 213, 216; postwar market and trends, 261n7, 262–63n16
Housing activism: California Committee for Fair Employment Practices, 109, 139; California FEPC movement, 266n64; Fair housing movement in California and in Santa Clara County, 92–93, 97–104, 108–21; Marcia Fein of, 212; Clarence Hudson and Tropicana Village, 110–11; Midpeninsulans for Fair Housing, 211–12; Herbert Mills and Unruh Act, 110; Berthina Nelson, 98, 263–64n24; San Jose's fair housing movement, 93, 111–13, 138–39, 155–56, 158, 160, 168; Mary Anne Smith, 98–102, 108, 264n25; Calvin Stovall and Bob Goligoski investigation, 210–211; J. S. Williams, 98. *See also* Eichler Homes; Sunnyhills, Milpitas, Calif.
Housing legislation and reports: California Fair Housing Act of 1963 (aka Rumford Act), 93, 108, 113–16, 120–21, 155, 199, 212, 267n81; Department of Housing and Urban Development (HUD), 212; Fair Housing Act of 1968, 93, 116, 119, 201–202; Federal Housing Act of 1950, 130; Federal Housing Authority, 75–76, 96, 109, 119, 129–31, 257n12, 257–58n14; Federal National Mortgage Association, 130; Fourteenth Amendment, 269n106; Hawkins Act, 105, 108–10, 112–13, 139, 266n68; Home Owners' Loan Corporation, 76; Kerner Commission report, 269n104; *Mulkey v. Reitman*, 118; National Housing Act of 1988, 212; *Shelley v. Kraemer*, 57; Veterans Administration, 96, 109, 131; Unruh Act, 105, 108–10, 112–13, 139, 267n76; U.S. Civil Rights Commission report, 267n82
Housing restrictions: blockbusting, 100; California Real Estate Association and the anti–fair housing movement, 115–19, 121, 138, 158–59, 269n99; Citizens League for Individual Freedoms, 111–12; housing discrimination at San Jose State, 171–72, 175; Proposition 14, 115–18, 268n95; redlining, 75–76; restrictive covenants, 57, 58
Hudson, James A., 221
Huizar, Pedro, 20
Hunter, Ed, 194

IBM, 119, 126, 128

Jackson, Cass, 165, 177, 195, 205, 207
Jackson, Inez, 85–87, 97–100, 107–108, 142, 165, 173, 180, 221, 263n22, 279–80n40
Jackson, Robert, 206
James, Ronald, 184

INDEX   333

Japanese. *See* Asian Americans
Jeffries, Leonard, 194, 295n67
Jones, Albert, 205
Jones, Octavia, 50
Juneteenth, 226–28, 297n91

King, Martin Luther, Jr., 1, 93, 136, 163, 166, 185, 201, 228, 229n1, 264–65n43

Labor: black businesses, 55–56, 84, 219; Cannery and Agricultural Workers Industrial Union, 63, 252n48; Clerks Union, Local 492, 157–58; Julia and Daisy Dollarhyde, letter to U.S. president, 82; early employment trends, 49–50, 52, 55–56, 59, 63–65, 70, 77; Executive Order 8802, 82–83; Fair Employment Practices Act, 157; Fair Employment Practices Committee, 82; Great Strike of 1934, San Francisco, 64, 253–54n59; Hendy Iron Works, 81, 83–84, 259n39; high-tech industry, 126, 215, 217; high-tech industry executive opportunities (Michael Sears, Howard Smith, John W. Thompson), 217–18; International Brotherhood of Boilermakers, 82; *James v. Marinship*, 80–82; Kaiser Shipyards, 80, 82; Libby, McNeil & Libby, 83, 247–48n6; Lockheed Aircraft, 119–26, 128; Moffett Federal Air Field, 81, 83, 110; Small Business Administration loans, 219; Taft-Hartley Act of 1947, 10, 123; Rosalind Taylor and early white-collar employment opportunities, 56; United Auto Workers, 10, 122, 124, 126–37, 139; "Working together to survive and thrive" concept, 31, 74, 77
Law enforcement, 219–22, 295n67
League of Women Voters, 99, 132
Leath, Dorothy, 89, 92
Libby, Jean. *See* Palo Alto–Stanford NAACP
Littlefield, John, 42
Los Altos, Calif., 120, 262–63n16
Los Angeles, Calif., 51–52, 73, 75, 97, 105, 168, 172, 189, 197, 205, 248n9; Watts, 5, 114, 118, 121, 162
Los Gatos, Calif., 47, 262–63n16
Luten, Shawn, 220
Lyman, Richard, 1

Madden, John, 32, 47
Marysville, Calif., 32
McNamara, Joseph, 220
Menlo Park, Calif., 1, 103, 262–63n16
Mexican Americans: Isais Aguilar, 159; Ray Belluomini, 282n74; Chicano movement, 194, 197; migration, 247–48n6; Proposition 14, 268–69n98; Santa Clara County, Calif., 3, 49, 52, 63, 75, 77, 83, 101, 117, 120, 122–23, 137, 139, 141, 156, 159, 198, 206, 221, 224–25, 277n7; United Farm Worker Movement, 194
Mexican-American War, 27
Mexico: slavery abolition, 21, 22; War for Independence, 20. *See also* Treaty of Guadalupe Hidalgo
Migration: Anderson family, 79–80; black flight, 209; black pioneers in San Jose and Palo Alto, Calif., 47, 53–54, 59; "black suburban spirit" concept, 208; Dollarhyde family (Edna, Gertrude, and Tom), 78–80; early-twentieth-century migration, 48, 52; "end of the line" concept, 52, 75; post–civil rights era, 215–16; post-Reconstruction era, 45. *See also* First Great Migration; Second Great Migration; Third Great Migration
Millner, Steven, 194, 197
Milpitas, Calif., 10, 47, 50, 93, 96, 106, 111, 120, 122–23, 262–63n16; Murphy Ranch, 29; Sunnyhills, 96, 103–22, 124–27, 205–208, 213, 222; as working-class suburb, 127
Milpitas Post, The, 126
Monterey, Calif., 15, 18, 163
Mosk, Stanley, 145–46
Moss, Thomas, 55, 57, 67–68, 84, 255n66
Mountain View, Calif., 59, 67, 120, 205, 214, 262–63n16
Murray, Charles, 194–95, 295n67

National Housing Act of 1988. *See* Housing legislation and reports
Native Americans, 15, 21, 26–27, 45
Naturalization laws, 49, 245n112
Newton, Nate, 220
Noel, Kenneth. *See* Revolt of the black athlete
Northside San Jose. *See* San Jose, Calif.

Oakland, Calif., 7, 32, 37, 73, 82, 85–86, 107, 125–26, 135, 182, 224
Oklahoma City, Okla., 77–81, 83–84, 86–87, 140–42
Orange County, Calif., 205, 262–63n16
Order of Eastern Star, 66–69, 89
Overton, Charles H., 55, 58, 250n32
Overton, Jacob, 34, 41, 45–46, 246n117; Afro-American League, 45; California Pioneers of Santa Clara County, 45; Colored Odd Fellows and Masons, 45
Overton, Sarah Massey, 34, 39, 45–46. *See also* Black women's club movement
Owen, J. J., 33, 43, 242n65
Owens, Alissa, 224
Owens, T. J., 107, 194

Palo Alto, Calif., 4, 9, 49, 59–60, 67, 85–86, 89, 96, 103–106, 110, 115, 125–26, 138, 143, 150–51, 204, 213–14, 222, 228, 262–63n16
Palo Alto African Methodist Episcopal Zion Church. *See* Churches
Palo Alto–Stanford NAACP: activism, 89, 103–104, 139, 150–51; Doris Jones, 103–104; Jean Libby, 150, 280–81n49; Muata Puryer, 150, 294n43; sneak out system in Palo Alto, 151
Palo Alto Times, 61
Panama, 38
Peckham, Robert F., 43
Perkins, Patricia, 79, 85
Pico, Antonio Maria, 21–22. *See also* Spanish California
Pleasants, Mary Ellen, 31
Plessy v. Ferguson, 139, 246n119
Political Equality Club, 45
Portland, Ore., 28, 82
Puerto Ricans, 63

Ray, Carl, 223
Reagan, Ronald, 183, 217
Record Hop, 141
Red baiting, 279n37
Republicans, 41 44, 67–70, 116; as New Right, 161
Revolt of the black athlete: Charles Alexander, 165–68, 198, 277n7; Muhammad Ali, 190–91; Stanley Benz, 179; Julian Bond, 193; Hobart Burns, 193; Mervyn Cadwallader, 180; John Carlos, 164, 190–93; Robert D. Clark, 178–87, 192–93, 198; conservative backlash, 183; Valerie Dickerson, 185; Educational Opportunity Program, 186, 198–99; Lee Evans, 172, 184, 193; *The Fire Next Time*, 186; general overview of, 162–65; the Good Brothers, 165–68, 170, 172, 196, 199; Good Brothers' Pad, 167, 173, 180; hearings on race relations at San Jose State, 185–87; Willie Jeffries, 189; Steve McKinney, 165; Walt McPherson, 179; NCAA, 164, 180, 182, 188–89; New York Athletic Club Boycott, 190; Kenneth Noel, 164, 177–78, 182–83, 187; Ray Norton, 165, 168; Olympic movement supporters, 184; Olympic Project for Human Rights, 189–93; Omega Psi Phi, 172, 285n14; Rally Against Racism, 179; recognition banquet, 193; Milt Rendall, 171; San Francisco State, 184; San Jose State College, 164–88, 193, 197–99, 210; Tommie Smith, 164, 171, 176, 189–93, 195; Smith's and Carlos's Olympic protest, 164; Speed City era, 172, 176–88; 2 Percent Rule, 176, 180; United Black Students for Action, 164, 178–88, 229; U.S. Olympic Committee, 188–90; Western Regional Black Youth Conference, 189. *See also* Black Power movement; Black studies; Edwards, Harry; Walsh, Bill
Ribbs, Clyde, 54, 56–57, 249n17
Ribbs, Henry, 54, 57, 65, 67–68, 249n17
Ribbs, William T., Sr., 68
Richmond, Calif., 7, 10, 124, 135, 137, 207, 209, 224
Roberts, Frederick M., 43
Rollins, Ellen, 226, 297n91
Ruffin, Herbert, 206–207, 218
Ruffin, Herbert, II, 206–207, 293n21
Ruffin, Sadie, 206–207
Rumford, William Byron, 92, 109, 115

Sacramento, Calif., 27, 29, 37, 112
San Diego, Calif., 205
San Francisco, Calif., 5–7, 15, 29, 32, 34–35, 37, 64, 69, 73, 82, 92, 94, 98, 101, 105, 107, 121, 126, 129, 172, 223–24, 228; Hunters Point, 5, 116, 162

San Jose, Calif.: Alum Rock, 59, 68, 85, 215; as Beacon City, 24, 248n9; as capital of Silicon Valley, 205; East Foothills, 206; East San Jose, 4, 49, 56, 85, 94–95, 102, 110, 120, 126, 140, 206, 213, 215, 220–21, 261–62n10; as El Pueblo de San Jose de Guadalupe, 18, 236n5; Guadalupe River, 9, 58; Northside, 4, 9, 47, 50–51, 58, 66, 75–76, 84–86, 89, 95, 97–98, 101, 120, 173, 180, 206, 209, 213, 224, 250n31, 257–58n14, 262–63n16; Piedmont Hills, 206; Southside, 58, 140, 148, 171, 223–24; West San Jose, 9, 100–102, 106, 113, 119
San Jose Council for Civic Unity, 92, 101–104, 132
San Jose Mercury News, 33, 37, 43, 108, 143–44, 148, 158, 160–61, 210
San Jose NAACP. *See* Civil rights organizations
San Jose Police Department, 182, 186, 220–21
San Juan Bautista Apartments, 270n116
Sankofa, 196
San Leandro, Calif., 122, 125
San Mateo, Calif., 228
San Mateo County, Calif., 61, 206, 262–63n16
Santa Clara, Calif., 15, 18, 47, 59, 94, 119, 205, 219, 262–63n16; as Mission Santa Clara de Asis, 15, 18
Santa Clara County, Calif.: East County, 8–9, 136, 205–206, 209, 213, 218; as Silicon Valley, 141, 199, 202, 204–205, 212, 215, 218, 223–24, 226; West County, 9, 59–60, 95, 102, 191, 205, 222; West County, as Mid-Peninsula, 213
Santa Clara County CORE. *See* Civil rights organizations
Santa Clara County NAACP: activities of, 86–91, 99, 100, 112, 142; Black History Month, 147; J. W. Byers, 87; Emmitt Dollarhyde, 84, 87–89, 141; Anna B. McCall, 87; minstrel shows, 88–89; Negro History Week, San Jose, 88, 138
Santa Clara University, 262–63n16
Saratoga, Calif., 119, 220, 226, 257–58n14, 262–63n16
Satterwhite, Frank, 1

Seattle, Wash., 82, 250n29
Second Great Migration, 74, 77, 84–85, 141, 233n17, 234–35n27. *See also* Migration
Shaw, James, 176–77, 180
Shorey, Julia A., 39
Silicon Valley. *See* Santa Clara County, Calif.
Slavery: Anna Maria Bascom, 240n49; Louis H. Bascom, 28; chattel slavery, 26–28, 239n39; Mattie Reed Lewis, 27–29; "natural limits" concept, 27; and John Sutter, 27
Smith, John Henry, 220, 295n67
Smith, Tommie. *See* Revolt of the black athlete
Spanish California: Afro-Mexicans, 16, 18; Tiburcio Basques, 17, 21; *californios*, 20; Charles IV, 19; Vicente Guerrero, 21; María Jacinta de la Bastida, 21; *Ladino* concept and early Mexican nationalism, 21; Mary, 23; Mission Santa Clara de Asis, 15, 18; Monterey, Calif., 15, 18; Negreto, Augustus, 239n41; the Ohlone, 15; Antonio Maria Pico, 21–22; *El Pueblo de San Jose de Guadalupe*, 18; Joseph Romero, 17, 22; Maria Petra Azebes Romero, 17, 22; San Francisco de Asis, 15, 18; settlers of African descent, 17–18; *sistema de castas*, 15, 18–20, 236n16; Spanish explorations of (Juan Bautista de Anza, Juan Crespi, Pedro Fages, and Gaspar de Portola), 15
Speed City era, 172, 176–88. *See also* Revolt of the black athlete
Stanford University, 1–3, 9, 40, 142–43, 150, 154, 196, 204, 210, 229n1, 230n7, 262–63n16
Stevens, Jerry, 220
Stockton, 32, 37, 78–80
St. Phillips Episcopal Church. *See* Church
St. Phillip's Mission School. *See* Cassey, Peter William
Stubbs, Orvella, 78, 140–41
Student Nonviolent Coordinating Committee. *See* Civil rights organizations
Sunnyhills, Milpitas, Calif.: AFL building trades, 133; American Association of

Sunnyhills (*continued*)
University Women, 132–33; American Friends Service Committee, 92, 103, 117, 129, 130, 132; Congress of Industrial Unions, 10, 123; development and life in, 4, 120, 123, 126–27, 130–31, 137, 139; Ford Motor Company, 10, 123–24, 126, 126, 130, 133; Ben Gross, 43, 127–28, 132–36, 207; housing law, 130; Joseph Kaufman, 129–30, 133; Vincent McKenna, 127–28, 135; Metropolitan Life Insurance Company, 130; William Oliver, 127, 133–35; Rancho Agua Caliente, Fremont, Calif., 129–34; Walter P. Reuther, 123–24, 127, 129, 134–35, 137; San Jose Council of Churches, 129–32; San Lorenzo Homes Company, 131–32, 134; Sunnyhills coalition, 132–33; Sunnyhills United Methodist Church, 135–36, 208, 264–65n43; Taft-Hartley Act of 1947, 10, 123; United Auto Workers, 10, 122, 124, 126–37, 139; United Auto Workers Local 560 Executive Committee, 127–29; "Working-class suburb" concept, 127
Sunnyvale, Calif., 106, 119, 211, 214, 22
Sweet, Tee, 209

Tanner, Francis, 107, 221
Third Great Migration, 200–202, 204, 207, 212–14, 218–19, 223. *See also* Migration
Thomas, Thurmond, 63–65
Thompson, Walter, 67
Tinsley, Ocie, 119–20, 269n113, 275n62
Treaty of Guadalupe Hidalgo, 23, 239n41

Unger, Bruce, 221
Unitarian Church. *See* Churches
United Auto Workers, 10, 122, 124, 126–37, 139. *See also* Sunnyhills, Milpitas, Calif.
United Black Students for Action, 164, 178–88, 229. *See also* Revolt of the black athlete

Urban development: desegregation of Santa Clara Valley, 193–94, 197–200; family disintegration and social disorientation theory, 251n43; inburbs, 205; late-blooming areas, 4, 138; Palo Alto–Stanford University Industrial Park model, 204; post-suburban construction, 91–96, 296n78; ring suburbanization, 94, 97; Santa Clara County as Valley of Heart's Delight, 48–51, 125, 142, 252–53n53; "underclass" concept, 204; working-class suburb, Milpitas, 127. *See also names of specific cities*
U.S. West: "African American West logic" concept, 5; Richard Dalfiume theory, 48, 246–47n2; misconceptualized as the North, 233n19; Gerald Nash theory, 48; older African American West histories, 232n15; Fredrick Jackson Turner theory, 6; Walter Prescott Webb theory, 6, 75, 232n14

Vietnamese. *See* Asian Americans

Wagner, Peter, 42
Walsh, Bill, 168, 195–96; Dennis Green, 196; NFL Minority Fellowship Program, 196–97, 291n139; John Wooten, 196. *See also* Jackson, Cass; Revolt of the black athlete
Ward, Anton, 220
Warren, William, 22
Washington, C. W., 77, 113, 146, 149, 161, 215
Washington, Keni, 1
Watson, Bob, 216
Welch, Robert, 151, 159
White supremacy: White Citizens Council, 115. *See also* California nativism; Housing restrictions
Williams, James, 29, 30, 137
Women International League for Peace and Freedom, 278n15
Woody, Alice, 222
World War II, 10, 73–86, 90, 259n39

www.ingramcontent.com/pod-product-compliance
Lightning Source LLC
Chambersburg PA
CBHW022102150426
43195CB00008B/236